D0193668

# The MADONNA Companion

# *The* MADONNA *Companion*

Two Decades of Commentary

*Edited by*

C A R O L   B E N S O N

*and*

A L L A N   M E T Z

782.42
c.1

Schirmer Books
*New York*

Copyright © 1999 Schirmer Books

All rights reserved. No part of this book may be reproduced or transmitted in any form or by any means, electronic or mechanical, including photocopying, recording, or by any information storage and retrieval system, without permission in writing from the Publisher.

Schirmer Books
1633 Broadway
New York, New York 10019

Library of Congress Catalog Number: 98-35861
Printed in the United States of America

Printing number
2 3 4 5 6 7 8 9 10

**Library of Congress Cataloging-in-Publication Data**

The Madonna companion : two decades of commentary / edited by Carol Benson and Allan Metz.
p. cm.
Includes discography (p. ), videography (p. ), filmography (p. ), bibliographical references (p. ), and index.
ISBN 0-02-864972-9
1. Madonna, b. 1958—Criticism and interpretation.
I. Benson, Carol.
II. Metz, Allen.
ML420.M1387M215 1998
782.42166'092—dc21 98-35861
CIP
MN

This paper meets the requirements of ANSI/NISO Z39.48–1992 (Permanence of Paper).

# Contents

*Preface* ix

*Acknowledgments* xi

*Introduction: Madonna* xiii
J. D. CONSIDINE

**PART ONE MATERIAL GIRL: Madonna on Record and Stage**

LIKE A VIRGIN (1985) 3
*PEOPLE* MAGAZINE

CONCERT REVIEW: UNIVERSAL AMPHITHEATER, LOS ANGELES (1985) 4
*VARIETY*

MADONNA IS NOBODY'S TOY (1986) 6
ROBERT HILBURN

LIKE A VETERAN: MADONNA'S TOUR REVEALS HER SAVVY, SHOW-BIZ SIDE (1987) 8
BRETT MILANO

EX-"BOY TOY" MADONNA TRANSFORMS HERSELF INTO ADULT ON *LIKE A PRAYER* (1989) 12
JONATHAN TAKIFF

CONCERT REVIEW: HOLLYWOOD LOS ANGELES SPORTS ARENA (1990) 14
*VARIETY*

WITHOUT THE VIDEOS, HER ALBUMS JUST AREN'T THE SAME (1990) 15
GREG KOT

THE MADONNA PORNUCOPIA: *SEX* FOR THE COFFEE TABLE AND *EROTICA* FOR THE EARS (1992) 16
RICHARD HARRINGTON

MADONNA GOES TO CAMP (1993) 21
RICHARD CORLISS

PILLOW TALK (1994) 23
STEVE DOLLAR

MADONNA CAPTURES THE MOMENT AND SEES THE SPIRITUAL LIGHT (1998) 24
JOAN ANDERMAN

**PART TWO OPEN YOUR HEART TO ME: Madonna and the Press**

MADONNA: SHE'S ONE LUCKY STAR! (1984) 31
*TEEN* MAGAZINE

MADONNA! (1985) 35
DENISE WORRELL

MADONNA CLEANS UP ACT BUT HER MUSIC REMAINS TRUE BLUE TO CONTROVERSY (1986) 48
STEPHEN HOLDEN

CONFESSION OF A CATHOLIC GIRL (1989) 52
BECKY JOHNSTON

FACE-TO-FACE WITH MADONNA (1996) 74
EDNA GUNDERSEN

NEW TUNE FOR THE MATERIAL GIRL: I'M NEITHER (1998) 79
ANN POWERS

**PART THREE PAPA, DON'T PREACH: Madonna as Phenomenon**

MADONNA RISING: THE WILD AND FUNKY EARLY YEARS IN NEW YORK (1991) 87
CHRISTOPHER ANDERSON

MADONNA ROCKS THE LAND (1985) 109
JOHN SKOW

A MAD, MAD WORLD OF "MADONNAS" (1985) 116
MARY ROURKE

VIRGIN TERRITORY: HOW MADONNA STRADDLES INNOCENCE AND DECADENCE (1985) 119
JOEL D. SCHWARTZ

SINGLE SEX AND THE GIRL (1991) 124
JOSEPH SOBRAN

MADONNA SELLS HER SOUL FOR A SONG (1989) 131
ED SIEGEL

WHY MADONNA CAN'T KEEP HER CLOTHES ON (1993) 134
WILLIAM CROSS

PLAYING THE SHOCK MARKET (1992) 137
MATTHEW GILBERT

MADONNA AND OTHER ARTHURS (1993) 142
MOLLY IVINS

MADONNA (1993) 144
STEVE ALLEN

**PART FOUR LIKE A VIRGIN: Madonna as Video Star**

VENUS OF THE RADIO WAVES (1990) 161
CAMILLE PAGLIA

IMMATERIAL GIRL? (1998) 167
TAMARA IKENBERG

LIKE A CRITIQUE: A POSTMODERN ESSAY ON MADONNA'S POSTMODERN VIDEO "LIKE A PRAYER" (1989) 171
STEPHEN E. YOUNG

FACE-OFF: MADONNA'S "LIKE A PRAYER": THIS VIDEO AFFIRMS RELIGIOUS PRINCIPLES (1996) 181
LIZ ROSENBERG

THIS VIDEO IS OFFENSIVE TO BELIEVERS (1996) 183
DONALD WILDMON

OUR LADY OF MTV: MADONNA'S "LIKE A PRAYER" (1992) 184
CARLA FRECCERO

JUSTIFY MY IDEOLOGY: MADONNA AND TRADITIONAL VALUES (1992) 204
JANELLE L. WILSON AND GERALD E. MARKLE

ANIMALITY AND ARTIFICE (1992) 215
CAMILLE PAGLIA

**PART FIVE JUSTIFY MY LOVE: Madonna and the Academy**

MAKE MY RAINY DAY (1992) 219
DANIEL HARRIS

GENDER POLITICS AND MTV: VOICING THE DIFFERENCE (1990) 226
LISA A. LEWIS

UNLIKE A VIRGIN (1990) 232
LUC SANTE

MADONNA (1992) 240
JANE MILLER

MADONNA'S POSTMODERN FEMINISM: BRINGING THE MARGINS TO THE CENTER (1992) 249
CATHY SCHWICHTENBERG

GUILTY PLEASURES (1996) 268
PAMELA ROBERTSON

ELECTRIFYING FRAGMENTS: MADONNA AND POSTMODERN PERFORMANCE (1996) 290
MARK WATTS

*Selected Discography* 303

*Videos* 309

*Filmography* 311

*Selected Bibliography* 313

*Chronology* 319

*Permissions* 321

*Index* 325

# Preface

Madonna is:

a. A teen-pop sensation whose career will be short-lived (1984).
b. A protofeminist who uses her sexuality as a commentary on the way society reduces women to sexual roles (1987).
c. A heretical ex-Christian who flouts the church and its authority (1989).
d. A ceaseless exhibitionist who can't keep her clothes on (1992).
e. A movie actress and chanteuse (1995).
f. A newly spiritualized artist (1998).

Well, you get the picture. Madonna has gone through many transformations in a long career as singer, songwriter, media sensation, actress, and agent-provocateur. To her critics, she is a shameless poseur, a true material girl who plays the media like a violin, while scooping up the adoration (and cash) of her fans. To her fans, Madonna stands ironically apart from the hoopla, controlling her own destiny while using the powers of her voice, physical presence, and video image to criticize social norms and common beliefs.

This collection tries to encompass the many Madonnas as viewed through different perspectives. With all the hysteria that has surrounded her as pop star, few have examined her now-considerable body of work. For this reason, in Part One we begin with a section of record and concert reviews to give the reader a grounding in the music itself. There would be no Madonna without the music—although some would argue that the music is merely a sound track to the phenomenon.

In Part Two, we offer an overview of key interviews that Madonna has given throughout her career, beginning with her teen-pop phase and then progressing through her years as idol, social critic, and finally new-age philosopher.

Part Three documents the Madonna phenomenon, examining the various controversies that have swirled around her during a long career. First came the Madonna as bad role model for teenage girls; then came the

Madonna as sacreligious icon who stole the imagery of the Christian church to pervert it to her own ends; then came the sexually provocative Madonna who launched a multimedia book-record-film assault on sex.

More than probably any other contemporary pop artist, Madonna has used video to promote her music. But her use of video goes further than that, as we will examine in Part Four. Here we realize that many of the songs are made far more meaningful through the use of the video medium. And, of course, much discussion is given to the controversial "Like a Prayer" video, perhaps Madonna's greatest achievement in the medium.

Finally, academics have long labored over the meaning of Madonna. For them, Madonna becomes a central image in new studies of feminism, gender roles, commercialism, the role of pop music in society . . . you name it. Part Five presents some of the more interesting academic stabs at defining Madonna.

At the book's end, thanks to the many Madonna fans on the World Wide Web, there is a rich selection of information about her albums, singles, videos, and film career. Finally, we include a selected bibliography and a useful chronology to put it all in perspective.

Like the other titles in this series, this book aims to serve both the Madonna neophyte and the longtime Madonna fan by bringing together many different perspectives on this most provocative pop star.

Carol Benson
Allan Metz

# Acknowledgments

I wish to thank Richard Carlin, Executive Editor of Schirmer Books for providing me with this opportunity and for his advice and patience in answering my many questions. I appreciate the contributors to this volume who corresponded with me. I also extend appreciation to the following libraries and their respective staffs for greatly facilitating my research: F. W. Olin Library, Drury College, especially Katherine Bohnenkamper and her student assistant Breanna Stauffer for interlibrary loan assistance; the Duane G. Meyer Library of Southwest Missouri State University as well as this university's music library; the Springfield-Greene County Public Library; and the staff of the Mid-Continent Public Library, Independence, Missouri, in particular the newspaper/periodical division personnel for their assistance, encouragement, and interest. (You know who you are!) I also conducted preliminary research on the theme of women in rock/pop music at the music libraries of the University of California at Berkeley and Stanford University.

Allan Metz

# Introduction

It may seem hard to believe now, but there actually was a time in her recording career when Madonna wasn't famous—in fact, wasn't even considered a contender. This was back in 1984, when Madonna's debut album, *Madonna,* was seen as a poor second to Cyndi Lauper's *She's So Unusual* in the Promising Female Artist sweepstakes. Both records sold well, and entered the *Billboard* Album Chart's Top Forty within a week of each other. But while *She's So Unusual* spun off four Top Five singles, Madonna merely slipped a pair of songs into the Top Ten.

Moreover, because those two singles—"Borderline" and "Lucky Star"—had crossed over from the dance market, most of the rock community saw Madonna as just another club-culture bimbette; video-savvy, sure, but hardly an artist of any import. Whereas Lauper not only had solid credentials (courtesy of her stint in the retro-rock act Blue Angel) and an interesting image (a sort of Betty Boop–meets–Laverne & Shirley chic), but actually seemed to be addressing important issues. After all, not only did she have the moxie to rewrite the sexist "Girls Just Want to Have Fun" as a tribute to feminine frivolity, but she even slipped a song about masturbation ("She Bop") into the hit parade. It was obvious, wrote the rock critic establishment, which of the two would turn into a truly major artist.

And as usual, the critical establishment got it exactly backward. It wasn't just that Madonna went on to greater chart success than Lauper, putting eighteen singles into the Top Five over the course of eight albums; by the end of the Eighties Madonna was a megastar, arguably one of the best-known women on earth and certainly one of the most talked-about figures in popular culture. She was written up everywhere, from *Cosmopolitan* to *Forbes* to the *Advocate;* her image was disparaged by Tipper Gore and Ellen Goodman, yet applauded by Germaine Greer and Camille Paglia; news of her latest controversy was as likely to turn up on *Nightline* as on MTV. She was, as her record company was proud to point out, Artist of the Decade.

Yet you couldn't really blame the critics for not seeing it coming, because in 1984 the pop world Madonna would rule hadn't been created yet. Back then, the dominant pop style was rock, rooted in the tradition-conscious sound of punk, and the dominant sensibility was camp, spun off from the Warholian adoration of TV and trash; naturally, Lauper had those qualities in spades. But Madonna was a creature of a different world. Her pop style was dance music, which had roots in funk and soul, but also in hip-hop and disco; her sensibility was ironic and postmodern, having grown out of the same media-saturated world that spawned graffiti artists Kenny Scharf and Keith Haring (and which, not coincidentally, would end up feeding the flames of MTV).

Like most denizens of that world, Madonna got there through a fairly roundabout fashion. Born comfortably middle-class in suburban Detroit, Madonna Louise Ciccone (she was named after her mother, who died of cancer when the singer was six) initially planned on a career in dance, studying briefly at the University of Michigan. Dropping out, she moved to New York with thirty-five dollars and an unflagging belief in her destiny. She continued to study dance, working with one of Alvin Ailey's secondary troupes, and drifted into music. Eventually she got a job singing backup with fading disco star Patrick Hernandez (of "Born to Be Alive" fame) and spent time in Paris; returning, she drummed with the Breakfast Club, formed her own group with pal Stephen Bray, and cut some demos with club DJ Mark Kamins. It was the Kamins-produced material that got her signed, and her first two singles, "Everybody" and "Burning Up," were solid club hits, though it wasn't until the Jellybean Benitez–produced "Holiday" that Madonna made any impression on radio.

Had she come along a decade earlier, this saga may well have ended there, but happily for her, Madonna emerged during the age of MTV. Although it would be oversimplifying to say that MTV made Madonna, providing her with a medium that would sell her image along with her music, it is obvious that video had an enormous impact on the singer's career. Her video for "Lucky Star," for instance, managed to turn Madonna's navel into a universal erogenous zone; "Borderline" established her as both a glamour puss and a romantic heroine, while "Material Girl" first introduced her version of the (Marilyn) Monroe Doctrine.

It was on a 1985 *MTV Video Music Awards* telecast, though, that Madonna made perhaps her most memorable appearance. Determined to introduce "Like a Virgin" even though the single itself was still weeks from release, Madonna hit the stage in a modified bridal gown and proceeded to writhe her way through the song. Yet it wasn't the apparent disparity between the song's virginal metaphor and the singer's decidedly carnal rendition that reeled in the home audience; it was the fact that Madonna had topped off the outfit with a customized belt buckle bearing the legend BOY TOY. Never had the iconography of Freud's madonna-whore complex been brought to bear so vividly.

Such apparent contradictions confused and outraged older viewers. Traditionalists, they were used to linear reasoning with all the important signs kept in context; they had no idea what to make of Madonna's clashing symbols. How could she be like a virgin, they wondered? How could she pose as both boy toy and bride? Was she selling sex or true love? Was she a feminist (as she said) or a bimbo (as she looked)? Just what in hell was going on here?

But the little girls understood. Children of the video age, they were used to logic-jarring jump cuts and context-shredding juxtapositions, inured to the white noise of advertising's sex-and-sizzle. Thus, where older observers saw blasphemy when Madonna wore rosaries and crucifixes, the younger fans—dismissively dubbed "Madonna wannabes" by their elders—merely recognized the icons as power-packed fashion accessories; likewise, the oldsters saw the singer's bra-baring brazenness as a slutty come-on, while the wannabes understood it as a statement of sex as power. Susan Baker, a cofounder of the Parents' Music Resource Center, griped that Madonna taught little girls how to act "like a porn queen in heat." But a seventeen-year-old wannabe quoted by *Time* begged to differ. "It's really women's lib," said the girl, "not being afraid of what guys think."

If *Like a Virgin* firmed up Madonna's stature as a pop power, it was her appearance in Susan Seidelman's *Desperately Seeking Susan* that established her as a "star" in the universal sense. Although hers was ostensibly a supporting role, Madonna stole the show from its putative stars, Rosanna Arquette and Aidan Quinn, and she made no secret of her eagerness to capitalize on that success. Here, however, Madonna would not be a particularly lucky star. Although she endured movie-star attention from the scandal sheets—which, clearly disappointed that Madonna had not been besmirched by the youthful, nude figure studies that ran in *Playboy* and *Penthouse,* hounded her and her hot-tempered then-husband, Sean Penn—her actual film career was shaping up as a flop, thanks to an execrable romantic comedy called *Shanghai Surprise* and the muddleheaded caper flick *Who's That Girl?* It wasn't until Madonna played Breathless Mahoney to Warren Beatty's Dick Tracy that she got any respect at all in Hollywood, and even then the praise was peppered with snickers over her offscreen relationship with actor-director Beatty.

By that point, however, Madonna was used to such comments. Ever since an early *Rolling Stone* cover story suggested that she had slept her way to the top by having romantic relationships with the men who helped her career, Madonna had been dismissed by detractors as little more than a conniving slut. "I have a sexy image," she explained in 1987, "and people with sexy images aren't supposed to have any integrity or intelligence." Madonna, though, had both—particularly the latter. *True Blue,* which followed *Like a Virgin,* not only was savvy and successful, generating three Number One singles, but had been entirely cowritten (except for "Papa Don't Preach") and coproduced by the singer herself. Obviously this boy toy was no producer's pet. Moreover, the album showed off the singer's fondness for genre jumping, allowing her to indulge both her balladry ("Live to Tell") and her club consciousness ("Where's the Party"), absorbing some conventions whole (like the Latin undercurrents in "La Isla Bonita") and gleefully upending others (the Sixties girl-group sweetness sent up by the title tune). Nor was music the only place Madonna proved to be a cultural chameleon; her image, too, was forever shifting, from Monroe sultriness to girlish precocity, to sassy sensuality, to boyish androgyny.

Yet for Madonna, unlike rock's other quick-change artists, each new image did not entail a complete reinvention of her character. If anything, the more Madonna changed her looks and sound, the easier it was to maintain a sense of who that girl was. An instinctive postmodernist, Madonna treated images, attitudes and ideas as artistic commodities, playing off the power of each icon while keeping the content of her work at a comfortably ironic distance. Thus, when Mary Lambert's video for "Like a Prayer" was attacked by religious groups for alleged blasphemy, the corporate conservatives at Pepsi may have blinked, backing out of a multimillion-dollar sponsorship deal, but Madonna's fans barely batted an eye. They, after all, knew the difference between an artistic statement and a special effect.

Because scandal so often worked to her advantage, Madonna took on a reputation as a media manipulator and shameless self-promoter. A typical example was the furor in 1990 surrounding the "Justify My Love" video, in which Madonna and boyfriend pro tem Tony Ward acted out a variety of sexual fantasies, including bondage, bisexuality, and voyeurism. Deemed too hot for MTV, it immediately mushroomed into a censorship scandal; an uncut commercial copy of the clip was rushed into record stores and sold millions. Madonna insisted that she hadn't caused the commotion intentionally (and the casual arrogance of her rationale—"Of course they'll play it; how could they not?"—was oddly convincing), but her critics accused her of planning the whole thing. Nobody doubted her intelligence then—they merely held it against her.

What her critics forget, however, is that manufactured sensation is usually short-lived, and contrived art is almost always conservative, while Madonna's career has been neither. Indeed, the multimedia contract she signed with Time Warner in 1992—a music-movies-publishing deal worth a reputed $60 million—seems tangible proof of her formidable cultural impact. "I like to push people's buttons," she admits in the backstage documentary *Truth or Dare* (1991), but breaking boundaries is more like it. Madonna changed the rules on almost every level, restructuring the relationship between image and content, realigning mass-culture perspectives on black and gay subcultures, and reducing to rubble traditional notions of sex and power. It would be hard to imagine a truer definition of star power.

J. D. Considine

Early '80s glamour pose. *Courtesy of Eric Watson, Star File.*

# *Part One*

## MATERIAL GIRL

MADONNA ON RECORD AND STAGE

*So much has been written about the myth of Madonna that it's easy to forget that the myth is based on (by now) a considerable body of music. It seems appropriate, then, to begin the book with a collection of reviews of Madonna's albums and stage shows, focusing on the "material" that made her famous. Many of these reviews are short, being originally written for daily newspapers or magazines, but they help track the critical reaction to Madonna from popster to icon to artiste.*—Eds.

# LIKE A VIRGIN

*People* magazine, 1985

*We begin with an early* People *magazine review of Madonna's second, breakthrough album, along with a reflection on the album from* Entertainment Weekly *written ten years later.*—Eds.

"[Boys] can beg and they can plead / But they can't see the light, that's right / 'Cause the boy with the cold hard cash / Is always Mister Right." Ah, yes, they sure don't write love songs like they used to, as those lines from *Material Girl* attest. Madonna Louise Ciccone does have a sense of humor, though, even if, like her sister singers of the Cyndi Lauper school, she is buried under so many layers of self-parody it's hard to tell sometimes. The lyrics on this album are on the primitive side. They might have been lifted off cave walls, full as they are of "oohs," "ahs" and "shoo bee doo bees." But Madonna, 24, can be subtle—"Shoo-Bee-Doo" is actually a quiet, romantic sort of song—and keeps the tone bright and airy. She's backed on this, her second album, by the reliable rhythmic touch of veteran producer Nile Rodgers. His contributions have helped her create a tolerable bit of fluff.
Grade: B+

Madonna and her producer, Jellybean, at Sigma Studios in New York, recording her first album, *Madonna*,1982. *Courtesy of Chuck Pulin, Star File.*

# CONCERT REVIEW: UNIVERSAL AMPHITHEATER, LOS ANGELES, MAY 8, 1985

*Variety*, 1985

*Madonna's early shows attempted to recreate her video image on stage, as this brief notice shows.*—Eds.

The power and influence of MTV was much in evidence as Madonna, music television's biggest star, strutted her stuff at the Universal Amphitheatre.

We do mean *strut*. Music was clearly ancillary to this show, with rock's trashy, somehow charming sex queen pulling out all her moves. The familiar, writhing, navel-stretching, girl-in-heat images of the videos were jacked up a risqué notch or two as Madonna figuratively made love to the infatuated SRO crowd.

Looking like she stepped off the cover of Prince's psychedelic new *Around the World in a Day* LP, with peacock paisley top, denim micro-mini, blue suede ankle boots and crucifixes hanging from all points, Madonna played the boy toy role to the hilt, wriggling and snaking on all fours, introducing her "box"—a stage prop that served no apparent purpose other than to support this double entendre—and breathlessly asking the paramour crowd between songs: "Are you excited? . . . How excited? . . ."

All this is not to downplay the music. Madonna's hits—of which there are already a remarkable number, considering her brief career—are bona fide hits, strong, catchy dance tunes sung in a voice that makes up in erotic personality for what it lacks in body and strength.

Renditions of the catalog were up to par with the records themselves, except for "Burning Up," a non-hit, but easily the hottest song of the night, sung with urgency that blew past all the singer's chronic teases.

But, for the most part, Madonna's singing was like a soundtrack to a more visceral display of herself, her persona, her nonstop dancing and her surprisingly explicit sexual dare, which included a visual climax—so to speak—to every song.

Somehow, despite the hard-core moves, Madonna did not really come off as naughty or menacing so much as solicitous and good-hearted, a kind of flirtatious, sugary sex fairy whose outrageous poses were really just a gift for the kids, a fantasy offering to help them grow up.

At show's end, Madonna made this explicit, revealing herself to be a good girl despite all, following a coolly corrupt rendition of "Material Girl" with a surprising, almost plaintive question: "Do you really think I'm a Material Girl? . . . I'm not. . . . Take it. I don't need money . . .," she cried, tossing handfuls of play bills to the crowd. "I need love . . ."

ROBERT HILBURN

# MADONNA IS NOBODY'S TOY

*Los Angeles Times*, July 6, 1986

*Madonna's* True Blue, *her third album, was the first to get critical attention. Distinguished music critic Robert Hilburn recognized it as a turning point in her career.*—Eds.

Wasn't this supposed to be the year that the pop world said bye-bye to Madonna?

All that media hype in 1985 about her teasing, gimmicky "boy toy" image was enough to turn off anyone. And the backlash was building well before the added exposure of the *Playboy* and *Penthouse* photo layouts.

But going against Madonna was a sucker bet. All along, she has shown hints of ambition and sharp show-biz instincts that suggested this cookie is a survivor: the brightness and punch of her hit singles, the good-natured sparkle of her live performances, and her disarming presence in *Desperately Seeking Susan*. Now, *True Blue* adds another strong credential.

New York club shot. *Courtesy of Bob Gruen, Star File.*

Some people will never take Madonna seriously—just as many never took Marilyn Monroe seriously. Novelty images—especially that of a sex symbol—are hard to erase. But talent far outshines novelty in Madonna's new LP.

The most obvious growth is in the control and character in Madonna's singing. Where she previously seemed dependent on clever record production, her vocals are so finely tailored that she actually extends the punch and appeal of the production touches. As cowriter and coproducer (with Patrick Leonard and Stephen Bray) of the album, Madonna also demonstrates greater confidence and direction musically.

Like David Bowie, Madonna visualizes music so that her best work seems equally designed with the stage or screen in mind—not just the jukebox. "Papa, Don't Preach" (written by Brian Elliot, with additional lyrics by Madonna) was tailor-made for video: the story of an unwed young woman wanting her father's approval after deciding to keep her baby. "White Heat"—which acknowledges its link to the gangster film of the same name by using a voice clip of James Cagney—is a playfully aggressive piece that will work great on stage.

Madonna also shares Bowie's ability to weave proven pop strains into a contemporary framework. The title song mixes the innocence of '50s R&B with the punch of Spector's '60s classics for a contemporary blend of "In the Still of the Night" and "Be My Baby." And "Jimmy Jimmy" has all the frisky fun and silliness of prime ABBA.

*True Blue* isn't revolutionary music, but it is imaginative, highly energized pop that recognizes the limitations and pleasures of Top 40 fare. There are flat spots: The outgoing "Open Your Heart" and message-bound "Love Makes the World Go Round" are equally uneventful. Still, the only bet I'd make after hearing *True Blue* is that Madonna's got at least four hit singles in the wings.

BRETT MILANO

# LIKE A VETERAN: MADONNA'S TOUR REVEALS HER SAVVY, SHOW-BIZ SIDE

1987

*Madonna's growth to stadium-sized attraction is documented in this tour preview for her 1987 shows.*—Eds.

Once it was easy to be a "Madonna wannabe." All you needed was a halter top, a few gold crosses, a bottle of blonde hair dye and a well-worn copy of the *Like a Virgin* album. But that was two years ago, when her trashy-classy persona got as much notice as her music, and there were doubts about how long she'd last.

But as time goes on, Madonna pulls new tricks from her sleeve: a successful film career, an ever-changing image and a stack of hit singles that hasn't let up. So nowadays, if you really want to be like Madonna, you have more of a challenge. You'll need to keep changing your style, from flashy pinup, to elegant film star, to dance club queen, to serious songwriter. You'll need an album *(True Blue)* on the charts, a film (the gangster comedy *Who's That Girl?*) on the way and a recent Latin-flavored hit ("La Isla Bonita"). You'll need 375 tons of equipment to carry around the world on a record-breaking tour. And you'll need to be one of pop's most recognizable faces while you're still only 28.

When Madonna arrives at Soldier Field on Friday, she'll bring a splashy show with her. Instead of a conventional pop concert, it's designed as a movable Broadway show—carried by a whopping 25 semitrucks.

Here's what's planned:

- Seven costume changes, ranging from formal gowns, to a "Material Girl" mink, to lingerie from "Virgin" days.
- Two giant video screens.
- An array of props and production numbers—including a Spanish fantasy for "La Isla Bonita" and a gangster takeoff on "White Heat."
- A troupe of six dancers.
- A band of studio aces, led by her keyboardist and cowriter Pat Leonard.
- A musical set heavy on greatest hits, including the movie themes ("Into the Groove" from *Desperately Seeking Susan*), the dance club favorites

("Holiday") and, most likely, next month's hit (the new "Causing a Commotion").

"She wanted a visual impact that would knock people out," says Madonna's publicist, Liz Rosenberg. "She was very determined about this. And she's the type that makes a lot of decisions quickly: If something doesn't work, she starts over. One day she might get sick of her bracelets and rip them all off. You'll see a different look this year, but it's still Madonna, still bigger than life."

The big question is whether Madonna's show can carry to large audiences. Two years ago, Bruce Springsteen drew criticism for moving from concert halls to football stadiums; this year U2 also moved to bigger-than-ever venues. But both had come up through the clubs and theaters and built a solid bond with their fans. For Madonna, this is only the second tour. Her initial fame came from records and video, not concerts or club gigs. Her debut LP, with the hits "Holiday" and "Borderline," created the intitial buzz; 1984's *Like a Virgin* album took her to No. 1. Fans saw her on film *(Desperately Seeking Susan)*, in magazines and on video, but they never saw her live until 1985's *Virgin* tour.

Madonna's last Chicago dates were in May of 1985, when she sold out two shows at the Pavilion. There were a total of 18,000 tickets sold. As of Tuesday, 42,500 of the 47,000 available tickets had been sold, according to Arny Granat of Jam Productions, which is promoting the Madonna show. Granat estimated he would sell 1,500 more by the end of the week, leaving 3,000 seats still available.

Did he have doubts about booking Madonna into Soldier Field? "I had second thoughts," acknowledges Granat. "I had second thoughts and third thoughts. She's a definite media star, but any show of that nature, with such big production costs, is a big [financial] risk. You want to be able to sell it out in a few days.

"But I decided to put the money down and book her, and it looks as if I'm going to be proved right, although it's going to be a tight deal with a very tight profit margin."

But questions remain: Is the real Madonna as exciting as the media image? Can she handle the new setting as well as the other superstars can?

The *Baltimore Sun*'s J. D. Considine, who caught her recent opening date at Miami's 60,000-capacity Orange Bowl, thinks she can. "I've seen the Springsteen stadium tour, I've seen Dylan and the [Grateful] Dead, and I was at Live Aid. Out of all those shows, Madonna's is the only one I'd want to see again," he said in an interview. "You need a larger-than-life show if you want to come off in a stadium, and Madonna does. She's not that large physically, but she holds your attention, just as Michael Jackson did in the best of the 'Victory' tour."

Not everyone was so impressed. Anne Ayers, the assistant entertainment editor of *USA Today,* saw the same show and found it high on glitz but low on emotional clout. "She's going for a certain kind of show: a Broadway, show-biz, song-and-dance spectacle. In that context it's hard to make a connection with the audience, and I'd have to say she didn't," said Ayers in an interview.

There also has been talk about the "new Madonna," a stronger and more intelligent but still sexual image. Here again, the jury is still out. "The important thing Madonna does is to demonstrate how female sexuality can be a source of strength," says Considine.

"Traditionally in pop culture, there are two roles women can play—the good girl and the bad girl, and the bad girl is never taken seriously. But Madonna shows up in the trappings of a bad girl, and demands to be taken seriously because she doesn't just roll over. Lately you get more sense of the strength and power that was under her image all along."

Some critics have charged that Madonna isn't much of a singer, just a charismatic actress who makes records. Musical director Pat Leonard, for one, disagrees.

"I've heard the talk about how Madonna can't sing, and I can tell you that's bull," says Leonard, the tour's bandleader who cowrote much of the *True Blue* album. "She's a natural, intuitive singer with great intonation; and she puts across a vulnerable quality that you can't copy, and I know, because I've heard people try."

Leonard's name may not be familiar, but he has had ample experience behind the scenes: as musical director for the Jacksons' *Victory* tour and as a hit R&B songwriter, cowriting Evelyn King's "Just for the Night" and Peabo Bryson's "There Ain't Nothing Out There." For Madonna's tour, he pulled together a band of seasoned studio players: James Herra (from the *Virgin* tour) on lead guitar, David Williams (from the San Francisco jazz circuit) on rhythm guitar, Cary Hatch on bass, Jonathan Moffitt on drums and Louis Conte on percussion. Leonard and Jai Winding share keyboard duties. With this group, Leonard does the near-impossible by bringing funky dance-club music into stadiums. "I wouldn't think it could work, but so far there's no problem. The stuff we do isn't Stravinsky, it's pop music, so you need to keep time and have some taste. People are familiar enough with the songs that they can fill in the parts that get lost in the wind."

Leonard also directed Madonna's first tour and said there's a major difference this time: Instead of following every note on the records, he's encouraging the players to branch out. So a number of songs sport new arrangements: There's a medley of three of Madonna's biggest hits—"Dress You Up," "Material Girl" and "Like a Virgin"—along with a surprising cover of the Four Tops' oldie "I Can't Help Myself." And the finale, "Holiday," now features a hard-rock lead guitar.

When he first heard Madonna, Leonard was skeptical about her talent. "When they first asked me to do her tour, I didn't recognize the name. So they said, 'You know, "Like a Virgin."' And I said, 'Right. No way.'" But his opinion changed when they met, and started writing songs together. "She's very charming. And she has a way of coming up with ideas people can relate to. When we did 'White Heat,' she looked up and said 'I've got it: Cagney.' And the idea developed, of doing the video like a gangster movie. She's very fearless, like all true writers."

One more Madonna myth needs to be debunked: that she lacks a social conscience. Two summers ago she performed at Live Aid, and sang the uplifting "Love Makes the World Go Round." But she's more remembered for making the day's most irreverent comment from the stage: A week before Live Aid, *Playboy* magazine had published some nude photos from her days as a struggling actress. So she taunted the crowd by wearing a full-length fur coat in the summer heat. "I ain't taking ____ off today," she announced. "I don't want to hear about it later on."

But in mid-July she played an AIDS research benefit at Madison Square Garden. "Her best friend died of AIDS last year," explains publicist Rosenberg. "When he was sick, the American Foundation for AIDS Research was very helpful. She made a vow that she would do a benefit as soon as she went on tour."

Rosenberg also disputes the idea that most of Madonna's fans are teenage girls—the "wannabes"—but says they are an important part of her audience.

"Madonna's fortunate in that the wannabes are growing up with her," adds Rosenberg. "She always talks about the audiences after the shows, about what each row was doing. She's always out there looking, because she wants them all to like her. She's always been happiest when she's onstage."

JONATHAN TAKIFF

# EX-"BOY TOY" MADONNA TRANSFORMS HERSELF INTO ADULT ON *LIKE A PRAYER*

1989

Like a Prayer *represented another step forward for Madonna as a performer/songwriter, as this critic begrudgingly notes.*—Eds.

On the Pop Tart Queen's new album *Like a Prayer,* a 30-year-old Madonna exposes her bruised child-self in full measure for the very first time. It's a bold and largely successful effort to explain both her "take me, I'm yours" exhibitionist nature and dark spiritual underpinnings, and to reshape her theatrical image again, for the umpteenth time.

*Like a Prayer* charts a new, more serious course for her future, rather like her recent stint on Broadway (in David Mamet's *Speed-the-Plow*) and her currently filming role as bad-girl Breathless Mahoney in Warren Beatty's *Dick Tracy* seem intended to do. Though Madonna is one of the highest-paid performers of the 1980s (with an income of $20 million during each of the last three years, according to *Forbes* magazine) she is not about to rest on her assets.

Certainly, her new album has its moments of gum-snapping, hip-swinging, hit-bound trash. The title track's controversial sacred/profane double meanings are an apt case in point. (Didn't Pepsi read the lyrics to the song before they got into bed with this viper?)

But there's a curiously moral tone to her spare, experimental duet with Prince on the self-denying "Love Song," a piece that doesn't sound finished at first, but grows on you with repeated listens. And I'm plumb crazy for the bouncier one-guy-girl ditty "Cherish," a guaranteed No. 1 hit for the warm-weather months.

Still, the hard core of this set is serious and reflective, at times heavily laden with psychic trauma. You might consider *Like a Prayer* to be her *Misfits* . . . or her hour in the confessional box.

Pointed songs direct our attention back to Madonna's working-class upbringing in Detroit and are heavily endowed with an aura of Catholic guilt. The album closer, in fact, is a bizarre recitation of the "Act of Contrition," done up in the warped psychedelic style of the Beatles "Revolution No. 9."

In "Oh, Father," a stark ballad scored with a serious string arrangement, she suggests a sad, sick relationship with an abusive father: "You can't hurt me now / I got away from you, I never thought I would / You can't make me cry, you once had the power / I never felt so good about myself."

A more sedate and poignant ballad, "Promise to Try," explores the psychological hangups Madonna evidently still feels about her deceased mother. Mom's death left Madonna (at age 7) without a much-needed confidante and supporter, and pressed Madonna to act as surrogate mother to a brood of younger sisters and brothers: "Little girl don't forget her face / Laughing away your tears / When she was the one who felt all the pain."

A couple of ironically chipper love-hate songs explore a topic familiar to scandal sheet devotees—Madonna's thoughts on marriage, directed to her abusive, self-absorbed ex-spouse, Sean Penn. In the anxious, erratic sounding "Till Death Do Us Part," she suggests that the sins of a father often are repeated by a husband—that we seek out familiar role models as marital partners no matter how warped or humiliating they prove: "I think I interrupt your life / When you laugh it cuts me just like a knife / I'm not your friend I'm just your little wife." And later, the sparks really start to fly: "He takes a drink, she goes inside / He starts to scream, the vases fly / He wishes that she wouldn't cry / He's not in love with her anymore."

Bloodied but unbowed, Madonna's bubbly "Cherish" kicks off Side 2 with a reaffirmation of romantic faith so sweet and happy you can't believe it's the same woman singing. As much a child of pop as of the church, Madonna is restored by music's healing power, in this instance with a mix of classic sweet soul and L.A. pop moderne. "Cherish" shows her hand with lyrics borrowed from Sam Cooke's "Cupid" and the Association's "Cherish."

In fact, musical allusions to her influences abound throughout this coming-of-age album. "Express Yourself"—in which she tells the girls to demand a lot more than sex in a relationship—spins off Aretha Franklin's "Respect." Madonna's reaffirmation of family loyalties, "Keep It Together," is a percolating funkster in the style of Sly Stone's "It's a Family Affair." Sparked with castinets and a florid rumba beat, the melodramatic "Spanish Eyes" sounds like a cross between Ben E. King's "Spanish Harlem" and something by Billy Joel. Her pastel-pretty, richly orchestrated children's song "Dear Jessie" could have fit easily into the sound track of the Beatles' *Yellow Submarine.*

Will Madonna's newfound maturity inspire her pack of wannabe emulators to look for something more serious to sing about than "I want to have some fun, move my body all night long"?

We can only hope.

# CONCERT REVIEW: HOLLYWOOD LOS ANGELES SPORTS ARENA, MAY 12, 1990

*Variety*, 1990

*Here is a less-than-enthusiastic review of a show from Madonna's 1990 tour.*—Eds.

Madonna's level of intentions doesn't quite mesh with their execution. Performance was noteworthy, considering what she is attempting to do—an 18-song set with seemingly million-dollar Broadway production values and nine dancers.

However, a set piece of "songs from and inspired by *Dick Tracy*" (as her upcoming Sire LP *I'm Breathless* is subtitled) should have been the showcase for the new Madonna. It remains to be seen whether she pulls it off in the film, but her rendering of Stephen Sondheim's "(Sooner or Later) I Always Get My Man" only calls attention to why she was well suited for a character named Breathless. The lyrics were rendered almost unintelligible by Madonna's gum-chewing moll interp and her lack of lung control.

She opened with a mechanical version of "Express Yourself," in which the set, replicating the Fritz Lang *Metropolis* milieu from the video, was more impressive than her performance. Her vocals sounded so much like the studio version one wondered how much was live and how much was Memorex.

Stabs at humor were inane. After "Causing a Commotion," she staged a mock fight with backup singers Donna DeLory and Niki Harris.

She tossed off her more "serious" material—"Oh Father," "Live to Tell"—in a medley, followed by "Papa Don't Preach."

The 90-plus-minute set ended with exuberant renderings of "Vogue" (featuring the sharp choreography of Vincent Paterson) and "Cherish." Madonna's final encore was a tightly choreographed "Keep It Together," marred only by the song's repetitive shortcomings.

GREG KOT

# WITHOUT THE VIL ALBUMS JUST AREN'1

*Chicago Tribune,* May 13, 199

*Here's an overview of Madonna's first six album lackadaisical* I'm Breathless.—Eds.

Madonna's sixth album, *I'm Breathless: Music from and I Film* Dick Tracy (Sire), is a pop trifle far removed from the i sonal, adult concerns of 1989's *Like a Prayer.* Madonna attem three relatively frothy, jazz-flavored Stephen Sondheim comp including a duet with Mandy Patinkin on the ballad "What Ca Lose," but sounds out of her league. She's more at home on the five cowritten with longtime partner Patrick Leonard, most of which so like cartoonish homages to the big-band era.

The album's ultra-hip lead single, "Vogue," doesn't fit with the retro sound of the 11 other cuts, and longtime fans may be disappointed that there aren't more heavy dance beats. But Madonna's wit and personality make this an amusing, if ultimately disposable, *Guys and Dolls* update.

#### The First Five

Forced to stand without their videos, Madonna's records are generally unremarkable but hardly empty of virtue, as some of her critics claim. Madonna's self-titled debut (Sire, 1983) contained tracks such as "Borderline" and "Lucky Star" that initially established her in underground dance clubs, but it wasn't long before she was living up to the words from "Burning Up": "Unlike the others I'd do anything / I'm not the same I have no shame."

Though her voice sounded thin, pinched, girlish, her personality was provocative, sexy and aggressive—qualities that her early singles hinted at, but which her videos fully exploited.

Her second album, *Like a Virgin* (Sire, 1984), was her breakthrough, playing off her self-conscious campiness with a series of hot dance tracks, attention-grabbing lyrics and steamy videos. The title track, "Material Girl," and "Dress You Up" didn't endear her to the critics, but the kids loved her rebel style and sassiness. In retrospect, it's clear that *Like a Virgin* doesn't so much glorify materialism as parody it, but at the time Madonna was hung out to dry by the critics.

Blue (Sire, 1986) expanded Madonna's musical horizons. With ...on't Preach," she confronted the difficulties of teenage pregnancy ...ense of yearning, determination and vulnerability that signaled her ...ion from pop star to pop artist. Even more compelling was "Live to ... a ballad about childhood scars that Madonna sang with moving ...iction.

*You Can Dance* (Sire, 1987), a retrospective released to fill the gap ...ween albums, is a fine collection of dance remixes.

*Like a Prayer* (Sire, 1989) is Madonna's most accomplished and ...ature record, with the title track, "Oh Father," and "Till Death Do Us ...art" reflecting her personal traumas. Her voice also had softened and deepened, dropping from the shrill chirp of the early days into a darker, more melodic mid-range.

RICHARD HARRINGTON

# THE MADONNA PORNUCOPIA: *SEX* FOR THE COFFEE TABLE AND *EROTICA* FOR THE EARS

*Washington Post,* October 21, 1992

*Madonna's sex period on book and record is reviewed.*—Eds.

Psssst! Wanna see some new Madonna product?

Yes, it's that time of the fiscal year when Madonna Louise Veronica Ciccone comes to liberate our libidos and lighten our wallets. The first installment of her $60 million, multimedia deal with Time Warner arrives in stores today: *Sex* (Warner Books), an oversized, overpriced coffee-table book of hard-core sexual fantasies sure to separate the wannabes from the wanna-be-faraways, and *Erotica* (Warner Bros./Maverick), a dance-pop album whose content is something of a tease. Meanwhile, MTV is giving post-midnight play to "Erotica," a video that is ostensibly for the album's first single, but is really a promotional sampler from *Sex*. Total Madonna investment: about $65, the price of a cheap trick in Times Square, but a lot safer.

With more than a million copies being shipped worldwide, *Sex*, priced at $49.95, will set a publishing record for a first printing. And you can touch, but you'd better not look: *Sex* comes encased in an impenetrable Mylar sack. The photos themselves sit between two thick aluminum covers. No voyeurs—paying customers only please.

While everyone knows that Madonna has been selling, celebrating and satirizing sex throughout her career, constantly pushing the envelope of acceptable imagery, *Sex* is her most explicit work so far, true blue indeed. It's almost an encyclopedia of sexual fantasies and fetishes, featuring 128 pages of artfully explanatory photos by Steven Meisel and *Penthouse* Forum–style texts by Madonna herself.

Is *Sex* shocking? Not really. Mostly because it's Madonna, and in a way we've come to expect this from her—Madonna being one of the few women or men with the nerve and savvy to publicly explore these particular territories. Maybe the only one. *Sex* would be a lot more shocking starring anyone else, but with Madonna, it's just another day at the orifice. For her, sex is play and this is still her playground.

Is *Sex* disturbing? Willfully so. Madonna is the biggest female star in the world, and this book is so hard-core that she's bound to lose some of her fan base, not to mention incite her detractors. Yet her brand of sensationalism is hardly out of step with the outer limits of today's pop culture, and Madonna is usually a step ahead in this area.

Is *Sex* pornographic? That decision, future court cases aside, remains in the eye of the book-holder. In a recent *New Musical Express* interview, Madonna said that for her, "pornography is a word that implies . . . some sort of violence, intrusion, abuse." By that definition, *Sex* is not guilty. Its explicit scenarios are based upon what Madonna describes in the book as the "mutuality" of sadomasochism, when "you let someone hurt you who you know would never hurt you . . . S&M can involve sex, but it doesn't have to. It's a head trip."

Still, if you use *Sex* as a flip book, the Motion Picture Association of America would probably want to rate it NC-17. That, of course, is the rating likely to be tagged on Madonna's upcoming film *Body of Evidence,* in which she portrays a dominatrix type who may be guilty of "pleasuring" her elderly husbands to death.

Is *Sex* boring? Actually, yes.

In recent years, it's usually been the videos of Madonna's songs that have sparked a fuss, and "Erotica" continues that tradition. In the video, Madonna becomes Dita Parlo, a masked, gold-toothed dominatrix from an indeterminate age, ready to help us cross the street at the corner of Pleasure and Pain. "My name is Dita, I'll be your mistress tonight," she says coyly, eventually singing "erotic, erotic, put your hands all over my body," assuming different dominatrix roles and investigating assorted bondage scenarios before finishing up with some nude hitchhiking on a busy street remarkably free of pile-ups. Shot in grainy black and white,

"Erotica" has the feel of stag film, though its quick cuts keep the viewer from seeing all that much.

But a good alternate title for *Sex,* the book, would be "Expose Yourself," which Madonna does with abandon. The roots of all this will undoubtedly be explored in future scholarly texts, but the obvious precedents are the videos for 1987's "Open Your Heart," a love song set in a tawdry Times Square peep show, and 1990's "Justify My Love," a study of a sadomasochistic relationship set in a sleazy hotel. Even the "Erotica" video doesn't give a clue about *Sex*'s explicitness.

Madonna's oft-stated position is that she wants people to confront their long-held beliefs about sexuality, gender and race. As Madonnatrix, she wants to help them overcome the Great Repression with a libertine sexuality. She does accept limits (you must be 18 to buy *Sex*), and the book's editor has pointed out there's no sex with children or religious objects, and no penetration (beyond market share, of course).

Other than that, anything goes. Here's a leather-clad Madonna dominated by a pair of bald, naked lesbians. Here she is sucking a toe. Here she is shaving a man's pubic hair with a straight razor. Here she is doing the hokey-pokey with Vanilla Ice, a discredited rapper from long ago. Here she is the white meat in a pumpernickel sandwich consisting of Naomi Campbell and Big Daddy Kane. Here she is in the middle of an otherwise male-only orgy. Here she is as a cheerleader, being raped by skinheads. Here she is as a teenager, discovering her own breasts for the very first time.

There are various takes on bondage, whose comfort Madonna traces back to "when you were a baby and your mother strapped you in the car seat. . . . She wanted you to be safe. It was an act of love." There are plenty of explicit and elaborate verbal fantasies as well, all written by Madonna, who could stand applying some of these skills to her lyrics.

Except for a clear feminist viewpoint, the verbal fantasies are not that different from what you'll find in letters to dirty magazines, though they're leavened to a degree by Mae West–like humor. As for Meisel's photos, their precedents are more varied, including Robert Mapplethorpe, Helmut Newton, Christopher Rage, Bruce Webber and those Calvin Klein pullouts. Sure, they're arty, technically excellent, provocative and all that, but as Ross Perot would say, that's irrelevant.

After all this, *Erotica,* the album, is something of a letdown. On many of its 14 songs, Madonna's dry, detached vocals reflect her current zeal for spoken passages (à la "Vogue," "Justify My Love" and 1–900 numbers), but this gets as tedious as a sax solo—call them sex solos. The vocals, thin already, are sometimes further submerged in the mix, waiting to be tarted up sonically in a remix. Given past history, this is quite likely.

Certainly, the sound is of the moment, incorporating hip-hop and house techniques into a familiar dance-floor aesthetic that's drum-deep, bass-heavy and spare in arrangements that feel as though they could stop on a dime (or a button). With few exceptions, *Erotica* is a rhythm-driven vehicle that will deliver its pure pop melodies to a variety of radio formats, but most of these songs will be made more interesting by their videos.

Only three songs seem to bare much relationship with *Sex:* "Erotica," of course, which is essentially a bondage update on "Justify My Love"; and the sultry "Where Life Begins," in which Madonna proves herself a cunning linguist in a metaphor-filled paean to oral sex ("Can you make a fire without using wood?" she asks).

And there's "Did You Do It?," a pure hip-hop cut by André Betts, who produced four tracks on the album. Oddly enough, Madonna appears on the track only incidentally via sampling; it's Betts who raps (in the style of Q-Tip and Black Sheep) in a sendup of macho bravado, detailing for disbelieving friends his sexual conquest of Madonna. (This is the only cut on the album that could be considered explicit; on a version of the album that does not include an "explicit lyrics" warning sticker, this cut has been removed.)

While some of the other songs on *Erotica* are likely to be recast in their meaning by sexually suggestive videos—an old Madonna trick—the album is more concerned with the pain and torment of the heart and the perils of romance. Mostly cowritten with producer Shep Pettibone, songs in this vein include the straight pop song "Bad Girl"—she masks her pain through debauchery while suggesting "I'm not happy when I act this way"—and "Bye Bye Baby," which borrows a hook from L. L. Cool J's "Jinglin' Baby," and kicks off with Madonna saying "this is not a love song." She uses a sonically filtered, detached and slightly taunting voice to talk about taking control rather than exacting revenge on a domineering, mind-game-playing partner ("It's your turn to cry, this time you have to say goodbye").

"Waiting for You" is a brooding ballad noir with a druggy pulse and obsessive ambiance in which Madonna is less certain of her course: "I wish I could love you or have the courage to leave you," she sings as a piano tinkles its own tears. And for Madonna, "Words" seems just as hurtful as sticks and stones: "They always attack, please take them all back," she tells a duplicitous partner. On a more positive note, "Rain" is an optimistic Peter Gabriel–like ballad in which water is a metaphor for love ("Work away my sorrow, take away my pain"). The video will probably be about golden showers.

Two songs with sexually charged titles are come-ons: "Deeper and Deeper" is about falling in love, and is blatantly self-referential musically. "Why's It So Hard" is about the difficulties in loving one another and a plea for better understanding between races and people, best expressed in the chorus "Bring your love / Sing your love / Wear your love / Share your love." On both songs, Madonna explores the bottom of her limited range, as she does on "In This Life," a lugubrious paean to friends who have died of AIDS. Heartfelt and well intended though the song may be, it unfortunately comes across as maudlin.

Among the least successful cuts are "Thief of Hearts," a mundane best-friend-steals-boyfriend scenario ("and now you'll have to pay") that sounds like an Exposé castoff; and Madonna's remake of Peggy Lee's classic "Fever." Lee's 1958 original was sly, sultry and as warm as its title; the new version is a cool mechanical recitation in which more attention is paid to the pulse of the music than that of the heart. A better title would have been "Headache Tonight."

The album's closing cut, "Secret Garden," is aurally intriguing but lyrically fatuous in the manner of Ingrid Chavez and Lenny Kravitz. In it, Madonna seems confused: "I wonder if I'll ever know / Where my place is / Where my face is / I know it's in here somewhere / I just wish I knew the color of my hair . . ." All this is played out over a neo-psychedelic ambiance tinged with jazz piano. Assuming the record-buying public may feel this $60 million woman is overexposed, there's also a question as to whether they'll continue to buy into Madonna songs that portray her as vulnerable—particularly after ogling *Sex*.

Ironically, the whole Madonna package brings to mind "Airotica," a dance number from the Bob Fosse film *All That Jazz*. "Fly us," the dancers-as-nearly-naked stewards and stewardesses say as they explore all manner of sexual coupling before a small, shocked audience of potential investors. "Our motto is we take you everywhere but get you nowhere."

That sounds about right.

RICHARD CORLISS

# MADONNA GOES TO CAMP

*Time* magazine, October 25, 1993

*The infamous Girlie Show tour is reviewed.*—Eds.

There she stood, a vision of tawdriness: blond hair, black skirt, red bra over taut white flesh. She was that odd-lot remnant of the '80s, a Madonna wannabe. But most of the other fans at the Toronto SkyDome last week for the North American opening of the singer's Girlie Show tour were dressed in civvies. For them, the star was only something to stare at. She is not a role model, not after a decade in the spotlight. These days, does anyone wanna be Madonna?

Does anyone even wanna see Madonna? Not on the movie screen. *Body of Evidence,* in which she played a woman accused of killing her lover with sex, earned just $14 million at the U.S. box office, less than her 1991 documentary *Truth or Dare.* Sales of Madonna albums have also had diminishing returns; the latest, *Erotica,* has sold about 2 million in the U.S., down from *Like a Virgin*'s 7 million. *Sex,* her notorious $50 diary and sado-catechism, enjoyed a frenetic first-day sale in bookstores but quickly reached climax, then rolled over like a sated lover and went to sleep.

It's true that her current caravan, traversing four continents and 20 cities (including New York last week, Philadelphia and Detroit this), is a smash. Biggest thing since the Who tour, you hear; biggest thing since the Rolling Stones. Alas, these fossils of Jurassic Rock are the merest nostalgia items; a fan wants to see them before they break up or crack up. Madonna sets herself the sterner challenge of being forever new, pertinent, shocking. But it's tough to stay on top by spanking somebody's bottom. In her recent work, Madonna has pursued dominatrix fantasies until she may be the only one getting off on them. She is in danger of going the blond widow in *Body of Evidence* one desperate step further, and loving herself to death.

She can also play the vulnerable diva. When two teddy bears from admirers landed at her feet in Toronto, she begged, "Just throw soft things at me, please." But Madonna is no Garland or Monroe, a prisoner to her poses. This is a woman in complete control of her career, canny about her image and ever protective of her shelf life. She made millions from going too far; it's just that for a while she went too too far. Now it is time for her to step back and appraise—what else?—herself.

The result is Girlie Show, an essay in retro show biz. As another star with some mileage on her said in *Sunset Boulevard,* "Not a comeback, a return." The show is a return to the womb of popular culture: a calculated peek at American innocence. The proscenium stage is fronted with red drapery suitable for a Louisiana bordello; the title promises and delivers burlesque. But burlesque in the older sense of parody, travesty, impudent fun. There is humid sexuality at the start of the two-hour extravaganza (topless acrobat on a phallic pole, Madonna easing a whip past her crotch, dancers gyrating in automassage), but it soon gives way to simpler, sunnier images.

For "Rain," Madonna dons demure black; the look says, "Listen to the sad ballad, the sweet harmonies." For "Express Yourself," she's dolled up in royal-blue bell-bottoms and a frizz wig, to pay homage to the gaudy innocence of the Cyndi Lauper era. The Wayback Machine keeps spinning until we are in Weimar Berlin, with Madonna in Dietrich drag warbling Teutonic twaddle: "Like a wer-gin, touched for the werry vurst time." She is Carmen Miranda ("Going Bananas"), Gene Kelly ("La Isla Bonita"), the Brigitte Helm robot goddess from the silent film *Metropolis.* She saves her best anachronistic joke for last: the steamy "Justify My Love" is performed in stately cadence and Edwardian morning coats. It might be the Ascot Gavotte from *My Fair Lady.*

Nostalgia, as wispy as the scent of marijuana that permeated the SkyDome, is itself decadent. By highlighting the past, Madonna is saying the present has little to offer. In doing so, she is also forging a bond with her loyal gay audience. It is an axiom of pop culture that no uncloseted gay man can be a star but that women can be stars by appropriating gay motifs. Bette Midler steals gays' jokes; Madonna steals their style. It's not just in the Nazified naughtiness of her night-at-the-Anvil routines, or the treatment of boys as toys (the Queen steps on their supine writhing bodies). It's in the dressing up as iconic actresses, the power plays and the nurturing of her brood. In a Pietá pose the star strikes with one dancer, she looks like a Mother Teresa to the emotionally homeless.

The fascinating thing about Madonna is that she is all-real and all-fake—in other words, pure show biz. Girlie Show—at once a movie retrospective, a Ziegfeld revue, a living video and an R-rated takeoff on Cirque du Soleil—opens with Smokey Robinson's "Tears of a Clown" and closes with Cole Porter's "Be a Clown." Pierrot is your silent host; the calliope music announces that this is a three-ring circus of clowning around. And Madonna, once the Harlow harlot and now a perky harlequin, is the greatest show-off on earth.

STEVE DOLLAR

# PILLOW TALK

1994

*Madonna's recent albums have been less commercially successful than their predecessors. Here,* Bedtime Stories *is reviewed in the context of Madonna's career.*—Eds.

Moreso than most pop singers, Madonna's albums function as accessories, items to adorn a newly minted persona or a blatantly manipulated image. When fans wonder, "Who is she this time?," a fresh batch of songs, recorded with a revolving roster of studio wizards, illustrated in rock videos and, usually, hyped with a burst of controversy, provides an answer. "Here's my story / No risk, no glory," Madonna sings on "Survival," the opening track of *Bedtime Stories,* which is due in stores today.

It's true that the new CD was steered, in large part, by Atlanta-based producers Babyface, cofounder of LaFace Records, and Dallas Austin, at his DARP Studios in Atlanta. Two of the smoothest operators in the field of contemporary rhythm-and-blues, the pair have independently structured hits for everyone from Whitney Houston to TLC, Toni Braxton to Boyz II Men.

Yet, rather than signify some bold new direction for Madonna, *Bedtime Stories* takes hardly any risks at all.

If it's not sensational, *Bedtime Stories* is comforting. Songs such as "Forbidden Love," "Sanctuary," and "Inside of Me" offer a kind of deluxe smooch music, with musings on the glory of love, the discontents of romance and the pursuit of pleasure. Though much of the music is generic—down to the samples of Blue Note jazz man Grant Green's guitar, so prevalent in recent hip-hop—it serves a purpose, allowing Madonna to speak as directly as she wants to.

"Who needs the light / With the darkness in your eyes?" she sings to a lover on "Sanctuary," while Austin samples bits of Herbie Hancock's "Watermelon Man" and what sounds like pygmy chants. On "Secret," she reveals that "Happiness lies in your own hand," and from her tone, it seems the lyric has to do with self-determination, not auto-eroticism.

It will be interesting to see how *Bedtime Stories* is received, since it offers neither the pop epiphany of *Like a Prayer* nor the shameless frolic of Madonna's dance hits.

"Oops, I didn't know I couldn't talk about sex," Madonna declares on "Human Nature," tweaking both audience and image. The irony is, this time she really doesn't.

**The Local Connection**

Though he kept quiet on the Material Girl while she was in town recording, producer Dallas Austin shared his thoughts the day before the album release. "Madonna is the kind of artist you really have to hang out with and get to know before you can start working with her," says Austin, 22. "Because she's who she is she might otherwise be sort of intimidating if you don't establish yourself with her beforehand. So we hung out, went to some ball games, that sort of thing before we started working. In the studio she could actually be very relaxed and playful, but also very outspoken about what she wanted," says Austin, who produced four of the 11 tracks. "We butted heads a few times, but all and all I have to say she is a perfectionist."

JOAN ANDERMAN

# MADONNA CAPTURES THE MOMENT AND SEES THE SPIRITUAL LIGHT

*Boston Globe,* March 1, 1998

*Madonna's 1998 album was well received critically. Here's an early, sympathetic review.*—Eds.

The release of a Madonna album—her new one, *Ray of Light,* is due Tuesday—amounts to so much more than a handful of new songs. To be sure, she no longer straddles the music/fashion/culture axis as she did in the mid-'80s, when—armed with not more than an ear for a dance track, a writhing midsection, and fierce belief in the power of her own personality—she transposed the New York club-music underground into the bouncy beat of pop superstardom. But even a string of forgettable films *(Shanghai Surprise, Who's That Girl?),* wildly inconsistent musical product (1989's exhilarating *Like a Prayer,* for example, was followed by 1990's abysmal *I'm Breathless*), and her drastically miscalculated publishing campaign to conquer America's final frontier with 1992's show-all book *Sex* and its aural aid, *Erotica,* haven't quieted the public's appetite for Madonna.

She remains, after all, the mainstream's most powerful magnet for camera-ready controversy. (Courtney Love is giving her a good run for her money, but Love's indie-girl acridness hasn't been entirely obliterated by the layers of stylists' perfumed paints, and that rock band of hers will never play in Peoria.) Madonna is the perfect modern pinup girl. She sells self-expression off the rack, blasphemy you can dance to, S&M for your coffee table, and most recently—in case anyone forgot along the way that she's got a heart—romance, in the form of 1994's tepid, soft-soul *Bedtime Stories.* Trouble is, Madonna's undulating persona, fueled in equal parts by savvy opportunism and true-blue creative juice, has almost entirely obscured her pop music voice. Carrying *Evita* lent her some of the post-disco queen/sex machine credibility she so desperately craves, but I'd rather listen to the trashiest Madonna cut than suffer through a block-buster refrain from Andrew Lloyd Webber's odes to the lowest common denominator. She's kept her audience, yes, but lost her way in the bargain.

Welcome back, girlfriend. *Ray of Light* (Maverick/Warner Bros.) is a remarkable album. It comes as no surprise that the record is awash in electronica; Madonna's great gift is to spot the cult trend of the moment, employ that sound's master craftsmen (in this case, the brilliant producer William Orbit), and overlay her own dance-pop sensibilities. What's extraordinary is how thoroughly Madonna has immersed herself in unfamiliar, and commercially unproven, musical territory. *Ray of Light* is no ambient-Lite project, no collection of Top 40 hits slapped with an occasional electronic flourish to prove its hipster quotient. It's a deeply spiritual dance record, ecstatically textured, a sumptuous, serious cycle of songs that goes a long way toward liberating Madonna from a career built on scavenged images and cultivated identities.

That said, one could argue that *Ray of Light* merely signals the arrival of her latest incarnation—Mystical Madonna, let's say, complete with long, wavy tresses and a dewy new look—which amounts to one more beautifully realized co-option carried out by a market-driven celebrity with limited potential for her own innovation. The difference is that Madonna's current musical journey is buoyed by an unprecedented interior odyssey.

Motherhood has been known to soften the hardest hearts; in Madonna's case it seems to have torn open a window-size hole. And that view of the artist, revealed in the first unforced, captivating singing I've heard from her, and words that aspire to something deeper and more personal than textbook emotions and dance-floor incantations, reverberates through *Ray of Light* as surely as her collaborators' finely honed musicianship.

"I traded fame for love / Without a second thought / It all became a silly game / Some things cannot be bought / Got exactly what I asked for / Wanted it so badly / Running, rushing back for more / I suffered fools / So gladly / And now I find / I've changed my mind" is the confessional (from "Drowned World/Substitute for Love") that opens the album. Sophisticated wordplay it's not. But it does sound like the truth, and that's a revelation for an artist notorious for being every sort of creature but herself. Here, as on the 12 following tracks, Madonna sings over shifting layers of sound that sift one into the next, emphasizing mood over structure. Airy, whirring tones and muted bells thicken into a melancholy, R&B undertow, gathering sprays of feedback and machine-gun drum fills as it swells to an industrial clatter, then drops off its own edge into a swirl of throbbing, buzzing points of sound. Orbit, the album's coproducer and cowriter (along with longtime collaborator Patrick Leonard, plus Rick Nowels and Susannah Melvoin), has made some of the most evocative trip-trance music on record with, among others, Massive Attack and his own *Strange Cargo* album series. On *Ray of Light,* he coaxes dazzling color and voluptuous contours from his knobs and buttons, which move in startling synchronicity with Madonna's newly colored, contoured voice.

Orbit deserves credit for the sheer artistry of sound on this album. But there's an art to Madonna's vision as well. She's an inspired navigator and cuts a tantalizing path through her newfound spiritualism, dance-club roots, and electronic soundscape. In "Shanti/Ashtangi," Madonna sings the praises of "the gurus' lotus feet" in an ancient Sanskrit text set to a dense mass of sampled sounds from India and Morocco, a rattling drum-and-bass groove, and gauzy blasts of electric guitar. Her ambition, clearly, hasn't been sacrificed to the inner journey. She set out to harness heaven and earth, and makes a valiant play of it.

My guess is that Madonna's dabblings in Eastern thought and music led her through the back door to this album's most exotic reference: the '60s. For such a post-everything girl, the heavy, psychedelic languor of "Candy Perfume Girl"—with its whimsical, Sergeant Pepper's pipe-organ break, stream-of-consciousness lyrics, and blaze of acid rock guitars (amid the heavy beats and futuristic noodlings)—is an arresting stretch. But from there it's a short passage to a dreamy trilogy ("Frozen," "The Power of Goodbye," and "To Have and Not to Hold") during which Madonna carries on a dialogue with herself about the path to divine openness.

Here her philosophical reach begins to exceed her songwriting grasp. Only "Frozen" (the album's first single) achieves a state of divine balladry, recalling the emotional pitch and simmering beauty of 1986's "Live to Tell" with a dark, lush string section, the smash and patter of a lone drum, and an ominous, pulsing buzz.

Mystical Madonna would surely appreciate the cosmic symmetry in the notion that her most adventurous outing yet doubles as a homecoming. The album's title cut is one of several disco-trance tracks (including "Skin" and "Nothing Really Matters") that are on a crash course with every late-night rave on the planet. For all its ambient glory, *Ray of Light* reminds us that the dance floor is her turf, and swaggering hooks her currency. That's not to suggest that a familiar fit invariably translates into a good song. With its slow, maudlin changes and copius clichés, "Skin" sounds uncannily like an Andrew Lloyd Webber number, heavy on the Orbit remix. It's simply a relief to find her—after so many years spent dodging the fallout of her own misguided expectations—doing what comes naturally.

# Part Two

# OPEN YOUR HEART TO ME

## MADONNA AND THE PRESS

*As an interview subject, Madonna has been a favorite among the media, from TV news to daily papers and glossy magazines. Although there are many glossy profile-interviews available, we've tried to select representative ones from various periods of the star's career for this roundup of Madonna in her own words.*—Eds.

# MADONNA: SHE'S ONE LUCKY STAR!

*Teen* magazine, 1984

*Here is a typical "fanzine" type interview from the early years.*—Eds.

"She's One Lucky Star!"

This set of lyrics from Madonna's single "Lucky Star" certainly can be used to describe her career—one that has been guided by unique style, talent and good fortune! Her 1983 debut album, *Madonna,* sparked more hits and praise than most performers can hope for in a lifetime! And now, with the recent release of her latest album, *Like a Virgin,* and two upcoming film roles, it looks as if all of Madonna's wishes have been answered. And her lucky star seems to be rising higher and higher!

Madonna is a fitting name for this dynamic beauty who has created her own self-styled fashion statement with uncombed hair, bracelets up to the elbows and a number of earrings on each ear. In a word, Madonna is unique. And, along with a small handful of other versatile performers, such as Sting and Prince, Madonna has become a one-name sensation!

Born Madonna Ciccone (named after her mother who died when Madonna was 7 years old), 24 years ago in Detroit, Mich., Madonna comes from a large Italian family with five boys and three girls. She describes the home environment as being very competitive.

"My father brought me up to be very goal-oriented—to be a lawyer or doctor and study, study, study. We didn't get allowances, but we definitely got rewards for achieving," she says. And with all those siblings to compete with, Madonna sought out every opportunity to be number one. "I got the best grades, straight As . . . and all my brothers and sisters hated me!" she jokingly adds.

On the lighter side, however, Madonna also describes her upbringing as being very musical. When she was very young, she studied piano for a

Early '80s. *Courtesy of Bob Gruen, Star File.*

year, but quit after convincing her father to let her take ballet lessons instead. And soon after, she became involved in everything from jazz and tap to modern dance.

Madonna's dance roots may seem like a strange beginning for someone who has blossomed into a dynamic singer, but as she explains, "I always had the idea that I wanted to be a performer, but I wasn't sure if I wanted to sing or dance or be an actress or what, so I concentrated on dancing."

And what began with her winning the lead roles in her high school's musicals such as *My Fair Lady* and *The Sound of Music,* soon earned her a dance scholarship to the University of Michigan. Yet after only a year, Madonna was filled with the desire to dance professionally and she set aside her studies and decided to go test her talents in the big time—New York City!

"I moved to New York in '78," says Madonna. "I was only 17. I had $35 in my pocket and knew no one. I told the taxi driver to take me to the middle of everything. I was let off in Times Square," she remembers.

Although this may have been a startling introduction for any other teenager, Madonna made this overwhelming environment work for her. And not long after her arrival, she auditioned for and won a dance scholarship with the Alvin Ailey American Dance Theater, and later studied the famous Martha Graham technique under the direction of one of Graham's dance soloists, Pearl Lang.

Madonna had a strong desire to dance professionally in New York, but as she explains, "There weren't many companies that I wanted to work for. The best ones didn't need anyone at the time. And I wasn't willing to wait five years for a break."

Therefore, when Madonna was offered the opportunity to sing and dance in a French disco singer's international tour, she jumped at the chance and caught the first plane to Paris.

She arrived back in New York six months later and came up with the innovative idea of combining her talents for music and dance. And after hanging out at various dance clubs, watching and picking up on the dancing she liked the best, Madonna put it all together and created her own choreographed music. At this same time, Madonna was briefly involved with a band called the Breakfast Club, in which she played the drums, but she soon broke away from the band so she could put all her energies into pursuing her solo career.

After recording a demo tape of original material, she convinced a disc jockey at a dance club called the Danceteria to play one of her songs. The song was "Everybody" and it was not only a pleasant surprise to the disc jockey and the dancers at the club, but it also happened to impress a record executive who was there. He signed her to a major recording contract that very evening! She was now on her way.

The immediate success of her debut album, *Madonna,* was solid gold proof that all her unique talents and stunning looks could come together and create a powerful and appealing package. And soon after the single "Everybody" was released, there was a string of crossover hits (on the dance and pop charts) that followed, including "Holiday," "Physical Attraction," "Burning Up" and "Borderline." In addition, the sophisticated "Burning Up" and "Borderline" videos helped establish Madonna as a star to be reckoned with!

Madonna describes her music as the kind that helps people to forget about the problems of the world. "It's just to cheer people up," she says. "People go out to dance to get away and forget about their problems, like a holiday, and that's what the music's about—to get together and forget."

On Madonna's latest album, *Like a Virgin,* she is following in the same formula. And with a powerful blend of dance songs on the album and a slick video to match, the package is hard to beat! Yet Madonna is not the kind to sit back and let success completely catch up with her, and that is why she's always thinking one step ahead of the game. That little girl is no longer inside of her who isn't quite sure in which creative direction to take her career. She has decided—and she wants everything!

"I want to keep on making great records and want to develop as a music artist, but also to get involved in other things, as well. I'd like to make more videos and to write music for other people and then I have a great interest in films," she says.

And in Madonna's go-getter style, she is exploring this great interest and will soon be seen in two films that will be released early this year—*Desperately Seeking Susan* and *Vision Quest.*

With all of her dreams falling perfectly into place, Madonna's schedule is extremely hectic. And although she finds it difficult to travel home to Michigan to visit the members of her family, they try to come to New York whenever they can. And during those rare moments when Madonna finds the time to relax, the things she enjoys doing most are reading, writing, eating, watching old movies and dancing.

As Madonna takes the time to reflect on her quick rise to super-stardom, she easily puts things into perspective. "Three to four years ago dancing was the most important thing—now it's music. That will lead on to something else . . . acting. Above all, I want to be an all-around entertainer. And happy," she says.

And judging from her self-confidence and mass appeal, it all seems to be in the stars for Madonna!

DENISE WORRELL

# MADONNA!

*Time* magazine, May 27, 1985

*Here Madonna spins her myths for the mainstream* Time *magazine.*—Eds.

"If people don't get the humor in me or my act, then they don't want to."

On the long bus ride from Houston to Austin, the green flatlands float past the window and Madonna settles down for an interview. She is wearing a Kelly green knit skirt, which is peeled down over her belly, and a Paisley shirt knotted above her waist. Her streaked blond hair is twisted into a bun and held in place by a big red bow. Her lips are painted bright red and exaggerated. Her voice is a little raw and raspy.

**FATHER** My father is first-generation Italian. He was the youngest of six boys. My grandparents came from Italy on the boat. They went to Pennsylvania, a town right outside of Pittsburgh, because the steel mills are there and there was a lot of work. They lived in sort of an Italian ghetto-type neighborhood, and my grandfather got a job in a steel mill. My grandmother and grandfather spoke no English at all. They are dead now, but when I was a little girl I would see them all the time. They weren't very educated, and I think in a way they represented an old lifestyle that my father really didn't want to have anything to do with. It's not that he was ashamed, really, but he wanted to be better. I think he was the only one of all my grandparents' children who got a college education. He got an engineering degree and moved to Michigan because of the automotive industry. I think he wanted to be upwardly mobile and go into the educated, prosperous America. I think he wanted us to have a better life than he did when he was growing up.

He was in the Air Force, and one of his best friends was my mother's oldest brother. Of course he met my mother, and he fell in love with her immediately. She was very beautiful. I look like her. I have my father's eyes but I have my mother's smile and a lot of her facial structure. She was French Canadian but she was born in Bay City. The reason I was born in Bay City is that we were at my grandmother's house. I'm the third oldest child and the oldest girl. There were six of us. Then my mother died and my father remarried three years later, and he had children with my stepmother.

My father was very strong. I don't agree with some of his values but he did have integrity, and if he told us not to do something he didn't do it either. A lot of parents tell their kids not to smoke cigarettes and they smoke cigarettes. Or they give you some idea of sexual modesty—but my father lived that way. He believed that making love to someone is a very sacred thing and it shouldn't happen until after you are married. He stuck by those beliefs, and that represented a very strong person to me. He was my role model.

I was my father's favorite. I knew how to wrap him around my finger. I knew there was another way to go besides saying, "No, I'm not going to do it," and I employed those techniques. I was a very good student. I got all As. My father rewarded us for good grades. He gave us quarters and 50 cents for every A we got. I was really competitive, and my brothers and sisters hated me for it. I made the most money off of every report card.

My father and I are still close. When I moved away for a long time we weren't really that close. He didn't understand what I was doing when I first moved away. First I was a dancer and I would call him and say, "Well, I'm dancing." He never, well, he's a sensible guy, and what's dancing to him? He can't imagine that you can make a living from it or work at it or be proud of it or think of it as an accomplishment. He could never really be supportive about it.

When I went to Paris, and I went from dancing to singing, I would call him and say, "Well, I'm in France." And he would say, "What are you doing there?" and I said, "I'm going to be a singer." And he said, "What do you mean you're going to be a singer?" I would always tell him not to worry and that everything was OK, and he would say, "How are you surviving? Who pays for everything?" I would say, "They pay for everything." And he wanted to know what I had to do for that, and I didn't have to do anything really.

I lived a hand-to-mouth existence. I relied on friends and on money I could get here and there on short stints at jobs which I could never keep.

It wasn't until my first album came out and my father started hearing my songs on the radio that he stopped asking me questions. I think now he has some conception of my success. He reads about me and people bother him and he has to change his phone number all the time. All of a sudden he's popular, and my brothers and sisters are popular in school because of their association. If he didn't know then, he knows now. He still works for General Dynamics. He's an optics and defense engineer, and he makes a lot more money now. I never considered my parents incredibly wealthy, but at least now they can travel. They go to Europe, and they have enough to have a good life.

**MOTHER** I was about six and a half or seven when my mother died. I remember her being a very forgiving, angelic person. I think my parents pissed a lot of people off because they had so many kids and they never screamed at us. My older brothers were very rambunctious and they would start fires in the basement or throw rocks at windows and my mother and father would never yell at them. They would just hug us and put their arms around us and talk to us quietly.

I have a memory of my mother in the kitchen scrubbing the floor. She did all the housecleaning, and she was always picking up after us. We were really messy, awful kids. I remember having these mixed feelings. I have a lot of feelings of love and warmth for her but sometimes I think I tortured her. I think little kids do that to people who are really good to them.

They can't believe they're not getting yelled at or something so they taunt you. I really taunted my mother. I remember also I knew she was sick for a long time with breast cancer, so she was very weak, but she would continue to go on and do the things she had to do. I knew she was very fragile and kept getting more fragile. I knew that, because she would stop during the day and just sit down on the couch. I wanted her to get up and play with me and do the things she did before.

I know she tried to keep her feelings inside, her fear inside, and not let us know. She never complained. I remember she was really sick and was sitting on the couch. I went up to her and I remember climbing on her back and saying, "Play with me, play with me," and she wouldn't. She couldn't and she started crying and I got really angry with her and I remember, like, pounding her back with my first and saying, "Why are you doing this?" Then I realized she was crying. [Madonna stops talking and covers her face with her hands and cries.] I remember feeling stronger than she was. I was so little and I put my arms around her and I could feel her body underneath me sobbing and I felt like she was the child. I stopped tormenting her after that. That was the turning point when I knew. I think that made me grow up fast. I knew I could be either sad and weak and not in control or I could just take control and say it's going to get better.

Then my mother spent about a year in the hospital, and I saw my father going through changes also. He was devastated. It is awful to see your father cry. But he was very strong about it. He would take us to the hospital to see her, and I remember my mother was always cracking up and making jokes. She was really funny so it wasn't so awful to go and visit her there. Then my mother died. I remember that right before she died she asked for a hamburger. She wanted to eat a hamburger because she couldn't eat anything for so long, and I thought that was very funny. I didn't actually watch her die. I left and then she died. Then everything changed. My family was always split up and we had to go stay at relatives'.

**STEPMOTHER** As soon as my father started hiring housekeepers we were all back together again. He just kept going through housekeepers because we never got along with them. Then he married one of our housekeepers. I don't really want to talk about my stepmother. I was the oldest girl so I had a lot of adult responsibilities. I feel like all my adolescence was spent taking care of babies and changing diapers and baby-sitting. I have to say I resented it, because when all my friends were out playing, I felt like I had all these adult responsibilities. I think that's when I really thought about how I wanted to do something else and get away from all that. I really saw myself as the quintessential Cinderella. You know, I have this stepmother and I have all this work to do and it's awful and I never go out and I don't have pretty dresses. The thing I hated about my sisters most was my stepmother insisted on buying us the same dresses. I would do everything not to look like them. I would wear weird-colored knee socks or put bows in my hair or anything. I also went to Catholic schools, so I had to wear uniforms that were drab. I guess that was the beginning of my style.

**KID STUFF** My father made everyone in our family take a musical instrument and go to lessons every day. I took piano lessons but I hated them. Finally, I convinced my father to let me take dance lessons at one of those schools where you get ballet, jazz, tap and baton twirling. Anyway, the dance school was really like a place for hyperactive young girls. I was pretty rambunctious.

I wasn't really a tomboy. I was considered the sissy of the family because I relied on feminine wiles to get my way. My sister was really a tomboy and she hung out with my older brothers. They all picked on me, and I always tattled on them to my father. They would hang me on the clothesline by my underpants. I was little, and they put me up there with clothespins. Or they'd pin me down on the ground and spit in my mouth. All brothers do that, don't they? I wasn't quiet at all. I remember always being told to shut up. Everywhere, at home, at school, I always got in trouble for talking out of turn in school. I got tape over my mouth. I got my mouth washed out with soap. Everything.

Mouthing off comes naturally. Every time there was a talent show or a musical in school, I was always in it. *Cinderella* and *The Wizard of Oz* and *Godspell* and *My Fair Lady:* the ingenue role was always mine. But when there was a role for, like, a forward, bad girl, everybody sort of unanimously looked over at me when they were casting it.

**VIRGINITY** I remember when I was growing up I remember liking my body and not being ashamed of it. I remember liking boys and not feeling inhibited. I never played little games; if I liked a boy, I'd confront him. I've always been that way. Maybe it comes from having older brothers and sharing the bathroom with them or whatever. But when you're that aggressive in junior high, the boys get the wrong impression of you. They mistake your forwardness for sexual promiscuity. Then when they don't get what they think they're going to get, they turn on you. I went through this whole period of time when the girls thought I was really loose and all the guys called me nympho. I was necking with boys like everybody else was. The first boy I ever slept with had been my boyfriend for a long time, and I was in love with him. So I didn't understand where it all came from. I would hear words like slut that I hear now. It's sort of repeating itself. I was called those names when I was still a virgin. I didn't fit in and that's when I got into dancing. I shut off from all of that and I escaped.

**DANCING** When I was in the tenth grade I knew a girl who was a serious ballet dancer. She looked really smarter than your average girl but in an interesting, offbeat way. So I attached myself to her and she brought me to a ballet class, and that's where I met Christopher Flynn, who saved me from my high school turmoil. He had a ballet school in Rochester. It was beautiful. I didn't know what I was doing, really. I was with these really professional ballet dancers. I had only studied jazz up to then, so I had to work twice as hard as anybody else and Christopher Flynn was impressed with me. He saw my body changing and how hard I worked. I really loved him. He was my first taste of what I thought was an artistic person. I remember once I had a towel wrapped around my head like a turban. He came over to me and he said, "You know, you're really beautiful." I said, "What?" Nobody had ever said that to me before. He said, "You have an ancient-looking face. A face like an ancient Roman statue." I was flabbergasted. I knew that I was interesting, and of course I was voluptuous for my age, but I'd never had a sense of myself being beautiful until he told me. The way he said it, it was an internal thing, much deeper than superficial beauty. He educated me, he took me to museums and told me about art. He was my mentor, my father, my imaginative lover, my brother, everything, because he understood me. He encouraged me to go to New York. He was the one who said I could do it if I wanted to.

**NEW YORK** I saved up enough money for a one-way ticket and flew to New York. It was my first plane trip. When I got off the plane, I got in a taxi and told the driver to take me to the middle of everything. That turned out to be Times Square. I think the cab driver was saying, like, "OK, I'll show her something." I think he got a chuckle out of that. I got out of the cab and I was overwhelmed because the buildings, you know, are really high. I walked east on 42nd Street and then south on Lexington and there was a street fair. It was the summer and I had on a winter coat and was carrying a suitcase. This guy started following me around. He wasn't cute or anything, but he looked interesting. I said hi to him, and he said, "Why are you walking around with a winter coat and a suitcase?" And I said, "I just got off the plane." And then he said, "Why don't you go home and get rid of it?" And I said, "I don't live anywhere." He was dumbfounded. So he said, "Well, you can stay at my apartment." So I stayed there for the first two weeks. He didn't try to rape me or anything. He showed me where everything was, and he fed me breakfast. It was perfect.

[In Southern-lady accent] I relied on the kindness of strangers. So then I auditioned and got a scholarship to the Alvin Ailey School. I wasn't worried about not getting anywhere as a dancer. I knew I was a decent dancer. It was great. I moved from one dive to the next, I was poor. I lived on popcorn, that's why I still love it. Popcorn is cheap and it fills you up.

**IDOLS** Growing up I thought nuns were very beautiful. For several years I wanted to be a nun, and I got very close to some of them in grade school and junior high. I saw them as really pure, disciplined, sort of above-average people. They never wore any makeup and they just had these really serene faces. Nuns are sexy.

I also loved Carole Lombard and Judy Holliday and Marilyn Monroe. They were all just incredibly funny, and they were silly and sweet and they were girls and they were feminine and sexy. I just saw myself in them, my funniness and my need to boss people around and at the same time be taken care of. My girlishness. My knowingness and my innocence. Both. And I remember Nancy Sinatra singing "These Boots Are Made for Walkin'" and that made one hell of an impression on me. And when she said, "Are you ready, boots, start walkin'," it was like, yeah, give me some of those go-go boots. I want to walk on a few people.

**AMBITION** I am ambitious, but if I weren't as talented as I am ambitious, I would be a gross monstrosity. I am not surprised by my success because it feels natural. When I was younger I never said, "OK, this is the plan. I'm going to be a dancer and that's going to lead to singing and that's going to lead to acting." My calculation was that I knew I had to apply myself and work. And that devotion—and that ambition and that courage—was going to take me to the next step. So, that's my calculation.

I don't see music and movies as being unrelated. I think when you are singing a song, you are making yourself very vulnerable. It's almost like crying in front of people. Acting is about that too—communicating and being honest and just projecting a feeling. It's just a different way of doing it. I also love making videos. They're like little movies. After I made my first video, it was just so great I wanted to make a movie. The next thing I want to do is make a really, really big movie, but nothing is definite. I see myself directing eventually. I will make more albums. I love performing, but the rock-star life on the road is a grueling thing for me. At the moment, with the music and *Desperately Seeking Susan,* I think I'm affecting people in the same way, either way. My personality is getting across. I really see myself as a comedian. In 20 years I know that I will be an actress. I aspire to be a great actress.

**IMAGE** My image to people, I think, is that I'm this brazen, aggressive young woman who has an OK voice with some pretty exciting songs, who wears what she wants to wear and says what she wants to say and who has potential as an actress. Sex symbol? That is such a weird question.

I guess I would be perceived as that because I have a typically voluptuous body and because the way I dress accents my femininity, and because a lot of what I am about is just expressing sexual desire and not really caring what people think about it. Maybe that would make you a sex symbol, I don't know. There is a very modest side to me too. How far away is the image from me? It's about 20 steps away.

**PHENOMENON** I'm not really sure what is going on. My fans come from a wide age range. I think it goes beyond sexuality. Maybe my fearlessness and courage give people a good feeling. I think I have a real sweetness inside and love for life and a good sense of humor. Maybe people see that. I think a lot of people are afraid to express themselves that way, so maybe they feel they can attach themselves to an innocence and joy. I believe that dreams come true: that you can do what you want to do. I don't mean that in a *Rocky III* kind of way either. I don't mean you have to go out and conquer the world and be a star. I mean, I came from a boring sort of middle-class lifestyle and a big family and I wasn't born with a perfect body.

It all has to do with an attitude and loving yourself the way you are. Think of all the anorexics and suicides. Young people seem to be obsessed with not liking themselves. I don't think that what I'm trying to say is hard to understand. I don't go overboard really in any direction. I don't shave the side of my head. My hair is not pink. I don't feel that I'm putting on a costume. It's part of my personality and the mood that I'm in. Also I think that for the last ten or 20 years, that part of a woman has been suppressed. There has been the feeling that it's not right to want to dress up and be feminine, because women think that if they indulge in that, men won't respect them or take them seriously. Maybe kids now see someone in the public eye doing what I do. Maybe that's the phenomenon and why young girls are dressing up like me—because finally someone else is showing that it's OK.

**FEMINISTS** To call me an antifeminist is ludicrous. Some people have said that I'm setting women back 30 years. Well, I think in the '50s, women weren't ashamed of their bodies. I think they luxuriated in their sexuality and being strong in their femininity. I think that is better than hiding it and saying, "I'm strong, I'm just like a man." Women aren't like men. They can do things that men can't do. If people don't get the humor in me or my act, then they don't want to get it. If ten-year-olds can get it and laugh, then an adult surely can.

**FAME** I love being onstage and I love reaching out to people and I love the expressions in people's eyes and just the ecstasy and the thrill. But I have to have a bodyguard around me for security reasons. When I finish a show I can't stop on the street and sign a few autographs because I would be there three years. Sometimes when I go back to my hotel room there are people hiding in the ice closet, waiting. That is scary.

1984 concert. *Courtesy of Bob Leafe, Star File.*

I feel caged in hotel rooms wherever I go. In New Orleans, after the show we took a cab to Bourbon Street. I put a hat on and pulled it down low, but I stepped onto the curb and one person said, "There's Madonna," and then everybody said, "There's Madonna." We started walking down the street looking in windows and watching some jazz groups, and the more we walked, the more people started to follow us. The people don't want to hurt me. They just want to be near me. Actually it hasn't gotten to the point where I never go out. I still go running on the street and shopping. I don't send people out to do everything for me. I want to try to do as many things as I can in that regard, because I think if you really separate yourself from people, you start to have a scary opinion of the world. I don't want to feel that way.

I don't sit around and contemplate my fame or how popular I am. I know my manager sometimes looks at me with dismay when he tells me I've sold 6 million records or sold out in 17 minutes, and I just say, "OK." I'm glad but that's not what interests me, numbers. What interests me is what happens in my confrontations with people every day and in my performances every night. Not figures on a piece of paper or how much money I have in the bank or any phenomenon. I don't think money has changed my life. I never had money until now, and I never felt the lack of it. I buy more clothes. Right now I live out of a suitcase. I don't own a car. Just before the tour, I took driver's ed and got a license for the first time. I rented a car and it was a thrill.

**DRUGS** I don't take drugs. I never really did. They don't do anything for me. All the feelings I think drugs are supposed to produce in you, confidence or energy, I can produce naturally in my body. The only problem is going to sleep. But I don't take sleeping pills. I drink herbal teas.

**THE NAME MADONNA** My mother is the only other person I have ever heard of named Madonna. I never had trouble with the name. Not in school or anything, of course. I went to Catholic schools. And then when I got involved in the music industry, everybody thought I took it as a stage name. So I let them think that. . . . It's pretty glamorous.

**CATHOLICISM** Catholicism gives you a strength, an inner strength, whether you end up believing it later or not. It's the backbone. I think maybe the essence of Catholicism I haven't rejected, but the theory of it, I have, if that makes any sense. I don't go to church but I believe in God.

I don't say my rosary but I think about things like that. The thing that has remained with me most, I guess, is the idea that you do unto others as they do unto you. It's not right to steal or lie or cheat. I think it's pretty creepy when guys cheat on their wives and the other way around, stuff like that. When I was little, I had all the usual feelings of guilt. I was very conscious of God watching everything I did. Until I was eleven or twelve, I believed the devil was in my basement and I would run up the stairway fast so he wouldn't grab my ankles. We had the kind of stairway where there were spaces between each step.

**CRUCIFIXES AND ROSARIES** I think I have always carried around a few rosaries with me. There was the turquoise-colored one that my grandmother had given to me a long time ago. One day I decided to wear it as a necklace. I thought, "This is kind of offbeat and interesting." I mean, everything I do is sort of tongue in cheek. It's a strange blend—a beautiful sort of symbolism, the idea of someone suffering, which is what Jesus Christ on a crucifix stands for, and then not taking it seriously at all. Seeing it as an icon with no religiousness attached to it. It isn't a sacrilegious thing for me. I'm not saying, "This is Jesus Christ," and I'm laughing. When I went to Catholic schools, I thought the huge crucifixes nuns wore around their necks with their habits were really beautiful. I have one like that now. I wear it sometimes but not onstage. It's too big. It might fly up in the air and hit me in the face.

**BELLY BUTTONS** The picture inside the dust sleeve of my first album has me, like, in this Betty Boop pose with my belly button showing. Then when people reviewed the album, they kept talking about my cute belly button. I started thinking about it and I said, "Yeah, well, I do like my belly button." I think there are other unobvious places on the body that are sexy and the stomach is kind of innocent. I don't have a really flat stomach. I sort of have a little girl's stomach. It's round and the skin is smooth and it's nice. I like it.

**BOY TOY** About four years ago, I used to live in the East Village. I used to love hanging out at the Roxy with all the break dancers and graffiti artists and the deejays. Everybody had a tag name they would write on the wall like "Whiz Kid" or "Hi-Fi." The thing was to see how much you could "throw up" [get your name up] everywhere. It was a very territorial thing. One day I just thought of "Boy Toy," and when I threw it up on a wall, everybody said they thought it was funny too. They understood the humor of it. I can see how the rest of the world thinks I'm saying "Play with me" and "I'm available to anyone." Once again, it's a tongue-in-cheek statement, the opposite of what it says. I had "Boy Toy" made into a belt buckle. Then I started doing stuff outside New York City and I kept wearing the Boy Toy belt, forgetting that no one outside of the Roxy was going to get it. I don't wear it any more because it's just become ridiculous. I think it's funny but not too many other people do.

**CLOTHES** I like to combine things but in a humorous way, like a uniform skirt and fishnets. Sometimes I like really expensive things. I like Vivienne Westwood, Commes des Garcons, and Jean Paul Gaultier. But I get a lot of stuff in thrift shops too. I really love dresses like Marilyn Monroe wore, those '50s dresses that were really tailored to fit a voluptuous body. A lot of stuff made now is for an androgynous figure, and it doesn't look good on me. I have always sort of elaborated with my dance clothes. I used to live in my dance clothes, my tights and leotards, but I always personalized them. I'd rip them all up and make sure the runs got really big and had a pattern to them. I started wearing bows in my hair because one day when my hair was long, I couldn't find anything to tie it back. So I took an old pair of tights and wound them around my head, and I liked the way that looked.

**MARRIAGE** I do want to get married and have kids. I don't know when, but I think getting married is probably something very exciting and very challenging, and I would definitely like to have a child. I've only heard wonderful things about it from people I know who are near my age. I'm saying it like it's baking a cake or something.

**LOVE** I'm at the end of my patience with this interview. I want to run down the hallway and finish writing a song. I won't sing it, but I'll tell you the hook. "Love makes the world go 'round." It's really trite, but that's what it is. Love makes the world go 'round and straight and square and squiggly.

Now leaning back, her dancer's legs straight up, with ankles crossed on the back of the seat in front of her, Madonna toys with the dial on her portable radio. She says, "I have to stop talking. I have to rest my voice." Would she add anything, maybe after the show tonight? She turns her head and looks out the window at Texas, then says slowly, "I can't focus after a concert. I have to talk to my boyfriend for a long time before I go to sleep."

Early '80s portrait. *Courtesy of Vinnie Zuffante, Star File.*

STEPHEN HOLDEN

# MADONNA CLEANS UP ACT BUT HER MUSIC REMAINS TRUE BLUE TO CONTROVERSY

*New York Times,* July 10, 1986

*Madonna comments on the controversy surrounding the video "Papa Don't Preach"—which, in hindsight, was fairly mild compared with what the Material Girl had up her sleeves.*—Eds.

New York—"I like challenge and controversy—I like to tick people off," Madonna boasted, tossing her head and flashing a mischievous half-smile. The 27-year-old pop star was sipping a diet cola in a conference room at the New York offices of Warner Bros. Records. She appeared almost demure in a pink-and-blue flowered dress and a very short haircut inspired by the late-'50s gamine look of Jean Seberg, Audrey Hepburn and Leslie Caron.

Gone along with most of her hair was the heavy makeup and jewelry that made last year's Madonna resemble a contemporary street version of Marilyn Monroe in *Gentlemen Prefer Blondes.*

"After awhile I got sick of wearing tons of jewelry—I wanted to clean myself off," Madonna said flatly. "I see my new look as very innocent and feminine and unadorned. It makes me feel good. Growing up, I admired the kind of beautiful glamorous woman—from Brigitte Bardot to Grace Kelly—who doesn't seem to be around much anymore. I think it's time for that kind of glamor to come back."

If Madonna's new upscale look represents a dramatic swing away from the provocative sex symbol who wore lingerie as outerwear and crucifixes like diamonds, it does not signal an end to her courting of controversy.

"Papa Don't Preach," the second single from her third album, *True Blue,* is bound to rile some parents of teenage girls. The protagonist of the song, which was written by Brian Elliot, is a pregnant adolescent who begs her father to bless her decision to keep the baby and marry her boyfriend. Madonna sings it in a passionate, bratty sob that makes the plea immediate and believable.

The song has also been turned into a compelling slice-of-life music video. Filmed on location in a working-class neighborhood of Staten Island, with Danny Aiello playing the father, it features a virtuoso performance by a waifish, saucer-eyed Madonna, who looks all of 15 as she quivers anxiously, awaiting her father's response.

Like Michael Jackson's "Billie Jean," the song and its video have an iconographic resonance that could push Madonna's career to an even higher plateau than the household-word status she attained last year with her 6.5 million–selling second album, *Like a Virgin.*

"'Papa Don't Preach' is a message song that everyone is going to take the wrong way," Madonna proudly predicted. "Immediately they're going to say I am advising every young girl to go out and get pregnant. When I first heard the song, I thought it was silly. But then I thought, wait a minute, this song is really about a girl who is making a decision in her life.

"She has a very close relationship with her father and wants to maintain that closeness. To me it's a celebration of life. It says, 'I love you, father, and I love this man and this child that is growing inside me.' Of course, who knows how it will end? But at least it starts off positive."

"Papa Don't Preach," for which Madonna contributed a couple of minor lyrical revisions, is the only song on the album that Madonna didn't have a strong hand in writing. The song was sent to her by Michael Ostin, the same Warner Bros. executive who discovered "Like a Virgin." Most of the album's eight other songs Madonna cowrote with Patrick Leonard, the musical director for her 1985 tour, or with her sometime songwriting partner, Stephen Bray. The three also coproduced the LP.

While *True Blue* lacks the gleaming ultrasleek aural surfaces of *Like a Virgin,* both its songs and Madonna's singing show a lot more heart. "Live to Tell," written for the sound track of *At Close Range,* the movie starring her husband, Sean Penn, was released in advance of the album and recently spent a week perched at No. 1 on the pop charts. It proves that vocally Madonna isn't limited to catchy novelties and disco tunes—she can carry off a weightier ballad. The rest of the album consists of highly commercial dance-pop whose lyrics convey an upbeat message along with casual autobiographical references.

*True Blue* takes its title from a favorite expression of Sean Penn, and is a tribute, according to Madonna, "to my husband's very pure vision of love." Musically, it also pays homage to Motown and to '60s "girl-group" hits like "Chapel of Love" that are the direct antecedents of Madonna's sound.

The happy Latin-flavored "La Isla Bonita" is Madonna's celebration of what she called "the beauty and mystery of Latin American people." The itchy dance tune "Jimmy Jimmy" commemorates her youthful fascination with James Dean.

"I used to fantasize that we grew up in the same neighborhood and that he moved away and became a big star," she admitted. "White Heat" is dedicated to another mythic rebel, James Cagney, whose voice opens the track in a snatch of dialogue from the movie of the same name.

"'Where's the Party?'" Madonna explained, "is my ultimate reminder to myself that I want to enjoy life and not let the press get to me, because every once in awhile it does." "Open Your Heart" is about "wanting to change somebody." And the album's final cut, "Love Makes the World Go Round," preaches a cheerfully simplistic humanitarianism: "Don't judge a man 'til you've been standin' in his shoes / You know that we're all so quick to look away / 'Cause it's the easy thing to do / Make love not war."

Obviously, Madonna is still much more significant as a pop culture symbol than as a songwriter or a singer. But the songs on *True Blue* are shrewdly crafted teenage and pre-teenage ditties that reveal Madonna's unfailing commercial instincts. And her singing, which has been harshly criticized as a thin imitation of the '60s girl-group sound, has strengthened.

"I grew up loving innocent child voices like Diana Ross, while she was with the Supremes, and Stevie Wonder when he was young, and I practically swooned when I heard Frankie Lymon's records," she said. "I don't know why, but I was always instinctively drawn to those voices. I don't think I sing like a woman. I sing like a girl, and it's a quality I never want to lose."

But even more than a girlish voice, the quality that defines Madonna Louise Veronica Ciccone is an instinct for rebellion that she traces to her parochial school girlhood in Pontiac, Michigan.

"When you go to Catholic school, you have to wear uniforms, and everything is decided for you," she recalled. "Since you have no choice but to wear your uniform, you go out of your way to do things that are different in order to stand out. All that rebellion carried over when I moved to New York eight years ago to become a dancer.

"At dance classes, all the ballerinas had their hair back in a bun, and so I chopped my hair off and ripped my leotard down the front and put little tiny safety pins all the way up just to provoke my teacher. After all, where is it written that in order to be a better dancer you have to wear a black leotard and pink tights and have your hair in a bun? Going out dancing with my girlfriends in New York clubs, we would dress for provocation. What I was wearing at the time I was signed to a record contract became my look.

"What kids see in me is another rebel kid who says what she wants and does what she wants and has a joy in life," Madonna went on. "The

Live Aid, 1985. *Courtesy of David Seelig, Star File.*

girls that dressed like me all got the joke—it was their parents who didn't."

A disciplined, immensely self-confident woman who doesn't eat meat, rarely touches liquor and rigorously trains her body every day, Madonna is a woman in charge of her life and career. She appeared to be uncowed by the voyeurism of a celebrity press that has dredged up vintage nude photos of her and made her recent marriage to Penn a running battle with the paparazzi.

Madonna's title role of a freewheeling bohemian vagabond in the Susan Seidelman film *Desperately Seeking Susan,* along with her music videos, has established her as a natural screen presence, and a larger movie career seems inevitable.

In her next film, *Shanghai Surprise,* she plays a staid young missionary from Massachusetts who falls in love with a petty swindler, played by Penn. The film, which is set in pre-revolutionary China, was shot in Hong Kong and is scheduled to be released this fall.

"I always thought of myself as a star, though I never in my wildest dreams expected to become this big," Madonna said bluntly. "But I knew I was born to it. I don't know why. I think people are named names for certain reasons, and I feel that I was given a special name for a reason. In a way, maybe I wanted to live up to my name."

BECKY JOHNSTON

# CONFESSION OF A CATHOLIC GIRL

*Interview* magazine, 1989

*This lengthy interview with Madonna is from Andy Warhol's* Interview *magazine and captures her at a creative highpoint.*—Eds.

By now, if you've glanced at half the magazines recently gracing the newsstands, you've probably noticed that Madonna—the New Madonna—has commanded front and center spot on the shelves. She is everywhere. The New Madonna has long, dark, center-parted hair, she's still as beautiful as the Old Madonna, but seems more approachable than the platinum-cropped, angular body-Nazi of recent past. British *Vogue* describes the New Madonna (who peers out in imperial splendor from the cover) as "stepping out of a Renaissance painting, a Mona Lisa. . . . This is the emergence of a new woman, an image that suggests culture clashes, and juxtapositions of old and new ideas." *Spin* magazine (on whose cover she also appears) says, "The New Madonna has dispensed with denials of her true self. The peroxide is gone, as are the other approximations of kaleidoscopic glamor. What you see is what you get." *Rolling Stone* (another cover) flatly states that she is "the world's most famous woman." Madonna herself says, "People have certain notions about me, and it is time for a change."

The occasion which precipitated this flurry of words and magazine covers was the release of Madonna's new album *Like a Prayer.* Simultaneous with its release was the highly publicized premiere of her sunny, upbeat Pepsi commercial and the unveiling on MTV of a dark, unsettling music video for the album's title song. In it Madonna witnesses a murder, falls in love with the black man falsely accused of committing it, dances in front of burning crosses, bears stigmata, and undulates in mesmeric rapture while a gospel choir belts out the song behind her.

Reports of outrage and protests were wildly exaggerated in the press. The video was not banned in Italy. Religious groups took umbrage but launched no organized protest. "This video is only one little narrow piece of a big pie," stated the Reverend Donald Wildmon, executive director of the American Family Association. "I'm not saying it's not offensive. It is offensive. But we don't plan on making a crusade of it." Rumors circulated that Pepsi intended to pull its Madonna commercial to avoid being mistakenly affiliated with the video, but those also proved to be inaccurate. After much internal debate, Pepsi officials decided to reaffirm their support of Madonna and the advertising campaign. Aside from their reputation, the $5 million reputedly paid to the world's most famous woman was at stake. In a world of happy endings, the controversy has been a godsend for everyone concerned. Publicity is the name of the game.

"Don't ask Madonna questions about her image," warns her publicist, Liz Rosenberg. "She hates that word." One might logically ask why image-making is irrefutably a key ingredient in the phenomenal success story of Madonna Louise Veronica Ciccone Penn. Born thirty years ago in Bay City, Michigan, the daughter of devout, strict Catholics, she was by her own description an outsider.

"I saw myself as the quintessential Cinderella," she once told *Time* magazine. At the age of seventeen, she left Michigan and headed to New York City, where she metamorphosed from scullery maid to princess of the grand ball. One could chart the rise of her immense star to the series of similar transformations which have guided it: from the early unkempt,

With Sean Penn, mid-'80s. *Courtesy of Vinnie Zuffante, Star File.*

crucifix-bedecked Boy Toy phase to the tongue-in-cheek Marilyn Material Girl phase to the svelte, silver-topped peep-shows chanteuse of "Open Your Heart." The unifying element in each of those image changes was the high level of irony articulating the form. Madonna may embrace female stereotypes, but it's more like a stranglehold than a caress. She seems always to be saying, "Don't take it too seriously. I don't." Which might lead one to believe that these image changes are not merely calculated career moves but forms of self-protection.

Certainly few public figures have had to withstand the same relentless hounding by emotional ambulance chasers as she has. When she married Sean Penn three years ago, a swarm of helicopters buzzed over the ceremony with all the proprietary arrogance of vultures. Every tiff and squabble in that volatile union was splashed in bold type on tabloid covers. In January of this year, Madonna filed for divorce from Penn amid more squawking and speculation about violence and abuse at their home in Malibu. Read any article on Madonna and there's usually some paparazzo freak lurking in the bushes, some horde of inquiring minds waiting outside the door. Madonna is more than a rock star or movie star or cultural queen. She has became a kind of international open territory—everybody feels entitled to a piece of her. It would seem only natural that one way of keeping the wolves at bay would be to change identities and remain elusive, out of reach.

But on the flip side, few public figures are such wizards at manipulating the press and cultivating publicity as Madonna is. She has always been a great tease with journalists, brash and outspoken when the occasion demanded it, recalcitrant and taciturn when it came time to pull back and slow down the striptease. Madonna is a self-created woman, no question, but it was not a virgin birth: her adroit handling of the press played a major part in the consummation. Publicity is the name of the game.

So, one might logically ask next, what is the New Madonna? Having achieved a monumental superstardom, which is roughly equivalent to creating a monster, what new identity has she carved out for herself this time? The cynics among as will probably hiss and snort and roll their eyes when the optimists among us tell them that Madonna has grown up, that the New Madonna is in fact a conscious renunciation of all image-making. The cynics will probably say, "Oh, please. Self-revelation is just the nice way of saying self-promotion."

Her new album, however, is the pudding in which to test the proof. *Like a Prayer* is an emotionally jarring collection of songs in which the focus turns consistently inward. Madonna emerges as a woman with battle scars, bewildered and saddened by personal losses of love, illusions, and the conviction that one can control all facets of one's life. Many of the songs are not about Madonna getting what she wants, they're about realizing she can't have it. Granted, there are some typical up-tempo life is a fab party tunes, but even those are imbued with a pervasive melancholia. It may be a party, but it's grueling real soon. Listening to the album, one is struck by how unprotected and vulnerable the world's most famous woman seems.

After two weeks of Madonna's having to schedule and then reschedule this interview, having to change dates and times and cancel at the last minute—all owing to the fact that she was busy preparing for her role in Warren Beatty's new film, *Dick Tracy*—I finally received the word: "Madonna can see you this Sunday. Four o'clock. Her house."

The house is perched high in the Hollywood Hills, and on first glance looks almost forbidding. There are no windows in the front. It feels like a fortress. I ring the doorbell. After a moment, Madonna answers the door. And lo and behold, it's not the New Madonna anymore. It's the Old Madonna, with a twist. Her hair has been bleached blond again. She's wearing cuttoffs and a T-shirt and slinky Brigitte

Portrait shot, 1986. *Courtesy of Danny Chin, Star File.*

Bardot sling-back pumps. She smiles warmly and says, "I'm sorry about all the scheduling mix-ups." I think, well, this is the New Madonna after all. Then she turns on her heels, and as I follow her through the house she says, "But it wasn't my fault."

***Becky Johnston:*** *Maybe, we should begin this interview with a verbal shit list. What don't you want to talk about?*

**Madonna:** No four-letter words.

***BJ:*** *I am assuming the ban on four-letter words includes any mention of your estranged husband.*

**M:** Yes.

***BJ:*** *Just as a footnote, I read in the* Los Angeles Times *that you're doing a big media blitz for the release of your new album,* Like a Prayer. *I'm sure you know the press will try to badger you with questions about your personal life, so how do you plan to deal with that?*

**M:** Well, generally I do interviews because I have something to talk about in terms of my work, and I try to keep it in that area. I mean, it's kind of an insult that they want to know those other things. It seems the most important thing to them is to find out [long pause] stuff I'd rather not talk about, things that don't have anything to do with my work. And it's nobody's business. But people always want to know what's not their business.

***BJ:*** *Do you care what people think about you in general?*

**M:** Yes, I do.

***BJ:*** *Are you vulnerable to criticism, to bad press?*

**M:** Absolutely. Definitely.

***BJ:*** *What about one of your other current projects? You're about to star in Warren Beatty's film* Dick Tracy, *playing Breathless Mahoney. What's she like?*

**M:** What's she like? She's [long pause] I don't know. She's a girl. She's scarred. She's a seductress in a lot of pain.

***BJ:*** *Have you spent the last couple of weeks preparing for the role?*

**M:** In terms of Breathless Mahoney, I've probably been preparing for that role all my life. [laughs] But superficially, yes . . . I mean, I had to dye my hair, pluck my eyebrows, have lots of fittings. Stephen Sondheim is writing songs of the period for the film, so I've been working on them, and they're quite difficult.

***BJ:*** *Why's that?*

**M:** Because Stephen Sondheim writes in a kind of chromatic wildness. They're very difficult songs to learn. I mean one song is written with five sharps. They're brilliant, but really complex.

***BJ:*** *Are they mostly torch songs?*

**M:** One is. There are three songs. One is a torch song and another one is more up-tempo. It's kind of like "Diamonds Are a Girl's Best Friend" or "Material Girl," where she keeps singing about how she wants more and more. It's about gluttony. And it's funny, its ironic. And then the third song is a kind of slow, sad song. I'm going to be singing it with Mandy Patinkin, who plays my accompanist at the nightclub where I work. It's the kind of song you sing at three in the morning, when the club is empty. It's very melancholy . . . just a piano and a voice. But they're all really different for me, and so I've been working very hard to get them right.

***BJ:*** *Do you feel this part is more demanding than a lot of the other parts you've played?*

**M:** [long pause] Yes and no. I'm different now from when I played those other parts, so *everything* is different for me. And I think there are a lot more subtleties to her character than it would seem on the surface. So in that respect it's more demanding for me.

***BJ:*** *You've just finished a much-talked-about commercial for Pepsi. It's apparently the longest television commercial ever made.*

**M:** Uh-huh. I just saw it. I love it.

***BJ:*** *Do they actually run the whole length of your song for it?*

**M:** It's an edited version of the song. The song on the album is five and a half minutes long. It would be great if they could run a commercial that long, but it's too much airtime to buy.

***BJ:*** *It's kind of a dicey proposition, doing a commercial, isn't it?*

**M:** I had a lot of apprehension about it at first, but we had several meetings, and in the end I got to collaborate with them, I had a lot of input, and they came up with a story that I found to be very touching. I don't feel I was used, if that's what you mean.

***BJ:*** *The first video off your new album uses the same song you chose to feature in the commercial, "Like a Prayer." How would you compare the two treatments of the same song?*

**M:** The treatment for the video is a lot more controversial. It's probably going to touch a lot of nerves in a lot of people. And the treatment for the commercial is, I mean, it's a commercial. It's very, very sweet. It's very sentimental.

***BJ:*** *It's the "lite" version. I saw the video. It's pretty shocking. What struck me most about it is that it's so unlike anything you've done before. It's frightening. It's dark. It's violent. And it's kind of bleak, despite the religious imagery.*

**M:** Well, originally, when I recorded the song, I would play it over and over again, trying to get a visual sense of what sort of story or fantasy it evoked in me. I kept imagining this story about a girl who was madly in love with a black man, set in the South, with this forbidden interracial love affair. And the guy she's in love with sings in a choir. So she's obsessed with him and goes to church all the time. And then it turned into a bigger story, which was about racism and bigotry. I wanted to put something in about Ku Klux Klan, use burning crosses . . . but then *Mississippi Burning* came out and I realized I was hitting the nail on the head a little too hard. Too obvious. So I thought I should take a slightly different approach. My original idea was much sadder. Kind of: this is reality, and reality sucks.

Then Mary Lambert got involved as the director, and she came up with a story that incorporated more of the religious symbolism I originally wrote into the song. The whole album has a lot of religious imagery in it. The video still has the sadness, but it's got a hopeful ending. I mean, I had these ideas about me running away with the black guy and both of us getting shot in the back by the KKK. Completely insane. So Mary made it more palatable.

**BJ:** *Still, it's not your standard MTV fare.*

**M:** Well, it's about something that I think is really tragic—not just in this country, but everywhere. My only fear is that people aren't going to get it. It's too complicated.

**BJ:** *Oh, I think they'll get it all right. They might be a little outraged or offended, though. You're not the Material Girl anymore.*

**M:** That's why I did it.

**BJ:** *You just turned thirty last August. How would you say you've changed in the last five years?*

**M:** I think . . . I don't know . . . I've changed.

**BJ:** *What do you think are your greatest strengths?*

**M:** [long pause] Well, I'm disciplined. And I'm persevering. And I don't give up very easily . . . and I'm reliable.

**BJ:** *And what would you say are your biggest flaws?*

**M:** [long pause] I'm impatient I'm intolerant of other people's weaknesses. And I'm really hard on myself.

**BJ:** *When you say you're intolerant of weaknesses, do you mean you find yourself expecting too much of other people?*

**M:** Yeah. Yeah.

**BJ:** *Is that because you set a standard for yourself and expect others to live up to that standard?*

**M:** Yes. That's true.

*BJ: What was your reaction to the Madonna "wannabe" craze a few years back?*

**M:** It was on my first tour that I first saw it . . . and I thought it was amazing, amazing that a certain way I chose to look and dress became an obsession. Certainly it was not what I set out to do. I think those things just happen by chance. I don't think you can set out to do something like that. But I thought it was really flattering.

*BJ: Aside from copying your style of dress, they looked up to you as a role model. What would you say, as a role model, your responsibility was to them?*

**M:** That's a tough question. Because in a way my first response is: I don't have a responsibility to them. They decided to look up to me, or use me as a role model. My only responsibility, I think, is just to be true to myself.

*BJ: But you said once before in another interview that you felt it was important for you to project a life-affirming point of view to your audience. That might be construed as a responsibility.*

**M:** Yes. Because it's important to me to be positive. I think there's too much negativity in the world. And I think there aren't a lot of things which give people relief from that negativity, something life-affirming to look to or look for. I know it sounds trite in a way, but I think it's important.

*BJ: You also said in the same interview that you didn't like yourself very much when you were a teenager. You said, "I didn't think I was beautiful or talented. I spent a lot of time loathing myself and not feeling I fit in, like every adolescent does. When I started dancing, having a dream and working toward that goal—having a sense of discipline—I started to like myself for the first time." Would you say work is a kind of internal monitoring system for you, a way of keeping the demons of self-loathing at bay?*

**M:** Yeah, but it has everything to do with feeling you can do something well. I mean, something to focus on takes you out of yourself—that's natural. You don't sit around all the time feeling you don't fit in or wondering what you're supposed to do with yourself for the rest of your life. And especially when you're a teenager, it's really important to fit in and feel there's a reason, for you to be on the earth. You start moving away from your family, feeling like you want to be somebody, do something. And when you find something that you can do, and you can do it well, it gives you reason for living.

***BJ:*** *I guess what interested me about that quote was the revelation of self-doubt or self-loathing and the incredible will to overcome it. You don't seem even remotely self-destructive.*

**M:** Yeah, well, that's why I work so hard. I work at not being self-destructive. I think my nature is to fight back, to fight those demons that want to bring me down. I have this motor inside of me that says, No, I will not go down. I feel it pulling at me, and sometimes it's stronger than at other times. But, yeah, working takes me out of that. And that's why I work so hard, because obviously I must have a lot of demons I'm fighting.

***BJ:*** *Do you do anything else to keep yourself on an even keel? Like meditate?*

**M:** Well, exercise is absolutely necessary for me, because I don't dance anymore. Dancing sort of brought me out of myself. Before I started dancing, I felt really physically awkward too. Not comfortable with my body. So what it does for me is twofold. I feel I can purge bad things when I exercise, and I also feel better physically. I feel superior, I feel like a warrior.

***BJ:*** *When you're everything, are you aware of your thought process, or do you sort of just blank out all thought?*

**M:** You have to concentrate on your breathing when you're exercising. You don't really have time to get tripped up on one thought. Everything goes through a processor and kind of gets cleaned out.

***BJ:*** *A little like praying?*

**M:** Yeah.

***BJ:*** *Do you pray?*

**M:** Absolutely.

***BJ:*** *As regularly as you exercise?*

Enjoying club life. *Courtesy of Bob Scott, Star File.*

**M:** Well, I don't pray every day at ten o'clock, but I pray a lot. It sort of happens on and off, whenever I feel like it, throughout the day or week.

***BJ:** You were raised a strict Catholic and went to Catholic schools all through your childhood, but you obviously rebelled against your upbringing at some point in your life.*

**M:** Yeah, I did.

***BJ:** At what age did you start to rebel?*

**M:** Probably when I was about ten.

***BJ:** And what form did the rebellion take?*

**M:** Well, when I was ten I started liking boys. That was the first form. I remember I wanted to chase after boys on the playground, and the nuns told me I couldn't: that good Catholic girls didn't chase boys. I didn't understand what was so bad about it, so I would do it anyway. And I would get punished for it. I also remember being really annoyed that I couldn't wear pants to school or church. My brothers could, and that seemed to me all locked up with the religion. I kept saying to my father, "But why can't I love God the same way if I have pants on?" [laughs] You know? And my father would always have these stock responses, like "Because I said so."

So often I would be confused about who I was worshiping, God or my father. Then, as I got older, I hated the idea that I had to go to church all the time. We used to get up every morning at six or seven and go to church for an hour before school. It just seemed like such torture—I mean, school was punishment enough. Then I got into this whole thing with my father about: Why do I have to go to church to pray? Why can't I take the basic principles of this religion—principles like being good and doing unto others as you would have them do unto you and *live* them? Why do I have to go to confession to confess my sins? Why can't I just tell God directly? These things didn't make any sense to me.

***BJ:** Did you ever actually break away from the church?*

**M:** Oh yeah. As soon as I left home. That was one of the great things about leaving home. I moved to New York when I was seventeen, and I had lots of terrible moments. I was afraid, I didn't know if I'd done the right thing. I missed my family, and then I'd say, well, at least I don't have to go to church every Sunday. So that was one of the rewards.

***BJ:** What aspects of Catholicism have remained with you and shaped your worldview as an adult?*

**M:** Well, I have a great sense of guilt and sin from Catholicism that has definitely permeated my everyday life, whether I want it to or not. And when I do something wrong, or that I think is wrong, if I don't let someone know I've wronged, I'm always afraid I'm going to be punished. I don't rest easy with myself. And that's something you're raised to believe as a Catholic. Everyone's a sinner in Catholicism, and you must constantly be asking God to cleanse your soul and begging Him for forgiveness.

I don't know if this was more my father or Catholicism, but I was also raised to believe that idle time wasn't good. You always had to be doing something productive, either your schoolwork or prayer or housework, never sitting around and never having too much leisure time. You always had to be challenging your mind or body, and that has definitely shaped my adult life. Also, I think in Catholicism there's a great sense of family and unity, and even though I've been through periods of time where I never wanted to see my family again, they're very important to me. Familes in general are important to me. I was also raised to believe that when you marry someone you marry him for life. You never give up.

***BJ:** You were the oldest girl in a family of eight, and spent most of your adolescence running the household and nursing the other kids after your mother died. Did you resent having to do that?*

**M:** I didn't resent having to raise my brothers and sisters as much as I resented the fact that I didn't have my mother. And that my ideal of my family was interrupted. My stepmother was very young, and she just wasn't ready for a billion kids who were extremely unwilling to accept her as an authority figure. So it was rough. We all resented it.

***BJ:** You were six when your mother died of cancer. You said in another interview that her death was a turning point in your life—you could either "be sad and weak and not in control, or say that it's going to be better." Was your mother a role model for you in that respect? Did she have the same kind of will and strength?*

**M:** I think she had a lot of strength. I didn't notice it as much when I was younger, but looking back on it . . . she was ill for a long time and she never allowed herself any sort of self-pity, you know. And we really tortured her when she was sick, because we wanted her to play with us. We wanted her to do things when she was tired, we picked on her all the time because we just didn't understand. But I don't think she ever allowed herself to wallow in the tragedy of her situation. So in that respect I think she gave me an incredible lesson.

But in reference to that quote about me not wanting to be sad or weak or not in control, that really came, I think, when my father remarried. Because for the three years before he remarried, I clung to him. It was like, OK, now you're mine, and you're not going *anywhere*. Like all young girls, I was in love with my father and I didn't want to lose him. I lost my mother, but then I was the mother, my father was *mine*. Then he got taken away from me when he married my stepmother. It was then that I said, OK, I don't need *anybody*. No one's going to break my heart again. I'm not going to need anybody. I can stand on my own and be my own person and not belong to anyone.

***BJ:** Would you say there was a definite change in your personality at that point? Did you go from being introspective to being much more extroverted? Or vice versa?*

**M:** Well, it was at the same time that I started to rebel against religion, to be conscious of what I consider to be the injustices of my religious upbringing. It kind of happened all at once. And yes, I think I was always very outgoing or outspoken. I think I just got even more fearless. Not afraid to say what I felt. Blunt. Lots of mouthing off. [laughs]

***BJ:** Are your brothers and sisters like that too? Or are you the only loudmouth in the family?*

**M:** Some of them are really outgoing. Some of them are very introverted. As in all big families, there's a whole hierarchy and lots of different personalities. There are the dominant forces and the submissive ones.

***BJ:** Growing up, were you closer to your sisters or your brothers?*

**M:** I didn't feel close to anybody in my family when I was growing up. I felt like an outsider in my own house. I didn't feel close to my older brothers, they were just typical older brothers who tortured me all the time.

And I didn't feel close to my sisters. There was a lot of competition in our family, and I was always vying for my father's attention and all that, so, I worked really hard in school. I was a straight-A student, and they all hated me for it because I did it more for the position I was going to have in my father's eyes than for whatever I was going to learn by studying. I just tried to be the apple of my father's eye. I think that everyone else in my family was very aware of it. And I kind of stood out from them.

Then when I got a little older—when I was in high school and started dancing really seriously—I'd say I got closer to my brothers. There was a lot of unspoken competition with my sisters. My oldest brother opened my eyes to lots of things, and I didn't see him as just my creepy older brother anymore. And my younger brother would come to dance classes with me.

**BJ:** *Are you close to your father now?*

**M:** Yes, I am.

**BJ:** *Did you have any heroines or role models when you were a kid?*

**M:** It's weird, people always ask me that question and I can't think of anybody specifically. [long pause] I think a few nuns, I thought they were pretty incredible. They seemed all powerful and perfect. Above everything. Really disciplined. And really clean. [laughs] For a while I was obsessed with being a nun, for those reasons. I just thought they were so superior. Then, when I realized that nuns didn't have a sex life, I was incredibly disenchanted.

**BJ:** *How old were you when you became aware of sex?*

**M:** Five.

**BJ:** *[laughs] Really? Do you have any specific memories?*

**M:** Well, I was always very precocious as a child, extremely flirtatious, I mean. I was just one of those little girls who crawled on everybody's lap. I flirted with everyone—my uncles, my grandfather, my father, everybody. I was aware of my female charm. Then, probably about the same time as I began to rebel against the church and my family, my breasts started to grow. I went through puberty before most of the girls in my class.

**BJ:** *They must have really loved you.*

**M:** [laughs] They hated me. So right around that time was when I really started to think about sex. About its presence, not about what I was going to do about it. The true sexual awakening,of course, happened much later. [pause] Last year.

***BJ:** [laughs] What would you define as the essence of femininity?*

**M:** The essence of femininity? To absolutely love being a woman.

***BJ:** It seems to me that one of the reasons you've had such a tremendous impact—on women, especially—is that you're saying it's time for women to use their sexuality as a strength and as a source of power.*

**M:** Right.

***BJ:** Can you elaborate on that subject at all?*

**M:** Well, it seems to me that one of the pitfalls of the women's movement was that women wanted to be like men. They felt they had to dress like men and behave like men to get anywhere, to be respected or to be in control. To have power. I think that's bullshit. I think women have always had the power; they just never knew it. And you can be just as powerful being feminine.

***BJ:** Would you say that women are stronger than men?*

**M:** That's a tough one. My first instinct is to say no. They have certain strengths, and men have certain strengths. But then I think that women are more durable. Emotionally, I mean, let's face it, we have our period every month. [laughs] That really makes you strong.

***BJ:** Is vulnerability an important quality to you? Most people equate vulnerability with femininity.*

**M:** Yes, it's absolutely important. And I think the most interesting men I've met are the ones who are in touch with their femininity. They are the strongest men.

***BJ:** So what would be the kind of man you dislike?*

**M:** I dislike men who totally suppress their femininity.

**BJ:** *Do you find that a lot of men feel threatened by you, by your self-confidence and sense of sexual challenge?*

**M:** I think only a few men are threatened by it. I think most men are inspired by it or entertained by it. Or may be challenged by it, but in a good way.

**BJ:** *Isn't it true that growing up Catholic you're cursed with the view of women as either virgins or whores?*

**M:** I was certainly aware of it, but I couldn't understand why you couldn't be both.

**BJ:** *[laughs] This is a quote from a* Rolling Stone *interview you gave. "I like to create a different character for each album I do." What motivates you to change your image or to create a new character?*

**M:** Well, I sort of get into certain kinds of moods. And then all the songs I write come out of that mood. I don't say to myself, Now I'm going to be in that mood. It just happens.

**BJ:** *Does the music change as a result of your changing the mood?*

**M:** Yes, I would say that.

**BJ:** *How? Can you give me an example?*

**M:** Well, listen to a song like "Like a Virgin," and then listen to "Live to Tell." There's a different mood in each one. They're the same person, but it's just my desire to focus on something different because of a mood I'm in. All the changes in my so-called image are just different facets of me. It's a matter of what you choose to focus on and how deeply you want to go into it. It's a matter of being specific, I guess.

**BJ:** *Does it annoy you that the press has devoted more attention to your image than your music?*

**M:** It used to annoy me, but now it doesn't anymore. Because somehow I feel that, as much as people complain and moan and groan and criticize me, they're affected by me. I've touched a nerve in them somehow.

**BJ:** *In your new album,* Like a Prayer, *it seems to me there's no character at play; it's the most revealing, self-exposed thing you've done, and you've addressed very personal issues.*

**M:** Yeah, well, that's the kind of mood I was in. And I have to say—even though I said I didn't want to talk about Sean—that he was extremely influential in encouraging me to reveal that side of myself.

**BJ:** *It's also much more experimental musically.*

**M:** Yeah, it is. I didn't have the censors on me in terms of emotions or music. I did take a lot more chances with this one, but obviously success gives you the confidence to do those things.

**BJ:** *How do you develop a song?*

**M:** All different ways. Sometimes, the music is sort of there, already written by either Pat Leonard or Stephen Bray. They give it to me and it inspires or insinuates a lyric or feeling. Then I write out the words in a free form, and we change the music to fit the form. Other times I'll start out with lyrics, or I'll have written a poem and I'll want to put that to music. Then I end up changing the words a little bit to make them more musical. Sometimes I'll hear the melody in my head. I don't write music and I don't read music, so I'll go to Pat Leonard, who is an extremely talented musician, and I'll sing it to him and make him play it, making chords out of it. Then I write the words to the song.

**BJ:** *Do you write the lyrics yourself? Or do your collaborators help?*

**M:** I write all the lyrics myself.

**BJ:** *Steve Bray said that one of the things that made this new album so different was the fact that you worked with live musicians in the studio.*

**M:** Well, I've worked with live musicians before, but this is the first time they were all together in one room, and we did most of the basic tracks with a band playing right there. I sang with them too, and we ended up keeping a lot of those vocals. It made it different, because obviously when the musicians are playing with you, you respond differently from when the track is already done, and you're by yourself with the headphones on, overdubbing things.

This approach was more integral to the music. I mean, we had every intention of going back and fixing the vocals, but then we'd listen to them and say, "Why? They're fine." They were a lot more emotional and spontaneous when I did them with the musicians. It's probably because I didn't feel the pressure of knowing that this was going to be the final vocal. So I decided not to go back and clean them up. There are weird sounds that your throat makes when you sing: *p*'s are popped, and *s*'s are hissed, things like that. Just strange sounds that come out of your throat, and I didn't fix them. I didn't see why I should. Because I think those sounds are emotions too.

**BJ:** *Did you work out the idea for the album in advance, or did it slowly evolve in the studio?*

**M:** I wrote a lot of songs for the album, and then I went through a process of editing what I was going to keep or not. I feel that there is something that links all the songs together, a common theme having to do with Catholicism, family, relationships thing like that. I had written a lot of other songs, but I didn't feel they went with the theme, so I cast them aside.

**BJ:** *How would you say you've matured as an artist with this record?*

**M:** Well, my first couple of albums I would say came from the little girl in me, who is interested only in having people like me, in being entertaining and charming and frivolous and sweet. And this new one is the adult side of me, which is concerned with being brutally honest.

**BJ:** *Do you think acting and making music are very similar? Do they require you to use the same aspects of your personality?*

**M:** Yeah. Definitely. I used to think they were different, because I felt with music you could be more revealing. I felt music was more of a personal statement, and acting was more about being someone else. But now I realize that acting is really about being yourself too. It's about being true to yourself, about being honest, and so is music. In music you can choose to be a certain kind of character, if you wish, but you use your experience to fill that character's shoes. So I think they are very similar.

**BJ:** *Of the films and plays you've done, which do you think best shows your abilities as an actress?*

**M:** None of them. Not yet.

***BJ:** Why?*

**M:** I don't think I've had a great part to play yet. There have been moments in each music where I feel I've really explored things or done what I set out to do, but nothing as a whole.

***BJ:** Is there any character you're dying to play?*

**M:** Yeah, Lee Miller. I think she was great. I love the idea of doing *Evita,* but that's just because she's just an incredibly complex and interesting woman I'm not dying to do it, but it's awfully intriguing to me.

***BJ:** I thought you were supposed to do* Evita.

**M:** I was, but it didn't work out.

***BJ:** What do you do to prepare yourself for a role?*

**M:** It's all emotional. If I'm attracted to the character, then I'm attracted to something emotionally. That's the main thing that helps me get into it.

***BJ:** Do you take the character home with you every night after work?*

**M:** No, but I'm incredibly affected by whatever role I'm playing. When I did *Speed-the-Plow* this summer, I felt the girl I played was extremely defeated. And I felt defeated all summer. I didn't feel she had a lot of focus or ultimately knew what she wanted to do with herself. And I felt that she lost in the end, she didn't have whatever tools she needed to get herself out of the situation she was in. And the effects of that really showed on me. I did some photo sessions last summer, and when I look at the pictures I see a totally different person. I didn't feel confident. I didn't feel my usual ballsy self. I just felt really, "defeated" is the best word to use. And that actually influenced everything I did, because it made me very sad.

I was writing my album during that time. Because of the state of mind I was in, I dealt with a lot of sadness in my life that I hadn't dealt with in a long time, things like my mother's death and certain relationships. I started to explore all of that every night when I would do the play. Especially for the last scene, when I had to walk onstage being really upset and frightened. I would sit in my dressing room with all the lights off, waiting for that scene, and I would force myself to think of something really painful. I did it every night, and I purged myself that way. It was like a goal I set. I would say, tonight I'm going to work this problem out. I need to think about this, or the possibility of this terrible thing happening. These little psychological exercises. Facing my fears.

***BJ:*** *What was it like working with Joe Mantegna and Ron Silver? Were they very supportive?*

**M:** Yeah. They were there for me, but they never went out of their way unless I asked for it. When I was doing the play I thought, God, they're not really very generous, or They're not really giving me that much. They made me stand on my own. They treated me like an equal. They didn't give me any training wheels.

***BJ:*** *What drew you to the play in the first place?*

**M:** It's weird. I have this thing about David Mamet, in spite of how chauvinistic he is. There's a sense of rhythm and music in his language that I think is beautiful. I'd written him a fan letter when I saw *House of Games.* I thought it was a great movie. And then, when I was in New York doing this movie called *Bloodhounds of Broadway,* I was having dinner with Mike Nichols, and he told me David Mamet had written a new play. He said, "You should do it." So I just kind of went for it.

***BJ:*** *And that was before you had even read the play?*

**M:** Yeah. And then I read it. I don't know, I can't even say why. I was driven. I was blindly driven to do it.

***BJ:*** *Do you think part of that has to do with the fact that you like to challenge yourself to try new forms?*

**M:** Yes. But things just come up in my life and I feel like I'm supposed to do them. I'm supposed to be doing *Dick Tracy* right now. I was supposed to write the songs for my album. I was supposed to do that play. And if I don't feel I'm supposed to do something, I won't do it. I believe there are no accidents, that everything happens for a reason.

***BJ:*** *This is one Catholic girl who believes in the preordained plan.*

**M:** Oh yeah, definitely.

***BJ:** Would you describe yourself as political, or politically involved at all?*

**M:** Well, I didn't vote, so I guess I'm not.

***BJ:** OK, let me rephrase the question. Are you motivated by political concerns?*

**M:** Yeah, I am. I would say that I am subconsciously more than consciously so. I'm aware of things. And my involvement has mainly been giving money to causes that I think are worthwhile. I have the resources to help people, so I do. But in the typical way that one would describe being political, I'm not.

***BJ:** You said in a recent interview that you're drawn to things that illustrate the sadness of life. Why is that?*

**M:** I don't know why. Because life is sad. And that's why I try to be happy, because life is so sad. And because sadness is a teacher, and happiness is really a gift.

***BJ:** And how would you define love?*

**M:** [long pause] Love is like breathing. You just have to do it.

EDNA GUNDERSEN

# FACE-TO-FACE WITH MADONNA

*USA Today*, December 11, 1996

*Madonna as mother-to-be and movie star (having just completed* Evita*) sat down for this typical mid-'90s-era chat.*—Eds.

Los Angeles—Madonna, our lady of constant makeovers, has added two new identities to her repertoire. Serious actress and mom.

She has the title role in *Evita*, Alan Parker's $59-million movie musical about Argentina's legendary first lady Eva Perón. It opens on Christmas. On Oct. 14, Madonna gave birth to her first child, Lourdes Maria Ciccone Leon, an arrival that upstaged her film coup.

"Everything I do is scrutinized so I shouldn't be surprised that it continued when I was pregnant," she says in her first postpartum interview. "I try to have a sense of humor about it, but it does irritate me. . . . My having a child is not for public consumption. It's not a career move. It's not a performance to be judged and rated. Nor is my role as a mother."

The coincidental timing of these twin feats "was incredibly poetic,"says Madonna, 38. "I waited so long for this movie, and it finally happened. I wanted so badly to have a child, and I got pregnant while making the movie. Suddenly, God gave me two gifts that were very important to me."

The singer/actress is sipping peach tea in the living room of her home, a 1926 Spanish mansion in the untrendy neighborhood of Los Feliz. Despite "major sleep deprivation," she is girlishly sexy, wearing tall boots, a short skirt, a sheer violet blouse and no makeup. Her blond-again hair is wet from the shower. Seven weeks after the delivery, she's trim again, save for a slightly bulging tummy.

"Don't crash my car, OK?" she jokes to the nanny, who has Lourdes and a bodyguard in tow for a visit to a park. Madonna would prefer pushing the stroller herself, but such an outing would provoke paparazzi frenzy.

Long a savvy self-promoter, Madonna draws the line at the nursery door. The media "turned my pregnancy into a spectacle," she says. "The media was at my gate 24 hours a day." Yet she and boyfriend Carlos Leon pulled off her stealth delivery at a low-profile hospital.

She'd rather shift public attention to *Evita,* a sweeping epic shot over 84 days (and 85 costume changes) in Buenos Aires, London and Budapest. It melds two of this century's most controversial women and provides a dazzling showcase that could reverse Madonna's track record of turkeys like *Shanghai Surprise* and *Who's That Girl?* A rave in this week's *Time* notes she "plays *Evita* with a poignant weariness" and "does a tough score proud."

The film, costarring Antonio Banderas and Jonathan Pryce, opens Dec. 25 in Los Angeles and New York, and goes nationwide Jan. 10. The soundtrack, featuring Madonna's finest singing to date, premiered at No. 6 on *Billboard*'s album chart.

Relaxed and upbeat, Madonna waxes rhapsodic on her career and motherhood:

*Your four-page letter to Alan Parker insisted only you could play Eva Perón. Why do you feel that way?*

I just knew that no one could understand what she went through more than I. I related to her commitment, discipline and ambition [and] that bravery required for a girl of 15 to come from the pueblos and go to Buenos Aires to find her way in entertainment and later in politics. Her suffering as a child was a catalyst to make a better life. I understood that.

*She was both beloved and reviled. Did you recognize yourself in that context too?*

Sure. Because of her enormous impact, her detractors tried to tear her down and desecrate her image. People were frightened of the power she had and undermined her accomplishments by calling her a whore. I can certainly relate to that. People intimidated by me feel the need to denigrate me.

*In past movie roles, your real persona seemed bigger than the characters.*

*Evita* is the first movie big enough to contain me. I know I have a very big presence. If I overpower the movie, the movie fails.

*Did your pregnancy pose problems on the set?*

I never had morning sickness. A couple times, I got dizzy and a little nauseous. I attributed that to the incredible heat in Argentina and the long hours. It was gone by the time I found out I was pregnant. I was more worried about my stomach showing. My only sense of terror was "I'm not going to fit into my costumes!"

*Did you have a comfortable pregnancy?*

It was great. I worked out. I didn't have any weird food cravings. I felt fine until the last couple of weeks, when you have to wheelbarrow yourself around. Your lower back starts killing you, and you don't want to get out of your pajamas.

*Was it hard to say goodbye to your waistline?*

I surrendered. It was cool to eat whatever I wanted. It was nice to have that freedom. Now that I've had the baby, I feel liberated in a sense. I don't feel I have to be a certain size or have perfect abs. I still exercise, but I don't care as much.

*Do you and Carlos Leon intend to get married?*

I don't see the need. I'm perfectly happy with the way things are.

*I barely caught a glimpse of the baby. Does she look like you or Carlos?*

She looks mostly like me, but every day she looks more like him. She has my shape of face and eyes. She's got his nose.

*Do you want more kids?*

I'd love to have one more. But not right away. I have to recover from this.

*Your mom died when you were 6, and you helped raise your siblings. Was that experience helpful in dealing with a first baby?*

To a certain extent. I knew how to change diapers and I spent many hours baby-sitting. My sister has a son, and I drew on her knowledge. She gave me tons of books, and I still call her up every five minutes.

*What have the past few weeks been like?*

For the first four weeks, I didn't do anything except take care of her: holding on to her, feeding her, looking at her. Then I slowly started getting back to work, sitting at my desk and talking on the phone and trying to run my record company. It was a huge adjustment. I used to make a list and know I'd get everything done. Now a lot of things don't get done, and that's OK.

*How radically will motherhood alter your future?*

It's a big question mark. I have no idea what I'm doing next. I'm reading a lot of scripts. I know I'll make another album. It's exciting that I don't have it all planned. I would like to spend less time working and more time with my daughter. And I will.

*Will Lourdes be raised a Catholic?*

I'm not really sure. I am baptizing her Catholic. There are things about Catholicism that I disagree with, but there are a lot of things I'm still intrigued by. I still go to church and light candles. The church provides a kind of sanctuary and a sense of community. I'll teach her about Catholicism, but also about all religions, especially Buddhism, Judaism and the Kabbala [ancient Jewish lore]. My own religion combines all those. I would rather present the Bible to my daughter as "some very interesting stories you could learn from" rather than "this is the rule."

*How will you shield Lourdes from the bad side effects of your fame?*

I would like her to have as normal a life as possible. I don't think I want her to go to school in L.A. I'd prefer New York, probably not Manhattan. I don't want her life to be chronicled, so I'll shield her as much as possible. Look at John Kennedy, Jr. He's been photographed since he was 2, and he turned out OK. He had a very strong, intelligent mother.

*What are your regrets?*

I wouldn't say I have regrets. I made mistakes and learned from them. Most people want to hear me say I regret putting out my *Sex* book. I don't. What was problematic was putting my *Erotica* album out at the same time. I love that record, and it was overlooked. Everything I did for the next three years was dwarfed by my book.

*Dennis Rodman wasn't a regret? In his* Bad as I Wanna Be, *he details your sexual encounters.*

First of all, it was untrue information. Second, I felt violated because I did consider him to be a friend, as crazy as he may appear. I know his depiction of our sex life was probably one reason the book sold so well, and that is highly irritating.

*Have you spoken to him since then?*

No.

*In* Rolling Stone, *he says he hopes you two can eventually be friends.*

[Laughs] Right. I think he's terribly delusional.

*In the documentary* Truth or Dare, *you made no secret about your crush on Antonio Banderas. Was it awkward making* Evita?

Not at all. Several years ago, when we were going to do *Evita* with a different director, we got together, had dinner and joked about the whole thing. We've become friends. It's way past the crush.

*Has the spotlight toughened your skin?*

I have a better understanding of humanity, but I'm still very hurt by personal attacks. I don't mind criticism of my work. As human beings, we have this need to tear people down, to enjoy other people's suffering. That makes me sad because it seems to be human nature. We'd rather watch people trip on the sidewalk than ascend to a great height.

ANN POWERS

# NEW TUNE FOR THE MATERIAL GIRL: I'M NEITHER

1998

*The newest new Madonna—Spiritual Girl—comments on her 1998 album,* Ray of Light, *and her newfound interest in yoga and spirituality.*—Eds.

Imagine Madonna in the most unlikely position she could take. Perhaps this: Alone in a silent room, lying face up on the floor in a yoga pose known as the corpse, crying uncontrollably. The 39-year-old singer, notorious for being the preeminent quick-change artist of her generation, found herself in this odd and vulnerable situation more than once in the two years that led up to the release of her new album, *Ray of Light.* She was not engaging in a kinky sex rite or a new performance style. She was doing what had not come naturally, she says—confronting herself.

"As my body was opening up and I was going into places that had been locked for so many years, it was releasing emotional things," she said on a recent afternoon in her Manhattan apartment, drinking ginger tea after her daily yoga session. "I'd be lying in shavasana"—the totally prone corpse pose—"and I'd be weeping. Or I'd do a forward bend and tears would come to my eyes. I'd sort of get embarrassed and think, why is this happening to me? But I realized that I was going through a catharsis."

Meet the newest new Madonna—a woman prone to uttering pearls of wisdom like "If you want something, give something," who admits that in the past she has been "selfish and disturbingly petulant," who has given over her impossibly taut physique to a discipline oriented toward letting things go. After the Caesarean-section birth of her daughter, Lourdes, two years ago, she tried yoga because her old regime of running and lifting weights was too painful. She just wanted to stay in shape but found the practice offered deeper lessons about, as she puts it, "desire and detachment." She started studying Sanskrit, the language of the yoga chants, and the Jewish mystical art of the Cabala. These new interests inform *Ray of Light*, an hour-plus look below the surface that will horrify those who prefer Madonna down to earth and out to win.

She expects negative reaction. "There are still a lot of people who are really uncomfortable with these topics, and they're going to go, 'We liked her better when she was hitchhiking naked in Miami. Where's the fun Madonna?' But I think that I have the ability now to have more fun and be happier than I ever have in my life."

It is tempting to view Madonna as just another star calling narcissism enlightenment. Famous seekers have proliferated since the 1960s, from the Beatles kneeling at the feet of the Mahareshi Mahesh Yogi to scientologists and Tibetan Buddhists like John Travolta and Richard Gere hawking their lifestyles today. Such explorations have given the world Shirley MacLaine's memoirs and the albums Bob Dylan made in his fundamentalist Christian phase. The average person struggling to grab a moment of reflection between work and family cannot help noticing that stars tend to take the higher path only after securing a good spot on the lower one. In this context, an inner sea change wrought by an exercise regime may seem no more than the luxury of a rich woman bored enough to keep looking for something, despite having it all.

But Madonna is not like other celebrities. If a deity can be defined as a force illuminating the world, then she is a secular goddess, designated by her audience and pundits alike as the human face of social change. Intellectuals have described her as embodying sex, capitalism and celebrity itself. She was a presence discussed on *Nightline*, enraged the Vatican and inspired countless articles and books—even one devoted to her appearances in people's dreams.

The last few years have seen Madonna's symbolic impact wane, along with her record sales, but lately she has landed at the center of another preoccupying public question: the uncertain maturity of the 1980s yuppie class. A generation that spent its young adulthood pursuing self-centered ambitions now faces questions of purpose and fulfillment. Madonna's recent moves—proudly becoming a single mother, expanding her career as president of her own label, Maverick Records, exchanging rock-and-roll outrageousness for the vaunted respectability of show tunes—have been scrutinized as signs of a new style of growing up.

"People have always had this obsession with me, about my reinvention of myself," Madonna said. "I just feel like I'm shedding layers. I'm slowly revealing who I am." *Ray of Light* is her testament to that process; not simply an inward-looking album, it is an inquiry into the nature of introspection itself. In songs flecked with phrases taken from proverbs and sacred texts, Madonna explores the terrain of the spiritual as she once investigated eroticism and social ambition. Once she borrowed sources and styles from gay drag queens and vintage Hollywood; now she mines Greek legends and *The Autobiography of a Yogi.* As always, she presents her own journey as a parable, something larger than herself.

"Even if I write about things in a personalized way, I also write about them in a universal way," Madonna explained. Madonna Ciccone, the individual, seems to have taken a genuine risk in opening herself up to self-examination and accepting that there is more to life than her own ambition. But *Ray of Light* is a risk for the other Madonna, the artist and star, whose genius has always lain in erasing the difference between her "personal" and everyone else's "universal," causing people to see themselves in her. Icons are flat surfaces; they do not have interior lives. Madonna's new music tries to imagine what it might sound like, and feel like, if one did. The woman who served as a channel for cultural myths about carnal pleasure and worldly accomplishment is trying to do the same for that most abstract and idiosyncratic of human yearnings. Stepping into a role that some will surely think is beyond her, Madonna is now manufacturing a fantasy of the soul.

She needed a sonic landscape for this new vision, and luckily for Madonna, one was bursting into view. "I had been listening to a lot of electronica and trance music," she explained. "It was just this blank canvas, a mood thing. It occurred to me that you could take it to another level by actually investing it with emotion."

Madonna is not the first superstar to adopt this music's cool language for her own purposes. U2 and David Bowie both explored it on recent albums but sounded out of touch and a bit desperate. Madonna courts similar accusations now. The electronica kingpins Tricky and Goldie scorned her advances for this project, and she ended up making a more mainstream album than most fans of this music will tolerate. It is easy to accuse her of jumping onto the cosmic bandwagon, merely to suit a new spaced-out sound.

Except that *Ray of Light* is not spaced out. Madonna treats her lofty subject matter with the same unceremonious ardor as she did unwed motherhood in "Papa Don't Preach."

Emotion is the key to *Ray of Light,* evident in the prosaic tone of Madonna's voice and her forthright professions. Collaborating with the longtime ambient music maker and pop remixer William Orbit, Madonna sought to link electronica's metaphysics with pop's empathetic heart. *Ray of Light* does not veer toward the cutting edge, but neither does it obscure.

Madonna's own frank sensibility is a jungle of beats and effects. The album gracefully connects current dance music sounds to older ones; its tracks recall early techno, Detroit house, disco and new wave, elements that Madonna used to create her own body of work.

Grounding it all is that familiar voice, which has strengthened considerably over the years. No longer chirping like a Betty Boop doll, Madonna now sings like a completely ordinary woman, and that quality turns her new songs into revelations. She renders their mystical pronouncements not as platitudes but as intimate prayers. They form a portrait of faith in the first person, connecting spiritual longing to the drive for sex and love, and to the sadness that comes with the knowledge of death.

"You can't help being sad and lonely when you're going through self-examination," Madonna said. "Because, at the end of the day, you're going to be buried alone." In the video for "Frozen," Madonna appears as a virtual angel of death beckoning viewers. *Ray of Light* repeatedly confronts the loss of a loved one; gossips and biographers will find references to the death of Madonna's mother when she was a child and the breakup of her relationship with Lourdes's father, Carlos Leon. But Madonna keeps aiming for the bigger picture. "Retaliation, revenge, hate, regret, that's what I deal with in 'Frozen,'" she said. "Everyone's going to say, 'That's a song about Carlos,' but it's not really; it's just about people in general."

In fact, *Ray of Light* is at its weakest when Madonna gets showily "personal." The ruminations on fame in "Drowned World" and the lover's farewell in "Power of Goodbye" come off as the stilted exclamations of a drama queen. "Mer Girl" is a more interesting mess; a long, amorphous tone poem in the style of Bjork, it builds Madonna's reflections on her mother's death into an apocalyptic vision. Images of the earth swallowing her and the stench of burning flesh are badly juxtaposed with saccharine pop-psychological insights. In such moments, Madonna comes perilously close to New Age gobbledygook.

Despite these weak points, *Ray of Light* wins its gamble, not by revealing Madonna's inner self—she has offered up plenty of confessions before, all as canny as the ones here—but by making her talent as an inspirational artist work in a more explicit way. The Roman Catholic references that have peppered her career from *Like a Virgin* on have always contained the seed of what the Rev. Andrew M. Greeley once called her "God hunger." Now, with a new metaphysical mood on the rise in America, Madonna is employing her goddess status to encourage the development of a spiritual sense that goes beyond ego. "The weirdest thing is, the more open you are to things, the more you suddenly become aware of people's divine nature," she said. Madonna has always encouraged her fans to express themselves. *Ray of Light* asks them to do it again, on a whole new plane.

"Boy Toy" at MTV Music Awards. *Courtesy of Chuck Pulin, Star File.*

# *Part Three*

## PAPA, DON'T PREACH

MADONNA AS PHENOMENON

*The Madonna myth has been exploited in many ways. Naturally, there has been an "unauthorized" biography that gives a far more titillating view of Madonna's pre-success years in New York than her official interviews do. When Madonna first hit, her fans (or Madonna wannabes, as they were colorfully called), immediately made her style of thirft-shop chic the "latest thing." But the wannabes soon faded, and Madonna had to find new ways to stoke the fires of controversy. Her controversial exploitation of religious imagery—discussed most thoroughly in the articles about her video for "Like a Prayer" in Part Four of this book—and her self-exploitation as sexual object (in both her* Sex *book and the related* Erotica *album) raised many hackles. The articles in this section address the Madonna phenomenon from many angles and at many different points of her career to show how she has kept herself a controversial figure before the public eye.*—Eds.

CHRISTOPHER ANDERSON

# MADONNA RISING: THE WILD AND FUNKY EARLY YEARS IN NEW YORK

*New York* magazine, October 14, 1991

*This selection from the "unauthorized" biography of Madonna appeared in* New York *magazine. It paints a less sympathetic portrait of Madonna in her early years than the one that she gives in her many interviews. While obviously written to appeal to the salacious, it gives much of the flavor of her days as dance-hall goddess.*—Eds.

On a warm July morning in 1978, nineteen-year-old Madonna Louise Veronica Ciccone ignored her father and flew from Detroit, where she had grown up, to New York; it was her first plane trip. With a suitcase and the clothes on her back, her dance slippers and only $37 in cash crumpled in her purse, Madonna hailed a cab. Unfamiliar with Manhattan, she simply asked the driver to take her "to the center of everything." The driver took her straight to Times Square.

Wearing a heavy winter coat in the middle of a New York heat wave, Madonna lugged her suitcase past the porno houses on 42nd Street, then took a right on Lexington Avenue. A few blocks farther downtown, there was a street fair. Making her way through the crowd, she realized that she was being followed. Rather than trying to dodge the man, she spun around and said hello. "Why don't you go home and get rid of it?" he asked.

"I don't live anywhere," Madonna told the man, who asked her to stay at his apartment. "I pretty much had to charm people into giving me things," she later said.

For the next two weeks, the stranger (whose name she no longer recalls) made her breakfast while she looked for a job and a place of her own. All she could afford was a fourth-floor walk-up at 232 East 4th Street, between Avenues A and B. "I really wouldn't go visit her there," Steve Bray, her boyfriend from Detroit, later confessed. "I thought I was going to be killed by junkies."

To pay the rent, Madonna got a job at Dunkin' Donuts across from Bloomingdale's but left after she heard that choreographer Pearl Lang, cofounder with Alvin Ailey of the American Dance Center in New York, was teaching a course in advanced technique at a six-week workshop in Durham, North Carolina. Several months before, when Lang was at the University of Michigan, Madonna had been mesmerized by her work.

Madonna scrounged up bus fare for the trip to Durham and was among the 300 aspiring dancers competing for one of a half-dozen scholarships to the workshop. "When we announced her name," Lang later remembered, "Madonna walked right up to the table and looked straight at me and declared, 'I'm auditioning for this scholarship so I can work with Pearl Lang. I've seen one of her performances, and she's the only one I want to work with.' Of course," said Lang, who had been lead soloist for Martha Graham before starting her own company, "Madonna's eyes popped out of her head when I told her I *was* Pearl Lang."

All of which came as a surprise to one classmate. "Pearl Lang was pointed out to her before the audition," she said. "Madonna knew *exactly* who she was talking to. Corny, but it worked."

At the end of the first week of classes, Madonna boldly asked if there was an opening for her in the New York company. "I was kind of taken aback," Lang said. "I told her I had to see but that we could probably make room. I asked her how she was going to get back to New York. She said, 'Don't worry—I'll manage.'"

Despite her later claims that she "performed with the Alvin Ailey dance company," Madonna began by taking classes with the American Dance

Center's third-string troupe. "I thought I was in a production of *Fame,*" she told *Rolling Stone.* "Everybody was Hispanic or black, and everyone wanted to be a star." Feeling very much alone in New York, Madonna often went to Lincoln Center, sat by the fountain, and cried. "I'd write in my journal," she said, and "pray to have even one friend. But never once did it occur to me to go back home. Never."

Faced with stiff competition, Madonna switched from Ailey's classes to Pearl Lang's Dance Company in late November of 1978. Lang was very disciplined and demanding, her approach to dance Spartan, dramatic, angular. Madonna called it "painful, dark, and guilt-ridden. Very Catholic."

Because Madonna was so skinny, her first appearance was as a starving ghetto child in the Holocaust drama *I Never Saw Another Butterfly.* "She was emaciated enough to pass for a Jewish child in the ghetto." Lang remembered. "And she danced marvelously."

Madonna also had an impetuous streak that appealed to Lang—for a time. Before long, Lang and Madonna were squaring off before the whole company. "It was like watching two tigresses prowling around, sizing each other up," one dancer remembered. "Pearl was very demanding of all her students, but Madonna was not one who took commands easily, particularly when she felt she was right."

Outside the dance studio, Madonna was struggling, relying on friends for meals and handouts. She had even taken to rummaging through garbage cans. If she spotted a bag from Burger King or McDonald's, she would, being a vegetarian, throw out the meat but eat the bun and the French fries. It was not unusual for her to go a day or more without eating.

To earn a few extra dollars, Madonna also began moonlighting as a nude model—which she had first done as an undergraduate at the University of Michigan. "I was in really good shape," she later recalled, "and I was slightly underweight, so you could see my muscle definition and my skeleton. I was one of their favorite models because I was so easy to draw. So I sort of made the rounds." She discovered she could earn up to $100 for a day's work—compared with $50 for eight grueling hours waitressing. Soon, she was modeling nude for private groups of three or four. "So I got to know these people in a friendly kind of way."

Martin Schreiber was in the middle of teaching a ten-week photography course at the New School in Greenwich Village when Madonna showed up on February 12, 1979. "Sometimes models would come in and be flamboyant and gregarious and talk with everyone," Schreiber said. "Madonna came in very quiet." Although he had no role in selecting her—the school hired all the models—Schreiber remembered that she was not "a welcome relief from the average, lumpy but sweet art-class model, but she was also one of the loveliest models I ever photographed. She came in wearing pajama bottoms, like a little girl. When she took off her clothes, she had a terrific body. It was beautifully proportioned, muscular, strong. She had lovely skin. She was an ideal."

After the class, Madonna gave Schreiber her phone number, and they started going out. Madonna accepted Schreiber's invitations to come to his loft: he bought her expensive dinners and hired her for his private advanced-photography class. At times, he found her bohemian personality off putting. "Once we went to a party in a loft on the Lower East Side, and she wore those same pajama bottoms! There were people of all ages there, and a couple of little kids. She preferred to sit on the wooden floor and play with them. I wanted her to be interested in me, but she wasn't."

In the spring of 1979, Tony Ciccone, a successful engineer, showed up unexpectedly on Madonna's doorstep. "When my father came to visit," she recalled, "he was mortified. The place was crawling with cockroaches. There were winos in the hallways, and the entire place smelled like stale beer." Predictably, Ciccone pleaded with her to return with him to Michigan to finish college. Just as predictably, she refused.

She was, in fact, mulling a career switch—the dance field was so crowded that it would take her at least three years to get a spot with a major company. Although she had never shown an interest in a music career before, Madonna began auditioning for singing and dancing parts in musicals and later videos, as well as for acting roles in films. Among the roles she would be turned down for were the lead in *Footloose* and a part in the TV series *Fame*.

At a party thrown by her friend Norris Burroughs, a graffiti artist, she met Dan Gilroy, a pleasant, goofy-looking musician/songwriter/comedian whose wardrobe of porkpie hats and slouchy coats were in sync with Madonna's own offbeat look. Sparks didn't exactly fly. She found Gilroy brusque: he found her depressing. But by the end of the night, Madonna turned to Gilroy and asked point-blank, "Aren't you going to kiss me?"

Not long after, they were making love in a former Corona, Queens, synagogue Gilroy shared with his brother Ed. The synagogue, with its carved-stone Stars of David and other Judaic symbols, also served as a studio for the brothers, who at various times worked as musicians or comics under the name Bil and Gil. That night, Gilroy strapped a guitar onto

Madonna and taught her her first chord. Something, she recalled, "really clicked something off in my brain." That "something" was the realization that music—not dance—might be her ticket to stardom.

Madonna's relationship with Dan Gilroy was barely two weeks old when Jean Van Lieu and Jean Claude Pellerin, the two French music producers behind the success of European disco star Patrick Hernandez, held open auditions in New York for young faces to back Hernandez. Though he was virtually unknown in the United States, Hernandez's single "Born to Be Alive" was a big international hit.

Madonna went to the audition, and after watching her dance and belt out a generic disco tune, Van Lieu and Pallerin offered to take her to Paris and turn her into a star. "We saw right away that she had more punch than the others," Hernandez said. "Instead of selecting her to dance like an idiot behind me, we separated her from the other performers. We wanted to bring her to France so she could record." Tired of sifting through garbage cans for her next meal, she accepted.

Madonna arrived in Paris in May of 1979 and was delivered by limousine to Pellerin's apartment on the Right Bank. In addition to lavish accommodations and a chauffeured limousine, her new employers supplied their find with her own maid, secretary, vocal coach, and unlimited wardrobe budget.

Evenings were spent ricocheting from one chic party to another, eating at Maxim's and Tour d'Argent, tearing up the dance floor at Régine's. Wherever they went, Madonna was promoted as "the next Edith Piaf." Van Lieu and Pellerin also took great pains to introduce her to the jet-set sons of some of France's oldest families. "They made me meet all these awful boys," she remembered, "and I would throw tantrums. They would just laugh and give me money to make me happy."

"She was very beautiful and dated a lot of French boys," Pellerin's wife recalled. "But she thought they were very old-fashioned, and she was very free. Very free. Very liberal. She wanted a lot of boys."

"Madonna went out every night in Paris," Hernandez said. "Concerning male friends at the time, let's just say she had a healthy appetite."

After three months in France, Madonna was feeling manipulated and neglected. She wanted out of the arrangement. The letters from Dan Gilroy, each more insistent than the last, buoyed her spirits but also reminded her that Paris might be costing her the chance to be a star back in the States.

She told her bosses that she wanted to visit her family. To prove that she intended to return, she asked for a round-trip ticket and left all her expensive new clothes behind at the Pellerins. "Madonna wanted only one thing," Madame Pellerin said, "to be a star. And when she left Paris, she promised that she would come back a star."

Patrick Hernandez credited Paris with "putting the bug in her ear that she could sing. Maybe if she had never come, Madonna would have continued taking dance lessons, going to auditions—and never even tried to make it as a singer!"

She arrived back in New York in August of 1979. Homeless, penniless, with no visible career prospects, she appeared no better off than when she left. Yet Paris had convinced her that she could make it as a rock star. Dan Gilroy was not entirely surprised when Madonna arrived back on his doorstep in Queens asking him to teach her an instrument. It didn't take him long to decide that she was best suited to the drums.

While Gilroy and his brother Ed were waiting tables during the day and performing their comedy gigs around town at night, Madonna used the synagogue to practice the drums. She had also begun writing songs, strumming tunes on Ed Gilroy's battered guitar. "It was one of the happiest times of my life," Madonna later said of that period. "I really felt loved. Sometimes I'd write sad songs and he'd [Dan] sit there and cry. Very sweet."

To help out, Madonna did occasionally take a job. One of them was as a coat-check girl in the Russian Tea Room. Manager Gregory Camillucci recalled the day he hired Madonna at $4.50 an hour. "I remember our first meeting vividly," he said, "because she was very striking in a kind of jungle way. Not that she was raw. She was a sweet thing, but rather like a sculpture that isn't quite finished yet."

He was also impressed by her name: "Even then it was just Madonna—such a striking, eye-opening, ear-awakening name." Physically, Camillucci remembered, she was "gaunt. She definitely had a dancer's body, and I got the impression that the one meal we fed her was the only food she was getting. She had very dark hair; she was very Italian-looking, very beautiful."

Sequestered in the tiny cloakroom to the immediate left of the restaurant's entrance, Madonna "was very quiet, never buddy-buddy with any of the other employees—a loner," Camillucci said. She was a "hard worker, conscientious," but she dressed in wild animal prints, ankle socks, and high heels. Madonna did not exactly fit the Russian Tea Room's uptown image.

After two months, Camillucci fired her. "She took it well," he said. "I didn't come right out and say she was terribly dressed or anything of that sort. I felt sorry for her. I felt badly because you could feel that she was alone. The others who work here—you know if they don't make it as actresses or singers, they will survive nicely. They have that sense of security, of having a family to fall back on. Madonna never gave that impression."

For three days straight, avant-garde filmmaker Stephen Lewicki had been holed up in his un-air-conditioned West Side studio, poring over hundreds of résumés to find an actress to star in his new feature. Despondent, he began tossing out résumé after résumé. When one of the envelopes fell out of the wastebasket, Lewicki bent over to pick it up, and a three-page handwritten letter fell out of it.

"Dear Stephen," it began, "I was born and raised in Detroit, where I began my career in petulance and precociousness. By the time I was in the fifth grade, I knew I either wanted to be a nun or a movie star. Nine months in a convent cured me of the first disease. During high school I became slightly schizophrenic as I couldn't choose between class virgin or the other kind. Both of them had their values as far as I could see."

Madonna got the part, and since he had to scrounge up financing as he went along, it took Lewicki two years to make the erotic thriller *A Certain Sacrifice,* the story of Bruna (played by Madonna), a Lower East Sider with her own family of three "sex slaves." No Sooner does Bruna find true love than she is brutally raped in a coffee-shop rest room. To avenge the crime, Bruna enlists the aid of her slaves, who hunt down the rapist, then drink his blood in a sacrificial ritual.

According to Lewicki, she was restless and distracted when the camera wasn't on her, but that certainly didn't stop him from being smitten by his star. Although they were never lovers, one afternoon while they sat on a bench in Battery Park, Madonna invited her director to lick blueberry yogurt out of her ear. He did. "That woman has more sensuality in her ear," he remembered, "than most women have anywhere on their bodies."

Madonna finally moved into the Gilroys' converted synagogue full-time and launched her campaign to be included in the new band the brothers were putting together. Despite his respect for her songwriting talent, Dan was not convinced that Madonna was enough of a musician to pull it off in front of a paying audience. He soon relented, however, and Madonna recruited Angie Smit, a dancer friend, to join their new group.

At Madonna's insistence, the band rehearsed, relentlessly. The all-night sessions spilled over into morning, when the exhausted musicians would stumble to a local coffee shop. The Breakfast Club, as they dubbed themselves, began doing gigs at all the "Lower East Side hell holes"—clubs with names like UK, My Father's Place, and Botany Talk House, and the star attraction was Angie Smit. Wearing little more than lingerie, the lithe dancer-turned-guitarist could barely sing an audible note. But she did sway seductively throughout most of the act, completely upstaging Madonna and the Gilroys. Madonna demanded that Smit leave the band.

She then pleaded with Gilroy to let her come out from behind her drum set and sing a couple of her own songs. Reluctantly, he agreed. She spent all day every day on the telephone, chatting up record producers, club owners, agents, and managers—anyone who could conceivably advance the band's fortunes with a record deal or club date.

Madonna's partners liked the fact that she was so good at drumming up business, but they were also taken aback. "They weren't as interested in the commercial end as I was," Madonna said. "It never occurred to me to get into this business and *not* be a huge success. I wanted the world to notice me, always have."

Audiences began to notice Madonna. It was hard not to when she jumped out from behind her drum set, grabbed a microphone, and belted out her songs, gyrating wildy across the stage. For more than eight months, Dan Gilroy had not only provided Madonna with a basic musical education but worked nine to five so that she could stay home and concentrate on honing her talents. Now that she had, in her own words, "sucked what I needed" from them, she announced to Dan that the affair was over and that she was moving from Queens back into Manhattan to start her own band.

Unexpectedly, Steve Bray, Madonna's boyfriend from Ann Arbor, called to say that he was fed up with life in the Midwest and ready to attack New York. Up until Bray's arrival, Madonna had been illegally squatting in a loft where she slept on a scrap of carpet and kept herself warm with three electric space heaters placed strategically around the room. One night, she woke up to find that one of the heaters had set her little piece of carpet ablaze and that she was surrounded by a "ring of fire." She doused the flames with water, but as she spun around to get more water, her nightgown caught fire. Madonna stripped it off, gathered what little she had together, and fled before the entire loft was in flames.

It was then that self-described "soul mates" Madonna and Bray rekindled their romance. "He was a lifesaver," she said. "I wasn't a good enough musician to be screaming at anybody about how loudly they were playing." Together they moved into the Music Building on Eighth Avenue in mid-Manhattan, a charmless, Depression-era structure that now houses dozens of recording and rehearsal studios.

"It was supposed to be like the Brill Building," said a musician who rented space there in the early eighties. "The only trouble was, the Music Building was filthy *and* dangerous—the neighborhood was crawling with cockroaches and addicts. The hallways smelled of urine; the place was truly disgusting." One morning, Adam Alter of Gotham Productions was walking briskly through the Music Building's shabby lobby when a gum-snapping girl in torn jeans stopped him. "Hey," she said before walking on, "you look just like John Lennon."

At the same time, unknown to Alter, his business partner, Camille Barbone, had met an offbeat young girl on the elevator. "We had the whole second floor to ourselves," said Barbone, an attractive, no-nonsense New Yorker who had worked over the years with such stars as Melba Moore and David Johansen and for such companies as Columbia, PolyGram, Buddha Records, and Arista. "When I got on the elevator one morning, I noticed this striking young lady. She had red hair, chopped off in a Prince Valiant style."

The next day, the girl showed up again. "Did you do it yet?" she asked.

"Excuse me?" Barbone replied.

"Did you *do* it yet?"

"No."

"Okay."

The bizarre exchange on the elevator was repeated for several days. "She was teasing me, and I was intrigued." Barbone admitted.

A week later, Barbone was searching for the keys to her office corridor when the same sassy young woman in dark glasses opened the door for her. "Don't worry," the mysterious girl said matter-of-factly. "You'll be opening doors for me someday."

Meanwhile, Alter had persuaded Barbone to listen to a demo tape recorded by this spectacular new talent he had discovered. Her name, he told his partner, was Madonna. Barbone thought most of the tape forgettable, except for one cut—an early rendition of "Burning Up." Alter then dragged Barbone to watch this Madonna woman rehearse. It was only then that Barbone realized that the Madonna on the tape and the mysterious woman she had been repeatedly bumping into on the elevator were the same woman. "I was shocked," she recalled. "Madonna had obviously planned this all along, and I never realized it."

Rather than feeling manipulated, Barbone was struck by Madonna's "waifish charm." "She had evolved as a personality even then," Barbone said. Barbone agreed to catch Madonna's act upstairs at Kansas City but didn't go because of a debilitating migraine. The pain she experienced that night was nothing compared with what was in store for her the following morning when Madonna paid her a visit.

"She came flying into my office," Barbone recalled. "'You're just like everyone else,' she screamed. 'How *could* you not show up? This is my *life*.'"

Barbone sat speechless on her side of the desk. "I was impressed," she conceded. "Here she was *screaming* in my face, but I admired her. No one had ever been so ballsy before."

Barbone apologized, agreed to catch the show the following Saturday, and reached across her desk for her datebook to make a note of the place and time. Madonna grabbed the book and shoved it into Barbone's chest. "No," she said, "you just *remember*." Then she left.

---

Barbone can still remember sitting in the audience at Kansas City when Madonna "poked her head out from behind the curtain looking for me. When she saw I was there, the show began. She wore men's gray pajamas with red stripes and the fly sewn up. She had dyed her hair from red to dark brown. The minute I saw her, I knew she was a megastar. Wow, I thought, what I could do with that face."

Afterward, said Barbone, "she came up to me and said she had a sore throat. So I got her some tea with honey in it. Then I said, 'How would you like a manager?' She screamed, 'Yeah!' and threw her arms around me."

On St. Patrick's Day 1981, Madonna sat on the floor of Barbone's office drinking green beer as her new manager explained each clause of her contract with Gotham Productions. Barbone then recommended a lawyer to approve the contract for Madonna. "I knew she would be big," she said, "so I did my best to forestall any trouble down the road. I didn't want there to be any misunderstanding when it came to our legal arrangement." The initial agreement called for Barbone to act as Madonna's sole manager for six months, then wound up being extended for three years.

First, Madonna needed a decent place to live. She found a room on 30th Street just across from Madison Square Garden for $65 a week, and Barbone wrote her a check for the apartment. Then Barbone gathered all Madonna's worldly possessions—a guitar with a broken neck, some soiled and frayed secondhand clothes—and piled into a cab for the ride to 30th Street. "When we got there, I was appalled at the squalid conditions," Barbone said. "This was not decent, this was not safe. But she was a free spirit, and she didn't seem to care at all."

At 29, Barbone was only seven years older than Madonna, but she definitely took on a maternal role. Following a break-in at Madonna's 30th Street apartment, Barbone and Alter agreed to set their new protégée up in a comfortable apartment on Riverside Drive and 95th Street (her roommates were a handsome middle-aged man and his grown-up twin sons), pay her a weekly salary of $100, allow her free run of their recording studio, and find her a housekeeping job. In return, she agreed to allow Gotham Productions to mold her act, select her musicians, guide her career—and collect 15 percent of the gross.

While Madonna vacuumed during the day and wrote songs at night, Barbone fired her ragtag group of backup musicians and put together a new band. It would take months ("I can still hear Madonna whining, '*I want* my *band*. I want it *now*,'" Barbone recalled); in the end, she signed up such respected sessions players as John Kaye (formerly David Bowie's bass guitarist), guitarist John Gordon, keyboardist Dave Frank, and drummer Bob Riley.

Still, Madonna wanted Steve Bray as her drummer. Barbone refused. Madonna already had a drummer, Bob Riley. Besides, Barbone knew that Bray and Madonna had been lovers. As a manager, Barbone strongly disapproved of love affairs among band members because of the friction created.

"I laid down the rules to Madonna," she said. "No romantic involvement with the band. There were so many heartbroken men running around, I didn't want to add to the list. She said, 'Don't worry about it' and then proceeded to go to bed with Riley." Confronted by Barbone, Madonna denied the affair at first, then demanded that Riley be fired and replaced with Bray. "I had to fire Bob," Barbone remembered, "and he was heartbroken." She then called the band members together. While Madonna sat there chewing gum, dangling her legs and blowing huge bubbles, Barbone told the other band members in no uncertain terms to "stay away from Madonna."

Barbone's motherly concern also involved keeping an eye on Madonna's health. When Madonna had four impacted wisdom teeth removed, Barbone paid the dentist's bills and put Madonna up at her home in Bayside, Queens. "She wanted to get it over with, so she had all four removed at once." Barbone recalled. "That night, Madonna was swollen, she bled all night, and she cried all night. She woke me up, and I held her and took care of her."

Barbone's involvement extended far beyond dental care. She even took Madonna to Planned Parenthood and arranged for birth-control pills. "The last thing I wanted," she said, "was a pregnant Madonna."

For nearly two years, Barbone would be the single most important person in her life, nurturing her talent, orchestrating her career, and massaging her ego. "Madonna would actually sit on my lap," Barbone said. "She needs to feel physically close to other women—she needs that nurturing. Her mother's death is still doing a number on her. She's still searching for Mommy."

They also spent weekends together going to art galleries, strolling through Central Park, or watching movies. As long as she did not have to pick up the check, Madonna seemed content. Barbone also took charge of Madonna's acting career, enrolling her in classes with the renowned drama teacher Mira Rostova. She quit after one day, saying that the experience was "too hard" and the teacher was "mean." According to Barbone, Rostova was happy to see her go. "This girl will never be an actress," Rostova told Barbone. "She is too vulgar, and she thinks she knows it all. Besides, I do not like her."

"The acting thing was a big bone of contention between Madonna and me," Barbone said. "I wanted her to evolve. She wasn't interested in the hard work it would take to become a real actress." Madonna seemed more content lolling around on the floor of her living room taking Polaroids of herself. "The character she would later play in *Desperately Seeking Susan* was Madonna," Barbone said. "I saw her do the things she does in that picture a thousand times."

For the moment, Madonna was interested only in landing a recording deal. Barbone circulated her demo, and by the autumn of 1981, agents, producers, booking agents, and packagers were vying for a piece of Madonna. At least nine record companies called Gotham to say that, on the basis of the demo, they were on the verge of signing up the hot singer with the provocative name. Barbone and Adam Alter were eager to sign a deal and replenish the company coffers that had been drained to support their up-and-coming star. (Unfortunately, those deals took too long, and ultimately she would leave Gotham and sign with Warner.)

Meanwhile, Barbone began to notice that her client was beginning to behave strangely. Madonna started speaking in hushed tones about the impact of her mother's death and the fierce competition within her family. One evening, she told Barbone she was convinced that Elvis Presley had died on her birthday "for a reason. His soul has gone to me and has given me the power to perform." Reincarnation aside (Madonna turned nineteen when Presley died on August 16, 1977), Barbone was quite convinced at the time that she was serious.

She was. Over the years, Madonna had also come to believe that she possessed powers. "Madonna was very sensitive, very attuned spiritually," said Christopher Flynn, a dance teacher and mentor. "There were things that other people might chalk up to coincidence, but we knew better."

Madonna was terrified that she would be assassinated onstage, like the country-and-western star who is gunned down before an audience in the movie *Nashville.* "She always felt that there was somebody out there in the audience who was going to jump onstage and shoot her," Barbone said. So Barbone hired Roman "Fundy" Fundador to be Madonna's bodyguard long before she had become a star. "She was already whipping audiences into a frenzy," Barbone said. "So when she was finished, Fundy would literally scoop her up and carry her above the heads of the crowd to safety. She was *terrified.*" Even after each performance, Madonna was "afraid of being alone," Barbone said. "So I would drive her around for hours until she felt safe again. She hated being alone.

"I was her mommy for over two years, and she was just grateful for the simple things I could do for her," Barbone recalled. "Then Madonna realized she could have anything she wanted. I watched her change from a really sweet girl into someone who really believed her own publicity. My efforts at building her confidence had backfired. I knew I was losing her. All the people I had introduced her to were now slipping her tickets to concerts behind my back and taking her out to dinner."

Tensions escalated as Barbone sought to protect her investment in Madonna. During one of their bitter arguments, "I screamed at her and told her she was manipulative, an egomaniac who didn't give a damn about anyone," Barbone said. Madonna cried, but her tears were unconvincing. "At that moment, I realized I had no control over her. I knew I had created a monster who would turn on me." Enraged by what she viewed as Madonna's betrayal, Barbone smashed her fist through a door, fracturing her wrist. Madonna did nothing to help. "She wouldn't hold the door open for me, or anything," Barbone recalled. "I was in tremendous pain, but she had no sympathy at all. Madonna has no compassion. To her, that would be a sign of weakness."

Finally, in a moment of desperation, Barbone told Madonna, "I can't ever do what you want, I can't please you."

Madonna agreed, "I'm a bitch." She shrugged. "I always want more."

"Madonna is a sponge, all right," observed Barbone. "She soaks up everything she can from you; then when you're totally drained, she goes on to the next victim."

The defection was devastating. "I risked my entire career on Madonna," Barbone said, "and she nearly destroyed me. But," she added years later, "I don't hate her. I miss her."

It was Erica Bell's first visit to the Continental Club, and everything she had heard about the place was true. "People said that the minute you walked in the door, somebody would thrust cocaine in your hand," said Bell, a strikingly attractive black dancer and NYU student who had just opened her own downtown nightclub on Ninth Street off Third Avenue, Lucky Strike. "It was worse than that. Outside the door, somebody offered me coke, which I didn't do."

Everything about that night in 1982 would remain clear in Erica Bell's mind. Once Bell passed through a billowing curtain into the main room, she was instantly struck by the blue-and-white high-tech décor. "It was straight out of the *Jetsons,*" Bell said. "There was a huge fish tank, a bar that went on forever, and these white, four-foot-high Corinthian columns for dramatic effect. It seemed like everything was covered in glitter. Very Hollywood."

"At the opposite end of the long bar, sitting cross-legged atop one of these columns, was "this woman, dressed all in white—wearing a white tuxedo suit with a very wrinkled white shirt. She had this dark hair sticking up all over the place, and, of course, she was surrounded by men."

It was Madonna. "My eyes went right to her." Bell recalled. "I just could not take my eyes off her. And she had such beautiful eyes. Incredibly gorgeous. She was staring at me and I was staring at her. To me it seemed like an eternity. It's one of those strange things that happen in your life. When you meet someone you fall in love with. It sounds so corny or trite, but it's like the movies when time stops. We've talked about it many times since."

Bell and Madonna had a lot in common, and Bell was very impressed with Madonna's resourcefulness—especially when it came to scrounging up a meal. "Even later, when she started to make it and we were driving around town in limousines," Bell claimed, "she'd point to an alley and say, 'I used to dig through the garbage can in there looking for food. It's amazing how much perfectly good stuff people throw away.' Delicatessen and restaurant owners would come up to Madonna, and she'd recognize them right away. 'Rica, I love this guy. He used to feed me, save food for me out back.' I mean, there were times when she'd have to decide whether she was going to eat an apple or take the subway. Hearing these stories made me want to cry."

But not Madonna. "She isn't the emotional type," said Bell, who soon became Madonna's closest female confidante. "Madonna has this force. She has the most phenomenal will of anyone I've ever met. How close were we? Well, we slept in the same bed," said Bell, who would recall Madonna's curious 6 A.M. ritual of gargling with saltwater—"for her voice, I think."

Most nights, according to Bell, she and Madonna went out to hot clubs like Danceteria. "We would go there on a date," Bell remembered. "We went terrorizing; that's what we called it because that's what we did—terrorize people. She would say, 'Rica, I am the best-looking white girl here, and you are the best-looking black girl here, so let's do it.' Then we'd push people off the dance floor and take over.

"We'd pick out the cute boys," Bell continued, "go right up, and without saying a word kiss them on the mouth. Then we'd take their phone numbers, walk away, and, while the guy was still watching, crumple up the number and throw it away."

"She must be good in bed, because she is so uninhibited and athletic," Camille Barbone observed, "but it's kissing that turns her on." Erica Bell says, "I was intrigued with Madonna before she kissed me. But I can tell you one thing: Once Madonna kisses you, you stay kissed."

When they weren't prowling the clubs, Madonna and Bell talked about everything. "She used to tell me that she wanted to be famous," Bell said, "that she *had* to be famous. Madonna would say, 'I don't just need attention. I need *all* the attention. I want everyone in the world to know who I am and to *love* me.' That was two years before she had a hit record. I think the strongest fear she had then was that she might die and be forgotten."

Madonna remained her own best PR woman, and unquestionably the single most important person she made herself known to at Danceteria was Mark Kamins. The Manhattan-born son of jazz aficionados, Kamins grew up listening to John Coltrane and Miles Davis. After he graduated from Ithaca College with a degree in film, he went on to postgraduate studies in Paris and Athens. Returning to New York in 1978, he capitalized on his lifelong love of music by doing a stint as a disc jockey at a club called Tracks. When Rudolf opened Danceteria, Kamins signed on, and his flamboyant style quickly earned him the reputation as king of the New Wave DJs.

What Kamins really wanted to do was produce records. "I was always the guy at the parties who played the records," he said. "But once I actually got inside a studio, I made the decision to become a producer." After writing a song called "Snap-Shot," he had landed a deal to produce an album for Capitol Records vocalist Delores Hall. He followed that up by working on a record with David Byrne.

It was at this point that Madonna sidled up to Kamins at Danceteria's DJ booth. "I'd been watching her dance," Kamins said, "but always from a distance—and she was spectacular. When she came up and introduced herself, I was struck by her innate sexuality. She is beautiful, but it is her sense of style, of individuality. She has this aura about her."

Before long, Kamins and Madonna became lovers. "She always was sexually aggressive, and it wasn't just her image," Kamins said. "She used her sexuality as a performer, but it's also how she got over offstage." Not that she left any doubts as to her intentions. "She was always straightforward. She always made it clear that she wanted to be a star. But there was also an innocence about her."

After a few days with him, Madonna felt comfortable enough to spring her demo tape on Kamins. He did more than just listen to the demo; he played it at Danceteria. The crowd went wild for the homemade tape. Kamins was convinced that she had the makings of a star.

Kamins took Madonna's demo to Warner Bros., where he had just completed work on the new David Byrne album and become friendly with Michael Rosenblatt at Warner's Sire label. At a time when most record executives were stumbling over one another to sign up the next snarling, leather-clad punker, Rosenblatt had championed upbeat dance-club acts such as the B-52s and the English duo Wham!

Kamins took Madonna to Rosenblatt's office at Warner headquarters in Rockefeller Center several days later. He placed a Sony tape recorder on the desk and switched it on. The first song was "Everybody." As they sat there, waiting for his verdict, Rosenblatt listened to the four songs on the demo, then rewound it and listened again, "The tape was good," he recalled, "but not outstanding. But here was this girl sitting in my office, radiating that certain something. Whatever it is, she had more of it than I'd ever seen."

Now all Madonna needed was the support of Sire president Seymour Stein. Less than an hour after Madonna and Kamins left, Rosenblatt took the tape to the mercurial Stein, who was in Lenox Hill Hospital recuperating from heart surgery. Stein was so excited by the demo tape that he told Rosenblatt to bring Madonna straight to him. The next afternoon, Madonna, Kamins, and Rosenblatt walked into Stein's hospital room to meet Stein, who greeted them, Madonna recalled, "in his Jockey shorts, with a drip-feed in his arm!"

Jean-Michel Basquiat was not yet 23 when he caught Madonna's eye at a party in 1983. The Brooklyn-bred son of a Haitian accountant and his Puerto Rican wife, Basquiat ran away from home when he was fifteen. His father—with whom, like Madonna, he had an intense love-hate relationship—found Jean-Michel four days later sitting on a bench in New York's Washington Square Park. Jean-Michel's head was completely shaved. "Papa," he said, "I will be very, very famous one day."

Leaving home for good at seventeen, he lived on handouts and slept on the floors of friends' apartments as he tried to gain a foothold in the art world. To survive during this period, he worked the streets as a male prostitute. And just as Madonna had forged vital contacts at downtown dance clubs, Basquiat hung out at Club 57, the Mudd Club, Hurrah's, M.K., Danceteria, CBGB, and other nightspots. By establishing the same sort of surrogate-parent relationship with art dealers that Madonna had established with Christopher Flynn, Pearl Lang, Camille Barbone, and others, Basquiat gained visibility. And by early 1983, he was selling his paintings for upwards of $10,000 to the likes of Richard Gere and Paul Simon. (A Basquiat can now fetch upwards of $600,000.)

"She came up to me at a party and asked me to introduce her to 'that beautiful black boy in the corner,'" recalled Ed Steinberg, who produced her first video, "Everybody." At the time, Basquiat, who would later become known for his wild dreadlocks, was sporting a dyed-blond punk hairdo. Their affair would be intense and brief, ending in part over his drug addiction. "Being seduced and abandoned by Madonna," said a friend, "is something I don't think Jean-Michel ever got over." Five years later, Basquiat would be found on the floor of his bedroom, dead from a heroin overdose.

In the early spring of 1983, Madonna added John "Jellybean" Benitez to the list. He was an ambitous young musician from New York's barrio who had already built a reputation as a mix master at the club Fun House. Benitez and Madonna, although from very different backgrounds, shared ambition and a knack for self-promotion. "Jellybean is the type of person," observed Johnny Dynell, a singer and friend of Madonna's during this period, "who walks in, says hi, then scans the room to see if there is anyone more important he should be talking to."

Benitez, like Kamins, wielded enough influence on the club scene to make him a worthwhile person for Madonna to know. "Madonna sought Jellybean out," Johnny Dynell recalled. "She had heard about him: she knew he could help her. So one night she walked right up to the DJ booth, grabbed him, and kissed him. They are so much alike. It was inevitable."

"Madonna always had at least three guys going at a time," Mark Kamins said."Each one of us was there to fulfill a separate need in her life. The cast of characters changed practically every week."

In the spring of 1983, Madonna was juggling at least a half-dozen boyfriends while managing to record her first album.

When Madonna walked into the Los Angeles office of Warner, jaws dropped. "She sounded black," said a former executive who had not seen her early videos, "and in pops this blonde. Everybody was stunned. She charmed the pants off everyone there."

Released in July of 1983, the album was dismissed by most critics as little more than a bland collection of disco tunes. But because it wasn't an instant hit, Madonna launched her own one-woman campaign. Through club exposure and radio airplay, the lead single from the album, "Holiday," crawled up the charts over the next eight months. By early 1984, two more cuts—"Lucky Star" and "Borderline"—had made it into the top ten.

Her agent, Freddy DeMann, quickly learned to defer to his headstrong client in all business matters, and she expected the same arrangement in her personal life. Her affair with Jellybean Benitez was punctuated with knock-down-drag-out plate-smashing rows.

"Jellybean was the only one who could drive Madonna crazy," Erica Bell contended. "The only time I ever saw her cry hysterically over a guy was after they had a fight and Jellybean had stormed out. She was devastated, really pathetic, on the floor on her hands and knees sobbing.

"It was totally unlike Madonna, of course, but he could really get to her."

A lot of people would credit Benitez for Madonna's early musical career, but "Jellybean was no rocket scientist," Bell said. "We had to tell him that osso buco wasn't a Japanese dish. Musically, Madonna knew way more than he did. He owes his career to her."

Johnny Dynell felt that Madonna and Jellybean Benitez were "meant to be together. They are true soul mates." Unfortunately their tempestuous on-again, off-again relationship, which lasted two years and nearly led to marriage, was undermined by one of the traits they shared: an undeniable aversion to fidelity.

Slightly built, standing barely five feet six inches tall, with shoulder-length hair, Benitez fancied himself a lady-killer. He was also hot-tempered, and he frequently flew into fits of jealous rage.

In mid-1983, Madonna was lip-synching onstage at a hip-hop club on New York's Union Square called Fresh 14 when Steve Newman, the editor of a struggling underground monthly called *Island Magazine,* saw her. "I thought, wow, she is great! My staff wasn't that impressed with her, but I wanted to put Madonna on the cover right away. For some reason I knew this girl was going far.

"At the photo shoot," Newman said, "I got really turned on." Several nights later, at a party given by Keith Haring, Madonna and Newman met again. "We danced, and she flirted outrageously," Newman remembered. "Afterward, I sat on one arm of this big chair, and she sat on the other. Then she crooked her finger at me, leaned over, and gave me this deep, deep kiss. Right then I fell head over heels."

Newman knew Madonna was a heartbreaker, and he didn't want a romance that would leave him "wounded. So I took Madonna out for a drink and told her that I wasn't interested unless she wanted something full-tilt, all or nothing—because I felt so strongly about her I knew that's the only way it could be." She said she was just as committed to a "full-tilt" relationship, and they began what Newman described as "the hottest thing you can imagine. She is unbelievably passionate, totally uninhibited. Madonna was wild. She liked to make love with the windows and shades open. I think even then she needed an audience."

Then, one morning, Benitez, to whom Madonna was by now officially engaged, arrived unannounced on Newman's doorstep. "I was sitting in the window with just my jeans on smoking a cigarette, because

Madonna didn't smoke," Newman recalled. "Suddenly Jellybean came bursting in, grabbed Madonna, and dragged her in the back room. I was in a daze, I just went in the kitchen and made toast. There was a lot of screaming. She and Jellybean were still engaged, and she was trying to get out of it. But he wouldn't let her."

Newman and Madonna continued to see each other, but the incident reminded him that he was far from the only man in her life. At one point, Newman said, he told her point-blank, "'I know your game, bitch, I know what you're doing. You're going to torture me.' Madonna indulges everybody's fantasies; then she moves on to the next man, or woman! She plays everybody every which way."

Around this time, Madonna met with with producer Jon Peters to discuss a possible role for her in his upcoming movie *Ruthless People.* Peters wound up hiring Bette Midler instead, but in September 1983, he was again looking for someone, this time to perform a small role as a club singer in *Vision Quest,* a romantic comedy about a teenage wrestler's affair with an older woman. "They didn't want to get someone they had to direct," Madonna said. "They didn't want to get an actress to pretend she's a singer. They wanted someone with a lot of style already."

Even Peters's former girlfriend Barbra Streisand was impressed by just how much style she had. Madonna arrived for dinner at a Chinese restaurant wearing a rag in her hair, a midriff-baring blouse, and her grandmother's lucky turquoise crucifix. Streisand pumped her for more than two hours: "She wanted to know everything about the way I dressed, the jewelry I wore, the way I sang, and how I grew up in Detroit."

Madonna walked away feeling they had had a genuine exchange—"as one singer to another." Streisand, however, was less than charitable in her assessment of her dinner guest. According to a friend who spoke with her shortly after the dinner date, "Barbra looked at Madonna as a curiosity. She admired the girl's chutzpa, but I got the impression she thought Madonna's singing was a joke."

That November, Madonna went on location to Spokane, Washington, with the cast and crew of *Vision Quest.* Bored, cold, and lonely, she called her agent's office and begged to have Benitez flown out first class to join her. When the shooting was finished, she phoned her father and announced that she would be paying the Ciccone clan a surprise visit. "Jellybean's with me, and we're coming to Detroit," she told him, "so be ready!"

As last-minute as it may have seemed. Madonna's decision to take Benitez home to meet her family was no chance occurrence. Rather than being put off by his flashes of jealousy, Madonna found them exciting. She was, by all accounts, in love with Benitez. More than once, according to Erica Bell, she said, "I'm going to marry Jellybean. And I'm going to have his baby."

She would ultimately do neither—although more than once she had the opportunity to have Benitez's child. "Madonna had several abortions when she was with Jellybean—at least three that I know of," Bell said. "She didn't make any secret about it. It wasn't something she tried to hide. She told all her friends."

Madonna was already proving herself to be a shrewd manipulator of the press. "She could lie very easily to reporters," recalled Bell. "It was fun for her—a game." On one typical occasion, Bell and Madonna drove to the Hamptons for the weekend with James Truman of Britain's *The Face* magazine (now the editor of *Details* magazine).

"He was going to do the first major piece about Madonna for a British publication," Bell said. "She called me up beforehand and said, 'Whatever you do, don't say a thing, just play along.' Then, on the ride out, she made up stuff, all these outrageous stories—how she grew up next to the slums, how her best friend was black, about these fights she got into and how she was arrested during a race riot and spent a week in jail. All untrue. We laughed our heads off when the piece came out. Madonna used to do that sort of thing *all* the time."

*Desperately Seeking Susan* had been floating around Hollywood for four years before it was optioned by Orion Pictures. Originally, the part of Susan had been conceived as sort of an aging hippie, to be played by Diane Keaton. Then the producers decided to go for a more modest movie, allowing the producers to trim the budget down to a bargain-basement $5 million. The project really gained momentum in June of 1984, when Rosanna Arquette signed up for the starring role of Roberta, the bored New Jersey housewife.

"Madonna was someone I knew about from the local club scene," director Susan Seidelman recalled. "I'd go to Danceteria and Paradise Garage occasionally, and I'd see her there—I knew who she was, what she looked like."

The trouble was that some 200 actresses had already read or been videotaped for the part of Susan, opposite Arquette. The list was impressive, including such women as Rebecca De Mornay, Melanie Griffith, Jennifer Jason Leigh, Ellen Barkin, and Kelly McGillis. "The executives at Orion had never heard of Madonna," Seidelman said. "Fortunately, one of the executives' sons had. So they said, 'If you're interested in this girl, why don't you give her a screen test?'"

When Madonna arrived for the audition, Seidelman recalled, "she got out of the cab, but she didn't have enough money to pay. So here she is meeting with a bunch of movie people for a job, and the first thing she does is hit us up for cab fare. It was exactly what Susan would have done!"

Even as early as their very first meeting, Madonna came across to Seidelman as "vulnerable, sweet, even a little bit nervous. There was none of the arrogance for which she was already becoming famous. And she had a sense of humor. Given what I'd been told about her, I wasn't at all sure she'd have one."

Seidelman was also surprised to discover that Madonna was "incredibly disciplined. When there was a 6 A.M. call, the rest of us would have to be rousted out of bed. The driver assigned to Madonna would pick her up at a health club every morning where she'd already done 50 laps by 6 A.M."

Nonetheless, Madonna was the indirect cause for the mounting turmoil on the set. No one, least of all Rosanna Arquette, could have anticipated Madonna's meteoric rise to superstardom that fall. "Rosanna was very upset," said Seidelman. "Imagine how awful it is to be hired as the star and then to be eclipsed by a novice. It made Rosanna crazy."

Madonna's own pressures during filming were more personal. Benitez's infrequent visits to her trailer invariably ended with his storming out. Benitez's anger was understandable: Between scenes, another boyfriend from the barrio, teenager Bobby Martinez, was also paying visits to her trailer. A worker on the set claimed Madonna's dalliances were no secret: "Her trailer would be rocking back and forth like there was an earthquake or something. *Like a Virgin* had just come out, so we all had a good laugh. But when it came to work," he added, "she was a total professional."

While Seidelman was editing *Susan,* Warren Beatty called up the director and asked to look at the dailies, film from each day's shooting. "He came to the editing room and watched some scenes," she recalled. "He was obviously intrigued by Madonna. Watching his face watching hers, I knew he wanted her. From that point on, I had a premonition that someday they would be together."

JOHN SKOW

# MADONNA ROCKS THE LAND

1985

*Madonna first attracted attention thanks to her legions of "Madonna-wannabes," girls who aped her thrift-shop chic look. The next two articles discuss the allure of Madonnaness, circa 1985.*—Eds.

Sassy, brassy and beguiling, she laughs her way to fame.

Now then, parents, the important thing is to stay calm. You've seen Madonna wiggling on MTV—right, she's the pop-tart singer with the trashy outfits and the hi-there belly button. What is worse, your children have seen her. You tell your daughters to put on jeans and sweatshirts, like decent girls, and they look at you as if you've just blown in from the

Broadway show debut in David Mamet's *Speed-the-Plow. Courtesy of Vinnie Zuffante, Star File.*

Planet of the Creeps. Twelve-year-old girls, headphones blocking out the voices of reason, are running around wearing T-shirts labeled VIRGIN, which would not have been necessary 30 years ago. The shirts offer no guarantees, moreover; they merely advertise Madonna's first, or virgin, rock tour, now thundering across the continent, and her bouncy, love-it-when-you-do-it song "Like a Virgin."

The bright side of this phenomenon is that these Wannabes (as in "We wanna be like Madonna!") could be out somewhere stealing hubcaps. Instead, all of them, hundreds of thousands of young blossoms whose actual ages run from a low of about eight to a high of perhaps 25, are saving up their baby-sitting money to buy cross-shaped earrings and fluorescent rubber bracelets like Madonna's, white lace tights that they will cut off at the ankles and black tube skirts that, out of view of their parents, they will roll down several turns at the waist to expose their middles and the waistbands of the pantyhose.

Does anyone remember underwear? The boldest of the Wannabes prowl thrift shops looking for ancient, bulletproof black lace bras and corsets,which they wear slapdash under any sort of gauzy shirt or found-in-the-attic jacket. They tie great floppy rags in their frazzled hair, which when really authentic is blond with dark roots.

To Madonna Louise Ciccone, who is 26, and her Wannabes, such getups somehow suggest the '50s, now conceived on the evidence of old Marilyn Monroe movies to have been a quaint and fascinating though slightly tacky time, rich in flirtatious, prefeminist sexuality. Although to her it's a joke, Madonna's "Boy Toy" belt buckle offends almost everyone except the Wannabes. Those who snoozed through the '50s the first time around are mystified. Some feminists clearly feel that Madonna's self-parody as an eye-batting gold digger, notably in her song "Material Girl," is a joke too damaging to laugh at. Somebody has said that her high, thin voice, which is merely adequate for her energetic but not very demanding dance-pop songs, sounds like "Minnie Mouse on helium." Other detractors suggest that she is almost entirely helium, a gas-filled, lighter-than-air creation of MTV and other sinister media packagers (these doubters have not felt the power of Madonna's personality, which is as forceful and well organized as D-Day). That mossy old (41) Rolling Stone Mick Jagger says that her records are characterized by "a central dumbness."

Kids born since the breakup of the Beatles, however, don't want to hear any of this. Can't hear anything else, at this tick of the clock except brassy, trashy, junk-jingling, state-stomping Madonna, who has been world famous for almost two months. Just now she is the hottest draw in show biz. Michael Jackson? History. Prince? The Peloponnesian Wars. Cyndi Lauper? Last week's flash, and besides, if you wanna be like Cyndi, you have to dye your hair orange and fuchsia, and your parents freak. No, Madonna is the full moon you see at this bend in the river, and never mind what is around the corner.

Her numbers, as they say, are spectacular. Her first album, a batch of dance tunes called simply *Madonna,* started slowly nearly two years ago, but now, at 2.8 million copies sold in the U.S., is closing in on triple platinum (in record-business jargon, 500,000 albums sold is gold, and 1 million is platinum). Her second, *Like a Virgin,* which includes five of her own songs, has gone quadruple platinum at 4.5 million copies in domestic sales, with 2.5 million more worldwide. Her singles have found 6.3 million buyers in the U.S. (or the same buyer 6.3 million times, exasperated parents may feel). "Like a Virgin" has sold 1.9 million copies as a single in the U.S., and the ballad "Crazy for You" recently dislodged USA (United Support of Artists) for Africa's "We Are the World" single from the top of the charts, though it has now slipped to sixth.

Audiences have been building, meanwhile, for *Desperately Seeking Susan,* a funny, likable film comedy in which Madonna costars (with Rosanna Arquette) as a rambunctious East Village vagabond whose free life becomes the obsession of a repressed New Jersey housewife. Madonna's current 28-city, 38-date concert tour, of which she is not only the lead singer and dancer but the director and driving force, has sold out almost instantly just about everywhere tickets have gone on sale. Sheer velocity of box office is watched very closely by concert promoters. Big stars are supposed to sell out, but stars whose shows sell out slowly may have peaked. When Madonna tickets went on sale for three June dates at Radio City Music Hall in Manhattan, fans who had huddled all night in the rain managed to slap their wadded-up, wet money on the counter fast enough to buy the 17,622 seats available in, yes folks, a new record of 34 minutes. (The old record was 55 minutes, jointly held by Elvis Costello and Phil Collins, who presumably are lolling by the pool somewhere, plenty worried.)

What is more, Madonna paraphernalia—posters, at least ten different kinds of shirts, bracelets and cross-shaped earrings like the ones Madonna wears in salute to herself for having survived a strict Catholic upbringing—are selling at concerts at a rate not seen even in the mega-meltdown tours of Michael Jackson and Prince. This is very important, and not just because it brings in money by the front-end-loader-ful. Fathers new to the bubblegum rock ramble (though they may have hung out at the Stones' concerts only a few years ago) may think that all they have to spring for is a pair of $15 tickets, a couple of $1.50 hot dogs and the parking fee. Not so. The young fans are telling their dads that they have to have some jewelry costing between $5 and $30, which is on display so that the dads can say no, feeling wise and fatherly lawgivers. Then the dads compromise on the shirts, which turn out to cost $13 to $22, and Jennifer has something to wear in school the next day to prove that she's seen Madonna.

Why the hard little hearts of all of the Jennifers, and quite a few of the Kevins, ache for Madonna is another question. Big-time show biz is three-fourths mass hysteria, especially when teenagers and rock music are involved, and anyone who thinks he can explain it fully is dreaming. But incredibly lucky timing is clearly part of the Madonna craze. As it happens, few other big rock stars are diluting media attention. Also the neo-conservative mood of the kid culture seems to be just right for an entertainer whose personality is an outrageous blend of Little Orphan Annie, Margaret Thatcher, and Mae West.

Madonna's best bit of luck may be her uproariously appropriate part in *Desperately Seeking Susan.* Here too, the timing was superb. As Director Susan Seidelman points out, when the movie was cast in the summer of 1984, Madonna was not quite a star. She was just another pretty pop singer, just beginning to be widely known. Madonna's style and attitude got her the part, though not without a lot of hesitation among male executives of Orion Pictures who had never heard of her. A year later she would have been too famous and too expensive for a nonsinging role in a low-budget comedy. Any film cast then would have been the usual rock-star exploitation flick, with songs, writhing dancers, guitarists with their shirts off and too much tricky camera work.

As things are, *Susan* gives Madonna an audience she can't reach with MTV or disco. When she sings she lacks the all-there quality of a great pop singer like Linda Ronstadt or Tina Turner. She disguises this with vocal intensity and good dance moves. The kids are so caught up in their own emotional storms that they don't notice it, but in the love songs Madonna is not in love, and in the heat songs, like "Burning Up," she is not in heat. But in the funny songs, like the pop-reggae "Material Girl," she is very funny. All-there people are not funny, most of the time, but detached, cool people like Madonna often are. And if you watch Madonna's video routines more than once, you begin to realize that almost all of her songs, as she belly-rolls her way through them, are sharply comic send-ups, mostly of rock 'n' roll sexual gyrations as delivered by male rockers from Mick Jagger to Prince.

In fact, Madonna is a talented, practiced comedian, who has been wising off constantly since grade school. And in the title role of *Susan* she proves it, playing a calamitous neohippy who clunks in and out of people's lives, and whose total self-absorption amounts to innocence. She dresses weirdly too; in one scene she parades through the streets wearing what appears to be men's boxer shorts, over which she has rigged a white garter belt, which holds up white lace stockings, which disappear into rhinestone boots. Madonna admits that Susan, except for her four-second attention span, is to some extent a self-caricature, and it remains to be seen what she could do with a role that required her to wear grown-ups' clothes. The guess here is that she would be very good. It does not take much imagination to see her in the Judy Holliday role in *Born Yesterday,* beating Broderick Crawford at gin rummy.

Hollywood thinks so too. Director Herbert Ross, who did *Funny Girl* and *Footloose,* is considering her, he says, for the lead in a movie about stripper Blaze Starr. Producer Ray Stark has talked with her about starring in a film about Libby Holman, the '20s and '30s torch singer. "Considering" and "talking with" do not cost much, of course, but Madonna's considering is moving in the same direction. "I don't think of myself as a rock star," she tells an interviewer as she cools out in her hotel room after her concert two weeks ago in New Orleans. The comment is not a gesture at modesty; Madonna is not modest. Nor, for that matter, is she puffed up with self-importance. She has a very clear, cold view of her strengths and weaknesses, and those of the wide world too. She got her first training as a dancer (she won a scholarship in dance at the University of Michigan, but she stayed only 1½ years). She became a fairly good rock drummer and guitarist during her knockabout years as a musician in New York City, then turned to rock singing because she realized she wasn't going anywhere in the dance world. She says that she might do another rock tour if her manager Freddy DeMann "puts a gun to my head," but clearly it is almost time for another career change.

She travels, just now, with a light load of baggage. Her physical possessions, she says, amount to not much more than the ragbag of goofy clothes that serve as her professional and private wardrobe, a ten-speed bicycle stored in New York and a Chinese rug in Los Angeles. No house, no apartment, no car, no rich-at-last jewels or stereo system. She seems to have passed through the lives of a lot of people and to have remained in not many. She sees her father and stepmother only rarely.

It can be hard, now, to get her to talk about her scroungy years in New York. She recalls being fired from a long succession of ratty jobs. She resents suggestions that she slept her way to the top. That is not because she didn't learn her trade from a succession of musicians and deejays, some of whom she slept with, but because the idea that she couldn't make it to the top on drive and talent alone is insulting. In fact the men in her life talk about her now without rancor; it seems to have been obvious even then that Madonna was just passing through. Mark Kamins, deejay at the Danceteria, a funky, four-floor Chelsea disco that caters to purple-haired punks in leather and other exotics, is credited with "discovering" Madonna in 1982, although like America before Columbus, she was there all along.

"She had this incredible sense of style," says Kamins. "She had an aura." She also had a four-track demo tape she had made with another boyfriend, a musician named Steve Bray. Kamins played it and got great response from the disco crowd for a song called "Everybody." Madonna's career began to gather momentum, and Kamins at one point thought she had agreed to let him produce her first album. Madonna instead chose a professional producer, Reggie Lucas. "At the time, I felt stepped on," says Kamins. "But I don't think there's a mean bone in her body. Maybe a mean knuckle but not a mean bone."

Madonna's current boyfriend is actor Sean Penn (*The Falcon and the Snowman*), whose name she shouts out with joyful exuberance when an interviewer asks her a plonking question about favorite actors. But Penn, 24, is about to start shooting a new movie in Tennessee, and she is grinding through her tour, and they do not see each other much, though Madonna calls for half an hour every night after her show. The dreary fact is that stars sometimes lead lives of chaste exasperation.

For Madonna on a show night, work begins at about 5, with a sound check at the arena to make sure the roadies have the equipment adjusted correctly. At about 7:20 the Wannabes start to file in. All of them head directly for the ladies' rooms, for a last mirror check on their getups. They are delighted with the two brand-new ancient games, dressing up and sexual teasing, that Madonna has taught them. Their dates look confused. Nobody under 40 has teased anyone sexually in the U.S. for something like 20 years. New Yorker Robert Shalom, owner of the video club Private Eyes, says, "The guys are scared of these girls. 'What do I do?' they ask. The girls come on so strong, dressed in their mothers' best fake jewelry, saying 'Don't touch me, I'm the material girl, spend money on me.' Waiting for a concert to begin, some of the boys who have tagged along will say that Madonna is, um, yeah, real sexy, but the cleverest, even as they scrape the ground nervously with one hoof, suspect that they are being kidded."

They could be right. When the Madonna show detonates at about 9 P.M., after a forgettable 30 minutes by a raunchy rap band called the Beastie Boys, the strongest impression is of being back in the '60s, listening to the Shirelles. This is no girl group; Madonna's two backup dancers are male and masculine. But they are small and unmenacing, dressed cheerfully in handpainted jeans and jackets, and when they frisk about the stage with Madonna the mood is light and childish. She wears spiked boots, black fishnet tights and a hip-slung miniskirt below her winking belly button. A loose-fitting hand-painted jacket swings free now and then to show a lacy purple shirt and the trademark black bra. She has a floppy purple rag tied in her hair. The costume is sexy, and light as she is, at 5 ft. 4½ in. and 118 lbs., her body is lush. But her movements to "Holiday" are skipping and prancing steps, mischievous kid stuff.

The show turns darker and funkier, with a lot of smoke bombs and jungle queen strutting in silhouette, toward something like a 14-year-old's florid conception of adult sexuality. Madonna comes onstage with a big portable stereo boom box and goes into a routine that sounds like the dirty jokes that eighth-graders giggle over. "Every lady has a box," she says. "My box is special. Because it makes music. But it has to be turned on." Adults wince, but the youngsters love it. "I like the way she handles herself, sort of take it or leave it," says Kim Thomson, 17, a Wannabe in Houston. "She's sexy but she doesn't need men, really. She's kind of there by herself." Says Teresa Hajdik, also 17: "She gives us ideas. It's really women's lib, not being afraid of what guys think."

What the guys think is sometimes seriously scrambled. Madonna comes onstage dressed in an elaborate bare-midriff wedding gown to do "Like a Virgin," the first of two high-spirited production numbers that close the show. "Will you marry me?" she asks the audience. "Yes Yes!" everyone screams. And in Dallas, one lovesick adolescent male stands up and yells, "I wanna have your babies!" Madonna sings, as she sashays about the stage, "You make me feel"—hip thrust—"like a virgin"—belly roll—"touched for the very first time." Mocking virginity, mocking sex, mocking, some might say, the solemn temple of rock 'n' roll itself.

Then she is back for her best number, carried onstage in a reclining posture by her backup dancers, looking like Madam Recamier in her salon, twirling a long rope of pearls and camping a mile a minute. "This is," she sings to a pop reggae beat, "a material world. And I am"—pause—"a material girl." Luxuriating in materialism, poking fun at greediness—she is performing for adolescents who feel deprived if their cars don't have quadraphonic cassette players—Madonna is singing that she is available to the highest bidder, then denying that. And at the end, she pulls wads of fake banknotes out of the top of her dress and tosses them all to the audience. Do the Wannabes see materialism glorified here, or mocked? Of course, they see both, and see no contradiction.

One last funny, sad, self-parodying joke as the lights go up: a loud, disapproving, male voice is heard over the loudspeaker, saying "Madonna, get down off that stage this instant!" And Madonna's recorded voice, whining, "Daddy, do I hafta?" Then the Wannabes, to whom the war between men and women is still far less real than the eternal skirmishing between parents and children, file out of the hall, dreaming of the time when they will be able to do anything in the world they want. Like Madonna.

MARY ROURKE

# A MAD, MAD WORLD OF "MADONNAS"

1985

It's getting so you can't wear your rhinestones anymore without someone screeching "Madonna Wannabe" from the window of a passing car.

That's Madonna talk for anyone who looks like a clone of the pop singer herself, whose junk jewels and boxer shorts, curvy skirts and corsets, lace leggings and lame blazers are causing something of a fashion sensation.

Until now her admirers have scavenged their Wannabe wardrobe from lingerie drawers, gym bags and thrift shops. But this spring they can purchase Madonna's flamboyantly feminine style prepackaged. Entertainers Merchandise Management Corp. is introducing the Boy Toy collection, named after the belt buckle Madonna wears on her "Like a Virgin " album cover. The line features a dress, a skirt, a crop top and cropped pants and an oversize sweat shirt in black or white, available at specialty stores such as Bullock's and Judy's. (Prices range from $18 to $30.)

But Madonna's tasty-trashy wardrobe was making waves well before it went mass market. By now, it is so often imitated that you can itemize it.

"The most important ingredients are the crop top, the bare midriff, a hip-hugger skirt or pants and lingerie straps showing under your top," Marlene Stewart says. She is the Los Angeles–based designer who styled Madonna's stage clothes for her U.S. tour this spring.

"Like a Virgin" live. *Courtesy of Danny Chin, Star File.*

Adriana Caras, a Madonnaesque sophomore at the University of Southern California, describes the look as "carefree, cute and young." But she tones down her idol's overtly outrageous stage style to fit student life. "Wearing lingerie in public like Madonna does can be obnoxious, but you can wear a tank top instead of a corset," she says.

Caras says she isn't about to accessorize her outfits the way Madonna does, with rosary-bead necklaces and Christian cross earrings. But junior-high student Tyla Ball says she wears them just because "the look is pretty rad."

No less rad than naming a child Madonna, as did the Italian-American Catholic parents of Madonna Louise Veronica Ciccone of Pontiac, Mich. "I couldn't believe it when I found out that Madonna is her real name," says Stewart, who got to know the "Material Girl" personally when she started designing her clothes. "The crosses and rosary beads she wears are a play on her cultural background."

There's a Wannabe beauty side to Madonna's look as well. The hair should be a shoulder-length mass of loose curls, with dark roots and blond tips. And true Madonna mavens draw a dark mole above their lips. "She's like Tina Turner, a female sex symbol," says Mimi Vodnoy, who wears a corset along with a Madonna 'do to work as a hair stylist at the Allen Edwards salon.

Vodnoy says she spends hours a day cutting the hair of girls who come into the salon carrying Madonna's picture on record albums and asking for the same look.

"Even women 35 years old want modified Madonna hairstyles," she says. They want a Madonna body too.

"Madonna isn't skinny, she's big. But she's voluptuous," says Vodnoy, who got a close look at those curves when she paid $100 to sit near the stage for Madonna's Los Angeles concert.

Tired of the leaner look, Vodnoy says: "Keeping up a body like Madonna's would make life a lot easier on a lot of girls." Caras already sees a trend toward more voluptuous figures on her college campus.

"A lot of girls now want muscle tone but not an anorexic body," she says. (Madonna maintains hers by lifting weights.)

For both fashion and beauty watching in the Wannabe way, Vodnoy says, the Glendale Galleria is a prime place to go.

She adds: "Beverly Hills girls dress like Madonna too, but they don't want to admit it."

Junior high school students Camille Weintraub and her friends Alice Bubman and Allison Silberkleit are three Beverly Hills girls who beg to differ. They used to dress like Madonna. But now, they say, the look is getting old.

"I've worn the rhinestones, the 10 or 15 bracelets on one arm, the scarf in my hair," Weintraub says.

"I like Madonna's look. But I like to dress more like fashion models." She now wears tight jeans, oversize sweaters and long, straight skirts.

Silberkleit says she may add a touch of Madonna to her dress style, but she'd wear a lace tank top like Madonna's with another tank top underneath it.

"If I wore a tight skirt like hers, I'd wear a big shirt over it. And I wouldn't think of wearing a lace bra that shows through a top for school. Nobody at my school would."

Bubman concludes: "It's her music we like. We don't try to dress like Madonna."

Diehards don't need to worry that Madonna has run out of outrageous fashion ideas for them to imitate. Stewart, who is still designing for Madonna, says there are layers of see-through pants and see-through tops to come.

And the look is going more commercial for fall. In New York, young designers are showing Madonna-like clothes that cross sweats with sweetie-pie style.

And then there is Betsey Johnson, the mother of it all, who's been designing what she calls "sexy-funky-curvy-body" clothes since 26-year-old Madonna was a baby.

JOEL D. SCHWARTZ

# VIRGIN TERRITORY: HOW MADONNA STRADDLES INNOCENCE AND DECADENCE

1985

*Here is a conservative reaction to the mid-'80s Madonna hysteria, along with some thoughts about how Madonna manipulates the media and her fans.*—Eds.

The predominantly female 13- and 14-year-olds who flocked to Madonna's Virgin Tour rock concerts went home loaded down with overpriced T-shirts, posters, and promo-magazines, all, of course, featuring their enigmatic, punked-out heroine. The most striking photograph in the 18-page, seven-dollar magazine shows the star lying on her stomach and looking back over her shoulder at the camera with a mysterious, sultry sneer. Her bleached hair is moussed to the max, and her red lips are painted to match the skimpy lace dress that might have been purchased at a remainder sale in the underwear department at K Mart. A rosary bearing an enormous, gaudy crucifix is draped conspicuously over her shoulder. And she is lying in the dirt. In fact, her face and back are covered with dirt. All in all, a fetching pose—a kind of cross between a tacky pinup for a fertilizer company calendar and a photo for a *True Detective* magazine article about a nun who was mugged by a motorcycle gang while gardening one morning in her Frederick's of Hollywood nightgown.

Madonna, as everyone who hasn't spent the last year in a coma knows, is the latest rock phenomenon. Her first album, *Madonna,* achieved double-platinum status, and her second album, *Like a Virgin,* whose title cut remained stationed on top of the *Billboard* charts for seven weeks, will certainly far exceed that accomplishment. At present she is selling discs at the nearly unbelievable rate of 75,000 per day. In addition to records and videos, she has made a successful full-length movie, *Desperately Seeking Susan,* and recently she's been on display, nude, in *Penthouse* and *Playboy.* Her popularity transcends the labels and factions that currently partition the adolescent rock scene, and it is just conceivable that she is on her way to becoming a latter-day Elvis—the central icon of mid-1980s teen popular culture.

It's often a mistake to overintellecturalize the psychological or cultural significance of popular rock entertainters. Madonna is a talented, sexy performer. Her concert is at once a scrupulously professional, Vegas-style show complete with well-timed entrances, choreography, costume changes, and special effects, and a spontaneous explosion of high-energy abandon. To say much more than this risks translating her appeal from the vernacular to the arcane, from the level of her fans' felt experience to the sterile platitudes of the tweedy, academic social critic. It is tempting for bewildered adults to want to "explain" the latest teen fad and thereby to impose a veneer of reassuring adult order onto the dark poetry of adolescence.

Still, a considerable amount of Madonna's appeal, captured beautifully in the ironic "dirty Madonna" photo, is that she (or her managers) has carefully constructed an intriguingly enigmatic image. With studied care, her blond hair and porcelain-white skin is contrasted with black dirt, her rosary juxtaposed to her red lips and matching cathouse dress. In fact, one of her accomplishments is that, at least until recently, she has nearly reversed the typical pattern of rock idolanalysis. The *Rolling Stone*–style critics have summarily dismissed her as top-40 schlock. This time it is the kids, whether in record stores or waiting in line to get into her concerts, who are engaged in a running debate over what she and her music stand for—what they mean. A fair measure of the seriousness of this debate is that it goes well beyond mere words to the very appearance and demeanor of her fans. For instance, the girls who have turned Madonna's concerts into Madonna look-alike costume parties wear their theories, as it were, on their backs. Some of them look like innocent bobby-soxers, some look like underage streetwalkers, but most look like an uneasy combination of the two.

Most of the rock stars who have captured the public's imagination since the 1950s have been social critics. While the most conspicuous of this criticism came in the political protest songs of the 1960s and early 1970s, by far the bulk of it, following established American patterns, has been much more personal in character. This personal or spiritual critique, in turn, has taken at least two forms. To one camp, a competitive, impersonal America is contrasted to a utopia of pastoral innocence characterized by puppy love and a triumph of virtue over crass materialism, of simple honesty and fidelity over hypocrisy and deception. This theme was introduced, often with substantial authenticity, by countless male and female balladeers in the 1950s, and it was continued, and often driven into the saccharine ground, by many folk groups in the 1960s and 1970s.

To the other camp, the same America—the same enemy—is contrasted to what only can be called a utopia of the libido, where boys can be boys, girls can be girls, and hormones can be hormones. From Little Richard (who had to censor his lyrics for popular consumption) to the Beastie Boys (Madonna's warm-up band), the theme has been not lost innocence, but sex, drugs, and rock 'n' roll. The choice many felt compelled to make a generation ago between the Beatles ("I wanna hold your hand") or the Rolling Stones ("I can't get no satisfaction") was drawn largely along these lines. What is the "real" human being buried beneath the artificial concrete of modern society? Is it a prelapsarian Adam in the Garden or a jungle animal grunting after its mate?

Madonna's talent is to join this debate without tipping her hand. Some of her songs sound like remakes of sweet-sixteen Connie Francis tunes dripping with old-fashioned, hand-holding romance. "It's so brand new; I'm crazy for you." This is the "Madonna" side of Madonna. The name fits the image so well that if she hadn't actually been christened with it (Madonna Louise Veronica Ciccone) she'd have had to adopt it as her stage name anyway. But she is also well known for hard-driving dance music, the kind with the senseless, non-sequitur lyrics and stirring rhythms that has proved to be so popular with the disco audience. It is this music that fits well with the image of almost vulgar sexuality that she often cultivates, and with her penchant for blurring the distinction between clothes and underwear.

The irony is perhaps most perfected in "Like a Virgin" and "Material Girl," her two best-known songs. On the one hand, "Virgin" is about a girl who has evidently been around the block a few times and is about to make yet another circuit. On the other hand, the song's theme is that now with "true" love, she feels pure again, "like a virgin, touched for the very first time." On the concert stage the tension is unmistakable. Is the message of recovered purity and chastity just a kinky put-on, as her lurid squeals and raunchy dances would imply? Or is it genuine? To finish the picture, she wears a white wedding gown for the number; but never before has a wedding dress looked more like a sleazy go-go outfit. Neither Debbie Boone nor Tina Turner could perform this song, because it works only for a performer who is an amalgam of the two.

Madonna's fans debate the meaning of "Material Girl" along similar lines. In this song, her straightforward message is that "we are living in a material world, and I am a material girl." Some boys offer their love and devotion, but she's only interested in the boys with the "cold hard cash." The fascinating point is that to about half of her devotees the surface reading of these lyrics is the accurate one. After all, Madonna can project the image of a no-nonsense, self-confident realist who knows what she wants and gets what she's after. But the other half sees the song as a satire, ridiculing materialism and exposing its shallowness.

So what will it be: cash and a good time at the disco, or romance and slow-dancing by the fireplace? Once again, it is in performance that the problem truly hits home. She prances around collecting cash, necklaces, and furs from various male suitors, and in the end she breaks from the recorded lyrics and proclaims, "No, it's only love that matters to me," and proceeds to strip off the jewelry and furs and to throw the money into the audience. With this new conclusion to the song, it appears the finally we know where she stands. She is playfully denouncing materialism—literally throwing it into the audience's face. Right? Well, not so fast. This, it develops, is only a false climax; she quickly returns to the stage to reclaim her cast-off furs. The enigma is restored.

The contradictions in the "dirty Madonna" photo exist, then, between her songs and within her songs, between the lyrics and the costumes, between the lyrics and the choreography. Inevitably, her concert becomes something of a game in which the audience is challenged to spot the double meaning in virtually every sentence and gesture. The phrase "I'll get down on my knees for you" has done long service in the pastoral-innocence genre as a statement of pure love and viruous devotion. To a "Madonna" raised in a devoutly Catholic family in Bay City, Michigan, the words must resonate with images of prayer. But as she vamps the words and slithers to her knees before the gyrating hips of her male dance partners, an altogether different meaning also suggests itself.

Everyone seems to agree that there is something puzzling and inscrutable about Madonna, and it is this quality that goes a long way toward explaining her cult appeal. My suggestion is that much of this is owed to an ironic dialogue that she half-consciously creates between two visions of human potential that are deeply rooted in American popular culture. What is the "real" American self struggling for survival in contemporary society? Is it Pat Boone or Little Richard? Karen Carpenter or Janis Joplin?

One unmistakable message that is transmitted to the audience is that there is an intense and necessary complicity between these two utopian visions. Virtue would soon lose its pristine luster if there were no vice to overcome, and the libido would quickly lose its prurient appeal if there were no rigid moral code to defy. The saint and the sinner nourish one another. Promiscuity may have become a commonplace in the modern world, but sex with a chaste "Madonna," with a "virgin"—that's another matter. Off-color lyrics and choreography hardly raise an eyebrow, but put the performer in a white wedding gown and you've got a superstar. To be sure, the surface reading of the "Material Girl" lyrics is grounded both in Yuppie aspirations and in punk cynicism. But at the same time, it should be interpreted as a Yuppie and punk reaction against the insipid sentimentalism of earlier eras—of the communal world of the 1960s social activist and the earlier familiar world of Robert Young and Jane Wyatt. Similarly, the "no, it's only love that matters to me" counterpoint requires an audience of materialistic Yuppies and cold hard punks to sustain its urgency. Just as the two sides of Madonna's image require each other, just as she uses each to set off the other in her act, we should not expect either vision of the hidden American self to even emerge triumphant in popular culture. Death to one means death to both.

But Madonna goes another step. Social criticism has always insisted on exposing the gap between appearance and reality; to criticize the artificiality and the hypocrisy of the modern world, to make the claim that it stifles our "real" selves, this distinction is crucial. But by internalizing both innocence and license within the same persona and by turning them on and off like faucets, Madonna suggests that they, too, are mere appearance, mere affectations. The appeal of rock 'n' roll at its best, from Buddy Holly to Bob Dylan to Prince, has always been its sincerity. Madona, in contrast, wears commitments like costumes, to be taken off and on at whim. Everything is a pose, everything a carefully scripted and choreographed part of the performance. To this extent, Madonna stands in satirical aloofness from both traditional camps, proclaiming them both naive to the core.

Younger audiences look to rock stars for role models, while older audiences, their personalities more fully formed, buy records and attend concerts more to satisfy their tastes in music. Since it is more Madonna's image than her music that is fascinating, it's not surprising that her audience is disproportionately adolescent and female—young girls who in many cases have spent hours literally doing themselves up like their heroine. There was a time when it was a serious criticism to say of someone that he or she is "just role-playing." But Madonna's fans are learning that maturity is superficiality, that to be grown-up is to have perfected one's repertoire of roles and the ability to manipulate them on call like a virtuoso actress. In this way, the walls of the concert hall are pushed out to include the world—a world, perhaps, soon to be populated with a whole chorus line of Madonnas who see their personalities as scaffoldings of affectations built on paper foundations of semblance—"like a virgin," or "like" anything else they please.

JOSEPH SOBRAN

# SINGLE SEX AND THE GIRL

1991

*Madonna's concert-documentary,* Truth or Dare, *perhaps unintentionally (perhaps intentionally) revealed a more cold side of Madonna as she acted as the Queen Bee to a retinue of dancers, hangers-on, family members, and even her then-beau, Warren Beatty, as this article describes.*—Eds.

In one scene in *Truth or Dare*—a documentary, of sorts, of her Blond Ambition concert tour—Madonna phones her father to ask if he's coming to see her perform. He says he understands her act is pretty "racy" and inquires as to whether she'll "tone it down" for him and the family. No, she answers; she won't "compromise my artistic integrity."

A few minutes later, we see that uncompromised artistic integrity as she lies on a bed onstage. The stage is dark, except for the bed. Standing beside her are two black male dancers wearing weird conical brassieres. As she sings "Like a Virgin," she vigorously massages her crotch, moaning and arching her back spasmodically. There's more, but you get the basic idea. The huge crowd goes wild.

Madonna is a genius at getting attention. Everything she does gets attention—her records, her videos, her movies, her marriage, her divorce, her amours (including a joke that she'd had a lesbian relationship with the comedienne Sandra Bernhard). When she showed up at the Cannes Film Festival with her hair dyed a new color, her face appeared on the front page of the *New York Daily News*. She has been on the cover of every magazine except *National Geographic.*

How does she do it? As she admits, she's not a great singer, a great dancer, or even—at least in repose—a great looker. She can't act. Yet she has the most flamboyantly theatrical personality since . . . well, who was the last one? Bette Davis? Joan Crawford? Tallulah Bankhead? Some people have what I can only call contagious vanity. You may even dislike them, but you can't take your eyes off them. Madonna is like that. In a country where people want to be liked (maybe even more ardently than they want to be loved), she dares you to hate her.

"Madonna is the true feminist," writes Camille Paglia, herself a sort of anti-feminist feminist. "She exposes the puritanism and suffocating ideology of American feminism. . . . Madonna has taught young women to be fully female and sexual while still exercising total control over their lives. She shows girls how to be attractive, sensual, energetic, ambitious, aggressive, and funny—all at the same time."

**Kink and Danger**

She's undeniably magnetic, but it's a calculating magnetism, a carefully constructed aura of kink and danger. If she seems to be shattering conventions, she's also there to pick up the pieces. One of her steamier videos, "Like a Prayer," shows her in a Catholic church adoring a statue of a black saint, who comes to life and kisses her passionately. She receives the stigmata, and there are burning crosses and things, and . . . well, again, you get the idea: a deliberate fusion of such themes as sex, race, and religion. These elements are combined in surreal montage, and the effect is eerie, shocking, Weimar decadent.

An even more explicit video, "Justify My Love," did succeed in outraging people, and even easygoing MTV refused to play it. "The video is pornographic," Miss Paglia writes. "It's decadent. And it's fabulous. MTV was right to ban it." But she chides Madonna for copping out on *Nightline* by pleading "her love of children, her social activism, and her condom endorsements." If you want to shock people, go ahead and shock 'em. But don't blame them for being shocked.

The trouble is that Madonna wants to have it both ways. (One problem in writing about her is that everything tends to sound like a double-entendre.) She clearly knows what she's doing, but wants to pretend she doesn't. Her calculation is shown in one sequence in *Truth or Dare* when her tour arrives in Toronto and she is told that the police are prepared to arrest her if she does the masturbation bit. She asks what the penalty is. She learns she'll probably just be booked, fined, and released. This, to her, is a cheap price to pay for the international front-page publicity she stands to get, so she goes ahead with it. The cops back down and do nothing. Never has the structure of incentives been so favorable to artistic martyrdom.

A similar event occurs in Italy, where she finds on her arrival that the Vatican has denounced her in advance. She holds a press conference, and says that as an Italian-American she resents this prejudicial treatment. Hers is no "conventional" rock act, but "a total theatrical experience." The note of pique sounds sincere enough, but she also knows that in her terms the Vatican has done her a favor. Madonna has a keen sense of whom it's profitable to offend and whom it isn't. She surrounds herself with blacks and homosexuals. She is heavy into AIDS education: "Next to Hitler, AIDS is the worst thing to happen in the twentieth century," she told *Vanity Fair* recently—a good, conventional, and convenient view to hold in her line of work. And when the Simon Wiesenthal Center in Los Angeles attacked her for including the phrase "synagogue of Satan" (from the book of Revelation) in one of her songs, she apologized.

In the film, one of her dancers worries that his scene of simulated sex with her will hurt his career. "In this country it works the other way around," she answers. "The more notorious you are, the more you are going to work! Don't you guys understand that?" Indeed. Nothing is more conventional than the daring. In *Truth or Dare,* she talks nonstop raunch, bares her breasts, gets into bed with a naked dancer and whoops about the size of his organ (it's all right, he's gay), and much, much more.

### The Good Christian

Raised a Catholic by devout parents (her mother died when she was six), Madonna's target of choice is Catholicism. Her concert and video performances abound in crucifixes, dancers dressed as priests fondling her, and so forth. It's exciting. It's outrageous. It sells. Naturally, much of her following consists of lapsed Catholics, typified by the columnist Pete Hamill, who calls her "a good Christian." You can write a Hamill column with your eyes closed: Jesus preferred Mary Magdalene to the Pharisees, drove the money-changers out of the Temple, hated prigs—a lot like Pete Hamill, come to think of it. This sort of approval (terribly smug, in its own way) implies that because Jesus forgave unchastity, he didn't regard it as a sin. Not only is this a non sequitur, it overlooks some very stern words in the Gospels, sterner, in fact, than anything in St. Paul, the favorite scapegoat of lapsed Christians who want to insist that it's only the Church they object to—nothing against Jesus, you understand.

Charity is of course the supreme Christian virtue, and those who fail in chastity often insist that they make up for it in charity. But there is more than one way of being uncharitable, and self-serving solicitude for today's accredited victims—"compassion," for short—doesn't necessarily cover a multitude of sins. In *Truth or Dare* we learn that Madonna leads her troupe in prayer before every performance. But the tone of her prayer is imperious and stagy. The viewer wonders if praying with the boss—or rather standing there submissively while she prays—is part of the job description of dancer. The question acquires a special urgency when the prayer turns into a chewing-out of some of those in the circle. She stops just short of demanding divine retribution against those who have offended her.

Madonna is even less charitable toward the Church itself. "I've always known that Catholicism is a completely sexist, repressed, sin- and punishment-based religion," she told an interviewer for *Us* magazine. She was even blunter to *Vanity Fair:* "I think it's disgusting. I think it's hypocritical. And it's unloving. It's not what God and Christianity are all about." Nearly every interview she gives includes bitter remarks about the Church and its "rules." It's the only subject, apart from herself, she regularly talks about.

But her father is still a faithful Catholic, and in *Truth or Dare* we see her fretting at the idea of his seeing her perform "Like a Virgin." In fact she does "tone it down" when he's in the audience, and she hales him onto the stage to be introduced to the crowd. He seems a mild fellow, confusedly proud of his famous daughter. Her anxiety about being seen by him *in flagrante* is puzzling: she seems bent on offending everyone who believes in the things he believes in, but not him. Why this exemption? If she hates the faith she was raised in, why doesn't she blame the man who raised her?

"She doesn't want to live off-camera," jokes Warren Beatty, her beau at the time of the filming. "Why would you bother to say something if it's off-camera?" Because Madonna finds everything about Madonna absolutely fascinating, that's why. Imagine a film in which it's left to Warren Beatty to sound the note of common sense.

"I find myself drawn to emotional cripples," Madonna says, explaining the odd assortment of characters she surrounds herself with. "I like to play mother." Oh. We see her visiting her own mother's grave (for the first time); naturally, she dresses in black for the occasion, brings a camera crew along, and lies down to kiss the tombstone. We see her backstage, complaining about a mike failure to a hapless technician. We see her dining with friends. We see her shopping in Paris. We see her meeting an old school chum, who she tells us once did something naughty to her at pajama party. (The school chum, now a mother of five, denies it when informed of it; she looks shocked by this ambush, having named a daughter Madonna.) We see her telling someone or other that her mission is to be "provocative" and "political." We see, in fact, two hours of this carefully staged "spontaneity," and two hours trapped in a dark room with that ego feels like a week.

### The Real Madonna

Talking to *Vanity Fair,* Madonna gets defensive: "People will say, 'She knows the camera is on, she's just acting.' But even if I am acting, there's a truth in my acting. . . . You could watch it and say, I still don't know Madonna, and good. Because you will never know the real me. Ever." You mean there's more?

Well, if we never know the real Madonna, we won't have Madonna to blame for it. She talks about herself volubly, incessantly; she poses for photo stills dressed up as Marilyn Monroe and other sexpots. It's as if her privacy might unfairly deprive us of something. Or rather, as if she wanted to become all the fascinating women of the past, and reveal their mysteries to us. Instead she creates the disconcerting impression that all the mystery may have been bogus; maybe those women were like her: self-absorbed little bores who talked in clichés about "art" and "truth," when they weren't talking about themselves. One would rather not know.

As for "truth," Madonna isn't interested in any that may inconvenience her. It never crosses her mind that there may be more to Catholicism than her spiteful parody of it, which is of an order of glibness that would embarrass Phil Donahue. For her there is no fundamental order in life, only arbitrary "rules." Do whatcha want, as long as you practice "safe sex," that mirage of those who think selfishness and sensuality can be calculating and civic-minded even at the peak of ardor. It isn't just that she's hopelessly banal whenever she tries to share an insight. It's that she has reached that pitch of egomania at which celebrity supposes itself oracular. That's when you say things like "Power is a great aphrodisiac," and you think it sounds impressive. (We may note in passing that the Me Decade is now entering its third decade.)

And as for "art," well, philosophers differ. But it's widely believed by wise people that art and ego sit uneasily together. The true artist, even if his ego is as muscular as Beethoven's, creates something outside himself. Art is not "self-expression" in the sense that its focus of interest lies in its

In concert, 1987. *Courtesy of Max Goldstein, Star File.*

creator; rather, it is self-contained. Its value doesn't depend on our knowledge of the artist. *Hamlet* is a great play no matter who wrote it. *Parsifal* is a great opera even if Wagner did compose it.

But for Madonna, art is defined by the censors: it's whatever they don't like. So someone who gets the censors howling must be an artist.

Silly, but a lot of people agree with her, and they buy tickets. Madonna offers something new under the sun: vicarious self-absorption. It takes a special kind of imagination to identify with a solipsist.

Madonna just doesn't glory in herself: she glories in her self. And *Truth or Dare* suggests a novel ambition: to make the self, even in its private moments, an object of universal attention. Who was the love of your life? someone asks her. "Sean," she murmurs, meaning her ex-husband, Sean Penn (of whom it was once said that he had slugged every photographer except Karsh of Ottawa). Sean, she explains, was madly jealous and domineering, but "at least he paid attention." Better hostile attention than none at all.

Like most pop music, Madonna's songs are about love. But love is the subject about which she shows no understanding at all. She is the perfect expression of an age that has reduced the erotic to the sensual: the gratification of the self rather than the yearning for union with another. "Lovers" become interchangeable and succeed each other quickly, each being merely instrumental to the self and its cravings. Real love is like art: it demands the subordination of the ego. Kinky, exciting, shocking: these are the attributes of love as she conceives it. It would make no sense to tell her that sodomy is at best a stunted and misdirected form of eros, since heterosexual love, as she exemplifies it, has the same character. The purpose of this love is neither permanent union nor procreation, but pleasure and ego-enhancement. For her, in fact, the erotic isn't all that different from the autoerotic, except that there happens to be another person present.

But the word "autoerotic" is self-contradictory. Being in love with yourself isn't love. And having sex with yourself hardly qualifies as sex. The Victorians thought masturbation led to blindness. If they'd said moral blindness, they might have had a point. At least Madonna seems to intimate a connection. "Masturbation," Woody Allen has said, "is having sex with someone you love." When we watch Madonna doing "Like a Virgin," clutching her private parts (if they can be called private any more), simulating ecstatic convulsions, we're seeing her having sex, as it were, with someone she loves, all right—maybe the only one she can love.

ED SIEGEL

# MADONNA SELLS HER SOUL FOR A SONG

*Boston Globe,* March 2, 1989

*Now long-forgotten, the "Like a Prayer" controversy began when Madonna made a commercial/video for Pepsi-Cola to launch the song. The original commercial was shown only once, preceded by much hoopla and promotion. It was then pulled when the "real" video for the song premiered, with its many controversial images. This article discusses how Madonna "sold her soul" to Pepsi. Ironically, she kept the huge fee she garnered from the soft-drink company even after it quickly dropped her as a spokesperson.*—Eds.

She appears like a vision to an Australian aborigine in the outback. It's a bird, it's a plane, it's . . . Madonna. Get thee to a television set on March 2, says the voice on the commercial that's been running on television lately, leaving the viewer wondering whether tonight will be (a) a great moment in music history; (b) a great moment in broadcasting history; (c) a great moment in advertising history; or (d) the end of Western civilization as we know it.

What you will see, should you be among the majority of Americans who watch *The Cosby Show* from 8 to 8:30, is a two-minute Pepsi commercial framing the release of Madonna's new single, the title track of her new album, *Like a Prayer,* not yet available in record stores or on radio stations and music-video channels anywhere.

The same two-minute commercial will air in 40 other countries at about the same time. "Showcasing our products alongside world-class celebrities in creative ads has always been a big part of our strategy," says Pepsi adman Alan Pottasch in a press release.

At least we know who or what's being showcased here. Not Madonna, but Pepsi. We know that Madonna hasn't acted like a virgin since arriving on the scene, maybe not even in her childhood memories. But this is the first indication that she's acting like a prostitute. Ironically, the cola company is using the program that showcases the No. 1 celebrity of its rival, Coca-Cola and Bill Cosby. "The global media buy and unprecedented debut of this long-awaited single will put Pepsi first and foremost in consumers' minds," says the Pepsi release.

Portrait, mid-'80s. *Courtesy of Mike Guastella, Star File.*

Here's where history comes in. More from the release: "The groundbreaking deal is expected to change the way popular tunes from major artists are released in the future. Traditionally, new songs have been made public through heavy radio airplay. In an innovative twist, the Pepsi-Madonna deal uses television to provide unparalleled international exposure for her new single . . . where Madonna takes a special trip back in time to revisit her childhood memories." After that, stripped-down 30- and 60-second commercials will air on television, the music video debuts on MTV tomorrow, the single is released March 7 and the album March 21.

Here's where the end of Western civilization comes in.

"There'll be some Pepsi visuals during the song," said a Warner Bros./Sire spokesperson. "It is clearly a Pepsi commercial." Madonna's not the first entertainer/artist to sell her body for her song, or her song for a corporation. Remember those avatars of the '60s, Eric Clapton and Steve Winwood? It's bad enough that the night belongs to Michelob; now all their songs do, too.

Of course, old prudes used to point to rock 'n' roll as symbolic of the end of Western civilization. Now it's commercialism that spells the death of rock music. Another avatar of the '60s, Bob Dylan, talked about the relationship between commercialism and the soullessness of contemporary music in the liner notes to *Biograph,* his five-record retrospective:

> Now it's just rock, no roll . . . it's now a highly visible enterprise, big establishment thing. You know things go better with Coke because Aretha Franklin told you so and Maxwell House Coffee must be OK because Ray Charles is singing about it. Everybody's singing about ketchup or headache medicine or something. In the beginning it wasn't anything like that, had nothing to do with pantyhose and perfume and barbecue sauce. You were eligible to get busted for playing rock 'n' roll. . . . There's an old saying, "If you want to defeat your enemy, sing his song." . . . I think it's happened and nobody knows the difference. . . . I think they killed something very important about it. The corporate world, when they figured out what it was and how to use it they snuffed the breath out of it and killed it. What do they care? Anything that's in the way, they run over like a bulldozer, once they understood it they killed it and made it a thing of the past, put up a monument to it and now that's what you're hearing, the headstone.

Nobody ever compared "Like a Virgin" to "Like a Rolling Stone," although "living in a material world" may define the '80s as well as "The Times They Are A-Changin'" defined the '60s.

There's obviously a place for corporate interest in arts and entertainment. Some classical albums and most public-television programs wouldn't be made without it. But to tie one's art to commercial interests crosses a very visible line. Thus we are treated to the pitiful spectacle of Eric Clapton. As David Bieber at WBCN points out, Clapton is a reformed alcoholic and drug user who now turns his songs into beer commercials and poses for an album cover smoking a cigarette. Camel cigarettes is another sponsor of his. Can we believe anything that Clapton says or sings through the green haze of what Bieber calls the growing trend of subliminal advertising through rock music?

It may be that rock music is now such a beacon of commercial interests that, as Madonna's show tonight suggests, there's no longer any difference between the two.

WILLIAM CROSS

# WHY MADONNA CAN'T KEEP HER CLOTHES ON

*McCall's* magazine, 1993

McCall's *magazine invited William Cross to comment on Madonna's tendency toward exhibitionism. The original article ended with a request to readers to send their comments to the magazine about the subject!*—Eds.

Since a scrappy little dancer (armed with far more ambition than talent) named Madonna Ciccone suddenly appeared in New York City in the late 1970s, she has never stopped surprising, delighting and repulsing her fascinated public. Above all, however, she has never stopped shocking her fans (and nonfans). Her latest and most inflammatory enterprise, published in October, is *Sex,* a Mylar-wrapped, $50 book that shows her eating pizza naked in public and engaging in various sadomasochistic acts. And this month she's slated to star in the thriller *Body of Evidence,* which originally received a rare NC-17 rating for its explicit erotic content.

But as Madonna scales heights of self-promotion that would put P. T. Barnum to shame, audiences are beginning to wonder: What is it with this woman? Is she a liberated crusader or a tortured exhibitionist? A brazen original or a pathetic narcissist? Her increasingly high-pitched attempts to be incendiary and explicit in all she does have begun to wear a little thin. Even before *Sex* appeared, people had started to ask: What makes her do what she does?

There are plenty of theories as to what fuels Madonna's surging exhibitionism. (Madonna herself has said, "All entertainers are exhibitionists, admitted or not.") Explains Peter Mezan, a New York City psychoanalyst, "Many different kinds of people can be exhibitionists, but they all have one thing in common: They have trouble believing in themselves. They require proof that they can thrill. Their actions are almost always based on the fantasy that seeing is believing. [Exhibitionism] arises at a stage in development when you believe that if others see something about you, it must be true.

"For many such people—and Madonna may be one—that means if they can inspire feelings of excitement in others, then they tend to believe they have some ability to thrill. And that is a certain kind of power."

### A Motherless Child

Some see in Madonna's behavior the desperate longing of a woman who lost her mother much too young. Madonna was five years old when her mother died—an event she readily acknowledges has affected her life in every way. Experts say that young girls who lose their mother often become extraordinarily self-sufficient or aggressive. They learn early that they are different from their peers and frequently exaggerate those differences.

"That way motherless children don't seem as much like victims," says Hope Edelman, who is writing a book about women who lost their mother at an early age. "They come off more as people who shape the world in which they live. And Madonna is in many ways the classic motherless child. She has a real need both to act like a caretaker and to seek attention.

"Madonna is constantly manufacturing new identities and tossing out the old ones," Edelman adds. "Many women without a mother do that. They have a question mark about who they are, about what their identity should be. Without a role model, it can be hard to know. So she can be viewed at least in part as constantly searching for something to grab onto. Something that works."

"Her life is like an addiction," says Jane Goldberg, a New York City psychoanalyst and author of *The Dark Side of Love,* which explores narcissistic relationships and romance. "She needs to shock. And each time the dose has to get higher to have the same effect it did before. I think there is some real fear in there: Will she lose her audience if she doesn't keep it coming, if she doesn't push the edge just a little harder next time?"

## Sex, Not Love

If it was ever hard to see inside the shell of bravado in which Madonna has encased herself, that ended with *Truth or Dare,* the stunning psychodocumentary of her 1990 Blond Ambition world tour. Audiences were shocked (by the scene in which Madonna lay down on her mother's grave), amused (by her sudden show of artistic integrity, when she stood up to the Toronto police, who threatened her with arrest if she performed her onstage masturbation routine), but also touched—by the pathos of a woman so obviously imprisoned by her own outrageous myths. As Warren Beatty (Madonna's boyfriend at the time) put it, "She doesn't want to live off-camera."

The Madonna in *Truth or Dare* is a woman with no deep personal relationships; her stage life is her life. "The key to her personality is in her attempt to simulate relationships that clearly don't exist," suggests Phyllis W. Meadow, executive director of the Center for Modern Psychoanalytic Studies in Boston. "She has never made it to the level where you form real relationships—there's all that sex and not much love. Perhaps she has had many lovers, but we do not often see her with a man for very long. In fact, we don't ever see her do any single thing for very long."

Like many psychoanalysts, Meadow thinks there was probably a central period in Madonna's early life—possibly even before her mother died—that damaged her, making intimacy nearly impossible and replacing it with the need to outrage. Meadow warns that the star is vulnerable to a severe depression should she fail to continue drawing the type of attention to which she has now grown accustomed.

According to this assessment, Madonna is an unstable woman heading for a fall. But Madonna's defenders, such as Camille Paglia, author of *Sexual Personae,* insist she is a healthy, fully formed woman who just doesn't give a damn about convention. "Madonna has taught young women to be fully female and sexual while still exercising control over their lives," Paglia has written. "She shows girls how to be attractive, sensual, energetic, ambitious, aggressive and funny—all at the same time."

"Madonna understands the power of sheer provocation," says Susan Rubin Suleiman, author of *Subversive Intent: Gender, Politics and the Avant-Garde.* "That is not a common trait, but it sets her squarely in the tradition of the avant-garde. Whatever else you say about her, Madonna knows how to do the outrageous thing. And just doing the outrageous thing has a tremendous power."

MATTHEW GILBERT

# PLAYING THE SHOCK MARKET

*Boston Globe,* October 11, 1992

The *Sex* scandal.

Where flesh meets flash, that's where you'll find Madonna. At the dawning of her second decade of celebrity, as her lucky 15 minutes stretch into an era of Blond superstardom, she persists in baring more and more of her Nautilized body and her transgressive soul. The presidential election may be heating up, but in coming months we'll see Madonna running hard for an even more incendiary office—that of the Most Sexually Daring Icon of This or Any Century Ever on Earth.

Later this month, the pop legend-in-her-own-time will set off her most brazenly risque multimedia barrage yet. On Oct. 20, *Erotica,* her first all-new CD since 1990's *I'm Breathless,* will slink into the record stores. Judging from the single, also titled "Erotica," the album will be dense with sexually playful, sadomasochistic lyrics. Over an irresistibly sultry dance groove, Madonna sings in a bedroom voice that recalls the

With Sandra Bernhard at the Rainforest Benefit, 1989. *Courtesy of Vinnie Zuffante, Star File.*

cooings of Prince: "I only hurt the ones I love." If you've always wanted to eavesdrop on Madonna's boudoir, this may be your chance.

*Sex,* her already infamous collection of hanky-panky "art" photos, will arrive safely in bookstores on October 21 wearing Mylar wrapping and warning stickers. The 128-page spiral-bound book, with weighty aluminum covers, is a visual essay on Madonna's far-flung sexual fantasies. Nude hitchhiking anyone? Striking poses in various stages of undress with Madonna will be such guests as model Naomi Campbell, actress Isabella Rossellini, and rapper Big Daddy Kane. *Sex,* shot by "cat in the hat" Steven Meisel, will sell for $49.95, with an optimistic first printing of 750,000 copies.

Most important, the Madonna blitz will commandeer screens big and small—her favorite media. MTV, the channel that banned "Justify My Love," is now airing the "Erotica" video, a montage of antiqued images of sexual flagrancy, but the video is restricted to late-night rotation. Along with future videos from the CD, we'll also see Madonna in the January 1993 feature film *Body of Evidence,* rumored to be heading for an NC-17 rating.

Timing an erotic landslide to the peak of an election season is, of course, Madonna-logic at its finest. Her people are staunchly withholding advance copies of *Erotica* and *Sex* from the press, to force a publicity rush two weeks before Election Day. Do they know there are few better distractions from political headlines than the Material Girl on an erogenous tear?

And you can bet that special-interest groups, and parents, will be newly appalled by her promiscuity, calling the teen idol irresponsible. *Entertainment Tonight* will document the tiny tempests, winning Madonna miles of free promotional attention. And once again we'll find ourselves debating her motives—is she a wizard of shock-hype or a First Amendment moralist opening America's mind to sexual variety?

But with this burst of Madonna-in-your-face approaching, we might ask another question. As her reputation as premiere provocateur grows, so does her international fame. But is Madonna really, truly shocking?

That our foremost commotion-meister is now, in effect, making soft-core pornography should surprise no one. Exhibitionism is the logical extension of Madonna's career, from her early slut-styled downtown days, through her ironic *Like a Virgin* romp, past her *Like a Prayer* blasphemies, right up to the more recent *Playboy* spread and the steamy "Justify My Love" video. During the course of her career, which began its ascent in 1983, she's worn underwear as outerwear, simulated masturbation onstage and produced a documentary that revels in revealing her own secrets. Her "Express Yourself" message has always had a far more superficial subtext: Expose Yourself.

As pop-culture critic Greil Marcus pointed out in a *Boston Globe* interview last year, we might even see Madonna having sex at some point: "I think it's in the rhythm of her work. It's gotta come." Madonna controversies wash in and out on promotional waves, and we've learned to expect sexual attention-getting from her. As an antidote to AIDS-era fear of sex, her libidinousness is curative. As stylistic flourish, it's appealing. But as provocation, it's lost its sudden electricity. There's little authentic surprise left.

When shaved-headed Sinead O'Connor rips apart a picture of the pope on *Saturday Night Live* after singing "War" a cappella, it is an unsettling act of hatred, and a stunned audience greeted it with nervous silence and a collective jaw-drop last week. When Ice-T portrays law-enforcement anarchy in the song "Cop Killer," official anxiety resulted in something very close to censorship, causing the artist to remove the song from future printings of his record. But Madonna flaps have become, in effect, enjoyably harmless. Unlike rap artists, or Sinead O'Connor, or Andrew Dice Clay, all of whom strike nerves in the American socioeconomic body, Madonna now elicits an "Oh my, look at what she's doing now" groan. She's evolved into a safe shocker, so utterly controlled about her public image that there's little possibility of sharp edges. While she dabbles in sleaze, and boasts about bondage, we don't imagine her living out these hardcore images. She's borrowing them to make her act more piquant, but she's not committed to their implications. She flirts with homosexuality, but she and former friend Sandra Bernhard never really answered The Question, did they?

Likewise, the sexual activity in videos for "Justify My Love" and "Erotica" has next to no shock value. With a gold tooth, slicked-down hair and heavily shadowed eyes in "Erotica," she does look very arch, particularly as she fellates a doll's arm. But as Madonna's faceless entourage frolics, with homosexual intertwinings and basement-bondage accouterments, the erotic impact is analagous to those ubiquitous jeans and underwear ads, what *New Yorker* editor Tina Brown calls "media wallpaper." They're everywhere you look. Madonna's videos are also not startling because they're all a pose. David Bowie in a dress on TV is eye-opening; Madonna and her troupe dressing up and undressing is attractive, but not challenging. Like the lush, homoerotic Calvin Klein campaign, it sells product. Vehemently, Madonna has defended her self-exposure with a freedom-of-speech riff that's hard for the liberal press to critique. She tries to portray herself as a Suppressed Artist whose goal is to break useless taboos. In Europe on the Blond Ambition tour, she achieved a publicity coup: The Vatican itself registered disapproval of her show, allowing her an International Photo Opportunity. Wearing glamorous I'm-in-a-historical-moment sunglasses, she met a gang of reporters to read a statement deploring censorship, supporting artistic freedom, etc. Talking to her Blond Ambition backup singers in *Truth or Dare,* she says: "I know I'm not the best singer and I know I'm not the best dancer. But . . . I'm interested in pushing people's buttons and being provocative. And being political." More recently, she tells *Vanity Fair,* "I'm out to open minds and get them to see sexuality in another way. Their own and others."

But Madonna's motive for baring her breasts to the public feels more like personal gratification, less like commitment to a cause. She's not out to change the world. Let's face it: Few people get erotic in front of millions of viewers for purely selfless political reasons. It's hard to escape the view of Madonna as a difficult Catholic adolescent aiming the finger at everything repressive. And many of her songs are addressed to an authority figure of her youth—from God and Jesus Christ to her own father. The heart of Madonna's outrageousness seems to lie beneath her liberal rationales, as if she's acting out something private and the world is her couch, not to mention her bank. Her politics are largely Electoral. Everyone gets silly with theory about Madonna, nevertheless. If she provokes anything these days, it's lots of press. For one thing, she's the best symbol of post-Warhol pop going. Few entertainment journalists will deny having spun out a few pretty puns courtesy of the lucky star, even when trashing her. Academia has adopted her, to the dismay of many old schoolers, featuring Madonna "texts" in Humanities, English and Women's Studies courses. Take her from a Freudian angle, look at her through a Postmodern lens. Is she or isn't she a feminist? *The Madonna Connection,* a forthcoming book from Westview Press, collects 13 very serious Madonna-themed essays. Sample sentence: "Vogue creates a memory link—a simultaneity—to specific historical times without constructing a place of memory; that is, we get a 'now' disjuncted from its 'here.'"

Simply watching Madonna cope with fame is a hobby for many. It's celluloid astronomy. After watching drugs and victimization destroy greats such as Marilyn Monroe and Elvis Presley, we understand the dangers of the public's love. Will Madonna survive the pressures?

Surely she is trying, all the more as the masses embrace her, prizing herself on her control-freakishness and her physical fitness. It's immediately gratifying, dissecting the making of an icon while it is actually occurring.

Most people, however, can't take their eyes off Madonna because she is an aesthetic wonder, reinventing herself repeatedly with uncanny sophistication. Who will she be next? Her sexual pranks may be predictable, but her fashion-savvy is awesome. She continues to appropriate shamelessly from classic historical high styles—the Marilyn look, the Brassai look, the Jean Harlow look. In the "Erotica" video, she's dressed as a Berlin Nazi-era master of ceremonies—Joel Grey with a whip, or early Annie Lennox. In the October *Vanity Fair,* she's a peachy 1950s teenager. "Beauty's where you find it," she reminds us in "Vogue." On top of her historical borrowings, Madonna adds glazes of avant-garde New York fashion, and gay culture in particular, never forgetting her roots in the disco, whose roots are in gay culture. Her hairstyles are endlessly intriguing, even more visually compelling than O'Connor's nubby egg head. She's aligned with the urban fashion elite, sporting her wardrobes with a deliciously cool attitude. In an MTV age, she's always on top of her own image, putting out songs and videos—and now a book—that feed one another and create a fetching world.

It's also eye-catching to find a woman in the music business blatantly trading in vulgarity and sexual power, yet always keeping charge of her career. It's a role most identified with male stars such as Mick Jagger and Jim Morrison. There have been other female pop precursors, including Tina Turner, Grace Slick, Janis Joplin, Bette Midler and Debbie Harry, but none has met with the raging success of Madonna. Madonna's sexual play may not be cutting-edge, or committed, but the way she manipulates attitude and style in her act is brilliant.

Is Madonna's promiscuity opening people's minds, rearranging public thinking about sex? Sex in its many variations is not something mainstream artists such as Madonna introduce to the world through coffee-table books. It's been there forever. It's all over MTV already; it's in the video stores and the movies; it's in magazines; it's on the calendars. Sex sells, and she's not the first artist to recognize that. And after all, if she were truly shocking, if she were truly breaking ground and causing us to re-view our lives, then we probably wouldn't talk about her so very willingly.

MOLLY IVINS

# MADONNA AND OTHER ARTHURS

1993

*Noted liberal columnist Molly Ivins comments on her own perplexed reaction to Madonna, sex, and other subjects.*—Eds.

I am worried about Madonna. Okay, actually I'm worried about Madonna and me. Because of this woman, I'm in danger of being consigned to premature Old Poophood.

On the subject of Madonna, I resemble the Senate Judiciary Committee—I just don't get it. I achieve positively Bushian levels of not getting it.

I went along fine for quite a while with Madonna, feeling vaguely fond of her on the slender grounds that I understand her Fashion Statement. Although a lifelong fashion dropout, I have absorbed enough by reading *Harper's Bazaar* while waiting at the dentist's to have grasped that the purpose of fashion is to make a Statement. (My own modest Statement, discerned by true cognoscenti, is WOMAN WHO WEARS CLOTHES SO SHE WON'T BE NAKED.) And Madonna's Statement is as clear as a Hill Country spring. It is: I'M A SLUT! What's more, it seems to be made with a great deal of energy and good cheer. I rather liked it.

But then Madonna took up *la vie litteraire,* invading my turf as it were, and I felt constrained to develop an opinion of her literary talents. Without, of course, reading her book, since no sane person is going to fork out fifty-seven bucks for her oeuvre. Even if she does have a comprehensible Fashion Statement. Careful study of the publicity about Madonna's book left me with a strong desire to say to her, "Young woman, stop making an exhibition of youself." Since Madonna makes a living by making an exhibition of herself, it seemed a singularly bootless impulse.

C. R. Ebersole of Houston, who happens to be my former Sunday-school teacher, passed along his opinion that Madonna has done more for dogs than anyone since Albert Payson Terhune. I did not inquire why my former Sunday-school teacher paid $57 for a book called *Sex.*

Thinking I might be of the wrong gender to appreciate Madonna, I called my friend Aregood in Philadelphia, whose taste in women is notoriously ecumenical. Aregood says you can tell you're out of touch with your fellow Americans when the reigning sex goddess is someone you wouldn't take home with you if she were the last woman left in the bar. He also says Sophia Loren is still his idea of a sex goddess.

I struggled with the concept of impending Old Poophood. I was, in my day, fairly with it, verging on hip. When I was in college, I carefully suppressed the fact that I knew all the words to every song Bob Wills ever wrote, and listened assiduously to Dave Brubeck and Edith Piaf. Later, I was among the first on my block to discover Bob Dylan, Janice Joplin, and The Band. You see, we're talking no mean record on the Cutting Edge Front.

I admit to recent slippage—both punk rock and rap slipped right by me. But with the large tolerance that comes from being a nonparent, I have been given to loftily assuring my offspring-impaired friends that every generation is entitled to some form of music that will drive anyone over twenty out of the room. I believe this is meet, just, and probably part of God's plan.

Several of my advisers on contemporary culture have tried to persuade me that Madonna's redeeming social value lies in her apparently premeditated pattern of pushing all known taboos to the limit and beyond, in order to force her fans to think seriously about their own choices. Her fans seem to consist largely of thirteen-year-old girls. I believe this is a reflection of how difficult it is to be a thirteen-year-old female in our society.

When I was thirteen, I yearned to be an arthur. As I understood it, arthurs got to live in New York or Paris and hang out in sophisticated places like the Algonquin or Harry's Bar with terribly witty people, all of them exchanging *bon mots* that would later be collected by literary historians. Sounded like a good deal to me.

Then I became an arthur. All that happened was my publisher sent me to a lot of radio stations in places like Garden City, Kansas, where deejays kept asking me, "So, Miss Ivv-ins, what is it about Texas?" No *bon mots* occurred.

Then I got sent to a literary tea in New York at the Waldorf Astoria, so my hopes were high. My fellow *litterateurs* on that occasion turned out to be Elmore Leonard, who writes those great tough-guy murder mysteries; Professor Henry Gates of Harvard, who is big on the multicultural circuit; and Ivana Trump, who paid somebody to write a book for her. My publisher says it is better than Marilyn Quayle's book.

We all addressed 350 blue-haired ladies at the literary tea, and I held up well until Ivana (she asked me to call her that) explained to the ladies that in addition to *la vie litteraire*, she is quite busy. She hass ze shildren, she bass ze sharities, and also she iss bringing out a new line of toiletries. I at once became enchanted with the marketing possibilities for *arthurs*.

Elmore Leonard can sell Eau de Detroit Funk, A Cologne for Men. Gates can retail a line of soul food, sort of like Paul Newman's Popcorn: Skip Gates's Pickled Pigs' Feet. I shall endeavor to sell Molly Ivins's BBQ-Flavored Vaginal Gel.

I dunno. You grow up, you finally get to be an arthur, and there you are with Ivana Trump and Madonna. What the hell would Albert Payson Terhune say?

STEVE ALLEN

# MADONNA

1993

*Pop song writer, comedian, and general cultural icon Steve Allen adds his thoughts to the Madonna debate, comparing her to now-forgotten comedian Andrew Dice Clay, who made a career out of four-letter words.*—Eds.

Madonna scrawls graffiti on the national dialogue. The saddest aspect of the present situation is not that she herself is the problem, any more than the Prince of Filth, Andrew Dice Clay, is the problem of the vulgarity and general ugliness that characterizes much of modern entertainment. These two pathetic individuals—and the scores like them who now market not beauty, the traditional province of the artist, but ugliness—far from being objects of contempt, as they would be in any truly civilized culture—are eminently successful in the marketplace.

Mr. Clay, at least as of several months ago, was able to fill Madison Square Garden, something that probably no other comedian, however gifted, could do at the time. Just so, Madonna's services are more in demand than those of other popular singers or entertainers who far surpass her in talent, a fact that speaks volumes about our social predicament.

There is one point, of crucial moral importance, that appears not to have impressed itself upon either the public consciousness or the circle of professional critics. No one assumes that there was ever a Golden Age of personal rectitude among creative people. The statistics about alcoholism, drug addiction, sexual promiscuity and emotional instability in the general population are tragic enough. They have always been higher in the arts, and particularly so in that branch of them referred to as show business. When, therefore, we say the present degree of moral turpitude is shocking and depressing, we are not being naive enough to compare it to some sort of moral never-never-land in which our singers, musicians, and entertainers were as righteous and heroic as the roles they played or the public images they manufactured.

But the sinners and offenders of earlier times at least attempted to keep their transgressions private, if only for selfish reasons. The popular comedian Fatty Arbuckle, in the 1920s, never worked again in the motion-picture business after his arrest in connection with an incident in which a prostitute died, apparently because Arbuckle, in a sexual context, had inserted into the poor woman's body a Coca-Cola bottle, which broke and cut her internally, after which she bled to death. If such a thing were to happen today, I would not be surprised if Arbuckle ended up doing a TV commercial for Pepsi.

It has become almost impossible to shame our public figures, given the general social sickness of our society and culture.

In the American past there was always, under the combined façade and reality of the sort of happy home depicted in the old MGM Andy Hardy films, a strain of social and moral illness, but formerly sexual perverts, sadists, masochists, and assorted other psychos and wackos at least scurried for cover when the lights were turned on, as do cockroaches and other insects in the middle of the night. Today, by way of contrast, the offenders, though they may become the butt of a few random jokes by late-night television hosts, are promptly surrounded and defended by those who stand to make money from their professional activities, and we are quickly told that even the most vile on-stage excesses are permissible because they are protected by the rights specified by the First Amendment in that most noble of documents, the American Constitution.

I do not take lightly the question of creative rights, and I'm certainly no abstract philosopher viewing the question from an impartial distance. I am myself the creator of a large body of poetry, short stories, novels, nonfiction books, plays, musicals, and songs, as well as an actor, vocalist, and pianist. But it would never occur to me to argue that simply because of my creativity I am entitled to introduce into the marketplace literally anything at all, however revolting.

The point here—again—is not that the present flood-tide carrying us all into the sewer is to be properly contrasted with a state of moral perfection. Even Shakespeare occasionally inserted a bawdy comment or joke into his magnificent plays. The Bible itself has passages that could hardly be considered suitable instruction for children.

The fundamental question as to the proper place of sex within the context of any even remotely civilized society is simply one of those ongoing dilemmas about which the ablest philosophers continue to differ. Relations between the creative community and the state, which through its laws is somehow supposed to represent the will of the people, have always been uneasy. But I deliberately return to the point, since it seems not to have been generally grasped, that we are by no means presently faced with one of those historic balancing-acts. In the past no artist has ever argued that literally *anything* is permissible. Henry Miller was not a complete moral anarchist. Today, however, *anything goes* seems to be the operative principle.

Am I exaggerating here? It is of the most crucial importance to understand that I am not. The marketing of the most depraved and disgusting material is now not only permitted—which would be bad enough—it is philosophically defended and dominant in the commercial marketplace. Millions of Americans have died, in various wars, presumably not on the classic justification that our borders needed to be defended—largely because of our two oceans, our mainland has traditionally not been in that sort of danger common to European and other nations around the world. That those millions of American deaths were justified as a defense of our economic system—which practically all Americans prefer—is part of the problem. Major national and international corporations are now making no distinction whatever between a dollar earned by marketing moral poison and a dollar made by marketing toothpaste or automobiles.

When, in the past, at least a segment of the public became aware that some of their favorite entertainers left a great deal to be desired in their simple capacities as human beings, they at least could respond, "Well, I wouldn't want my daughter to marry the fellow, but I like this singing (clarinet playing, acting) so much that I'll just turn a deaf ear to his personal faults." And indeed, this is a perfectly reasonable attitude as regards individuals possessed of true artistic talent.

Although I understand the reasons behind the U.S. government's campaign to ban Bach, Beethoven, and other great German composers from our airwaves during our wars against Germany, it was always my private opinion that there was something stupid in the practice. It is, after all, possible to thrill to the music of a German genius while still despising the Nazis, or to enjoy an Italian opera while still loathing Mussolini and his Fascists.

But such equations do not apply to our present predicament, and this is nowhere as clearly illustrated as in the case of the young woman who calls herself Madonna, for the simple reason that her talents are quite modest. She has never been considered a great singer, and she is certainly not a gifted dancer. She has a certain modest ability as an actress, but given that so do many three-year-olds and other untutored individuals, including a few animals, she is not noteworthy at that capacity either. Many performers achieve success because of their remarkable gifts. Barbra Streisand, Meryl Streep, Robert De Niro, Al Pacino and Robert Duvall come to mind in such a connection.

Madonna does not. She has succeeded for a reason that reflects no credit upon the rest of us. She has succeeded because of her neurosis, her moral weaknesses, her willingness to prostitute herself for fame and money, to shame her family. She is not, like the rest of us, simply someone who almost daily falls short of the moral standards we sincerely profess. She does not hide but flaunts her disdain for those standards. No doubt there are women working in offices, restaurants, or other workplaces who are equally as depraved, but *they are not role models to millions of impressionable teenagers.*

It is precisely at this point that the terrible work of the Madonnas of our time is done. I now hear seven-year-olds using vile terms and references that not so many decades ago did not enter into the American consciousness and vocabulary until the age of 14 or 15. It has never been suggested that Madonna is solely to blame, but it cannot be denied that her name is high on the list of those responsible.

In this general connection I am reminded of the evening, some years ago, when at a small dinner party in her apartment in New York, former Congresswoman and social critic Clare Boothe Luce, who was an admirer of *Meeting of Minds,* a television show I had created for the PBS network, recommended that I consider booking the Marquis de Sade as a guest. (*Meeting of Minds* was a television talk show, though scripted and rehearsed, in which important figures of history came together to engage in philosophical debates.) For a moment I thought that Ms. Luce was joking. "Oh, no," she said. "I'm quite serious. Sade was the most despicable person imaginable, but his views are very influential in today's society."

Ms. Luce was quite right, needless to say, and the two one-hour shows in which Sade was permitted to advocate his depraved positions were both stimulating and sobering. Madonna is the Marquis' ablest and most influential present defender, although because she has been poorly educated she may never have consulted his works.

One clue to the profound seriousness of our present predicament concerns the term *deviant behavior.* The concept, which for centuries has had legitimate application among social philosophers, is obviously based on moral distinctions between more-or-less common modes of behavior, not all of them necessarily highly virtuous, and other forms of conduct that represent dangers to society. But that classic and common-sense difference is not, in the public consciousness, as clear-cut as it formerly was. Indeed, those guilty of blatantly deviant behavior are now unapologetic, even defiant, and if they happen to be celebrities, their very game seems to provide at least a degree of immunity from public criticism. Some such criticism is there, of course, though largely because there is an unappealing appetite for scandal. But there is so much of it, such a daily flood, in fact—the public's attention span apparently now being comparable to that of a gnat—that there is not only little likelihood that the offenders will suffer professional harm, it is quite likely that they will profit by rather than suffer from their escapades.

Although it would not matter to me in the least if I were the only person in the entertainment field to express such views, the important thing is that I am not.

Although standards of beauty are notoriously personal—as are judgments as to what constitutes sexual attractiveness—Madonna cannot be sensibly defended on the ground that, through no fault of her own, she is simply a highly desirable creature to members of the opposite sex. There are women of whom this is true, Marilyn Monroe being a classic example. Although I met Marilyn on only one occasion (she had just started work on her last picture), I had long admired her work in films. She exuded that always mysterious trait referred to as "star quality," and was, in person, as breathtaking as she appeared to be on screen. Because of the tragic circumstances of her early upbringing, she always seemed to me a helpless puppy desperately in need of attention and love. It makes no sense whatever to marry such individuals, as Joe DiMaggio and Arthur Miller were to learn to their sorrow, but they are naturally lovable. Dolly Parton, Sophia Loren, and a few of today's young actresses might also be cited in this connection. But as against this real sexuality there has always been the pseudosexuality of the professional prostitute. It may come as a shock to 15-year-old boys, but the fact is that the average prostitute does not enjoy sex, and certainly not with the parade of johns who purchase her temporary services. In the film *Klute* Jane Fonda struck just the right note, in the role of a whore, when, pretending to be emotionally moved by one of her clients, she suddenly look at her wristwatch as if to say, "How soon can we wrap this up?" It was a moment of both high comedy and important insight. Madonna's sexuality is, to put the matter quite simply, that of the professional prostitute. She does not really look like Marilyn Monroe. Her hair is black and her features considerably less than ideal; she simply *imitates* Monroe's true beauty. As contrasted with Dolly Parton's cute, ultra-natural country girlishness, Madonna presents a hard, tough attitude. She may make legitimate claims on our sympathy, since we all emerge from the shell of childhood as products of genetics and environmental conditioning, but there is no reason for the rest of us to accept as genuine the illusory merchandise that has been so cleverly marketed. Even as a sex object the young woman is simply not the real article.

There is a clue to this in the sort of wardrobe and costume she affects. There is nothing in it of the sweet, feminine, even Victoria's-Secret sort, in which the purpose is to glorify and enhance the natural factor of womanly beauty. What we see in Madonna, by way of contrast, is much use of black and of leather, of the sort associated with sadomasochism. Then there are the absurd conical, metallic-looking brassieres, a dehumanizing element when contrasted with the natural beauty of the well-formed breasts with which some women are gifted by nature.

To sum up, Madonna has not become arguably the most commercially successful performer of her time because of her ability to sing, dance or act; in all three categories her gifts are minor. Nor has she become successful because of her beauty, the illusion of which is largely a matter of the contributions of makeup people and hairdressers. She has become successful because of her willingness—even eagerness—to resort to the grossest sort of vulgarity.

There has never been any such thing as a universally popular entertainer. The only American who came close was the brilliant and naturally lovable Will Rogers. It is therefore not particularly noteworthy that Madonna has her detractors. But it is instructive to consider what it is, very specifically, that makes her repulsive to millions. A few examples:

- On the night after a throat ailment caused her to cancel a concert, she announced to an audience in the Washington, D.C. area, "I don't care what anyone says, I'm fucking hot tonight."
- In the presence of a performer dressed as a Catholic priest, Madonna not only starts to disrobe but smashes a crucifix—the most sacred of symbols to hundreds of millions of Christians—to the ground.
- Asked why she chose to use a sacred religious symbol as a trademark/logo, Miss Class actually replied, "Crucifixes are sexy because there's a naked man on them."

Truth or Dare tour. *Courtesy of J. Mayer, Star File.*

On tour. *Courtesy of Danny Chin, Star File.*

- After nude pictures of her were published in *Playboy* and *Penthouse,* she explained, "It was like when you're a little girl at school and some nun comes and lifts your dress up in front of everybody and you get really embarrassed." Were there no journalists present to ask for the identity of the nun and the name of the school where the alleged incident took place?
- It is also relevant that most Christians resent the young woman's choice of a stage name, given that the word *Madonna* has traditionally referred to the Virgin Mary, Mother of Jesus.
- A concert in Texas included one number about sadomasochistic spankings and another in which masturbation was feigned.
- Another number features seven cross-dressed male dancers wearing brassieres.

Given that no other entertainer in modern history has consciously conveyed so many destructive and perverted messages, is it perhaps possible that the young woman's own intentions are virtuous but that she has fallen under the influence of some evil guru of the sort connected with the infamous "Children of God" cult? The answer is *no*. It's difficult to dig out clear answers to certain kinds of questions, but not in this instance. The evil done by Madonna is entirely of her own volition. As her close associate songwriter Stephen Bray has put it, "This is a woman who is in complete charge of her life. She calls her own shots." This is perhaps the one point about her that is not a subject of controversy.

Despite the entertainer's success, which is formidable, her eager willingness—no, determination—to shock does occasionally affect ticket sales. When she appeared in Italy in the summer of 1990, sales were low, and one performance in Rome was canceled after Catholic spokesmen, quite correctly, termed her show blasphemous.

The ancient debate pitting the Past against the Future is meaningless except as regards specifics, but even then the debate is impossible to resolve because it is not so much a matter of science as of opinion and taste. Literally every professional critic on earth could assure us that the music created by Jerome Kern or George Gershwin is vastly superior to that of this week's shocker-punk group, but to those who simply prefer the latter such unanimity of opinion would mean nothing. There are, however, certain factors of the large argument that have nothing to do with opinion and are therefore demonstrable as matters of fact. It is simply the case that in earlier decades entertainers achieved success largely by having actual talent. Sometimes other elements contributed—dumb luck, physical beauty, connections, sleeping with a studio executive—but talent was dominant. This is no longer the case.

The greatest art has traditionally appealed to the best elements of human nature. It did not disguise the reality of evil. Quite to the contrary it called evil by its right name. What Madonna presents—one can certainly not call it art—is very much the opposite. She appeals to sickness, to perversion, to the worst elements of human nature. In one of her 1990 concerts she stomped her female dancers, again and again. Was the crowd shocked into silence as sometimes happens to comedians or talk show hosts who have "gone too far"? Sadly, no. The crowd *approved* of what it was seeing and, in fact, as critic Richard Goldstein put it, "went wild."

Says Goldstein "At another point, she stopped the show to give a speech about Keith Haring, a friend she admired for his candor about being gay and having AIDS. Polite applause."

And Goldstein, I must make clear, is no Michael Medved. He is not only not neutral about the chiefly male performers he calls sexual outlaws; he greatly admires them. In his defense it should perhaps be explained that he is talking about theatrical representations, since it is obvious enough that judged purely as human beings—which is to say as faithful lovers, husbands, fathers, citizens—such people are utter failures. I am afraid that to critics like Goldstein the ideal of sex within the context of romantic love and/or marriage simply eludes them.

It might be instructive for Time Warner executives to consider a few of the audience segments the woman called Madonna has alienated:

- Feminists do not like her.

Eighty percent of Americans report being affiliated with one Christian denomination or another. Catholics, in particular, despise her because she has directly attacked the church and its symbols. But Protestants too, strongly disapprove of her.

Explains Christian columnist John Lofton, "The opening excerpt from the video shows some scumbag, of indeterminate sex, sucking on the face of a blonde woman. And this androgynous something mounts this woman and as sexual intercourse is simulated we see, fleetingly, pressed between these two riding bodies, a cross with the crucified Christ on it . . . what we're seeing here is plain, old-fashioned, blasphemous sacrilege. . . . Just how bad is this video? Well, it's so bad, so slimy and sleazy, that it's been banned by MTV—the cable network that, 24-hours-a-day, is already an open sewer."

Girlie Show, 1993. *Courtesy of Max Goldstein, Star File.*

Since the Jewish community has historically had relatively elevated cultural tastes and has distinguished itself by its support of the true arts, the Jews have understandably not been conspicuous among Madonna fan clubs. In January of 1981 Rabbi Abraham Cooper, Associate Dean of the world-famous Simon Weisenthal Center in Los Angeles, described a track of Madonna's *Justify My Love* CD as "dangerous and an insult to every Jew."

The passage in question is from the Revelation of St. John and is commonly translated as "and the slander of those who say they are Jews, but they are not, they are a synagogue of Satan." "The notion," Rabbi Cooper said, "that an icon of American pop culture should, for whatever reason, zero in on the most notorious anti-Semitic quote in the Bible is totally unacceptable. . . . The idea of the synagogue of Satan was a very powerful weapon used against Jews in the Middle Ages, and the Nazis depicted Jews with horns in the image of the devil."

The Anti-Defamation League (ADL), commenting on the case shortly thereafter, said that lyrics of the song and anti-Semitic slurs spray-painted on three California synagogues in December, bear a "painful resemblance."

In a letter to an executive of Warner Brothers Records, which released the CD, the ADL expressed the "hope that the influence that you and your company have on the shaping of American youth can be used to impart a more positive and hopeful message."

I would not advise that any of us hold our breaths until the record industry starts to take that recommendation seriously.

Over half a century ago James Thurber wrote a prescient short story that had not a funny line in it but made, in a bitter, Swiftian way, a powerful point that, had Thurber not shared his insight with us so early, would almost certainly never have occurred to those modern critics of culture who would appear to have abandoned whatever taste they might originally have had and permitted it to be replaced by a lemming-like submission to the dominant mob-mood of the present.

The protagonist of Thurber's story is a young hero-of-the-moment who has attracted the attention of the nation by making a remarkable airplane flight. So hysterical is the acclaim that greets this achievement that a number of national leaders convene in a room, high in a Manhattan skyscraper, to share the young favorite's company. Unfortunately they discover that the daring young fellow is, to use the simplest possible language, a total jerk who appears to have not one redeeming feature that might justify and sustain his incredible fame. The shocking ending of the story comes when the high government officials, perceiving that the young fellow—by a combination of his social idiocy and popularity—is actually a threat to the nation, contrive, by unspoken agreement, to push him out an open window.

Thurber was, of course, not seriously recommending such a course of action, but the story is instructive because it is based on the sobering realization that the world would really be better off had some people never lived, whatever the degree of their momentary popularity. Today, so compulsive have we become in our adoration of The Celebrity that Thurber's solution to the problem, even as a purely literary exercise, would simply never come to mind. The result, God help us, is that the pantheon of American heroes has now admitted so high a percentage of jerks that we are—well, getting the culture we deserve.

In the 1950s and '60s there were hundreds of critics, in their middle years, who had no doubts whatever that Cole Porter, let's say, was vastly superior at the songwriting art to, oh—Mick Jagger or Bob Dylan. Why, then, did they so rarely say as much? I submit that the reason was a sort of social cowardice. The critics, though they knew better, held their tongues because they did not want to seem un-hip.

I make a distinction here between middle-aged, generally well-informed critics and the teenage fans then attending rock concerts. The young people could be forgiven on the classic grounds that they simply didn't know what they were doing. They were not consciously rejecting Porter, Kern, Gershwin and the other representatives of the glorious Golden Age; they simply had never consciously heard them in the first place. Eventually a small minority of the younger generation who happened to be, for the usual mysterious and genetic reasons, gifted with the ability to write, used the ability to express their taste, vulgar as it was.

The point is that even these aesthetically compromised modern critics have turned against Madonna.

But Madonna seems not to understand the essential message her critics are now transmitting. When asked by the *Today* show's Bryant Gumbel about the barrage of public criticism to which she has been subjected, Madonna referred only to "bad reviews," showing that she either entirely missed Gumbel's point—or pretended to.

By the time of the release of her film *Body of Evidence,* in January of '93, quite a distinct phase of Madonna's career had been entered upon. Even the usually tolerant popular media had begun to treat her not so much as a femme fatale, socially dangerous because of her willful assault on conventional morals, but as a laughing stock. *People* magazine, a Time Warner subsidiary, unwilling even to take the film seriously, ran a feature headed *Madonna's Movie Misadventure,* in which it was pointed out that film critic Roger Ebert gave the picture half a star, Susan Stark of *The Detroit News* called it "trash," and in Peoria, Illinois, "52 people gathered in a 237-seat theater and giggled." At a Loews theater in Cambridge, Massachusetts, the audience reaction was "belly laughs that dwindled to snorts and cackles." One theatergoer was quoted as describing the picture as "stupid and confusing." An audience in New York city, according to the feature, applauded when Anne Archer called Madonna a "coke-head slut." It is important to grasp that audiences all over the country were not so derisive simply because the film was of such low quality; scores of pictures every year may be so described. What audiences were contemptuously rejecting, even with laughter, was precisely the merchandise that is Madonna's stock-in-trade.

No society can long endure that has abandoned its ideals. Granted that ideals are rarely achieved, they are nevertheless vitally important compass points. It might even be argued that in a society of liars, Truth and Honesty are needed more than ever. The relevance of this to Madonna's unhappy story is that for a very long time, and by no means only in Western nations, one purpose of social education was to prepare young people to assume the status of lady or gentleman. Granted that there has never been any shortage of sluts, whores, pushovers, rogues and rakes, it was nevertheless considered important that a society produce as many actual ladies and gentlemen as surrounding circumstances permitted.

Madonna and her kind run precisely counter to such an honorable tradition. It would be as ludicrous to refer to her as a lady as it would be to describe her as nun or princess.

Traditionally theatrical criticism relates to specifics—singing, dancing, acting, playing an instrument, or, at the more creative level, writing, composing, directing. It is important to understand, in this context, that no performer ever lived who was not occasionally negatively criticized. But no professional critic, theatergoer, or television viewer ever made much of a fuss about the simple quality of a performance. In any event, such traditional considerations have nothing to do with the barrage of criticism to which Madonna has been quite properly subjected. What outrages millions is not the quality of her singing, dancing or acting. This particular young woman is criticized because she has made a conscious, calculated decision to debase herself. There are those who work as whores, but we may safely assume there has never been a case in which a young woman, having had the opportunity to choose among dozens of professions and trades, decided that the best of them all was prostitution. As regards those who work in what are called strip joints, the same may be said. They are uniformly women with no particular talent, with nothing, in fact, except impressive bodies. If they could make good money working at McDonald's or the neighborhood dime store, they would no doubt be quite willing to do so. But that's not where the big money is. So they go where it is; it's that simple.

In the case of Madonna, she's a megamillionaire and indeed at present is probably making so much money she herself doesn't have an accurate accounting of it. She has, therefore, no excuse whatever for deciding to become a public slut.

Those presently reaping enormous profits from deliberately marketing anything-goes sex and violence are, judged morally, equally as loathsome as the purveyors of tobacco or cocaine, although the latter can at least be excused of hypocrisy in that they know that they have made a conscious choice to become criminals, whereas tobacco companies, in common with the marketers of much popular culture, actually attempt to justify their trade.

Girlie Show, 1993. *Courtesy of Max Goldstein, Star File.*

# *Part Four*

## LIKE A VIRGIN

MADONNA AS VIDEO STAR

*More than any other recent pop star, Madonna has used MTV and music videos to establish her popularity and to enhance her recorded work. It's hard to imagine discussing many of her songs* without *referring to the related video. Most of the controversy surrounding her most-discussed songs, notably "Like a Prayer," has to do with the video images created to promote the song, rather than with the song itself. In fact, many of her songs seem more significant than they are because of the impact of the accompanying videos. This part of the book considers Madonna's contributions to the music-video medium.*—Eds.

CAMILLE PAGLIA

# VENUS OF THE RADIO WAVES

1990

*Camille Paglia, the famed "I'm no feminist" feminist critic, was an early champion of Madonna as feminist symbol, primarily based on her performances on video, as this article relates.*—Eds.

I'm a dyed-in-the-wool, true-blue Madonna fan.

It all started in 1984, when Madonna exploded onto MTV with a brazen, insolent, in-your-face American street style, which she had taken from urban blacks, Hispanics, and her own middle-class but turbulent and charismatic Italian American family. From the start, there was a flamboyant and parodistic element to her sexuality, a hard glamour she had learned from Hollywood cinema and from its devotees, gay men and drag queens.

Madonna is a dancer. She thinks and expresses herself through dance, which exists in the eternal Dionysian realm of music. Dance, which she studied with a gay man in her home state of Michigan, was her avenue of escape from the conventions of religion and bourgeois society. The sensual language of her body allowed her to transcend the over-verbalized codes of her class and time.

Madonna's great instinctive intelligence was evident to me from her earliest videos. My first fights about her had to do with whether she was a good dancer or merely a well-coached one. As year by year she built up the remarkable body of her video work, with its dazzling number of dance styles, I have had to fight about that less and less. However, I am still at war about her with feminists and religious conservatives (an illuminating alliance of contemporary puritans).

Most people who denigrate Madonna do so out of ignorance. The postwar baby-boom generation in America, to which I belong, has been deeply immersed in popular culture for thirty-five years. Our minds were formed by rock music, which has poured for twenty-four hours a day from hundreds of noisy, competitive independent radio stations around the country.

Madonna, like Venus stepping from the radio waves, emerged from this giant river of music. Her artistic imagination ripples and eddies with the inner currents in American music. She is at her best when she follows her intuition and speaks to the world in the universal language of music and dance. She is at her worst when she tries to define and defend herself in words, which she borrows from louche, cynical pals and shallow, single-issue political activists.

Madonna consolidates and fuses several traditions of pop music, but the major one she typifies is disco, which emerged in the Seventies and, under the bland commercial rubric "dance music," is still going strong. It has a terrible reputation: when you say the word *disco,* people think "Bee Gees." But I view disco, at its serious best, as a dark, grand Dionysian music with roots in African earth-cult.

Madonna's command of massive, resonant bass lines, which she heard in the funky dance clubs of Detroit and New York, has always impressed me. As an Italian Catholic, she uses them liturgically. Like me, she sensed the buried pagan religiosity in disco. I recall my stunned admiration as I sat in the theater in 1987 and first experienced the crashing, descending chords of Madonna's "Causing a Commotion," which opened her dreadful movie *Who's That Girl?* If you want to hear the essence of modernity, listen to those chords, infernal, apocalyptic, and grossly sensual. This is the authentic voice of the *fin de siècle.*

Madonna's first video, for her superb, drivingly lascivious disco hit "Burnin' Up," did not make much of an impression. The platinum-blonde girl kneeling and emoting in the middle of a midnight highway just seemed to be a band member's floozie. In retrospect, the video, with its rapid, cryptic surrealism, prefigures Madonna's signature themes and contains moments of eerie erotic poetry.

"Lucky Star" was Madonna's breakthrough video. Against a luminous, white abstract background, she and two impassive dancers perform a synchronized series of jagged, modern kicks and steps. Wearing the ragtag outfit of all-black bows, see-through netting, fingerless lace gloves, bangle bracelets, dangle earrings, chains, crucifixes, and punk booties that would set off a gigantic fashion craze among American adolescent girls,

Madonna flaunts her belly button and vamps the camera with a smoky, piercing, come-hither-but-keep-your-distance stare. Here she first suggests her striking talent for improvisational floor work, which she would spectacularly demonstrate at the first MTV awards show, when, wrapped in a white-lace wedding dress, she campily rolled and undulated snakelike on the stage, to the baffled consternation of the first rows of spectators.

I remember sitting in a bar when "Lucky Star," just out, appeared on TV. The stranger perched next to me, a heavyset, middle-aged working-class woman, watched the writhing Madonna and, wide-eyed and slightly frowning, blankly said, her beer held motionless halfway to her lips, "Will you look at this?" There was a sense that Madonna was doing something so new and so strange that one didn't know whether to call it beautiful or grotesque. Through MTV, Madonna was transmitting an avant-garde downtown New York sensibility to the American masses.

In "Lucky Star," Madonna is raffish, gamine, still full of the street-urchin mischief that she would portray in her first and best film, Susan Seidelman's *Desperately Seeking Susan* (1984). In "Borderline," she shows her burgeoning star quality. As the girlfriend of Hispanic toughs who is picked up by a British photographer and makes her first magazine cover, she presents the new dualities of her life: the gritty, multiracial street and club scene that she had haunted in obscurity and poverty, and her new slick, fast world of popularity and success.

In one shot of "Borderline," as she chummily chews gum with kidding girlfriends on the corner, you can see the nondescript plainness of Madonna's real face, which she again exposes, with admirable candor, in *Truth or Dare* when, slurping soup and sporting a shower cap over hair rollers, she fences with her conservative Italian father over the phone. Posing for the photographer in "Borderline," Madonna in full cry fixes the camera lens with challenging, molten eyes, in a bold ritual display of sex and aggression. This early video impressed me with Madonna's sophisticated view of the fabrications of femininity, that exquisite theater which feminism condemns as oppression but which I see as a supreme artifact of civilization. I sensed then, and now know for certain, that Madonna, like me, is drawn to drag queens for their daring, flamboyant insight into sex roles, which they see far more clearly and historically than do our endlessly complaining feminists.

Madonna's first major video, in artistic terms, was "Like a Virgin," where she began to release her flood of inner sexual personae, which appear and disappear like the painted creatures of masque. Madonna is an orchid-heavy Veronese duchess in white, a febrile Fassbinder courtesan in black, a slutty nun-turned-harlequin flapping a gold cross and posturing, bum in air, like a demonic phantom in the nose of a gondola. This video alone, with its coruscating polarities of evil and innocence, would be enough to establish Madonna's artistic distinction for the next century.

In "Material Girl," where she sashays around in Marilyn Monroe's strapless red gown and archly flashes her fan at a pack of men in tuxedos, Madonna first showed her flair for comedy. Despite popular opinion, there are no important parallels between Madonna and Monroe, who was a virtuoso comedienne but who was insecure, depressive, passive-aggressive, and infuriatingly obstructionist in her career habits. Madonna is manic, perfectionist, workaholic. Monroe abused alcohol and drugs, while Madonna shuns them. Monroe had a tentative, melting, dreamy solipsism; Madonna has Judy Holliday's wisecracking smart mouth and Joan Crawford's steel will and bossy, circus-master managerial competence.

In 1985 the cultural resistance to Madonna became overt. Despite the fact that her "Into the Groove," the mesmerizing theme song of *Desperately Seeking Susan,* had saturated our lives for nearly a year, the Grammy Awards outrageously ignored her. The feminist and moralist sniping began in earnest. Madonna "degraded" womanhood; she was vulgar, sacrilegious, stupid, shallow, opportunistic. A nasty mass quarrel broke out in one of my classes between the dancers, who adored Madonna, and the actresses, who scorned her.

I knew the quality of what I was seeing: "Open Your Heart," with its risqué peep-show format, remains for me not only Madonna's greatest video but one of the three or four best videos ever made. In the black bustier she made famous (transforming the American lingerie industry overnight), Madonna, bathed in blue-white light, plays Marlene Dietrich straddling a chair. Her eyes are cold, distant, all-seeing. She is ringed, as if in a sea-green aquarium, by windows of lewd or longing voyeurs: sad sacks, brooding misfits, rowdy studs, dreamy gay twins, a melancholy lesbian.

"Open Your Heart" is a brilliant mimed psychodrama of the interconnections between art and pornography, love and lust. Madonna won my undying loyalty by reviving and re-creating the hard glamour of the studio-era Hollywood movie queens, figures of mythological grandeur. Contemporary feminism cut itself off from history and bankrupted itself when it spun its puerile, paranoid fantasy of male oppressors and female sex-object victims. Woman is the dominant sex. Woman's sexual glamour has bewitched and destroyed men since Delilah and Helen of Troy.

Madonna, role model to millions of girls worldwide, has cured the ills of feminism by reasserting woman's command of the sexual realm.

Responding to the spiritual tensions within Italian Catholicism, Madonna discovered the buried paganism within the church. The torture of Christ and the martyrdom of the saints, represented in lurid polychrome images, dramatize the passions of the body, repressed in art-fearing puritan Protestantism of the kind that still lingers in America. Playing with the outlaw personae of prostitute and dominatrix, Madonna has made a major contribution to the history of women. She has rejoined and healed the split halves of woman: Mary, the Blessed Virgin and holy mother, and Mary Magdalene, the harlot.

The old-guard establishment feminists who still loathe Madonna have a sexual ideology problem. I am radically pro-pornography and pro-prostitution. Hence I perceive Madonna's strutting sexual exhibitionism not as cheapness or triviality but as the full, florid expression of the whore's ancient rule over men. Incompetent amateurs have given prostitution a bad name. In my university office in Philadelphia hangs a pagan shrine: a life-size full-color cardboard display of Joanne Whalley-Kilmer and Bridget Fonda naughtily smiling in scanty, skintight gowns as Christine Keeler and Mandy Rice-Davies in the film *Scandal.* I tell visitors it is "my political science exhibit." For me, the Profumo affair symbolizes the evanescence of male government compared to woman's cosmic power.

In a number of videos, Madonna has played with bisexual innuendos, reaching their culmination in the solemn woman-to-woman kiss of "Justify My Love," a deliciously decadent sarabande of transvestite and sadomasochistic personae that was banned by MTV. Madonna is again pioneering here, this time in restoring lesbian eroticism to the continuum of heterosexual response, from which it was unfortunately removed twenty years ago by lesbian feminist separatists of the most boring, humorless, strident kind. "Justify My Love" springs from the sophisticated European art films of the Fifties and Sixties that shaped my sexual imagination in college. It shows bisexuality and all experimentation as a liberation from false, narrow categories.

Madonna's inner emotional life can be heard in the smooth, transparent "La Isla Bonita," one of her most perfect songs, with its haunting memory of paradise lost. No one ever mentions it. Publicity has tended to focus instead on the more blatantly message-heavy videos, like "Papa Don't Preach," with its teen pregnancy, or "Express Yourself," where feminist cheerleading lyrics hammer on over crisp, glossy images of bedroom bondage, dungeon torture, and epicene, crotch-grabbing Weimar elegance.

"Like a Prayer" gave Pepsi-Cola dyspepsia: Madonna receives the stigmata, makes love with the animated statue of a black saint, and dances in a rumpled silk slip in front of a field of burning crosses. This last item, with its uncontrolled racial allusions, shocked even me. But Madonna has a strange ability to remake symbolism in her own image. Kitsch and trash are transformed by her high-energy dancer's touch, her earnest yet over-the-top drag-queen satire.

The "Vogue" video approaches "Open Your Heart" in quality. Modeling her glowing, languorous postures on the great high-glamour photographs of Hurrell, Madonna reprises the epiphanic iconography of our modern Age of Hollywood. Feminism is infested with white, middle-class, literary twits ignorant of art and smugly hostile to fashion photography and advertisement, which contain the whole history of art. In the dramatic chiaroscuro compositions of "Vogue," black and Hispanic New York drag queens, directly inspired by fashion magazines, display the arrogant aristocracy of beauty, recognized as divine by Plato and, before him, by the princes of Egypt.

In my own theoretical terms, Madonna has both the dynamic Dionysian power of dance and the static Apollonian power of iconicism. Part of her fantastic success has been her ability to communicate with the still camera, a talent quite separate from any other. To project to a camera, you must have an autoerotic autonomy, a sharp self-conceptualization, even a fetishistic perversity: the camera is a machine you make love to. Madonna has been fortunate in finding Herb Ritts, who has recorded the dazzling profusion of her mercurial sexual personae. Through still photography, she has blanketed the world press with her image between videos and concert tours. But Madonna, I contend, never does anything just for publicity. Rather, publicity is the language naturally used by the great stars to communicate with their vast modern audience. Through publicity, we live in the star's flowing consciousness.

Madonna has evolved physically. In a charming early live video, "Dress You Up," she is warm, plump, and flirty under pink and powder-blue light. Her voice is enthusiastic but thin and breathy. She began to train both voice and body, so that her present silhouette, with some erotic loss, is wiry and muscular, hyperkinetic for acrobatic dance routines based on the martial arts. Madonna is notorious for monthly or even weekly changes of hair color and style, by which she embodies the restless individualism of Western personality. Children love her. As with the Beatles, this is always the sign of a monumental pop phenomenon.

Madonna has her weak moments: for example, I have no tolerance for the giggling baby talk that she periodically hauls out of the closet, as over the final credits of *Truth or Dare*. She is a complex modern woman. Indeed, that is the main theme of her extraordinary achievement. She is exploring the problems and tensions of being an ambitious woman today. Like the potent Barbra Streisand, whose maverick female style had a great impact on American girls in the Sixties, Madonna is confronting the romantic dilemma of the strong woman looking for a man but uncertain whether she wants a tyrant or slave. The tigress in heat is drawn to surrender but may kill her conqueror.

In "Open Your Heart," Madonna is woman superbly alone, master of her own fate. Offstage at the end, she mutates into an androgynous boy-self and runs off. "What a Tramp!" thundered the *New York Post* in a recent full-page headline. Yes, Madonna has restored the Whore of Babylon, the pagan goddess banned by the last book of the Bible. With an instinct for world-domination gained from Italian Catholicism, she has rolled like a juggernaut over the multitude of her carping critics. This is a kaleidoscopic career still in progress. But Madonna's most enduring cultural contribution may be that she has introduced ravishing visual beauty and a lush Mediterranean sensuality into parched, pinched, word-drunk Anglo-Saxon feminism.

TAMARA IKENBERG

# IMMATERIAL GIRL?

*Los Angeles Times*, April 9, 1998

*This review of the "Frozen" video (1998) includes an overview of Madonna's video career.*—Eds.

A mystical creature. The embodiment of female angst.

This is how Madonna describes her look in the new video "Frozen,"from her recently released album *Ray of Light*.

In "Frozen," her hair is decidedly raven, she's clad in black from fingernail to foot, and her hands are decorated with trendy mehndi temporary tattoos.

But this look isn't as vogue as we expect Madonna to be, observers say. It may even mark the end of her days as pop's No. 1 fashion icon.

The newest Madonna incarnation has a name: "Veronica Electronica," a spiritual alter ego whose style is suspiciously similar to the

Goth look, a black, brooding, club-kid fashion staple that's been around for well more than a decade.

"Don't say Goth," Madonna said on a recent MTV special. "The director won't like that at all."

But Leon Hall, cohost of E! Entertainment Television's *Fashion Reviews,* knows a Goth when he sees one. Madonna may disguise it under the moniker "Veronica Electronica," but Hall prefers to recognize the Morticia Addams–ish attire for what it is.

"Goth is tired, and why would Madonna pick up on a tired trend?" says Hall, who also is host of E!'s *Fashion Emergency.* "You expect her to be an originator, not a follower."

It's simply out of chameleonic character for Madonna to take anyone else's lead. It's her fashions that have been faithfully copied since she bounced onto the pop scene in 1983 with a crucifix and a dream.

The music on her new album may be hailed as progressive, but the look of "Frozen" is regressive.

It's her first video since giving birth to baby Lourdes, and Madonna watchers looked for signs that her latest role as mother had impaired her trendsetting powers.

But despite Hall's negative reaction to "Frozen," he and other critics concede it will cause a temporary resurgence in mehndi tattoos and the Goth look.

"Madonna has influence, be it good or be it bad," Hall says.

At 39, Madonna's not the same person who simulated sex on the stage 14 years ago at MTV's *Video Music Awards* when she debuted "Like a Virgin" in a thrift-store wedding dress.

You won't see that innocently trashy aesthetic so obviously at work anymore, now that she's heavily reliant on high-end haute couture designers such as Versace, Gaultier, Dolce & Gabbana and Galliano.

Duplicating her style has become increasingly difficult. Once it was as easy as plucking a Madonna-inspired rubber bracelet or a PG-13 bustier off the rack of your local Contempo Casuals. But when her looks began to change from video to video, a concrete image became harder to pin down, says David Wild, senior editor for *Rolling Stone,* who has chronicled Madonna's influence through the years.

Today, Madonna's look is more indefinable and reflects her many symbiotic relationships with fashion designers.

Although she's gone from thrift-store to Dior, as Hall says, Madonna can still peripherally influence a purchase and lend momentum to a fad, depending on what she's seen wearing. The fur-collared Dolce & Gabbana coat she wore on magazine covers and talk shows in the early '90s spawned hundreds of knockoffs around the world. And not long after the release of her "Human Nature" video—an S&M sendup—black vinyl adorned the racks of even the most mainstream retailers.

While she still has power in the fashion world, some of Madonna's core audience wishes she'd never abandoned her sincerely slatternly fashion statements.

GiGi Guerra, associate editor of the fashion magazine *Jane,* targeted to women ages 18 to 34, was part of the fan base that Madonna inspired to lip-sync to "Like a Virgin" in the living room, wearing their mom's old bras.

"She doesn't appeal to me like she used to," Guerra says. "She was my idol for so many years. She and [Duran Duran's] Simon LeBon. That's all I thought about. She almost annoys me now. She keeps chugging along, doing it over and over."

Fans such as Guerra, who idolized Madonna in her first phases, are far past the stage of mimicking rock stars.

"It's pretty embarrassing to have kids of your own and still try to be her. She's not that kind of icon anymore," Wild says. "The remarkable thing is, she's still in the game. It's a testament to her ingenuity."

Madonna has held the world's attention for 15 years and weathered many fashions in the time between "Material Girl" and mehndi makeup. She has shifted looks more times than Susan Lucci has lost at the Emmys.

*Rolling Stone*'s Wild would like nothing more than to see Madonna return to the vampy virgin look for a video or two. Guerra also sees Madonna returning to fun and flirtation.

But *Fashion Emergency*'s Hall, who regards the Goth look of "Frozen" as a low point, will only be satisfied "if she did something uniquely her that still had that edge, within the parameters of being a 40-year-old mother."

#### From Video to Video, the Many Looks of Madonna

Madonna's videos have always been a powerful fashion pulpit. Here's a review of classic videos featuring Madonnas whose looks run the gamut from Marilyn to Morticia.

"Borderline" (1984): Bows, baggy pants and spray paint are the tools of the new girl on the block. Her style is solid, but the thin, pop candy music leaves many critics wondering whether it's enough to sustain a career.

"Like a Virgin" (1984): Vintage Madonna in beads, lace and teased hair at her writhing, moaning, trashiest best shows that style may be enough. As an urchin tart rolling in a gondola at one moment and a deceptively innocent bride being carried over the threshold the next, Madonna cements her sexual split personality.

"Material Girl" (1985): First out-and-out outing as Marilyn Monroe in an ironic, cleverly choreographed showcase. In diamonds and a nostalgic pink satin gown, she struts her stuff through a sea of black-suited suitors. Icon established.

"Open Your Heart" (1986): Madonna heralds the lethal lingerie period as a peep-show dancer wearing a spiked bra with tassels in a seedy strip club. Cropped ultra-platinum hair and dark eyebrows further distinguish the look that also encompassed "Papa Don't Preach," "True Blue," and that whole "Who's That Girl?" fiasco.

"Like a Prayer" (1989): A brunet Madonna with stigmata, getting cozy with a black saint statue in a church, makes Catholics cringe and Pepsi pull the video from an ad campaign. But before they can do that, she's already repopularized visible bra straps.

"Express Yourself" (1989): Monocled, in designer power suits, with exposed bras and in clingy dresses, Madonna alternately laps up milk and grabs herself authoritatively in this update of Fritz Lang's *Metropolis*. The look spurred a resurgence in tailored women's fashions coupled with peekaboo lingerie.

"Vogue" (1990): Ultra-retro Hollywood at its glammest. In suits and Hollywood-starlets-of-yore costumes, Madonna pays homage to Greta Garbo and Monroe, Dietrich and DiMaggio, among others. As she urges observers to"strike a pose," she brings a dance trend from the black gay underground to light.

"Erotica" (1992): Relegated to late-night play on MTV (which was more exposure than the racy "Justify My Love" video ever got), Madonna dominates with a whip, tongue-kisses girls and goes S&M manic in this "fantasy" that left many a fan more irritated than offended.

"Take a Bow" (1994): As a bullfighter's babe circa 1930, Madonna stuns visually with fitted, classic suits by Galliano and exquisite hats. She also does some of her best lingerie-clad writhing since "Like a Virgin."

"Frozen" (1998): Madonna's latest incarnation is as a Goth–Morticia Addams with black nail polish and mehndi henna hand tattoos. She morphs into multiple Madonnas and makes weird, flowy movements with her hands that are supposed to look spiritual but actually look like slow-mo voguing.

STEPHEN E. YOUNG

# LIKE A CRITIQUE: A POSTMODERN ESSAY ON MADONNA'S POSTMODERN VIDEO "LIKE A PRAYER"

1989

*The controversial "Like a Prayer" video gets its day in the academic sun.*—Eds.

"[Performance artist Cindy] Sherman abandoned the film-still format for that of the magazine centerfold, opening herself to charges that she was an accomplice in her own objectification. . . . This may be true; but while Sherman may pose as a pinup, she still cannot be pinned down" (Owens 75).

"We are faced then with mimicry imitating nothing. . . . There is no simple reference . . . signifieds and signifiers are continually breaking apart and re-attaching in new combinations. Not matched pairs (signifiers/signifieds), but couplers or couplings. A person or thing that couples or links together" (Derrida, *Dissemination* 206; Ulmer 88–89).

Postmodernism, in the arts and culture more generally, has been variously defined, discussed, and debated. In this essay, it is defined as any text that is highly ambiguous, basically nonnarrative, and concerned with presenting a visually and/or aurally exciting surface, characterized by colorful images, rapid movement, and provocative juxtapositions of ideas that much of American (in this case) culture views as separate and oppositional. Postmodernism is clearly a stage that follows and presupposes the death of modernism. Where modernism pretended to mean something, if only itself, postmodernism (as if influenced by semiotics and poststructuralism) revels in ambiguities and its refusal to take a stance. It uses images from many different times and places, and borrows styles from the museum of history, all to create an exotic surface of color and flash where the images and styles have lost their original meaning, if indeed they ever had one.

Postmodernism has been both praised and damned by critics. Jean Baudrillard sees it as an empty display of surface flash that refers only to itself, not to any form of the "real."[1] Fredric Jameson characterizes it as a pastiche, an imitation of dead styles. More positively, critics like Eric Salzman[2] and Gregory Ulmer view it as an exciting and welcome freedom from the sterile intellectualism of modernism with its false reification of the art object, as in modernist works of Stravinsky, Joyce, and Proust. Postmodernism has also been viewed rather warily, as a "blurring of hitherto sacrosanct boundaries and polarities" (Kaplan 126) that leaves "the viewer perplexed as to how to read the images" (142). And the complexities and multiple readings of postmodernism go far beyond what I have suggested here.

Postmodernism also blurs other distinctions, particularly that between high and pop culture. Modernism was built on one side of a chasm, wider than at any other time in history, constructing an ivory (or ebony) tower on its side, leaving its potential audience at first hostile and eventually uncaring, completely untouched on the other side. Postmodernism in music, for example, replaces the abstract and difficult rhythms and dissonances of modernism (Schoenberg, Elliott Carter) with a steady pulse and elements of tonality (Philip Glass, Steve Reich). In doing so, it makes a rapprochement with rock and punk through the Talking Heads and others. Contemporary music journals increasingly review contemporary "art" music and jazz next to punk and even mainstream rock.[3]

All of this activity coincides with changes and growth in the field of cultural theory, which increasingly sees its role as creative and even subversive in deconstructing, revealing new meanings and possibilities in the texts it discusses. Since signifiers (texts of any kind) no longer have signifieds, we find ourselves in a world where the reader/viewer is potentially as creative as the author of the text.

The intent of this essay is to identify one particular music video as postmodern, to explore some of the complexities and ambiguities it inevitably presents as a postmodern text, and to tentatively propose a positive, even subversive reading. The essay itself is postmodern in that it reinforces that ambiguity; in fact it declares it to be the content and form of both texts (video and critique). The essay also juxtaposes things that are normally separate, if not oppositional (pop culture/high culture and serious critical writing/wordplay and puns).

The critique consists of two tropes, interpolations which amplify and embellish "Like a Prayer," Madonna's music video advertising the album (or CD) of the same name. The video received heavy rotation on the music video channel, MTV, in the first five months of 1989. The first trope, a verbal description of the events of the video, already stands at a distance

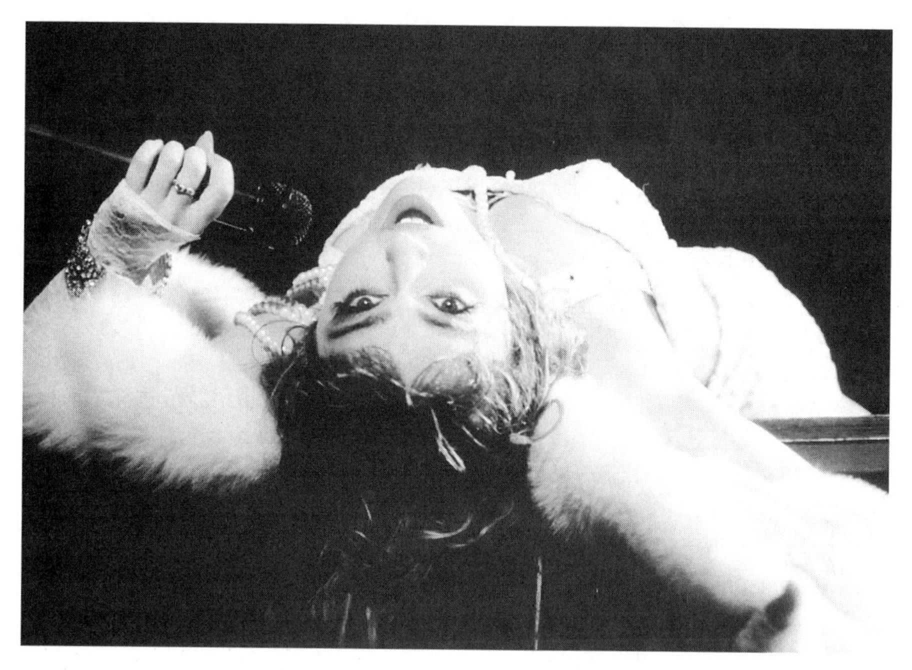

Glamour shot. *Courtesy of Danny Chin, Star File.*

from the video, as its two language systems, music and film, are converted into words. The second trope is even further removed from the original as it interprets and explores possible meanings in the video both as a text and as it is received by the viewer. Yet this second trope will also come closer to the video, completing the circle as persons and things (the viewer and the video) find potential couplings in and from the original text.[4]

**Trope 1**

We see bright flames, for one second (almost subliminally), as the video begins. Madonna (M) is lying on her stomach, half-raised, her face towards us as if she has fallen while fleeing. She is wearing a black coat, pulled on and around her as if in haste. She witnesses (has witnessed) a group of white men beating up (raping) a girl. One of the attackers, a blond German type, looks up and clearly sees her (us) as a witness. Back to where she has fallen, M gets up and flees to a wooden country church (appearing Southern and Protestant) with lighted windows (the same color as the flames). A black male (B), back at the scene of the crime, looks uncertain and perhaps fearful. Then inside the church, M removes her coat to reveal a red negligée, looks around and sees a black saint statue behind barred gates, now as in a Catholic church. The saint statue is the same person as the black male (B). Although apparently lifeless, he cries tears. M comes up to the barred gates, kneels before him, and then lies on her back on a pew. She closes her eyes and suddenly is seen falling through a blue sky. A smiling black female in choir robe throws M back *up* into the sky. M kisses the feet of the statue, who rises and opens the gates. He moves and whispers to her, kisses her on the forehead, as if in benediction. He leaves the church, and M picks up a knife lying by the red roses the statue had been holding (at some point, perhaps as the sharp edges of the knife cut her and she receives stigmata on both palms, one notices that almost everything is black or red). A black gospel choir appears on the other side of the church, singing and moving. The scene shifts to the men moving to beat up the girl and fills in details. Several men push her up against the wall, swinging fists, and one knifes her in the abdomen. She falls to a bench and we see how much she looks like M. The attackers run and B is seen running down some interior stairs as if he has heard the struggle outside. He tries to help the girl, the police arrive and arrest him. We see that M sees it happen.

Suddenly, M is dancing in her red negligée in front of several burning crosses. In the longest scene of the video (30 seconds) we see her close up and then back, caressing herself and dancing erotically before the flames.

Back in the church, the choir now includes a little boy, who gestures for M to join them. M kneels before the female choir leader, who blesses her with her hand on M's forehead. There is a cut to the black saint, who kisses her on the mouth, then a close-up of his face becoming waxy (statue-like) as he sheds tears, now of blood. M dances with the choir and the saint returns to his statue position, resumes holding the red roses and the gates shut. M gets up from the pew, sees the choir, still moving and singing. The black saint, now in his role as the innocent human, is in jail, behind barred gates. M appears before the officer in charge and her brief word frees him. She walks up to the bars. She briefly appears in front of the flames again as in a flashback, and a red curtain falls. It rises as the entire cast takes a bow. It descends and rises again for the solo bows of M and B. It then descends the final time as all dance and celebrate. "The End" appears written across the screen in classic Hollywood fashion.

### Trope 2

Confusions and ambiguities dominate the video; the pace of cutting is rapid (often a cut every two seconds) and a narrative line or thread is hard to find. Clearly, the apparently oppositional dyads of sex/religion and black/white are everywhere, as are the two dominant colors of the film (black/red) cutting across both dyads, unifying the visuals at the same time as they confuse by forming a third dyad of colors (a red herring?). And yet these digital pairs (0, 1) also blend together, or seem so to do. The black choir sings the same music as Madonna's white, multitracked voice. It's the same song and makes us almost forget the historical distinctions of the 1950s and 1960s in which the sound of a black choir was seen to be profoundly different at both musical (more tremolo, emotion, sliding into pitches, etc.) and cultural (sense of community, authenticity, etc.) levels from a white female pop singer (less tremolo, right on the notes, clear diction, more studied and weaker emotion). As Robert Pattison points out, the value judgements evident in these stylistic summaries have become a myth (30–55). And like most myths, there is both historical "truth" and "nontruth" in them. Truth—because many white singers of the '50s and '60s *were* more stilted and less emotional than their black counterparts; nontruth—because white singers like Jerry Lee Lewis ('50s) or Janis Joplin ('60s) had all the stylistic traits attributed to blacks above, and black singing groups like the Platters ('50s) or the Fifth Dimension ('60s) the stylistic traits of whites. The myth of emotional, authentic black culture providing salvation for uptight whites plays throughout the video, being both supported and negated at various points.

The black saint-Jesus-statue kisses Madonna both brotherly-sisterly on the forehead and later erotically on the mouth, not because anything happened in the video to change their relationship, but to present the union of black/white and sex/religion. Several people, including rock star Peter Gabriel, believe that Madonna and/or her producers borrowed (stole) from the film *The Last Temptation of Christ* and wonder about her (their) goals in so doing (qtd. in Baird 40). But these surmisings are probably unverifiable and less interesting than the realization of the existence of a network of condemnation of the video (and the film) among conservative elements in our society, a network that seems to spread in direct proportion to having never seen the video (or the film).

Madonna saves the innocent black who was falsely jailed for the rape-attack, and yet the choir seems to save her. The white singer is more emotional and real, because she is the superstar and up front—both her and her breasts. She is closer to us in space (the black choir is often behind her) and in on-screen time, and yet less emotional and real, because of the cultural myth mentioned above that black people—and especially black gospel choirs—exude a passion and religious sincerity that whites can only weakly emulate. One result of this shifting back and forth between

Madonna and the black choir as the dominant source of emotion and reality, is that they cancel each other out, and both become neutral.

When Madonna flies through the blue sky, she descends into the arms of the female black gospel choir leader, only to be smilingly thrown back up into the sky again. Is this the Assumption, the bodily taking up into heaven of the Virgin Mary (Madonna)? If so, it is performed by the black female, as if Madonna as her individual self were falling helplessly to be transformed by her sister into the ascension as her sacred Self. When Roman Catholic parents name their children after saints, the Virgin, or Jesus, it is an honoring, dedicating act, but it is also at another level a recognition of the divine Self within all of us. Madonna the individual thus becomes the heroine of world myth, who is transformed by the aid of another into the self-realized Madonna.

Yet no sooner do we arrive at this interpretation than we realize the video does not give us a chance to think about that scene (8 seconds), or any other. As Kaplan reminds us, the whole fundamental nature of music videos is their continuous immersion into a 24-hour, never-ending flow (31). Pleasant—or profound—reflections on an 8-second scene can only occur when our memories freeze-frame it; and the whole postmodern nature of the video, with its surface flash of images and rapid movement to the next more tantalizing or ecstatic scene, seems to be set up to oppose such relaxed ruminations as the above on the Assumption.

The crux/cross of the video, the climax point, is by far the longest single scene of the video (30 seconds). The Golden Section of the entire video occurs during this scene, at 200 seconds, which neatly coincides with the Golden Section of the scene itself.[5] This placement appropriately marks the heart of the piece, where the true meaning should be revealed. It is the most ambiguous and meaning-less place of all, thus neatly fulfilling its classical function, since the video is "about" ambiguity. (A) M(m)adonna is there in red negligée—moving, dancing, jiggling the fullness of her upper breasts, at one level signifying red-fire-lust-sin—or openness. But this is ob-scenity in the Baudrillardian sense, since there is nothing "real" to be revealed, only images referring to themselves and each other; we are in the presence of the postmodernist hyperreal. M dances against the backdrop of several burning crosses—Ku Klux Klan crosses, perhaps. In "reality" the scene is probably a collage, or given the extravagant budgets for superstar videos, perhaps she is "really" there in front of the fiery roods. But such determinations are impossible to make and therefore increasingly irrelevant, which further undermines the question of "reality."

The relations of Madonna to the crosses are as many as the crosses themselves. She triumphs over them, she joins with them, she negates them; they triumph over her, join her to themselves, negate her. And when this image is succeeded by the next one, we realize that the fire has not ebbed, the climax does not go out, the desire did not die, it is only replaced as always, followed by the next image, and the next and the next.

Another fascinating place is at the very end of the video, and by virtue of being The End—at the end—perhaps impresses itself on our memory better than some interior section. Kaplan has commented on music video producers' fascination with Hollywood clichés from the '50s (46). This is another aspect of postmodernism, to use elements from the past without any commitment to their historical context, just as images. The curtained ending implies that perhaps the whole video was "like a play" or even a joke. The actors: Madonna, the black male both as saint and innocent victim, and the others were just that, actors. The reference to a vintage ('50s or earlier) Hollywood movie tells us it was fun; to a teenage viewer, old movies are corny (like the popcorn) and less real than modern, sophisticated videos and films. The modern ones don't end that way, by admitting that it was all an illusion. Young people don't often go to plays anyway, so the curtain and the bows are even more artificial. If any bit of seriousness or "message" might have threatened the viewer's somnambulent state for a moment in this video, no problem, it was all just a play anyway—not to mention that history or the past is only an image to be played with, never a lived experience from which one might learn. In Baudrillardian terms, the video is no longer a scene or a spectacle, because it is caught in a loop, meaning only itself, referring to nothing but the instantaneous ecstasy of communication.

### In Place of a Conclusion

Is the blending of sex and religion, at the crux (this cruci-al scene) and elsewhere, some higher, cosmic linking of eroticism and religion that the rest of society is not yet ready for (now even pop artists can be out-in-front-avant-garde), as the model of Prince clearly suggests (he is of course a participant on the *Like a Prayer* album)? The packaging and the photos certainly stress this, as do the lyrics.

Is the cross by Madonna's bellybutton flesh on the cover of the album emblematic of a new, more holistic understanding? Little in our culture seems to reinforce that. Fundamentalist religion takes a strong stand against sex and religion together, as in *The Last Temptation of Christ* film protests, not to mention Jerry Falwell. From whence then, cometh our help? Is it from one's own intuition, evidence in the video (the text), or other corroborative signs around us? The specter of no meaning that reared its frightening head for many intellectuals when they first understood—via semiotics—that there are no assigned meanings, is now showing itself to many more people via postmodernist videos and other art forms. How do we know with what/whom to couple? The question presupposes that it makes a difference. Which meaning one chooses to couple with—perhaps the one that gives warmth and understanding, *must* comfort (or signify) at some level, or we would not choose it. But this choice does not imply that another coupling would not work as well, and that realization is scary and threatening. So sex/religion gives way to a deeper dyad, multiple/single.

We long for, desire, the single in sex; contemporary love songs are filled with lyrics calling for a relationship that will last "for the rest of your life" (Chicago), or "is this the eternal flame?" (The Bangles) and so on. We also long for the single in religion: "I am the Way, the Truth, and the Life; no man cometh unto the Father but by me" (John 14:6). Besides excluding the feminine twice, not to mention all the other world's actual and potential religions, statements like this have been incredibly powerful political signs in our Western culture.

Conversely, we fear the multiple—in sex and religion. And that fear is reinforced by many things that are happening in the world around us. Ironically, the conservatives (and their neoconservative intellectual allies like Daniel Bell) blame modernism for the ills they see in contemporary society and culture (Habermas 6). They then desperately erect walls against something that is already dead (Baudrillard, *Simulations* 131–4) and do not acknowledge the products of postmodernism at all.

But this leaves the way open for the videos themselves (the postmodernist texts) to provide a solution to their and our fears, or at least their temporary easing. A reminder here that popular culture, *any* culture, encodes its behavioral models in its music and other artistic, nonverbal, expressions. These models are seldom resisted because they are not perceived. If the Madonna video shows an almost seamless blending of the various apparently oppositional dyads, black vs. white, sex vs. religion, multiple vs. single, into ambiguities, which reveal the lack of one signified meaning, then as viewers, we may take that first step, even if only tentative, toward the freedom to choose for ourselves, a choice that because it can change tomorrow is threatening yet is ultimately liberating because it subverts the power of the dominant ideologies all around us.

Some would doubtless argue that this reading is naive, that the clear presence of the Madonna video as a part of mainstream culture makes a subverting reading into a kind of oxymoron. But the subverting possibilities are just as potentially powerful as the reinforcing ones because both messages are part of the "non-said," sub-texts that do not give us the opportunity to put up defenses against them, because we do not normally (except in deconstructive readings) know they are there. In a world of multiple meanings and couplings, the positive, nonhierarchical subverting meanings are just as potentially active on the reader as the hierarchical reinforcing ones.

In 1981 Jameson asked, "can [postmodernism] resist the logic of consumer capitalism?" (125). It would seem unlikely, but a positive answer is at least possible. As we take pleasure in ambiguity, increase through exposure our experience of "false realisms," "images about images," we are being informed about toleration of differences, and we are being subverted into a world where hierarchies can blur and perhaps even dissolve.

No one meaning is guaranteed to work—"like a prayer" is more and less than a simile, close to and yet far from a metaphor. The same as a prayer and yet only seeming to be a prayer, both flow from the word "like" as well as our pleasure, as in we "like" it, we approach it, it is comfortable. Or perhaps it is a command, a series of commands: "Take pleasure in prayer, in spoken words to God." "Take pleasure in the pray-er, the person who prays, Madonna herself." "Be fascinated by her as a self-realized heroine, with her message of the unity of black/white, sex/religion." "Be fascinated by her as a superstar, purchase her album, look like her, or desire her."

Although this essay has concentrated on the visuals of the video, it is important to remember that the viewer is also hearing both the music and the lyrics of the song. In fact it is the music and its lyrics that he/she is being encouraged to purchase. The lyrics reinforce the postmodern nature of the video; the wonderfully ambiguous word "like" appears numerous times. The blurring of distinctions between a human lover and God as the signified of the lyrics is frequent and unresolved ("Like a child you whisper softly to me; when you call my name / it's like a little prayer; I hear your voice / it's like an angel sighing"). Ironically, the video mitigates this particular ambiguity by strongly directing the signified toward the religious dimension, and away from the possibility of a human lover. The music, however, has to be described as unambiguous. It is very much a mainstream contemporary pop sound with no real subtleties or surprises. As such, its role is probably a mitigating one, blunting and softening the harder edges, the more challenging content of the lyrics and video. It caresses and reassures the listener like the proverbial "warm bath." Yet by being predictable and steady in sound and rhythm, it creates a "groove," an unchanging sound environment that partially ceases to be the object of our attention. It can then function as a vehicle on which one can ride into the world of fantasy, back toward the imaginary, open to the ambiguities and pluralities of the postmodern video, precisely because it is so safe and predictable as music. Our minds and feelings whirl in a vertigo of conflicting messages, yet we are somehow secretly happy, because we have been like children at play in the world of "as if" (Campbell 28–9).

Like a virgin (also the title of her first superstar album and hit single), Madonna gets off her feet to lie on her back on the pew, to humble herself, to submit to a lover, to pray, to sleep, to think. Both commanded and not, we like this prayer/virgin; we like the idea of a prayer/virgin, and we like someone who is like a prayer/virgin, and like someone who likes the idea of being like a prayer/virgin, and yet we always know that there never was/is a prayer virgin nor a virgin prayer.

## NOTES

1. Although Baudrillard only rarely uses the term "postmodernism," he often refers to a postindustrial phase, the "third order simulacrum, our own" (*Simulations* 105–6). See all of his *Simulations* and the first section of *The Ecstasy of Communication.*

2. See especially Chapters 18–21. Salzman defines postmodernism more narrowly and relates it specifically to music.

3. See recent (1988–1990) issues of *Option* or *Fact Sheet Five.*

4. As Derrida so beautifully states it, "[language must ultimately function as a sign], not only because all that desire had wished to wrest from the play of language finds itself recaptured within that play, but also because, for the same reason, language itself is menaced in its very life, helpless, adrift in the threat of limitlessness, brought back to its own finitude at the very moment when its limits seem to disappear, when it ceases to be self-assured, contained, and *guaranteed* by the infinite signified which seemed to exceed it" (*Of Grammatology* 6).

5. The Golden Section (GS) is an aesthetic principle "recognized since ancient times as important in architecture, painting and natural organic growth" (Howat 1). Its use is believed to provide instinctive satisfaction "whether the (creator) applied it merely by instinct or by careful design" (1). The GS is expressed as "the way of dividing a fixed length in two so that the ratio of the shorter portion to the longer portion equals the ratio of the longer portion to the entire length" (2). The GS is thus found by multiplying the whole length by 0.618, which is then taken to be the center of gravity of the work.

## WORKS CITED

Baird, Jock. "Peter Gabriel's Tickle Therapy." *Musician* (June 1989): 35+.

Baudrillard, Jean. *The Ecstasy of Communication.* Trans. Bernard and Caroline Schutze. New York: Semiotext(e), 1988.

———. *Simulations.* Trans. Paul Foss, Paul Patton, and Philip Beitchman. New York: Semiotext(e), 1983.

Campbell, Joseph. *The Masks of God: Primitive Mythology.* Rev. ed. 1969. New York: Penguin, 1976.

Derrida, Jacques. *Dissemination.* Trans. Barbara Johnson. Chicago: U of Chicago P, 1981.

———. *Of Grammatology.* Trans. Gregory Spivak. Baltimore: John Hopkins UP, 1976.

Foster, Hal, ed. *The Anti-Aesthetic: Essays in Postmodern Culture.* Port Townsend: Bay Press, 1983.

Habermas, Jürgen. "Modernity—An Incomplete Project." Foster 3–15.

Howat, Roy. *Debussy in Proportion: A Musical Analysis.* Cambridge: Cambridge UP, 1983.

Jameson, Fredric. "Postmodernism and Consumer Society." Foster 111–25.

Kaplan, E. Ann. *Rocking around the Clock: Music Television, Postmodernism and Consumer Culture.* New York: Methuen, 1987.

Owens, Craig. "The Discourse of Others: Feminists and Postmodernism." Foster 57–82.

Pattison, Robert. *The Triumph of Vulgarity: Rock Music in the Mirror of Romanticism.* New York: Oxford UP, 1987.

Salzman, Eric. *Twentieth Century Music: An Introduction.* 3rd ed. Englewood Cliffs: Prentice-Hall, 1988.

Ulmer, Gregory L. "The Object of Post-Criticism." Foster 83–110.

LIZ ROSENBERG

# FACE-OFF: MADONNA'S "LIKE A PRAYER": THIS VIDEO AFFIRMS RELIGIOUS PRINCIPLES

*USA Today,* 1996

*In these two related "guest columns" in* USA Today, *Liz Rosenberg, vice president of Warner Bros. Records, "faces off" with Donald Wildmon, executive director of the ultraconservative American Family Association, as they discuss the merits—or lack thereof—of Madonna's "Like a Prayer" video.*—Eds.

New York—As with any work of art as striking and evocative as Madonna's music video "Like a Prayer," it's understandable some would take exception or offense to images and themes juxtaposed to a contemporary pop song. What's striking in light of the ongoing Salman Rushdie uproar is that ad hominem, Khomeini-esque calls for censorship continue unabated.

"Like a Prayer" portrays a dramatic situation in which hate-mongering bigots murder an innocent woman, a crime which Madonna's character witnesses. Is this an implicit endorsement of bigotry or murder? Of course not, no more so than any theatrical presentation condones a character's actions or point of view.

Madonna's character, in peril, seeks refuge in a church, which represents sanctuary. This is a story about positive religious beliefs, human equality, religious symbolism. It's about being good, not about evil.

And what of the saint who comes to life in the dream sequence? Isn't Madonna making a statement about the innocence and guilt we all share? As a mortal, this man is charged with a crime he didn't commit. In the confines of the church, inspired by a saint and full gospel choir, Madonna experiences an epiphany leading her to set aside concerns for her own safety to clear an innocent man.

That's the story line and one, albeit educated, interpretation. Doesn't Madonna, or any artist, have the right to tell a story using imagery and ideas most resonant to the creative process? Madonna's brave video affirms the eternal biblical covenant: "Love thy neighbor." Though some object to the way she has chosen to make her statement, who can deny her constitutional right to do so?

At Warner Bros. Records, we stand by our artists' right to free expression, a hallmark of an open and tolerant society. While that expression can be one of despair or vitriol, it is ironic that in this instance an uplifting story of redemption and hope is damned by self-appointed arbiters of decency. Kudos to Madonna and the millions who will not be frightened away from her positive message by those who make no effort to transcend their own ingrained prejudices.

DONALD WILDMON

# THIS VIDEO IS OFFENSIVE TO BELIEVERS

*USA Today*, 1996

Tupelo, Miss.—Madonna's new video, "Like a Prayer," is an extension of a disturbing trend by some in the media, that of disrespect and disdain for the religious beliefs of millions of Americans.

The video is steeped in Christian symbolism in general and Roman Catholic symbolism specifically. The freeing of the priest from the bondage of being locked in the church is good. Christianity should not be locked up in the building. The symbolism dealing with racial injustice is good. A person's race should not be a source of hatred or injustice. But the video's symbolism of sexuality, suggesting that priests (and indeed all Christians) are sexually repressed, is blatantly offensive.

In the video, Madonna, who represents Christ, is shown in a scene suggesting that she has sex with the priest, obviously to free him from sexual repression. That is absolutely repugnant to Christians. It brings back shades of *The Last Temptation of Christ*—and that is no doubt the intent.

Christian symbolism is nothing new for Madonna, once quoted in *Penthouse* as saying, "Crucifixes are sexy because there's a naked man on them." Famous for her "Like a Virgin" song and open sexuality, Madonna once starred in a low-budget porno film. Pepsi rewards her by giving her millions of dollars to promote her as a role model for our youth.

Coca-Cola, not to be outdone by Pepsi in the race to denigrate Christianity, gives George Michael millions of dollars to be its role model. In "I Want Your Sex," he sings that he "don't need no Bible" when he gets ready to have sex.

I am solidly behind the First Amendment. There is, however, another issue. Columnist Charles Krauthammer stated it: "American [religious] pluralism works because of a certain deference that sects accord each other. . . . In a pluralistic society, it is a civic responsibility to take great care when talking publicly about things sacred to millions of fellow citizens."

For the next year, I will not drink Pepsi. If enough others join me, perhaps respect for religious beliefs of others will be helped tremendously. At least it is a start.

CARLA FRECCERO

# OUR LADY OF MTV: MADONNA'S "LIKE A PRAYER"

1992

*Here are further academic ruminations about Madonna, the video, Pepsi-Cola, MTV, etc.*—Eds.

White academic feminists and feminist intellectuals are currently enacting the wanna-be syndrome of Madonna fans, analyzed, along with fashion, by Angela McRobbie, and more recently by Lisa Lewis, as the complex and specific mode of interpretation, appropriation, and revision belonging to "girl culture" in Britain and the United States.[1] What better way to construct an empowered performative female identity than to claim for ourselves a heroine who has successfully encoded sexiness, beauty, *and* power into a performing embodiment? You can have it all, Madonna suggests, and be credited with a mind, as well. For her girl fans, Madonna has suggested ways of appropriating rebellious masculine youth culture, both preserving and subverting femininity, mitigating the adolescent disempowerment of the female position. It is Madonna's ambition, hard work, and success, as she moves into her thirties, that her women fans appreciate. Thus, Lisa Lewis and Susan McClary, abandoning the intellectual feminist's suspicion of popular cultural representations of female empowerment, argue for a feminist reclamation of Madonna on solid intellectual and feminist, if overly celebratory, grounds.[2]

While impressed with their insights and sympathetic to their "defense" of Madonna against her detractors (all of whom, to my knowledge, deploy traditional elite or masculinist *topoi* in their attacks), I am skeptical of their and my own desire to appropriate Madonna for intellectuals, if only because "she" responds so easily to this desire and fits so well into the progressive white feminist fantasy I am about to explore in her text. Since I am interested in practicing cultural politics, in strategically locating and developing what Andrew Ross calls the "protopolitical" in popular culture, particularly in those media that have been derogatorily designated as "mass culture" or the "culture industry" by left- and right-wing intellectuals alike, it will be important to consider my investment in this reading, as a patrilineally Italian American academic, antiracist (multiculturalist) feminist, whose micropolitical positioning is peculiarly adapted to the cultural representations called *Madonna*.[3]

Much has been made of MTV's postmodern style: the fragmenting of images, the blurring of generic boundaries between commercial, program, concert, and station identification, the circulation of commodities wrenched from their marketplace context, the sense of play and carnival; the attention to fashion; and the de-centered appropriation of images without regard for context or history. Now, there is even a show called *Postmodern Videos.* Its advertised de-centeredness, its "semiotic democracy" (John Fiske's term), its refusal of national boundaries, are, however, like postmodernism itself, far from innocent, and most comparisons that foreground MTV's postmodernism neglect its project, a sort of global cultural imperialism that is nowhere more clearly demonstrated than in its own self-advertisement: "ONE WORLD, ONE IMAGE, ONE CHANNEL: MTV." I call this *imperialism* because MTV is not a democratic medium, equally available to all cultures and nations for use, but a specific creation of the United States for the incorporation of "world music" into itself and for the creation of global desires to consume the products of U.S. popular culture.

The global preparation for Madonna's Pepsi commercial testifies both to MTV's success in having colonized cable and to some of the more concrete goals of this capitalist medium (for MTV models itself on television advertisements and airs commercials for songs and albums). A commercial appeared around the world, featuring an aborigine running across the plains of Australia (in reality, California) into a bar, arriving just in time to see, you guessed it, Madonna's Pepsi commercial version of "Like a Prayer." The commercial itself aired in forty countries on 2 March 1989. Madonna is, like George Michael and other relatively recent stars, one of the "corp-rock" generation, as the *Village Voice* puts it, untroubled by Nell Young's accusations of sell-out as they take directorial control over multinational commodity advertising to the tune of $3 to $5 million.[4]

I point out these things to emphasize that it is not a question of holding these stars to some kind of moral or political "standards"; the portrait of the folk/rock artist as an oppositional figure does not apply to the same extent in the domain of pop. Rather, if resistance, or opposition, is to be found, it is in the subordination of the multinationals' interests to the promotion of an individual; both George Michael and Madonna made long, seminarrative minimusic videos out of Coke and Pepsi bucks that de-centered the corporation's product (Diet Coke and Pepsi) relative to their own. Madonna's piece is that of an *auteur* inscribing a thoroughly private autobiography as a masterpiece of global interest in its own right.[5]

It is often said of the postmodern that its messages are both reactionary and leftist; certainly popular texts must occupy at least both those positions to be "truly" popular, for the clearer the *partis pris,* the narrower and more specific the addressee.[6] Madonna aims for a wider audience, the widest possible, as her changing image indicates. One song that quintessentially illustrates this political both/and position is Madonna's "Papa Don't Preach," a song about a girl who decides against having an abortion but articulates this decision in assertively pro-choice terms.[7]

I start from the position that these products of late capitalism are, with almost no embarrassment, reproducers of dominant ideologies; I then ask whether there is anything else to be found in them. Fiske, in his studies of television, of Madonna, and of television audiences, argues for a *reading* of television that emphasizes not only the dominant ideology's efforts to reproduce and maintain itself, not only the representation of hegemonic forces, but also the active and empowering pleasures that are negotiated in television by subcultures, by the marginalized and subordinate. "Television and its programs do not have an 'effect' on people. Viewers and television interact," he asserts, which is another way of saying that viewing television is, for its viewers, an act of reading and that the cultural text is that which is produced by these acts of reading.[8] Television, Fiske argues, is an open text, one that enables "negotiated," resistive, and oppositional meanings to be read even as it promotes the values and serves the interests of the ruling classes. I propose to read the ways in which several of Madonna's music videos enable some oppositional readings, and I want to go a step further in describing a theologico-political discourse that moves into and out of focus in these videos. I want to make an argument for deliberately locating elements of resistance in cultural texts produced, as in this case, squarely within a patriarchal and capitalist hegemony. Of course, it is difficult to gauge whether such elements are indeed resistive, or whether, through their staging of rebellion, they, in fact, contribute to hegemony.

*The Village Voice,* given to a great deal of highbrow sneering when it comes to Madonna, remarks nastily of her autobiographical album, *Like a Prayer,* "You don't need Joseph Campbell to untangle her personal mythos."[9] I am suggesting, however, that there is a specificity to Madonna's mythos and that the specific cultural semiotics of Madonna's lyric and visual production are located within the history and popular spiriitually of an Italian American cultural imagination. Robert Orsi, in *The Madonna of 115th Street: Faith and Community in Italian Harlem, 1880–1950,* describes the mythos of the immigrant community, its relationship to the homeland and to spirituality, as well as the relationship of the second generation (the immigrants' children) to this mythos, fundamentally centered on the *domus,* household or family, as its significant unit.[10] Orsi argues that one must understand Italian immigrant culture to understand the sometimes "strange" forms its popular piety takes. The visual images of "Like a Prayer," and those of an earlier video, "Open Your Heart," bring this Italian American culture into focus so as to articulate Madonna's feminocentric street theology. Critics of "Like a Prayer" accuse it of sacrilege and even heresy. Orsi notes that there is a similar response to the forms of popular spirituality in the communities he studied, and he adds, "There is a spirit of defiance in popular spirituality . . . it allows the people to claim their religious experience as their own and to affirm the validity of their values" (Orsi, 221). Furthermore, Orsi provides a key to the central role played by the Madonna, or heavenly mother *(mamma celeste),* in Madonna's theology and provides, as well, a key to her staging of a daughterly discourse within a patriarchal family context.

Madonna Louise Veronica Ciccone was born in 1958 and grew up in Pontiac, Michigan. Her father is a first-generation Italian American, whose parents came from the Abruzzi in the twenties or thirties to work in the steel mills of Pittsburgh. Like many Italian Americans of his generation, he was upwardly mobile. Silvio Ciccone went to college to become an engineer, and he moved to the Detroit area to work in the automotive industry. Like many "patriotic" Italian Americans, Silvio Ciccone served in the U.S. military. In interviews, Madonna talks about his ambition, his work ethic, and his will to succeed materially, all of which bequeathed a legacy that is embodied in the nickname critics give to Madonna and that is also the title of one of her most famous songs, "Material Girl."

Madonna takes her name from her mother, a French Canadian woman, who lived in Bay City and who died when the singer was six. Madonna is the third of six children, the oldest daughter. After high school, she won a dance scholarship to the University of Michigan, where she remained for a year or so. She then left for New York and "worked in a donut shop" until she joined the Alvin Ailey Dance Co., after which she went to Paris, where she began to sing. Hers is a typical and typically romanticized immigrant story, an American dream come true. She affirms this myth at the beginning of the Virgin tour, where her voice-over prefaces the concert tape with the following story: "I went to New York. I had a dream. I wanted to be a big star. I didn't know anybody. I wanted to dance. I wanted to sing. I wanted to do all those things. I wanted to make people happy. I wanted to be famous. I wanted everybody to love me. I wanted to be a star. I worked really hard and my dream came true."[11]

The autobiographical album, *Like a Prayer,* makes explicit the traces of a Roman Catholic Italian American family ethos in Madonna's work.

Family is the major theme of the album: from "Till Death," an account of the violent dissolution of her marriage; to "Promise to Try," a child's hymn of mourning to the lost mother and an appeal for guidance to the Virgin herself; to "Oh Father," an indictment and a forgiving of the severe patriarch; to "Keep It Together," a song that asserts the necessity of family ties. The album also includes a distorted rendering of the Roman Catholic Act of Contrition that turns into a sort of child's parody of this frequently recited confessional prayer. The album itself is dedicated to her mother, who, she writes, "taught me how to pray." The cover playfully exploits Roman Catholic religious themes and reinscribes Madonna signifiers, most notably her navel, from her earlier work.[12] The album cover of *Like a Prayer,* which reveals Madonna's naked midriff and the crotch of her partially unbuttoned blue jeans, imitates the Rolling Stones' *Sticky Fingers* album cover. Above the crotch is printed her name, Madonna, with the **o** (positioned where her navel should be) surrounded by a cruciform drawing of light and topped with a crown (the Virgin's, presumably).[13]

Understanding Madonna in this context depends on three aspects of these video texts. First, Madonna plays with the codes of femininity to undo dominant gender codes and to assert her own power and agency (and, by extension, that of women, in general), not by rejecting the feminine but by adopting it as masquerade; that is, by posing as feminine.[14] She takes on the patriarchal codes of femininity and adds an ironic twist that asserts her power to manipulate them. The second salient aspect of Madonna's text depends on understanding a subculture that goes unread, for the most part, by the dominant culture: a connectedness to Italy—in name, of course; in tradition; and in relation to theology, to femininity, and to exile, departure, and immigration. Madonna represents herself as doubly, if not triply, exiled: She has lost her homeland (as a second-generation immigrant), she is a woman, and she is motherless. She also figures herself in a relation of generational conflict (as the oppressed daughter) within the severely patriarchal structure of the household, represented by her Italian American father.[15] The inscription of the daughterly position is a market strategy, as well, for it sets up an identification with adolescent girls, who initially constituted the majority of Madonna's fans.

These motifs appear strikingly in two videos: "Papa Don't Preach" and "Open Your Heart." "Open Your Heart" presents an early version of Madonna's musings about her Italian heritage, explicitly brought out by the 1987 Ciao Italia tour, where she attempts rudimentary conversation in the language and makes a pilgrimage to the home of her Italian relatives.

In this video, Madonna also works, dreamlike, through her relationship to an actress she idolizes, Marlene Dietrich in the *Blue Angel,* and to Dietrich's dark sister Liza Minnelli (another Italian American) in its remake, *Cabaret.* The relationship to Italy, to the father, and to her own commodification as a female sex object and a performing star are all deeply ambivalent.

The video opens with a small boy trying to gain admittance to a sort of cabaret/peep show that displays out front photographs of naked women (with black bars covering breasts and pubes) and a blue-tinted poster of Madonna, who wears a black wig. The ticket-taker will not admit the boy. We move inside, then, to Madonna's "strip show" number, where she manipulates a chair and sings, while onlookers sit in coin-operated booths that enable them to watch the show (this video also includes, for the first time in Madonna's videos, the gay spectator—a woman rather than a man). The video plays with the notion, made famous by Laura Mulvey, of the male gaze in cinema, the construction of the camera's "look" as male and its object as female. Madonna is clearly the object of these voyeuristic gazes, yet, at the same time, she fractures the monolithic nature of the camera's look with the opening and closing barriers of the booths, her direct countergaze into the camera's lens, and the cuts in the video to the little boy standing outside, placing his hands over the various body parts of the pinup women as if to cover them. Thus, the video makes the audience uncomfortably aware of the voyeuristic aspect of our enjoyment of the performance, while nevertheless staging that performance for us to watch. The camera cuts to the young boy, who, looking in a mirror, dances in a manner imitating Madonna's dance inside the cabaret, thus establishing an identification between them. When Madonna comes outside, she is dressed like the boy, with her hair similarly disheveled. McClary argues that "the young boy's game of impersonating the femme fatale and Madonna's transvestism at the end both refuse essentialist gender categories and turn sexual identity into a kind of play," a visual effect echoing the musical resistance to closure in the song itself.[16] Madonna gives the boy a chaste kiss, and they run off together. The ticket-taker runs after them and mouths some words that appear as subtitles in the video. The two "children" go skipping off into the distance.

The subtitles without translation, "Ritorna . . . ritorna . . . Madonna. Abbiamo ancora bisogno di te" [Come back . . . come back . . . Madonna. We still need you] literalize Louis Althusser's description of how ideology functions by "hailing" the subject; here, Madonna is hailed by what is represented as Italian patriarchy. In the Virgin concert tour, her real-life dad comes on stage during the song and says, "Madonna, get off that stage right now!" Madonna looks around and out into space, as if puzzled, and says: "Daddy, is that you?"

The father is figured as in the role of service to a clientele (he is a ticket-taker) and thus not in the dominant position, clueing us in on the immigrant or subcultural status of "Italian" in this context. "We" is, of course, a symbolic utterance: "We," uttered in Italian, suggests that the "we" has to do with being Italian, with "serving," and with profiting from the woman's prostitution. It is not, in other words, the "we" of the clientele. It is also a private message. Subtitles, which are meant to make what is foreign intelligible, here refuse to translate for the Anglophone viewer, staging, instead, the private in a public place; like the cabaret act and the children's flight from both it and the camera, subtitles permit voyeurism but reject voyeuristic mastery by the viewer. Meanwhile, what is also staged is the flight from an interior space (coded as "feminine" in music video) to the exterior (coded as "masculine" and "free"), with its explicitly drawn vanishing point.[17] The family triad of Madonna, child, and interpellating father, who is resisted and refused, uneasily alludes to the absent mother, who is both sacrifice (Madonna as commodity) and savior (fantasy of escape), the homeland, or motherland.

Madonna says that her father was socially ambitious, focusing on his own, and his children's, upward social mobility. This video stages Madonna's ironic resentment of the hostility and rejection she receives as a "bad woman" (whore, slut, skeezer, etc.) within the very culture that uses her for profit; and she marks that culture as Italian. The ambitions are figured as her father's. She stages, as well, the typical second-generation resentment of the make-it-in-America materialist mentality (*and* her willingness to serve those ends). Madonna is thus "martyred" to the male gaze, but she escapes into preadolescent innocence. Yet, this martyrdom is simultaneously a recognition of her power to rake in profit, to fix and fragment the male gaze, and to control men.

A third important aspect of Madonna's text is the way in which the relation to exile becomes displaced in "Like a Prayer," so that the position of exile without a home, pariah, or outsider comes to be occupied not by Italian immigrants but by African Americans. This displacement has become even more pronounced in her recent work, which consistently features Black gay dancers. This, too, has its microcultural history: Italian Harlem shared borders with Black Harlem in New York, as in many urban communities across the United States, and Italians and African Americans share a long American history of similarities and differences, conflicts and cooperations. For Madonna, there is, additionally, a personal narrative of guilt assuaged, in that Steven Bray, an African American R&B musician, composer, songwriter, and producer, gave her her first break into the business and established her on the R&B charts before she ever crossed over into pop. She subsequently abandoned him for a producer with more prestige but has since then provided him with opportunities for fame and has reunited with him to collaborate in songwriting.[18] Finally, of course, what traverses many white popular musicians' work is a sense of indebtedness and collective guilt about R&B, or Black, music, whose deliberate exclusion from avenues of mainstream stardom and, until recently, MTV itself, is well documented.[19]

"Like a Prayer" is the now-notorious video that occasioned Pepsi's withdrawal of the Madonna commercial featuring the same song but different visuals. Fundamentalist religious groups, in the United States and abroad, protested that the video was offensive, and they threatened to boycott Pepsi.[20] In part, their reaction stems from a long-standing dominant culture hostility to Italian Catholic popular spirituality: statues coming to life, bleeding (an old tradition called *ecce homo,* whereby Christ's, or a saint's, face becomes bathed in blood), stigmata, sexuality coupled with religious worship, as well as the demystification involved in developing an intimate and personal reciprocal relationship to the divine (Orsi, 225). There is also the fact that Madonna is inserted as an active agent in a story and in a role reserved for men, and in so doing, she challenges the patriarchal stranglehold on the Catholic church. The video of "Like a Prayer" can also be read as an indictment of a white male patriarchal Christianity in the name of what has happened to "white" women and to Black men.

Here, then, is Madonna's (and the video's director, filmmaker Mary Lambert's) account of the plot for "Like a Prayer":

> A girl on the street witnesses an assault on a young woman. Afraid to get involved because she might get hurt, she is frozen in fear. A black man walking down the street also sees the incident and decides to help the woman. But just then, the police arrive and arrest him. As they take him away, she looks up and sees one of the gang members who assaulted the girl. He gives her a look that says she'll be dead if she tells. The girl runs, not knowing where to go, until she sees a church. She goes in and sees a saint in a cage who looks very much like the black man on the street, and says a prayer to help her make the right decision. He seems to be crying, but she is not sure. She lies down on a pew and falls into a dream in which

> she begins to tumble in space with no one to break her fall. Suddenly she is caught by a woman who represents earth and emotional strength and who tosses her back up and tells her to do the right thing. Still dreaming, she returns to the saint, and her religious and erotic feelings begin to stir. The saint becomes a man. She picks up a knife and cuts her hands. That's the guilt in Catholicism that if you do something that feels good you will be punished. As the choir sings, she reaches an orgasmic crescendo of sexual fulfillment intertwined with her love of God. She knows that nothing's going to happen to her if she does what she believes is right. She wakes up, goes to the jail, tells the police the man is innocent, and he is freed. Then everybody takes a bow as if to say we all play a part in this little scenario.[21]

The puns, reversals, and circularities of this video, in combination with the lyrics, are dizzying. The name *Madonna* and "the voice" are constantly referred to yet never named: "When you call my name it's like a little prayer." The name is Madonna, heavenly mother, here also embodied in the singer herself. Calling the name Madonna is "like a little prayer," a prayer to the Virgin, "little," presumably, because the big one would be the "Our Father." Yet, it is "like a" prayer as well, suggesting the deep irreverence familiar to us from a former context, Madonna's "Like a Virgin." It is and it is not a prayer, the name-calling referring devoutly and daughter-like to the absent mother (whose name was Madonna) and narcissistically to the star herself. When she enters the church, she is singing: "I hear you call my name . . . and it feels like . . . Home," whereupon she closes the door to the church. Orsi mentions how the women of East Harlem called their church *la casa di mamma* (Momma's house), grafting together their real mothers in the lost homeland, Italy, and their heavenly mother (the Madonna) (Orsi, 206–7). Madonna does this, and goes a step further, returning the name Madonna to herself. The strange distortion of pronouns in the song can be attributed to this circularity: Madonna is both mother and child, both divine intervener and earthly supplicant.

After witnessing a double crime that is equated with a burning cross, Madonna falls into a dream. That this is a dream is of utmost importance, for it signals that the character Madonna is not really putting herself in the place of the redeemer but imagining herself as one (note the insistence on dreaming in the script). At this point, Madonna sings the words, "Oh God, I think I'm falling" and "Heaven help me," clichés that in the context of a dream flight and a divine encounter become literal. A Black woman catches her; the woman is a figure of divinity (a heavenly mother) and assists Madonna. She plays this role throughout; meanwhile, similarities of hair, halo, and voice establish an identification between the two women.

Back at the church, Madonna encounters the black icon (apparently a representation of Saint Martin de Porres), who comes alive through the praying Madonna's faith and who, after conferring upon the character Madonna a chaste kiss (like the chaste kiss in "Open Your Heart"), leaves the church.[22] The scene of the encounter between mortal and saint epitomizes Orsi's description of "popular religion" and the hostile reaction it provokes from the established church:

> When used to describe popular Catholic religiosity, the term conjures up images of shrouds, bloody hearts, bilocating monks, talking Madonnas [!], weeping statues, boiling vials of blood—all the symbols which the masses of Catholic Europe have found to be so powerful over the centuries and which churchmen have denigrated, often while sharing in the same or similar devotions. (Orsi, xiv)

After the icon comes to life and departs from the church, Madonna picks up his dropped dagger and receives the stigmata that mark her as having a role to play in the narrative of redemption. Stigmata, with their obvious phallic connotation, are a sensual sign of contact with the divine, a kind of holy coupling, which the film *Agnes of God* has made clear in the popular filmic imagination. This reciprocity between the worshipper and the divine is a common feature of popular piety (Orsi, 230–31 ).

During the (second) scene of the crime, an identification is established (through the camera's line of sight, through hair color and style) between Madonna and the victim. The woman's death is compared to a crucifixion (arms out, Christlike knife wound in her left side) and, perhaps, to a rape.[23] Madonna first sings the lines, "In the midnight hour I can feel your power," in the scene with the icon; now these words are given a sinister reinterpretation, suggesting the collusion between patriarchal and racist power rather than the more traditionally lyric "seductive power" of woman. The woman cries out while the lyric line is "When you call my name." The look between the ringleader and Madonna sets up a complicity (one commits a crime, one remains silent about it) that is also a challenge. The scene sets up a parallel: White men rape/kill women, white men blame it on Black men; or, women are raped/killed for being on the streets at night, Black men are thrown in jail.

With the line, "Life is a mystery, everyone must stand alone," the scene cuts to Madonna singing in front of a field of burning crosses, a visual citation of the film *Mississippi Burning,* as is the young boy in the white choir gown (referring, perhaps, to the only Black person represented in the movie as speaking out against Klan violence), who beckons to Madonna. She prays. This scene, which marks the dramatic center of the video, uses the privileged "sign" of Madonna (the cross, or crucifix, which she always wears) to set up the religious and political discourses of the text.[24]

Back at the church, Madonna is brought into the community of worshippers by the female deity. With the laying on of hands, Madonna is "commissioned," or slain in the spirit; the community is an African American community. The scene of erotic union with the saint sets up the syntax for a sentence: We see the kiss; a burning cross; Madonna; a field of burning crosses; Madonna's face looking shocked; the bleeding eye of the icon, all of which seem to suggest: Black men have been martyred for kissing white women.

At this point, the dream ends, and the choir files out. The icon returns to its position, and the bars close in front of him. Madonna wakes up, and the camera cuts to the jail cell, which is the church, now without the altar and with the American flag in its stead. We see Madonna mouthing the words "He didn't do it" to the police, who then free the Black man. A red curtain closes on the scene, which fades to Madonna in the field of burning crosses. Next, the curtain rises on the church, with all the actors—the criminals and victim and police—gathered, seated or standing in the foreground. They take a bow; the camera moves in to focus on the Black woman. Madonna and her costar, Leon Robinson, come center stage, holding hands, and they take a bow. The camera pulls back and the credit comes up: "Madonna/'Like a Prayer'/*Like a Prayer*/Sire Records." We see the actors dancing, and the curtain comes down again. Finally, "The End" is written in script on the curtain.

How can we read the political and spiritual in this melodramatic medieval morality play? On the one hand, there is the displacement of a predicament: A woman's disempowerment in relation to a religious tradition is displaced by a story about how a white woman, with the help of a female Black divinity, saves a Black man. Madonna stages the predicament of the Italian American immigrant daughter within the patriarchal institutions of family, church, and state and enacts a feminine fantasy of resolution and mediation, the quintessential Roman Catholic fantasy of sacrifice, redemption, and salvation. This feminine fantasy of resolution resembles that of the popular religious *feste* that constitute the spiritual experiences of the East Harlem women described by Orsi, as well as those of most southern Italian immigrant communities in cities all over the United States, with their specific focus on the divine intercession of the Virgin. It is the temporary empowerment of sacrifice that connects the woman to the Madonna and that allows her to play a central role within the Italian spiritual community. This role is also a trap, however, for it perpetuates an ethos of self-sacrifice and self-abnegation. The video suggests Madonna's rebellion against this entrapment by presenting the image of a successful heroine. In this fantasy of female empowerment, the mother, as divine intercessor, empowers the daughter to play the son's salvific role. The narrative attempts to break the cycle, whereby the mother's centrality to the *domus* also disempowers, by finding a place of empowerment as the mother, as the *mamma celeste,* the omnipotent woman—Madonna herself. In other contexts, Madonna will figure herself as playfully and parodically phallic, but here she remains emphatically feminine, even while enacting the son's castration in the stigmata.[25] Yet, the trace of a self-wounding sacrifice remains, for at the end of the play there is a corpse, the young woman, who is also a double for Madonna, thus reminding us that phallic power also kills.

There is clearly guilt here, a guilt Madonna shares with many white rock and pop musicians who have been making "Black America" the subject of their videos, for theirs is a musical tradition grounded on a violation and a theft, the appropriation of musical forms originating with African American musicians who were unable, in racist America, to profit. That appropriation made millions of dollars for these white musicians. But if we take seriously the cultural specificities of this particular white woman (Madonna), cultural specificities that may be applicable to communities larger than the private fantasies of one individual, then the mixture of religious traditions in the video and the intertwining of two political histories may constitute a different sort of text.

Orsi points out that southern Italian immigrants were often associated with Africans by their northern compatriots, by the Protestant majority, and by the established Catholic church.[26] Chromatically black Madonnas and saints abound in southern Italian and Catholic worship. The video, too, sets up a chromatic proximity through the racial indeterminacy of the woman who is killed and, most markedly, through hair: Madonna's hair is her natural brown (she says it makes her feel more Italian) and curled into ringlets, the female deity's hair is similarly brown and curly, while the female victim's hair is black and curly. The only blond characters are the white men who attack. Madonna says she grew up in a

Black neighborhood and that her playmates and friends were Black. In a *Rolling Stone* interview, she notes apologetically that when she was little she wanted to be Black.[27] Likewise, there is a tradition of African Americans in northern urban settings who identify themselves as "Italian" in order to pass or to protect themselves from the full force of U.S. racism in the majority community.

This fantasy thus attempts to reach out beyond the private ethnic imagination to create a bridge to another culture's popular piety, itself grounded in an experience of exile and oppression. McClary notes how the song merges the traditional solemnity of Catholic organ music with the joyous rhythm of gospel, thus musically reinforcing the fusion of the two communities.[28] More ethnographic research might reveal the ways in which these communities met or meet (East and West Harlem) in the neighborhoods of New York City or Detroit and might also reveal what is produced from the similarities in their family structures, spiritualities, and their historical experiences. The media, the press, and even resistive subcultural narratives, such as Spike Lee's film *Do the Right Thing,* suggest that the dominant representation of intercultural relations is a narrative of conflict. The alternative vision of community presented in this video challenges the complicity with hegemonic violence of Spike Lee's cultural politics. I wonder to what extent the rareness of this fantasy is related to the fact that it is a feminine fantasy of mediation, a woman's representation of the possibilities of connectedness rather than conflict. In other words, one difference between the cooperative interaction narrated here and the representations of violent conflict is that this representation is feminocentric and grounded in a spiritual vision. Points of contact between communities are imagined not only in terms of conflicting and competing ethnicities but also in terms of communicative openings, the affirming interactions and the potential for communication between contiguous cultural groups who also share some experiences of oppression within a majority community hostile to their presence.[29]

The visual bridges that connect the two communities are identity and icon. Identity connects Madonna and the Black priestess, the Madonna, a phallic woman, the "muse," who answers Madonna's prayers and assists her, who participates as her mirror in the narrative. The identification, furthermore, extends beyond two individuals; Madonna does not redeem alone, she seeks assistance from her Black double and from the community of worship whom the woman represents and leads. The icon is the Madonna icon par excellence: The cross, or crucifix, the calvary for African Americans, and the burning cross of the Ku Klux Klan all remind us that Catholics and African Americans (as well as Jews) were targets of this nationalist project conducted in the name of the cross. It is no wonder, then, that the first to speak out about this video, condemning its irreligiosity and sacrilege, were fundamentalist religious leaders and televangelists—Jimmy Swaggart, Donald Wildmon, Bishop Gracida of Texas, and the American Family Association.[30]

This story of how a white girl learns to "do the right thing" and succeeds, with the help of a Black woman and the Black community, depends on the scapegoat and the saved being Black and in a position of even more radical disempowerment relative to the police and to "America." As the recognition of a predicament, the narrative is politically progressive; in its resolution, however, it participates in the myth of the great white savior, marked here as a traditionally feminine wish fulfillment in its simultaneous desire for power and approval. The absent-mother-returned-as-divine-intercessor-become-Black mitigates that usurpation, covering also for the guilt of the white woman's erotic appropriation of the man she saves (the Black woman says "I'll take you there" just before the camera cuts to the kiss). The narrative itself signals this irony through the explicit reference to fantasy and dream as the contexts for wish fulfillment and through the framing device of the play, which distances the events from anything that might occur in "real life." Madonna's hyperfemininity in the video and her association with the children in the choir attempt to convince us that she is, indeed, a daughter, a mediator, and not the powerful superstar Madonna, so that we can "believe in" the power and agency of the other woman. But the governing irony of the text as a whole, an irony that remains unstated, is that the mother, the Madonna, *is* Madonna; the Black woman is "merely" a screen.

It is in its relation to the "Other woman" then, to use Gayatri Spivak's term, that the political blind spot in the narrative, and in its reception, appears.[31] We would not expect a Madonna commercial to assume any subject-position other than that of its protagonist, Madonna. Though in the media we can see interviews with Leon Robinson and hear him speak about his role, with regard to the other woman there is silence, so much silence that I do not know her name. This necessarily questions the gender/race empowerment of the representation in its interaction with a hegemonic racism that traditionally suppresses nonstereotypic representations of women of color. The erasure of the embodied African American woman, the Madonna of the narrative—Madonna's double—is even more marked, because she is the only character other than Madonna to have a solo part in the song. The Pepsi commercial merely reinforces the interchangeability of that image, for the gospel solo is sung not by the woman we see here but by a more stereotypical—maternal and desexualized—member of the choir who is, therefore, more "fitting" for the traditional worship setting of the service.

A bold fantasy of intercultural relatedness that will not obey the rules of the dominant culture's narrative of necessary interracial conflict; a fantasy of self-aggrandizement that recognizes itself as such; a world where women are both heroic and omnipotent, where female agency can be effective. A world, too, where the authorities are benign, where police will admit that they have made an honest mistake. A world where Black women approve of white women's desires for the leading role in the narrative of African American salvation. As Andrew Ross has insisted, "We cannot attribute any purity of political expression to popular culture, although we can locate its power to identify areas and desires that are relatively opposed, alongside those that are clearly complicit, to the official culture."[32] In celebrating the proto-political of Madonna's texts, academic feminists must recognize, as well, the self-aggrandizement these fantasies serve. Madonna is not, after all, a revolutionary feminist (*pace* Camille Paglia); she is a female multimillionaire.[33] MTV reveals its political inadequacies in the very postmodernism of its premise: It is the individual, or the private subject, who makes cultural meaning, rather than communities or collectivities, and individuals may become empowered through those meanings.[34]

So why read MTV, and why read it in this way? For one thing, it's pleasurable—pleasurable because these texts are there to be read and talked and gossiped about publicly in the culture. They often bridge class gaps and, at least in my experience, have made for some interesting interracial, intergenerational, and interfaith conversations that have served as occasions for political debate. Almost anyone can participate in such debates and conversations, since Madonna, MTV, and television, in general, are available to the many rather than the few. If the news constructs, produces, and mediates hegemonic national fantasies under the guise of a reality principle, why not frankly confront and contest it with alternative fantasies explicitly produced in the name of pleasure?

At the same time, the Left cannot retreat into anachronistic puritanism with regard to what it calls the new opiate of (young) people—"mass" culture—or else it cedes a strategic terrain of cultural politics all too clearly recognized as such by the New Right. These texts may suggest strategies for the empowerment of the subordinated, marginal, and decentered in advanced capitalist culture, strategies that are not anachronistic but born of the medium of advanced capital and the gaps that are produced within it. I am interested in the ways such strategies, and such technology, may be used to produce significant counterhegemonic forces within a culture whose ruling classes seem to have perfected the art of containment. If Gil Scott-Heron is correct in claiming that "the revolution will not be televised" (and I am no longer convinced that he is), it may, nevertheless, be the case that through strategic articulations of these popular cultural texts, something "like a" revolution can be imagined.

## NOTES

The use of initial caps in writing "Black" is a deliberate political gesture on my part, referring not to a color but to a political designation.

1. Angela McRobbie, *Feminism and Youth Culture: From "Jackie" to "Just Seventeen"* (Boston: Unwin Hyman, 1991); Lisa Lewis, Gender *Politics and MTV: Voicing the Difference* (Philadelphia: Temple University Press, 1990). See also Simon Frith and Angela McRobbie, "Rock and Sexuality," *Screen Education* 29 (1978–1979): 3–19. I owe a debt of gratitude to numerous people who have assisted in this study of Madonna: Nancy Vickers, in particular, for her studies of the lyric tradition, MTV, and popular music; Tom Kalin (see "Media Kids: Tom Kalin on Pussy Power," *Artforum International* [September 1991]: 19–21); Charles Hamm; the audiences, mainly students, who have heard and criticized this paper; and Cirri Nottage and Melinda Weinstein, whose research assistance has been invaluable.

2. See, in particular, Susan McClary, "Living to Tell: Madonna's Resurrection of the Fleshly," *Genders* 7 (March 1990): 1–21; and Lewis, *Gender Politics and MTV.*

3. Andrew Ross, *No Respect: Intellectuals and Popular Culture* (New York and London: Routledge, 1989); see also his "Hacking Away at the Counterculture," in *Technoculture,* ed. Constance Penley and Andrew Ross (Minneapolis: University of Minnesota Press, 1991), 107–34: "The significance of these cultures lies in their embryonic or *protopolitical* languages and technologies of opposition to dominant or parent systems of rules. If hackers lack a 'cause,' then they are certainly not the first youth culture to be characterized in this dismissive way. In particular, the left has suffered from the lack of a cultural politics capable of recognizing the power of cultural expressions that do not wear a mature political commitment on their sleeves" (122). For a critique of the too-rapid dismissal of neo-Frankfurt School leftist intellectuals' suspicion of mass culture, see Meaghan Morris, "Banality in Cultural Studies," in *Logics of Television: Essays in Cultural Criticism,* ed. Patricia Mellencamp (Bloomington: Indiana University Press, 1990), 14–43: "There is an active process going on in both of discrediting—by direct dismissal (Baudrillard) or covert inscription as Other (cultural studies)—the voices of grumpy feminists and cranky leftists ('Frankfurt School' can do duty for both). To discredit such voices is, as I understand it, one of the immediate political functions of the current boom in cultural studies (as distinct from the intentionality of projects invested by it). To discredit a voice is something very different from displacing an analysis which has become outdated, or revis-

ing a strategy which no longer serves its purpose. It is to characterize a fictive position from which anything said can be dismissed as already heard" (25).

4. Leslie Savan, "Desperately Selling Soda," *Village Voice* 34, no. 11, 14 Mar. 1989, 47. See also Bill Zehme, "Madonna: The *Rolling Stone* Interview," *Rolling Stone,* 23 Mar. 1989, 52.

5. Lewis points out how the traditional opposition between rock and pop (serious/frivolous, political/apolitical, etc.) has often been used to marginalize female vocalists by trivializing the genre with which they are most frequently associated. See Lewis, *Gender Politics and MTV,* 29–33. For an analysis of the Madonna Pepsi commercial, see Nancy Vickers, "Maternalism and the Material Girl," in *Embodied Voices: Female Vocality in Western Culture,* ed. Leslie Dunn and Nancy Jones (Cambridge University Press, forthcoming).

6. John Fiske, "British Cultural Studies," in *Channels of Discourse: Television and Contemporary Criticism,* ed. Robert C. Allen (Chapel Hill: University of North Carolina Press, 1987), 254–89: "The television text can only be popular if it is open enough to admit a range of negotiated meanings, through which various social groups can find meaningful articulations of their own relationship to the dominant ideology. Any television text must, then, be polysemic, for the heterogeneity of the audience requires a corresponding heterogeneity of meanings in the text" (267).

7. For an interesting and suggestive survey of audience response to this video and to "Open Your Heart," see Jane D. Brown and Laurie Schulze, "The Effects of Race, Gender, and Fandom on Audience Interpretations of Madonna's Music Videos," *Journal of Communication* 40, no. 2 (Spring 1990): 88–102.

8. John Fiske, *Television Culture* (London and New York: Methuen, 1987), 19; see also his "British Cultural Studies," 260. Much of Fiske's discussion here is taken from Stuart Hall, "Encoding/Decoding," in *Culture, Media, Language,* ed. Stuart Hall et al. (London: Hutchinson, 1980): 128–39. I take to heart the critique offered by the "disgruntled" Morris in "Banality in Cultural Studies" with regard to Fiske's and others' "making the best of things" approach to popular culture as a way of salvaging leftist energy from mass media, yet I also find it necessary continually to rehearse arguments for attending at all seriously to elements of resistance within these texts. At the same time, my own project takes some distance from Fiske's particular approach to cultural studies and Madonna by its in-depth focus on an "ethnic" and "female" subcultural specificity. In this regard, it resembles more the "new philological" project of cultural critics such as Stephanie Hull, though our (political) conclusions diverge significantly ("Madonna's Vogue," Paper presented at session number 504: "Essentialism, Philology, and Popular Culture," Modern Language Association Annual Meeting, San Francisco, 29 Dec. 1991). In one of the most intellectually serious treatments of Madonna as a postmodern text, Ramona Curry cites Richard Dyer's discussion of stars as composite images and argues that one should read Madonna as an "intertextual conglomerate": "Meanings of any given text arise not predominantly in readers' experience of its construction but in their discursive interactions with it in the context of myriad associated texts" (see "Madonna from Marilyn to Marlene—Pastiche and/or Parody?" *Journal of Film and Video* 42, no. 2 [Summer 1990]: 15–30; in particular, 16).

9. Steve Anderson, "Forgive Me Father," *Village Voice,* 4 Apr. 1989, 67.

10. Robert Anthony Orsi, *The Madonna of 115th Street: Faith and Community in Italian Harlem, 1880–1950* (New Haven and London: Yale University Press, 1985); hereafter cited in my text as Orsi. Luc Sante, in "Unlike a Virgin," *New Republic,* 20 Aug. and 27 Aug. 1990, 25–29, modifies his acerbic tone when he discusses Madonna's Catholism: "If, at this point, there is any aspect of Madonna's act that seems independent of calculation, it is her preoccupation with the Catholic mysteries" (28). For a high theological reading of Madonna, especially "Like a Prayer," see Andrew Greeley, "Like a Catholic: Madonna's Challenge to Her Church," *America,* 13 May 1989, 447–9.

11. "Madonna Live: The Virgin Tour," Warner Music Video, Boy Toy, Inc., 1985.

12. For a meditation on Madonna's navel, see Harold Jaffe, *Madonna and Other Spectacles* (New York: PAJ Publications, 1988), 7–12.

13. The cover design also puns on the Elizabethan meaning of **o** as a designation for female genitals; on this cover, Madonna makes a joke about her phallic power by combining the Rolling Stones blue jeans, which "contain" the phallus, with the **o** of her own phallic absence.

14. For the notion of femininity as masquerade, see Joan Riviere, "Womanliness as a Masquerade," and Stephen Heath, "Joan Riviere and the Masquerade," in *Formations of Fantasy,* ed. Victor Burgin, James Donald, and Cora Kaplan (1986; reprint, London and New York: Routledge, 1989), 35–61; see also Mary Russo, "Female Grotesques: Carnival and Theory," in *Feminist Studies/Critical Studies,* ed. Teresa de Lauretis (Bloomington: Indiana University Press, 1986), 213–29. Lewis *(Gender Politics and MTV)* convincingly argues the case for female empowerment and gender code manipulation in the works of several female pop musicians from the point of view of authorial control and production, on the one hand, to fan response and the issue of female address, on the other hand; Fiske ("British Cultural Studies") points to the evidence of female fan response; while McClary's study (*Feminine Endings: Music, Gender, and Sexuality* [Minneapolis: University of Minnesota Press, 1991]) traces, among other things, a genealogy of female musicianship and struggles for empowerment that "culminates" in Madonna.

15. This notion of the household could be extended to include not only the family but the music industry, as well, for this upstart female has not always been well received in the traditionally white male bastion that is MTV.

16. McClary, "Living to Tell," 13. See also Curry's reading of "Open Your Heart," which makes the argument that the video constructs an "alternative audience address" that champions "oppressed social and racial groups" (see "Madonna from Marilyn to Marlene," 19–20). Brown and Schulze found that white girls did not react to the pornographic performance as parody, although they did interpret the final scene as an escape into childhood innocence (see "The Effects of Race, Gender, and Fandom," 97–99).

17. Lewis discusses the coding in music videos of male and female spaces and the creation of female address videos through an initial appropriation of what is coded as "male space," primarily the street. See "Female Address in Music Video," *Journal of Communication Inquiry* 11, no. 1 (Winter 1987): 73–84; also "Form and Female Authorship in Music Video," *Communication* 9 (1987): 355–77. She develops this dis-

cussion at greater length in *Gender Politics and MTV*. For a feminist critique of subculture study that focuses on the street as a site of youth activity, see Angela McRobbie, "Settling Accounts with Subcultures: A Feminist Critique," *Screen Education* 34 (Spring 1980): 37–49. McClary, in "Living to Tell," 12–13, and Lewis, in *Gender Politics and MTV*, 141–43, also provide (different) interpretations of "Open Your Heart."

18. Christopher Connelly, "Madonna Goes All the Way," *Rolling Stone*, 22 Nov. 1984, 15–20, 81. Subsequent to the making of "Vogue" and *Truth or Dare*, there has been a dispute about Madonna's business relationship to dancers José Gutierrez and Luis Camacho; here, too, the politics of race plays a subtextual role. See "Madonna's Boyz Express Themselves to Jonathan Van Meter," *NYQ* 13, 26 Jan. 1992.

19. See the NAACP's pamphlet *"The Discordant Sound of Music": A Report on the Record Industry* (Baltimore: The National Association for the Advancement of Colored People, 23 Mar. 1987). I thank Nancy Vickers for providing me with this document.

20. James Cox, "Pepsi Cans Its Madonna Ad under Pressure," *USA Today*, 4 Apr. 1989; Karen Phillips, "Madonna Canned: Pepsi Pulls the Plug on Controversial Ads," *New York Post*, 5 Apr. 1989; "Madonna's 'Like a Prayer' Clip Causes a Controversy," *Rolling Stone*, 20 Aug. 1989. Pepsi denied the charge (see Bruce Haring, "Pepsi Denies Pulling Madonna Spots," *Billboard*, 18 Mar. 1989), but this commercial, unlike George Michael's Diet Coke commercial, no longer appeared on television.

21. Cited by Stephen Holden, "Madonna Re-Creates Herself—Again," *New York Times*, Sunday, 19 Mar. 1989, Arts and Leisure section. There are many imagistic, verbal, and thematic resemblances between the video "Like a Prayer" and Mary Lambert's earlier film *Siesta*, starring Ellen Barkin, indicating that intertextuality occurs on the directorial level, as well, so that not only the star but also (at least) the director contributes to the composite, or conglomerate, text that is Madonna. The centering of female subjectivity in *Siesta* also supports an argument for Lambert's important role in constructing the structure of address in "Like a Prayer." I thank Nancy Vickers for drawing these similarities to my attention and Mary Lambert for her corroboration of my reading of these texts as feminocentric.

22. Sante, "Unlike a Virgin," 28.

23. Freud refers to experiments finding sexual symbolism in dreams about stabbing and shooting in *The Interpretation of Dreams*, vols. 4 and 5 of *The Standard Edition of the Complete Psychological Works of Sigmund Freud*, trans. James Strachey (London: Hogarth Press, 1953), 419.

24. *Home*, an important, if not central, term of the text, is repeated again in this scene (Madonna in the field of burning crosses), referring back to and reinterpreting the scene in which she enters the church. There, *home* seemed a relatively positive term, although the conflation between the church and the police station at the end of the video suggests an ambivalence about the positioning of the institution of the church. In this scene, however, *home* is ironic and constitutes an indictment of racist and patriarchal America.

25. The *Rolling Stone* photographs of Madonna (Zehme, "Madonna: The *Rolling Stone* Interview") focus on the phallic Madonna with shots of her crotch and the now-infamous "phallic woman" gesture—first used parodically by Michael Jackson, then deployed (post-Madonna) by Roseanne Barr—of crotch-grabbing. On the parodic use of this gesture, and on Madonna's "imitation" of Michael Jackson, see Marjorie

Garber, "Fetish Envy," *October* 54 (Fall 1990): 45–56. On Madonna's later phallicism, see also Sante, "Unlike a Virgin," 27: "Oh yes, and there were those male dancers adorned with breasts that flopped like so many pairs of flaccid phalli while her own looked like armor-plated projectiles."

26. Orsi, *The Madonna of 115th Street,* 160: "Americans and American Catholics distinguished the northern Italian racial type ('Germanic') from the southern ('African'), a tendency that may have contributed to the identification of East Harlem with West Harlem. In 1912, Norman Thomas admitted that American-born Protestants in Harlem did not appreciate the presence of Italians in their churches." Sante cannot resist a racist remark about Madonna's ethnicity, though he says it isn't one: "In her 'Ciao Italia' video, decked out in various gymnastic outfits and body-pumping to the screams of tens of thousands in a soccer stadium in Turin, Madonna looks perfectly able to make the trains run on time. (Do not mistake this for an ethnic slur: her last name could just as easily be O'Flanagan and the setting Oslo or Kalamazoo.)" ("Unlike a Virgin," 27).

27. Zehme, "Madonna: The *Rolling Stone* Interview," 58: "'When I was a little girl, I wished I was black. All my girlfriends were black. I was living in Pontiac, Michigan, and I was definitely the minority in the neighborhood. White people were scarce there. All of my friends were black, and all the music I listened to was black.'"

28. McClary, "Living to Tell," 14–15.

29. Mark D. Hulsether, writing for the Left progressive Christian journal *Christianity and Crisis,* forcefully affirms his sense of the radical message of "Like a Prayer": "This video is one of the most powerful statements of the basic themes from liberation theologies I have seen in the mainstream media. It sharply rejects racist perversions of Christianity such as the Ku Klux Klan; emphasizes Jesus' human solidarity or identity with victims of oppression; places the cross in the context of sociopolitical struggle and persecution; and presents the church as a place of collective empowerment toward transforming justice. In the context of racism, it promotes African-American culture and combats both police violence and the scapegoating of black males. In a way that converges with some feminist theology, it stresses the importance of the erotic in conceptualizing faith" (see "Madonna and Jesus," *Christianity and Crisis,* 15 July 1991, 234–36, especially 235).

30. Cox, "Pepsi Cans Its Madonna Ad under Pressure."

31. Gayatri Chakravorty Spivak, "Imperialism and Sexual Difference," in *Contemporary Literary Criticism: Literary and Cultural Studies,* ed. Robert Con Davis and Ronald Schleifer (New York and London: Longman, 1989), 517–29.

32. Ross, *No Respect,* 10.

33. Camille Paglia, "Madonna—Finally, A Real Feminist," *New York Times,* 4 Dec. 1990. Both Paglia and Madonna are called feminists by the press, but feminists *sui generis.* In my own understanding of feminism this is not possible, since *feminism,* by any political definition, implies collective political struggle, distinguishing it from a liberal bourgeois ideology of individualism, even when the individual is marked as female.

34. Perhaps this is a sign of capitalism's triumph from within the postmodern, for the construction of the private subject as addressee and agent seems to be simply the extension of bourgeois individualism.

JANELLE L. WILSON AND GERALD E. MARKLE

# JUSTIFY MY IDEOLOGY: MADONNA AND TRADITIONAL VALUES

1992

*This is a close, academic reading of the video for "Justify My Love," which was banned by MTV and holds the distinction of being the first-ever "video single" released for sale.*—Eds.

*I present my view on life in my work. The provocation slaps you in the face and makes you take notice, and the ambiguity makes you say, well, is it that or is it that. You are forced to have a discourse about it in your mind.*

*—Madonna (Arrington 58)*

*[Madonna's] personality is an outrageous blend of Little Orphan Annie, Margaret Thatcher, and Mae West. (Skow)*

**Introduction**

Some view Madonna as a serious artist; others see her as an outrage; still others think she is both. The Vatican has denounced her. Teenage fans, called "Madonna Wannabes," idolize her. The Queer nation beatifies her. Some feminist scholars praise her, while others damn her work. She has been described as "The pop-tart singer with the trashy outfits and the hi-there belly button;" "brassy, trashy, junk-jiggling, stage-stomping"; "queen of oxymoron"; "flesh and blood become pop archetype: Vamp, Tramp, Star, Madonna"; "the world's most famous—and infamous—female entertainer." Scholars "spin doctoral dissertations based on her canon" (Arrington 56).

Madonna is a cultural icon. Our intent is neither to praise nor to bury. After a brief discussion of Madonna and her work, we focus on perhaps her most controversial video, "Justify My Love," a work which was banned from MTV. Our intent is to engage in ideological criticism: to analyze this work and assess the values and ideology which underlie it. In so doing, we hope to contextualize Madonna's work and show the degree to which it supports, and the extent to which it departs from, dominant American values.

### Madonna

"Madonna," a name which would provoke outrage among some, is her real name. Madonna Louise Veronica Ciccone was born on August 16, 1959 in Bay City, Michigan. "Madonna is a strange name," she said, "I felt there was a reason. I felt like I had to live up to my name" (qtd. in Arrington 57).

Growing up as the eldest girl in a strict Catholic family, Madonna saw herself as the "quintessential Cinderella." Her mother died when she was a child, and later, her father married their housekeeper. Eventually, she won a dance scholarship to the University of Michigan and later worked with the Alvin Ailey dance company. At Danceteria, a Manhattan club, she launched her career by combining song and dance into a successful act.[1]

Madonna's Catholicism has played an important role in her life. "Once you're a Catholic," she has said, "you're always a Catholic—in terms of your feelings of guilt and remorse and whether you've sinned or not" (qtd. in Zehme 180). Her rebellion, she claims, is not theological, but institutional: against "the priests and all the men who made the rules while I was growing up" (qtd. in Arrington 56). She claims that her use of religious symbols is not sacrilegious. Her motive for using the crosses and rosaries, she continues, is to

> take these iconographic symbols that are held away from everybody in glass cases and say, here is another way of looking at it. . . . The idea is to bring it down to a level that everyone can relate to. (qtd. in Arrington 58)

She may have discarded strict Catholic doctrine, but she retained—or developed—"a unique kind of spirituality that . . . permeates her life and work" (Murphy B-14).

Madonna's success and popularity are linked to the birth of the cable television music network (MTV) in 1981. According to the *New York Times,* "Music video has created a new kind of star, exemplified by Madonna, whose meticulously crafted four-minute fantasies shake the electronic media as easily as she shimmies her hips" (Pareles 1). She has been called "the firstborn child of MTV" (Campbell D3). The new MTV format and Madonna's style are especially suited for one another: "The quick cuts and brash iconoclasm that made MTV the voice and look of a generation found a perfect match in Madonna" (Ayers 21).

Works such as "Like a Virgin," "Material Girl," "Like a Prayer," "Papa Don't Preach," and "Express Yourself" represent Madonna's rebelliousness toward conventional, limiting notions of sex, femininity and religiosity. Madonna "has always reveled in making the establishment gasp. And every time she's done it, she's used video" (Ayers 22). Describing her concert performance of "Like a Virgin," one critic concluded that she was "mocking virginity, mocking sex, mocking, some might say, the solemn temple of rock 'n' roll itself" (Skow 77). Her 1991 *Truth or Dare* version of this song/video features Madonna simulating masturbation while two male dancers on each side of her attempt to win her attention. Her denial of the men and her ability to satisfy herself expressed both female independence and sensuality.[2]

**"Justify My Love"**

Madonna's videos have dealt with controversial themes such as teen pregnancy, voyeurism and bondage. Her work in general—and this banned video, in particular—has generated a considerable amount of commentary from writers for popular magazines. One critic sees the video as "a soft-core portrayal of an omni-sexual interlude in a hotel room" (Johnson). Still another terms it "sleek, fairly harmless stuff," yet admits that it is "a tad more risqué than the usual MTV fare" (Cocks).

The video, released in the fall of 1990, was banned by MTV because "the cable television station deemed it too sexually explicit to broadcast" (Philips G13). According to MTV vice-president Abbey Konowitch, the network has "frequently" had concerns about the content of the star's videos. "You take the black lingerie, sex scenes and flesh out of 'Justify My Love,' and you've got 10 seconds of ill-focused dancing" (Hinckley A6).

Because it was banned, the video received considerable media attention. There is nothing "like censorship, real or imagined, to create headlines and create lineups at the box office" (Gordon 13). In December, 1990, the banned video was shown on *Nightline*. The program, which received excellent ratings, promoted the sale of the video, as well as *The Immaculate Collection,* the album on which "Justify My Love" was the lead single (Cocks 74). Madonna also sold "several hundred thousand copies" of the video, each at $12.99, through Warner Reprise Video (Goodman 55).

## Method

Our analysis of "Justify My Love" was naturalistic. We recorded observations under two headings: "lyrics" and "action" and produced the "Video Analysis Flow Sheet" shown in Table 1. In the first column, "Lyrics," we simply recorded the actual words of the song. In the second column, "Action," we recorded the actors' actions and interactions and attempted to interpret their role-related and other meanings. We were particularly interested in the relationship between the lyrics and the action and sequences of events (the plot), of the video. Each column—lyrics and action—of Table 1 can be analyzed separately (i.e., "down"), but the table can also be read "across" for a more holistic interpretation of the video.

## Video as Text

The video begins with the blurred image of a male dancer, who appears effeminate and moves smoothly and expressively. He sometimes masks his face with his sweeping movements, which creates a mystical aura about him. This dancer serves as a transitional tool: Between dramatic scene changes, his elastic movements ease the viewer from one scene to the next.

The setting is a hotel. Madonna, looking as though she might faint, walks unsteadily down a long corridor. She drops her suitcase and then holds her head. The opening lines of the song are quite romantic: "I wanna kiss you in Paris, I wanna hold your hand in Rome, I wanna run naked in a rainstorm, Make love in a train . . . cross country."

A male protagonist enters the picture. She looks at him, caresses his face, and says: "Wanting, needing, waiting, for you to justify my love. . . ." She begins to take her long, black coat off and, underneath, she wears only a black lace bra, black stockings and stiletto heels. As their faces move closer together and they begin to kiss, the image is momentarily blurred.

The scene shifts to the bedroom. Madonna is sitting on the bed, and the man is standing in the doorway. After she says "okay," he comes toward her. This man—Madonna's lover—has a masculine and rough appearance. He has the start of a beard, his collar is up, his shirt is unbuttoned, and he has a tattoo. Madonna is in bed with her lover. Then, suddenly, she is in the bed with an androgynous individual who wears dark eye makeup and has a smooth face; Madonna's lover sits and watches.

Madonna is explicit about the kind of relationship she wants with the androgynous character: "I don't wanna be your mother, I don't wanna be your sister either. I just wanna be your lover. I wanna have your baby." They kiss and the scene then shifts to the dancer, followed by Madonna in bed with the "original" (who initially greeted her in the hall) lover.

**Table 1**
Video Analysis Flow Sheet

| Lyrics | Action |
|---|---|
| | Male dancer; Madonna walks down hall of hotel, carrying a suitcase and looking faint. |
| | Female in doorway—men's haircut, breasts showing. |
| | Madonna drops suitcase, holds her head. |
| . . . | She has her back against the wall, hands on neck. Facial expression relaxes. |
| I wanna run naked in a rainstorm | Hands on face, neck, chest. |
| Make love in a train . . . cross country | Crouching on the floor, touching her thighs; starts taking off her jacket. |
| You put this in me. | Man enters the picture. |
| So now what? | Looks pleadingly up at man. |
| | Stands up and faces man. |
| . . . | Caresses his face. |
| | Kisses him (image blurs). |
| | Man and woman in other room. |
| | Dancer (by window). |
| | Bedroom—Madonna on bed. Madonna's lover takes his shirt off. He wears two crosses around his neck—one with Jesus on it. |
| | He begins to lay her down. |
| | She holds him back. |
| | Dancer. |
| . . . | Faces close different person (androgynous). |
| | Turns her head to the side |
| | Faces him again; they kiss. |
| I wanna have your baby | |
| Kiss me, that's right, kiss me | |
| Waiting, needing, waiting | Kissing. |
| For you to justify my love | |
| Yearning, burning for you | |
| to justify my love. | Dancer (crucifix on wall). |
| | Man and androgynous person. |
| . . . | The "original" man is in bed with her now. |
| | Dancer. |
| | She is standing, looking in the mirror and looking troubled, serious. |
| Talk to me, tell me your dreams | Looks seductively at him. |
| Am I in them? | The woman with a man's appearance having no shirt on walks into the room, aggressively grabs the man, tilts his head back, and touches him up and down. |

| | |
|---|---|
| Tell me your fears—Are you scared?<br>Tell me your stories<br>I'm afraid of who you are<br>We can fly | Madonna is lying on her back, alone; she stretches her arms out as she says "fly"; her arms extend past her head and her hands are crossed. The scene shifts to an image of Jesus in the sacrificial position. |
| | Dancer. |
| | Two people—trina and woman?— |
| . . . | He is looking at her sympathetically like something is wrong. |
| Love me, | Dancer. |
| That's right, love me.<br>I wanna be your baby | Madonna is on top of the man in bed. |
| | Madonna smiles; there is a close-up of androgynous person, blurred at first, then clear; shifts to Madonna and lover in a blurred fashion. |
| . . . | He runs his hand and face down her body. |
| | Man with mustache. |
| | Dancer. |
| I'm hoping (?) | Two androgynous persons paint mustaches on each other and Madonna giggles. |
| Ready, for you to justify my love<br>To justify my love | Kissing. |
| Wanting, to justify | Another couple is shown—He has his hand on her jaw and she is looking away from him. |
| | Dancer (crucifix on wall in background). |
| | Two men on couch, one woman lying down with her head on one of the men's laps. |
| Praying, to justify | Madonna comes around the corner. |
| To justify my love | Her lover reaches out toward her. |
| | She hurries down the corridor, laughing, excited, happy. |

When Madonna stands in front of the mirror and says, "What are you gonna do? What are you gonna do?" her facial expression takes on a more serious, scared look. She says, "talk to me, tell me your dreams—am I in them?" Her facial expression changes from distressed to playful; she looks seductively at her lover. A woman with a man's appearance—and wearing suspenders but nothing above the waist—walks into the room and aggressively grabs the man, tilts his head back, and touches him. The image blurs as she does this.

Madonna says to her lover: "Tell me your fears—are you scared? Tell me your stories; I'm afraid of who you are. We can fly." The scene then shifts to an image of Jesus on the cross.

Madonna shyly smiles and says to her lover, in bed: "I wanna be your baby." There is a close-up of an androgynous person, blurred at fast, but then clear. The scene shifts again to a blurred Madonna and lover. She repeats: "Wanting, needing, waiting, for you to justify my love" and he runs his hand and face down her body. The dancer is shown and then two androgynous persons paint mustaches on each other and Madonna giggles at them.

Another couple is shown briefly—the man with his hand on the woman's jaw. She looks away from him and then the dancer is shown. The most obvious portrayal of a homosexual couple comes near the end of the video: Two men are sitting together on the couch and another woman is lying down on the couch with her hand on one of these men's laps, and she is laughing.

### Analysis

This video is sensual, spiritual and romantic all at once. But, most importantly, it is erotic. Madonna's tone and bodily movements are seductive. Words such as "wanting," "needing," "waiting," "hoping," "yearning" and "burning," expressed in her tone and accompanying her apparent "ever-readiness" to have sex, create one erotic scene after another. Such eroticism is, by traditional standards, non-normative. The effeminate dancer, the homosexual behavior and the action and appearance of the masculine woman in the video also represent behavior outside the accepted norms.

Yet there is a flip-side to this eroticism. In both the lyrics and the actions, the more obvious erotic and sensual themes are interwoven with traditional themes. The very notion of "justifying love" has traditional, Christian roots. Not only is Madonna "wanting, needing, waiting," and "hoping" for the man to justify her love, she is also "praying" for this justification.

One of the lines in the song is "I wanna have your baby." What greater justification for making love—from a biblical standpoint—than to make a baby? She explicitly says: "Love me, that's right, love me." The traditional notion of love being a precondition and a justification for sex is depicted here. She next says, "I wanna be your baby." Again, a traditional gender role characteristic—that the seductress is actually a man's possession.

The entire sexual interlude begins as Madonna gives permission—and thus takes control—for her lover's entry into the room. As soon as she says "okay," he begins to walk toward her. The next line, "I wanna know you," reflects a traditional requirement for making love, atypical of casual sex. Just as obvious, however, is the pun on the biblical meaning of "knowing."

One of the lines in the song seems entirely out of context: "Poor is the man whose pleasures depend on the condition of another." Nevertheless, its biblical tone and style fit into a video which features so many religious allusions. About halfway through the video, Madonna lies down on her back, alone, and says "we can fly." She extends her arms past her head and her hands are crossed.

The scene directly shifts to an image of Jesus on the Cross. The crucifix is a dominant symbol in the video. Madonna's lover wears two large crosses around his neck; one of these crosses has the suffering Jesus on it. There is a small crucifix on the wall which is shown two different times in the background. The words of the song that precede the crucifix scene may serve to attribute God-like characteristics to her lover—or, at the least, these words produce a spiritual dimension to lovemaking: "Tell me your stories. I'm afraid of who you are. We can fly."

The black and white filming, the long corridor of the hotel and the sometimes blurred images give the video a style reminiscent of Alfred Hitchcock. Black and white may symbolize right and wrong, good and bad. Feeling the need to justify something is indicative of one's desire to at least feel that she is doing the right thing. The blurred images in the video, such as when Madonna and her lover first begin to kiss in the hallway, may symbolize the opposite: A lack of clarity regarding what is right and what is wrong.[3] The video's grainy character, in conjunction with Madonna's voice, also makes it seem somewhat like a cheap porno clip. This song is "talked" rather than sung, and Madonna's voice is very "throaty," which contributes to the image of Madonna as seductress.

### Justify My Ideology

Our analysis of "Justify My Love" is an ideological criticism. The point of ideological criticism is not to find:

> unadulterated truth or unbridled manipulation "beneath" or "behind" a given text or system of representation, but to understand how a particular system of representation offers *us* a way of knowing or experiencing the world. (White 141)

We view the video as an open "text," with potential multiple meanings. It is interpreted not only by its contents, but by the particular reading of given viewers. Thus we treat this particular video as a "discourse"—"a socially located way of making sense of an important area of social experience" (Fiske 277).

Madonna is a phenomenon of postmodernist culture. In her analysis of Madonna's video "Material Girl," Kaplan notes the absence of typical bipolar categories, such as male/female. The "ambiguity of enunciative positions within the video," according to Kaplan, "is responsible for the ambiguous representation of the female image" (246). The ambiguity and contradiction in Madonna's work parodies conventional representations of women; such parody effectively questions dominant ideology by defining features of the ideology's object, exaggerating and making them, and thereby mocking those who "fall" for its ideological effect (Fiske 277).

Madonna's parody of culture goes even further: "She parodies not just the stereotypes," according to Fiske, "but the way in which they are made." Her excessiveness of jewelry and makeup, for instance, causes the viewer to question ideology. "Too much lipstick interrogates the tastefully made-up mouth, too much jewelry questions the role of female decorations in patriarchy" (277).[4]

She is a feminist,[5] she is a traditionalist; she is a vamp, she is an angel; she is radical, she is conservative. "Madonna's provocative and wholesome at the same time, nice and naughty, strong and vulnerable" (Racine F5). Madonna challenges "the categories with which we neatly cordon off the world: male and female, gay and straight, erotic and pious, political and playful" (Hochman G8). Madonna's concerts are "something of a game in which the audience is challenged to spot the double meaning in virtually every sentence and gesture" (Schwartz 32).

Madonna provokes multiple and contradictory meanings. Madonna can be taken "straight," as conforming to patriarchy's positioning of women, or as resisting that subordination. She can be taken as pure commodity ("sex sells") or as independent auteur evading the culture industry's commodification of female sexuality. (Brown and Schulze)

The greatest irony is that, while she calls herself Madonna, she dresses and acts in manners quite at odds with the holiness associated with Jesus' mother. In "Justify My Love," Madonna portrays seemingly contradictory messages. With her throaty voice and assertive sexual behavior, Madonna is a seductress. Yet her desire to justify her love and her submission to her lover as his "baby" gives her the image of the traditional girl next door. Both of these images—seductress and girl next door—have long been on opposite sides of the same gender role, with virtually nothing permitted in between.

### Conclusion

"Justify My Love" was banned from MTV because of its explicit and unorthodox sexuality. The video exalts values of nonconformity, individual freedom and sex, as well as themes of eroticism and homosexuality. A closer look at the script and the actions, however, illustrates that the video is, in many respects, morally acceptable—even commendable in terms of traditional ideology. In this particular video, then, traditional values are espoused, albeit in an unusual, erotic kind of format. She is icon, and she is iconoclast. "Like a virgin one minute, like a Marilyn the next," Madonna justifies her ideology—and (mostly) justifies the traditional American ideology.

## NOTES

1. Madonna's film career has also been a success, most notably, *Desperately Seeking Susan* (1985) and *Dick Tracy* (1990). Madonna also runs her own business affairs. She was the top-earning female entertainer in America in 1990.

2. Murphy succinctly catalogued Madonna's controversial behaviors. She has: crawled across the floor on all fours and lapped cream from a saucer (the "Express Yourself" video); developed stigmata ("Like a Prayer"); said she wore crucifixes because they were "sexy"; cavorted with transvestites and been banned from MTV ("Justify My Love"); paid tribute to sadomasochism (the Top Ten song "Hanky Panky"). Finally, she has simulated oral sex with a water bottle in her film *Truth or Dare* (B14).

3. It is also a film technique to capture the viewer's attention and imagination. When an image begins to blur, the viewer becomes more intent. An action begun but not completed clearly demands intervention of the imagination.

4. Schwartz strikes a similar chord in suggesting that Madonna's internalization of both innocence and license and her ability to turn them "on and off like faucets" is indicative of her implication that they are mere appearance; "[e]verything is a pose" (32).

5. Madonna is a true feminist," according to Paglia. "She exposes the Puritanism and suffocating ideology of America feminism. . . . Madonna has taught young women to be fully female and sexual while still exercising total control over their lives." She has "a far profounder vision of sex then do the feminists. She sees both the animality and the artifice." "Feminism says, 'No more masks,'" Paglia concludes, whereas "Madonna says we are nothing but masks" (A39).

## WORKS CITED

Arrington, C. W. "Madonna in Bloom: Circe at Loom." *Time* 137 (1991): 56–58.

Ayers, A. "TV's In-Vogue Vamp." *TV Guide* 38 (1990): 20–22.

Brown, J. D., and Schulze, L. "The Effects of Race, Gender, and Fandom on Audience Interpretations of Madonna's Music Videos." *Journal of Communication* 40 (1990): 88–102.

Campbell, R. H. "Breathlessly Seeking Madonna." *Pennsylvania Inquirer*, 18 June 1990: D3.

Cocks, J. "Madonna Draws a Line." *Time* 136 (1990): 74–75.

Dougherty, S. "Madonna Exposes, MTV Opposes: Is Her Naughty Video Art or Just a Boy Toy Marketing Ploy?" *People Weekly* 34 (1990): 54–55.

Fiske, J. *Channels of Discourse: Television and Contemporary Criticism.* Ed. R. C. Allen. Chapel Hill: U of North Carolina P, 1987.

Goodman, F. "Madonna and Oprah: The Companies They Keep." *Working Woman* (Dec. 1991): 52–55.

Gordon, C. "The Unimportance of Being Earnest." *Maclean's* 20 (May 1990): 13.

Hinckley, D. "Why Vid Didn't Have a Prayer." *Daily News* (New York) 28 Nov. 1990: A6.

Hochman, A. "Is Madonna a Feminist?" *The Oregonian* (26 May 1991): G7.

Johnson, B. D. "Madonna!" *Maclean's* 104 (1991): 44–50.

Kaplan, E. A. *Channels of Discourse: Television and Contemporary Criticism.* Ed. R. C. Allen. Chapel Hill: U of North Carolina P, 1987.

Murphy, R. "Madonna-rama." *Miami Herald*, 28 April 1991: B14.

Paglia, C. "Madonna—Finally a Real Feminist." *New York Times*, 14 Dec. 1990: A39: 1.

Pareles, J. "As MTV Turns 10, Pop Goes the World." *New York Times*, 7 July 1991: sec. 2: 1.

Philips, C. "Anger over Madonna Single." *Los Angeles Times*, 4 Jan. 1991: G13.

Racine, M. "Who's That Girl? Madonna Lets the Astrodome Know." *Houston Chronicle*, 26 July 1987: F5.

Ritts, H. "Madonna!" *Rolling Stone* (15 Nov. 1990): 92–97.

Skow, J. "Madonna Rocks the Land." *Time* 125 (1985): 74–77

Wurtzel, E. "Heavy Breathing." *New York* (14 May 1990):110.

Zehme, B. "Madonna" (interview). *Rolling Stone* (23 March 1989): 50–53.

CAMILLE PAGLIA

# ANIMALITY AND ARTIFICE

1992

*The controversy over "Justify My Love"—and Madonna's somewhat self-serving self-defense—is analyzed here by Camille Paglia.*—Eds.

Madonna, don't preach.

Defending her controversial new video, "Justify My Love," on *Nightline* last week, Madonna stumbled, rambled, and ended up seeming far less intelligent than she really is.

Madonna, 'fess up.

The video is pornographic. It's decadent. And it's fabulous. MTV was right to ban it, a corporate resolve long overdue. Parents cannot possibly control television, with its titanic omnipresence.

Prodded by correspondent Forrest Sawyer for evidence of her responsibility as an artist, Madonna hotly proclaimed her love of children, her social activism, and her condom endorsements. Wrong answer. As Baudelaire and Oscar Wilde knew, neither art nor the artist has a moral responsibility to liberal social causes.

"Justify My Love" is truly avant-garde, at a time when that word has lost its meaning in the flabby art world. It represents a sophisticated European sexuality of a kind we have not seen since the great foreign films of the 1950s and 1960s. But it does not belong on a mainstream music channel watched around the clock by children.

On *Nightline,* Madonna bizarrely called the video a "celebration of sex." She imagined happy educational scenes where curious children would ask their parents about the video. Oh, sure! Picture it: "Mommy, please tell me about the tired, tied-up man in the leather harness and the mean, bare-chested lady in the Nazi cap." Okay, dear, right after the milk and cookies.

Sawyer asked for Madonna's reaction to feminist charges that, in the neck manacle and floor-crawling of an earlier video, "Express Yourself," she condoned the "degradation" and "humiliation" of women. Madonna waffled: "But I chained myself! I'm in charge." Well, no. Madonna the producer may have chosen the chain, but Madonna the sexual persona in the video is alternately a cross-dressing dominatrix and a slave of male desire.

But who cares what the feminists say anyhow? They have been outrageously negative about Madonna from the start. In 1985, *Ms.* magazine pointedly feted quirky, cuddly singer Cyndi Lauper as its woman of the year. Great judgment: gimmicky Lauper went nowhere, while Madonna grew, flourished, metamorphosed, and became an international star of staggering dimensions. She is also a shrewd business tycoon, a modern new woman of all-around talent.

Madonna is the true feminist. She exposes the puritanism and suffocating ideology of American feminism, which is stuck in an adolescent whining mode. Madonna has taught young women to be fully female and sexual while still exercising control over their lives. She shows girls how to be attractive, sensual, energetic, ambitious, aggressive, and funny—all at the same time.

American feminism has a man problem. The beaming Betty Crockers, hangdog dowdies, and parochial prudes who call themselves feminists want men to be like women. They fear and despise the masculine. The academic feminists think their nerdy bookworm husbands are the ideal model of human manhood.

But Madonna loves real men. She sees the beauty of masculinity, in all its rough vigor and sweaty athletic perfection. She also admires the men who are actually like women: transsexuals and flamboyant drag queens, the heroes of the 1969 Stonewall rebellion, which started the gay liberation movement.

"Justify My Love" is an eerie, sultry tableau of jaded androgynous creatures, trapped in a decadent sexual underground. Its hypnotic images are drawn from such sadomasochistic films as Liliana Cavani's *The Night Porter* and Luchino Visconti's *The Damned*. It's the perverse and knowing world of the photographers Helmut Newton and Robert Mapplethorpe.

Contemporary American feminism, which began by rejecting Freud because of his alleged sexism, has shut itself off from his ideas of ambiguity, contradiction, conflict, ambivalence. Its simplistic psychology is illustrated by the new cliché of the date-rape furor: "'No' always means 'no.'" Will we ever graduate from the Girl Scouts? "No" has always been, and always will be, part of the dangerous, alluring courtship ritual of sex and seduction, observable even in the animal kingdom.

Madonna has a far profounder vision of sex than do the feminists. She sees both the animality and the artifice. Changing her costume style and hair color virtually every month, Madonna embodies the eternal values of beauty and pleasure. Feminism says, "No more masks." Madonna says we are nothing but masks.

Through her enormous impact on young women around the world, Madonna is the future of feminism.

# Part Five

## JUSTIFY MY LOVE

MADONNA AND THE ACADEMY

*It's hard to believe that Madonna was once considered to be a bubble-gum, teeny-bopper pop singer, somewhat less talented than Cyndi Lauper, to whom she was first compared. Madonna's work has spawned an entire industry of academic commentary, and several collections of academic articles have already appeared, discussing her impact on music, feminism, sexuality, and dozens of more issues. This part of the book collects some of the classic academic pieces, beginning with Daniel Harris's overview of Madonna's impact on the academy.*—Eds.

DANIEL HARRIS

# MAKE MY RAINY DAY

1992

*An overview of the academic reaction to Madonna written by a critic who is none too sympathetic to the academy.*—Eds.

Within an entertainment industry expressly designed to absorb and commodify even the most unconventional talents, up-and-coming performers must face the fact that growing recognition of their work will ultimately compromise their integrity by forcing them to tone it down and smooth out the rough edges of their idiosyncrasies as they attempt to appeal to wide audiences. In the case of Madonna, however, the exact opposite has occurred. If co-optation involves the appropriation of a marginal artist by the mainstream, reverse co-optation involves the appropriation of a mainstream artist by a marginal group—in this case, the increasing numbers of academics who are currently flooding the country's journals and small presses with a glut of scholarship on the stylistic flamboyance—the glitz, guts and pure raunch—of a celebrity who has borne much of the brunt of the university's restless and uncertain engagement with popular culture. Madonna has been drafted into the staggeringly implausible role of spokeswoman of the values and professional interests of university instructors! Her academic admirers spend a great deal of time studying how she embodies the fantasies of other people; they devote remarkably little time, however, to discussing how she embodies their own.

A quick survey of the variety of responses to what mass-media pundit E. Ann Kaplan identifies in all seriousness as the "MP," the "Madonna Phenomenon," offers a fascinating look not only at contemporary academics' attempts to counteract their own marginality by making desperate forays into popular culture but also at the inadequacies of postmodernism itself and the conceptual limits of its application to specific uncanonized forms of lowbrow entertainment. There is a Madonna for virtually every theoretical stripe—the Lacanian Madonna of Marjorie Garber, who says that the singer's recent tendency to squeeze her crotch like a man while singing "emblematize[s] the Lacanian triad of having, being, and seeming"; the Foucauldian Madonna of Charles Wells, who claims that in her videos she "is instructing us with a Foucauldian flair in the 'end of woman'"; the Baudrillardian Madonna of Cathy Schwichtenberg, who reads "Madonna's figuration against the backdrop of Baudrillardian theory"; or the Marxist Madonna of Melanie Morton, who says that Madonna singlehandedly undermines "capitalist constructions" and "rejects core bourgeois epistemes." There is even the Freudian Madonna of Cindy Patton; in reference to the fact that the voluptuous members of Madonna's male dance troupe often appear on stage in the steamier numbers grinding and groaning as they massage outrageous strap-on falsies with masturbatory intensity, she claims that "the gendering of the breast is problematized through the evocation of breast envy . . . and implicitly [through the evocation of] men's desire to be lesbians." In Barbara Bradby's close reading of the lyrics of the song "Material Girl," titled "Like a Virgin-Mother?: Materialism and Maternalism in the Songs of Madonna," she, like Patton, plumbs the depths of our collective musical ids when she psychoanalyzes the lines "Only boys that save their pennies / Make my rainy day" in an effort to buttress her theory that Madonna is not passive and victimized but in fact nurturing and mothering:

> We may note that teaching children to save pennies (in piggy-banks, etc.) is an important function of mothers, if their children are to be successful. However, in this nursery context of early training, "saving pennies" evokes its opposite, "spending a penny," which little boys may think of as like "making rain." In this sense, potty training is about learning to "save pennies," or the ability to control the activity of "spending a penny." The lines "Only boys that save their pennies / Make my rainy day" can therefore be taken as expressing the mother's approval of the boy who has learnt to pee in the appropriate situation.

Just as members of the left often sentimentalize the proletariat, so academics have begun to sentimentalize popular culture by ascribing to it all sorts of admirable characteristics that it does not have—in particular, the potential to radicalize the huddled masses by providing typically quiescent MTV viewers with what it is now fashionable to term "a site of contention" (or, in Charles Wells's marvelous malapropism, "a cite of contention"), a subversive forum within the mainstream where socially conscious performers can actively challenge reactionary patriarchal ideologies. In the inflationary rhetoric of the MP, however, the tail inevitably begins to wag the dog and Madonna emerges not simply as a pop star but as "the most significant artist of the late twentieth century," who, in the acknowledged masterpieces of her oeuvre, songs like "Cherish," "Papa Don't Preach" and "Like a Prayer," demolishes assumptions "foundational to liberal humanism," "rewrit[es] some very fundamental levels of Western thought" and even defies "the ongoing dominance of 'Western' culture by Protestantism." In "Madonna's Postmodern Feminism," Cathy Schwichtenberg strikes the apocalyptic note characteristic of the whole extravagant tenor of Madonna scholarship when she speculates wistfully about the sexual utopia that would result in American society if the performer's agenda of unbridled hedonism, her uncanny ability to "pluralize sexual practices" and transgress "the lines and boundaries that fragment gender polarities," were actually implemented. In Schwichtenberg's view, the world according to Madonna would be so emancipated, so polymorphously perverse, that we could all "'come out' and participate in a range of identities such as a lesbian heterosexual, a heterosexual lesbian, a male lesbian, a female gay man, or even a feminist sex radical."

The meteoric growth of the MP reflects changes that are occurring in the perception of popular art not only among academics but among mainstream pop critics as well. In the past few decades, there has been an ironic switch of roles between the two major sectors of cultural commentators in our society. Mainstream reviewers are gradually assuming the mantle abandoned by academics, that of the custodian of High Art, criticizing Madonna as a talentless opportunist, a monster created by the publicity machine, a nasty scourge in an unmitigatedly vulgar pop music scene; while academics are wrapping themselves in a populist flag and interpreting Madonna as nothing less than a grass-roots revolutionary.

The psychological mechanism behind this recent orgy of slumming in the university has, in my view, little to do with its participants' genuine interest in popular culture and even less with the real pleasure it is possible to take from it. Rather, it is motivated by professional factors within the academy—specifically, by many academics' desire to prove their social relevance. The MP is really not about Madonna at all but about dissatisfaction with insulting stereotypes of the Ivory Tower, stereotypes some academics reject by flouting the decorum of traditional fields of study in what often seems, at least in the kitschier examples of postmodern scholarly extremism, to be a magnificently executed practical joke on the conventional disciplines of the liberal arts. Madonna scholars see themselves as iconoclasts rebelling against the suffocating strictures of High Art, as devilish pranksters shocking prudish humanists who hurl themselves melodramatically in front of the canon in order to shield it maternally from assault. It is one of the great ironies of the whole phenomenon of slumming that the perception of radicalism on the part of those who go rooting around amid the rubbish of popular culture, defying the ordinances of the classical definition of the humanities, derives from their increasing contacts with conformist mainstream culture, a forum that is anything but radical—or more precisely, that is radical only within the context of divisive skirmishes occurring within the university itself.

Despite this new tendency to sentimentalize popular culture and exaggerate its subversive content, Madonna studies in fact represent the ultimate act of cultural imperialism in the sense that Madonna simply provides a lift into the saddle for the inevitable ride on academics' all-too-predictable hobbyhorses. Such theorists are often quite frank about the naked opportunism of their pillaging of lowbrow art. In her preface to the forthcoming (Westview, October 1992) anthology *The Madonna Connection,* Schwichtenberg states explicitly that "this volume demonstrates Madonna's usefulness as a paradigm case to advance further developments in cultural theory." Kaplan, the acknowledged torchbearer of Madonna studies, refers to the performer's contributions to MTV as "an especially appropriate proving ground for postmodern theories." This tendency to turn Madonna into a classroom aid becomes most obvious when one examines the basic methods by which her admirers interpret her songs and videos—in particular, the intensive close readings they perform with the grisly clinical efficiency of autopsies. These astonishing note-by-note and frame-by-frame vivisections of Madonna's work, which surely constitute some of the strangest intellectual curiosities to have emerged from the university, reveal the devastating insufficiency of postmodernism as a vehicle for cultural analysis. Academics interpret even the melodies of these conventional pop hits as "strategies" for effecting revolutionary changes in listeners, as if Madonna were capable of rousing the slumbering masses from their oppression with unoriginal Top-40 songs postmodernists take quite literally as clarion calls for action.

In "Living to Tell: Madonna's Resurrection of the Fleshly," Susan McClary examines the "brave new musical procedures" of each bar of

"Like a Prayer" in order to show that Madonna, who is "as much an expert in the arena of musical signification as [Teresa] de Lauretis is in theoretical discourse," "offers musical structures that promise narrative closure at the same time that she resists or subverts them," thus "destabilizing the male gaze" and rendering the coup de grâce to patriarchy. Similarly, in "Don't Go for Second Sex, Baby," a deconstructionist analysis of the song "Express Yourself," Morton transforms a pop hit into a rabble-rousing postmodernist anthem, the "Internationale" of the dance floor, which "takes as its object the general logic and various practices of domination most prevalent in Western culture." Subverting melodic authority by challenging oppressive tonal hierarchies, Madonna decimates "patriarchal, racist, and capitalist constructions" simply in the way she bellows out "self" in the line "Express yourself."

[The word becomes a meditation] on the constitution of a de-centered subjectivity. "Self" is first sung on G, then on F sharp, moving to F natural, then on G, moving back to F sharp, and lastly (not counting repeated bars) self is sung on F sharp to E. The word as well as the concept gets divided and put in motion, articulating agency through positions which remain partial and temporary. . . . [Madonna's melodies thus] prevent what we would call in narrative terms an ideological closure. There is no recapitulation which fixes power and establishes (or re-establishes) any element as dominant.

As seen here in the way academics overinterpret Madonna's songs, close reading represents the inappropriate transfer to low culture of habits of study derived from high culture, habits that assume that the work of art under scrutiny is so complex that it deserves to be examined in all of its nuances. Because such techniques presuppose conventional notions of authorship, as well as misconceptions about the density of artistic intentions in commercial entertainment, they are suffused with the humanistic reverence for canonical art that postmodernists flatter themselves they have long since outgrown. In the very act of turning away from high culture and spurning the pieties lavished on the canon, academics demonstrate how incomplete the postmodernist break with traditional forms of artistic analysis has been, how abysmally they have failed to take popular culture on its own terms and how unimaginatively they insist on studying one set of cultural artifacts exactly as they study an entirely different and more literary set. Their treatment of popular culture is inherently elitist. At their most postmodern, academics remain dyed-in-the-wool humanists.

That critical theorists simply borrow the methodology of traditional scholars can also be seen in the way they attempt to create a unified artistic form out of the fragmented rock video, whose deconstructed "text" inevitably provokes frantic efforts to fuse all of its component parts into an integrated composition. Intolerant of the cinematic confusion of MTV—the non sequiturs, the jump cuts, the decontextualized images, the random breaks in visual syntax—scholars like Kaplan and John Fiske engage in spectacular feats of overinterpretation to restore seamless narrative continuity to something that is by nature disjunctive. Concluding that Madonna's videos lack "closure" and therefore liberate the female viewer by allowing her to interpret the images as she chooses, thus leaving her in "a position of power vis-à-vis the text" Kaplan and Fiske paradoxically recycle the high-art concept of organic unity. They distill from a wide range of very disparate pieces a single encompassing idea, the master theme, the skeleton key that unlocks every door—the absence of ideological and narrative resolution, an interpretation they apply indiscriminately, oblivious to the irony that works of art purported to have such little closure should become in their hands so hermetically closed.

This never-ending attempt to silence the clamor of incoherence with pat, reductive readings about empowering "syntagmatic gaps" that produce a malleability of form academics describe as somehow intellectually nutritious for the viewer shows how determined postmodernists can be in quarrying out of the garbled obscurities of MTV themes as monolithic, invariable and all-inclusive as those developed by New Critics in the cribs and trots with which they once led their readers through the enigmas of modernist art. Moreover, "lack of closure" is in itself a high-art concept, for what is this mystifying property that academics bestow so sanctimoniously on popular culture but the New Critical concept of "ambiguity" in disguise, a quality that critics have long reserved as the highest form of praise for canonical works of art?

But perhaps the clearest example of the way postmodernists cling tenaciously to the values and procedures of conservative scholars is the tendentiousness with which they examine every pose Madonna strikes for the taint of ideological corruption. In "Images of Race and Religion in 'Like a Prayer,'" Ronald Scott scours the song's video for "the positive social messages imbedded" within it, agonizing over such questions as whether the black character in the piece is actually lying on top of Madonna as she sprawls defenselessly over a pew, an image that may be contaminated with negative stereotypes. In "'Material Girl': The Effacements of Postmodern Culture," Susan Bordo takes this didactic political nitpicking one step further when she describes Madonna as a kind of antifeminist scab, an unprincipled collaborator with the opposite sex, who recently rejected the voluptuous proportions of the full-figured female when she submitted to a punishing exercise and diet regimen in an effort to satisfy the patriarchal ideal of svelte feminine beauty. This moralizing of every bump and grind that Madonna makes, of every inch of cleavage she bares and every glimpse of navel she flashes, demonstrates the full extent of the intellectual chauvinism implicit in the academics' engagement with popular culture.

While Madonna scholars share the philosophical posturing and muddled politics characteristic of contemporary critical discourse as a whole, her admirers' wild exaggerations of her subtlety as an "author" are even more untenable than the evasive generalities found in theoretical work on conventional literary subjects. It is even tempting to enter into the Swiftian spirit of overstatement that suffuses the books and articles about her and conclude apocalyptically that postmodernism is Madonna, that the banality of Madonna is in some sense its fate, the logical conclusion of its aims and assertions. As she is remade into Theory incarnate and invested with a radicalism that her public image as a mainstream performer cannot, by any stretch of the imagination, sustain, she becomes the ultimate realization of many postmodernists' most cherished tenet—that words have only an arbitrary relationship with the things they signify, and that there is no stable and empirically verifiable "reality" behind the vagaries and impermanence of language. As E. Deirdre Pribram put it in her analysis of last year's documentary *Truth or Dare,* "Madonna, this chameleon-of-appearances . . . refuses all fixed meanings . . . there is no definitive 'real,' no authentic Madonna beyond the person(a) we already know through her various incarnations." When a signifier becomes as "free-floating," as unmoored from the thing it signifies as Pribram suggests that Madonna has become, the consequence is what some would call "slippage" but might be more aptly characterized as outright detachment, a state of intellectual anarchy that sanctions willfully perverse misreadings. Some theorists have even gone so far as to justify the poetic license with which they treat their subjects by suggesting that, as Charles Wells writes in his master's essay on Madonna, titled "Like a Thesis," "rationality is a patriarchal trick. . . . All readings, in some way, are misreadings. All interpretation is misinterpretation. Though the page you are now reading appears to be flat, that is an illusion." Such skeptical caveats go a long way toward explaining the literature of the MP: Although it appears to be about Madonna, that is an illusion.

LISA A. LEWIS

# GENDER POLITICS AND MTV: VOICING THE DIFFERENCE

1990

*Madonna's life and career are seen from a political/feminist point of view.*—Eds.

*It doesn't matter who you are,*
*It's what you do that takes you far.*

Madonna Ciccone grew up outside Detroit, Michigan, in a large Italian-Catholic family headed by her father, who worked as an engineer in the auto industry. Her mother died of cancer when Madonna was six years old; her father remarried the family's housekeeper two years later. Both events, Madonna has remarked in interviews, left her with a sense of abandonment that fueled a fierce desire for attention, eventually driving her to pursue stardom (Connelly, 1984). But the desire for attention was not only a product of psychological trauma, it was also a result of the social system of gender inequality that denies recognition to intelligent and talented girls and women. Lacking a sympathetic mother, the rule of the patriarch in the family intensified in the form of her father's strict enforcement of Catholic morality. The presence of her numerous brothers demonstrated to Madonna the double standard that formed his parenting routines: "I had a traditional Catholic upbringing, and I saw the privileges my older brothers had. They got to stay out late, go to concerts, play in the neighborhood. I was left out" (Phillips 1987, p. 24).

Born in 1958, Madonna is five years younger than Pat Benatar and Cyndi Lauper. She entered adolescence during the heyday of the women's liberation movement in the early and middle 1970s, and her desires and actions are representative of the pressures brought to bear on gender definitions at the time. The movement's rhetoric called on girls to be career-oriented and to seize equality by pursuing the male vision. But opportunities lagged behind rhetoric and the mixed signals caused considerable conflicts for young women poised at the start of life. The pathway to personal achievement had to be paved from within the confines of female lives.

Madonna recalls discovering at an early age the proven female attention-getting strategy of flirtation: "The power of my femininity and charm, I remember it was just something I had, that I'd been given. . . . From the age of five I remember being able to affect people that way" (Fissinger 1985, p. 34). But pleasing does not ultimately lead to self-development and equal treatment. To achieve as a woman takes the will to violate expectations of female service. As she grew into adolescence, Madonna accepted the role of "bad girl" in an effort to accumulate experiences and focus her yearning for recognition. She rebelled against her father's rule, despite her desire for his attention, and pursued male-adolescent privilege despite its alienating effects on her peers: "Boys didn't understand me, and they didn't like me because I wasn't stupid, and I *was* blunt and opinionated, but I was a flirt at the same time. They took my aggressiveness as a come-on. They didn't get it" (Fissinger 1985, p. 36). Years later, she would equate her treatment by adolescent boys in junior high school with her treatment by press reviewers.

Barred from the leisure activities of her brothers and male-adolescent peers, Madonna adopted dance as her primary mode of expression and took ballet classes regularly. Dance provided a socially accepted mode of channeling her desires for control and pleasure. Dance meets social requirements by making the female body into an object of admiration, but, as Angela McRobbie (1984) has argued, it also produces a number of benefits for girls themselves. The discourse of the prima-ballerina, as represented in fiction designed for girl readers, introduces girls to the idea of career commitment and the hope that rewards and recognition are available to girls who work hard. Madonna credits her dance training with teaching her the discipline needed to handle the rigors of her music and acting careers (Stanton, 1985). As she became successful, she borrowed from the discourse of dance to characterize her achievement for critics and fans, saying, "I had a dream and I worked hard and my dream came true" (Stanton 1985, p. 60).

When Madonna was a girl, the discourse of dance converged with her allegiance to the discourse of pop. Pop ideology was attractive because it provided the fantasy of stardom, a symbolic solution for her female-adolescent craving for recognition. The rhetoric of the women's movement helped instill the sense of possibility and the drive to make over the fantasy into a career direction. Committing to dance was the first available step. But the odds against succeeding in a dance career, and the increasingly restrictive regimen imposed by a classical ballet training program, reportedly led Madonna to consider combining dance with music creation, and to relinquish a four-year dance scholarship after only a year and a half at the University of Michigan in favor of the New York City dance-club scene (Connelly, 1984; Fissinger, 1985).

In New York, Madonna's musical training was first fostered by a boyfriend's garage band. She sang, learned to play guitar and drums, and wrote songs with Dan Gilroy and his brother, who lived and practiced their music in a rented synagogue in Queens. They formed a band together, Breakfast Club, but Madonna was not given the opportunity to sing as much as she wanted, and she soon left the band to start her own. Schooled within a garage band, rock's primary training ground, Madonna sang rock and roll in her new band, aided by black rhythm-and-blues musician Steve Bray, an old boyfriend from Michigan. A manager signed the band, but balked when she began to veer away from rock toward funky, urban (black) dance music. Finally, Madonna quit the deal and, along with Bray, started writing dance music and attending dance clubs at night with demo tape in hand, trying to charm and entice club deejays to play it. She found a willing prospect in Mark Kamins, a respected deejay at the club Danceteria. Kamins played the song and, taking note of the audience's response, helped her produce an improved version. He took it to Sire Records, which offered Madonna a recording contract in 1982 (Connelly, 1984; Fissinger, 1985; Bego, 1985).

The string of events in New York before Madonna's "big break" became the subject of much scrutiny in press accounts of her rise to fame. Early articles focused on Madonna's sequential sexual relationships with Gilroy, Bray, and Kamins, the three men who figure in her development stages (Connelly, 1984; Fissinger, 1985; Skow et al., 1985). In a reversal of the ideology of sexual favors, the articles positioned Madonna in the role of an exploiter who sleeps with men as a calculated measure to steal their musical knowledge and contacts. *Rolling Stone*'s first cover story on Madonna in 1984 (titled with the sexual innuendo "Madonna Goes All the Way") raised the issue directly: "She's an unqualified success. But did she exploit people to get there?" (Connelly 1984, p. 81). The implied accusation punishes Madonna for her apparent inversion of the female role of service, for putting men in the position of serving her career rather than the other way around. The extent of Madonna's success and the three men's relative lack of success at the time made it difficult to sustain the usual interpretation of women as the vehicle of male talent and control. Instead, it was the men who began to take on the color of victimization as frustrated reviewers lamented the ideological crisis Madonna's ambitious progress created. Madonna herself resisted the efforts to create a new ideological model to deny the value of her accomplishments. *Time* magazine was obliged to convey her feelings on the matter in its 1985 cover story: "She resents suggestions that she slept her way to the top . . . because the idea that she couldn't make it to the top on drive and ambition alone is insulting" (Skow et al. 1985, p. 76).

*Rolling Stone*'s story also examined Madonna's career path for evidence of her violation of rock discourse. The centerpiece of the biographical account was her choice of Reggie Lucas, an experienced producer, to produce her first album, and not Bray or Kamins. The choice of an experienced producer over inexperienced ones is the prerogative of a professional, a sign of Madonna's mature assessment of her needs at the time, yet because it violated the loyalty imperative of the rock discourse (as well as the practice of female service to men), the decision became a point for criticism.

Madonna, in fact, embodies *not* rock discourse, but pop discourse. Rock's ideology of authenticity demands an absence of image or, in other terms, correspondence between public image and personal subjectivity. But image and representation, Pat Benatar's nemeses, are Madonna's playground. She revels in self-promotion, in the creation of an image or images, in being a personality, a celebrity. She accepts artifice as an integral feature of music production and promotion and is comfortable with textual production. Madonna breaks with the preferred ideology of rock by equating image-making and acting, image and character: "For most people, music is a very personal statement, but I've always liked to have different characters that I project. . . . The problem is, in the public's mind, you are your image, your musical image, and I think that those characters are only extensions of me" (Gilmore 1987, p. 87). Revealing image to be a construction does not entirely disable the capacity of image to function as a personal statement of the musician's subjectivity. Symbolic practices can yield authentic expressions. Madonna has verified that the characters she creates spring in part from her own experiences. And it is her ability to represent gender experience symbolically in the characters she creates that provides points of identification for a female audience.

Predictably, Madonna's association with pop music was interpreted as an alignment with industry control and was used, at least at the beginning of her career, as an excuse to undermine her authorship. Perhaps the best illustration of how the puppet metaphor circulates in the popular arena has been provided by Madonna herself, who described in an interview how she first encountered it:

> I was making this movie, *Desperately Seeking Susan* [in 1984]. One of the drivers that took me to the set every day was this kid, and one day he said to me, "I have this bet going with my friend, he told me that all the music

> you do was done by someone else and they picked the songs and did it all, and all they needed was a girl singer and you auditioned and they picked you. And Madonna isn't your real name and all of it is fabricated." And I said, "WHAAAAAAT?? Are you out of your mind??!" But that's what his friend told him, and it suddenly hit me that's probably what a lot of people think. It hit me. (Fissinger 1985, p. 36)

Although Madonna's revelry in pop discourse made *Rolling Stone* defensive at first, the magazine did decide to place her photo on the cover of issues in four consecutive years (1984–1987), implementing a shift in attitude toward a reevaluation of pop and the disintegration of the rock/pop dichotomy.

Madonna's image constructions, which she develops in her video promotion, zero in on the most controversial and conflicted images of women: bad girl, virgin, pregnant teen, glamour queen, and stripteaser. There is a sexual edge to all of her "characters" and this, again, resulted initially in the interpretation that Madonna was operating in collusion with the industry and with patriarchal ideology to reproduce the standard of female representation. But gradually, Madonna's manipulation and critique of the codes of female representation began to be acknowledged in the press, having already been recognized by female audiences. Her appropriation and resignification of the standard of female representation was a fundamental upset to the standard's ability to function as a strategy to thwart female musician authorship and subjectivity. The story of Madonna's exercise of creative control over her own representation began to be a subject of discussion in feature articles, and the discovery of her authorship over her image(s) eroded the tendency to portray her as a puppet of commercial manipulation.

By laying claim to symbolic self-determination, Madonna prompted a backlash, a reassertion of patriarchal entitlement to modes of female representation. The publicity industry proved to be its messenger, reacting to her assertions of control over representation by stalking her in an attempt to take unauthorized photographs. Madonna herself has equated the unsolicited picture-taking with male acts of aggression against women, with the violation of her body, and seems to appreciate the ideological stakes that are at issue:

> It's not even the taking of pictures that bothers me, it's the element of surprise I always encounter every time they jump out of the bushes or jump from behind a corner. . . . They're always scaring me. . . . Every time they

> jump out to take a picture, the way they take them—it's like they're raping me. (Stanton 1985, p. 63)

When nude photographs of Madonna (taken when she was modeling for artists to support herself in New York) were published by *Playboy* and *Penthouse* in September 1985, it was her lack of control over the situation that Madonna found most disturbing: "The thing that annoyed me most wasn't so much that they were nude photographs but that I felt really out of control—for the first time in what I thought to be several years of careful planning and knowing what was going to happen" (Schruers 1986, p. 60).

Madonna entered the music business with definite ideas about her image, but it was her track record that enabled her to increase her level of creative control over her music. By negotiating authorship through informal collaborations, she was gradually able to parlay unofficial collaborative liaisons into a sanctioned credit as producer:

> On my first album, the demos we made were not as close simply because I didn't have as much direct involvement with the production of my album. I didn't know enough to speak out. It wasn't until my first album *[Madonna]* was three-quarters of the way done that I realized, hey! I know a lot more about this than I'm allowing myself to speak out about. So I started going backward and stripping the songs down and making them more sparse. Until then they'd been layered with a lot of stuff. Then when we got into the second album *[Like a Virgin]*, I had a lot more confidence in myself and I had a lot more to do with the way it came out soundwise. I really worked side by side with Nile Rodgers. . . . Nile was very open with me, he gave me the feeling we really were collaborating and I felt free to say what I wanted. (Stanton 1985, p. 66)

By her third album, *True Blue*, the reports place Madonna more firmly in control. Bray, her collaborator on a number of songs, is quoted at the studio during the production of the album: "If you just talk in the hallway for more than twenty seconds, you hear, 'You guys! Get in here'" (Schruers 1986, p. 60). Pat Leonard, with whom Madonna writes and produces, describes the confidence and daring in her musical decision-making: "We'll do something and I'll say, 'Let's go to the next chorus and repeat it,' and she goes, 'Why? Where do these rules come from? Who made up these rules?'" Leonard applauds her musical sensibilities: "If you listen to what she says, it instantly becomes a 'Madonna' record—her instincts just turn it into that, no matter what producer she's working with" (Schruers 1986, p. 60). Madonna's proven ability to create songs that become hits has facilitated her involvement with record producing and promotion. It has enabled her to negotiate authorship in the form of official credit for her album sound (the producer credit), to penetrate the discourse of rock, and to be treated by the music press as an author.

LUC SANTE

# UNLIKE A VIRGIN

1990

*This critique examines Madonna as a capitalist.*—Eds.

After two or three months of ceaseless barrage upon the American continent, the winds of Madonna have shifted and besieged Europe. Not that the American public is likely to banish her from memory for even a second, especially since The Movie is playing in every minimall and multiplex and is still being considered from every angle in Sunday supplements throughout the land, and The Album is prominently on display in retail outlets of every demographic. The Tour, however, has left these shores, taking with it the unilateral media saturation that brought Madonna into every room of every house and caused her to hover in the periphery, at least, of every consciousness. Is there anyone, at large or in stir, who does not know the details of Madonna's latest look, with its kewpie-doll ponytail and dominatrix affectations, its nose-cone brassieres and pin-striped suits with breast slits? Or of her stage show, complete with tubular-breasted males, wriggling mermen, and a kickline of Dick Tracies?

Of course, Madonna dwells among us at most times, and her presence is felt in record shops and T-shirt boutiques and on MTV and in the sheets and rags that draw all their material from speculation on the hidden lives of celebrities. But in this late-century version of the dog-and-pony show, her face and body and the attributes of her legend appeared on and in every general-interest magazine and newspaper and magazine-format television program, her name was heard as a reference and a figure of speech in the routines of comedians, the banter of TV news coanchors, the fulminations of media moralists, in bar-talk and gym-talk and water-cooler-talk and supermarket-line-talk. In the night sky of the American imagination, Madonna looms.

For the time being, at least. Will she endure as a figure to color forever our idea of fame, to become the little picture accompanying the definition of "media star" in the illustrated dictionaries of the future? Will she enter the domain of clip-art imagery as a badly printed blob on shopping bags and paper placemats whose muddy outlines are nevertheless as instantly recognizable as those of the Marilyn of the dress-flipping-up-over-steam-vent or the Brando of the peaked cap and motorcycle jacket?

Such, after all, is her ambition. Madonna is not out for mere money or mere glory; even less is she in pursuit of the perfect beat or the sublime hook. It is not for her to achieve international respect and then disappear into genteel privacy in Switzerland or New Mexico, to define a song or a movie role and then suffer that title's parenthetical accompaniment of her name in every printed citation. She does not want to make her pile and cut out—she does not want to cut out. Madonna wants to conquer the unconscious, to become indelible.

She has already taken steps toward this end. There is, for example, the matter of the single name, which in America is usually an abbreviation conferred by the public over time as an accolade and a sign of affection. Madonna has taken the shortcut of lopping it off herself. And there is the image. In her canny way Madonna realized that in this day and age success results less often from imposing a spectacular figure on the public than from erecting a screen upon which the public can project its own internal movies. So she invented herself as a mutable being, a container for a multiplicity of images. She could be anything, with only the one unchanging grace note: the mole just above her lip.

Madonna Louise Veronica Ciccone hails from Michigan, came to New York in the late 1970s or early '80s, studied dance, hung out heavily, began her career as a photographer's model (some mildly dirty pictures from this period surfaced a few years ago, and some of the tabloids were weak-minded enough to think they could make a scandal out of them), appeared in a small role in at least one low-grade exploitation movie, and then began making a name as a "track singer" (a lost term from that brief *inter regnum* between live performance and the total electronic environment, referring to vocalists who appeared in clubs singing to taped accompaniment).

On the New York club scene she appears to have gone from decorative nobody to new face on the rise in a sort of Ruby Keeler minute. She persuaded Mark Kamins, a deejay at Danceteria, the club of that hour, to produce a song for her ("Everybody"), then persuaded Seymour Stein, the godfather of New York "New Wave," to issue it on his Sire Records label, and it hit the charts. In those days (1982), when Reaganism was still young, dance-party records made by ambitious white semi-bohemians might be viewed as artistic and even political statements merely by virtue of their genre. By eschewing rock 'n' roll jingoism in favor of bass out front, wide backbeat, and lyrics that in essence always said, "Let's everybody party down," they made a gesture of calling out to the whole world, especially to its third part. It was a year or two before this stance became generic.

So it was that Madonna's early records, blasting out over such stations as WBLS in New York, stations that were then just beginning to be referred to by the demographic euphemism "urban contemporary," sounded like more than mere product. The very simple lyrics of her second 45, "Holiday" ("We should take a holiday, some time to celebrate . . ."), had a utopian flavor, however soft. Her voice, with its nasal tough-girl inflection by Ronnie Spector out of Minnie Mouse and related by blood or marriage to the throw-down quality exuded by such chanteuses as Teena Marie and Evelyn "Champagne" King, made the invitation sound uncompromising, almost brave. After three or four hits in succession, Madonna was a downtown singer with proven crossover ability.

Still, the likelihood of her achieving any further distinction seemed remote. Madonna, however, was not one to accept any predetermined view of her career. She immediately raised the stakes, and in rapid order began advancing one marketing theme after another, in the process revealing that while she had a small talent as a pop singer, as an image strategist she possessed something approaching genius. Her first order of business was to jettison the appealing but limited waif look featured on the cover of her eponymous first album, to replace its whisper with a shout. For this purpose she initiated a hostile takeover of the sartorial repertoire of her older rival Cyndi Lauper, an original who had taken the hippie-punk scavenger aesthetic to an extreme point and assembled herself as a living collage of old and newstyles, clashing colors, mismatched fabrics, accessories contrived from the most unlikely objects.

Madonna, of course, was no original; she was, like her role model David Bowie, a magpie with a flair for highlighting the critical elements of the styles she appropriated. She dispensed with the self-mockery implicit in Lauper's presentation and zeroed in on its fetishistic sexual aspect. Hence the bras-as-outerwear, the "Boy Toy" belt buckles, the junk jewelry by the pound. The look titillated boys of all ages, while teenage girls found in it a form of rebellion that could be safely assumed and doffed outside parental ken, since it involved nothing drastic or irreversible. The look instantly propelled Madonna into the national image bank. She had taken her first beachhead.

A measure of the success of this image was that it lasted much longer in the consciousness of the public than it did in Madonna's own career. Its early crudity can be assessed in her Virgin Tour video, which shows her looking askew and even a bit chunky, missing notes and flailing around on stage, but evidently learning on the job. This, however, was her live show. At the same time, she was displaying a precocious understanding of the nascent power of the video clip, becoming one of the first pop stars to issue songs that were inseparably entwined with the visual imagery of their MTV illustrations in the minds of consumers.

Her first successful salvo in this direction was "Like a Virgin." "Should go over big in Italy," quipped a friend of mine at the time; sure enough, the video was shot in Venice, and it contained the first glimmers of her now-trademark Catholic-transgression sideline. Of course, it also possessed all of the grace of a "Girls of the Adriatic" *Playboy* feature, along with the patented MTV significance-trigger of staggering slo-mo, but it can be said to have made its point. Her follow-up was "Material Girl," which may have sounded a bit like Carmen Miranda. What everybody noticed, however, was the video, in which Madonna shamelessly reinvented the wheel, lifting wholesale Marilyn's courtroom dance sequence from *Gentlemen Prefer Blondes* and flushing it of its satire. Subtlety, Madonna well knew, butters no parsnips in the pop marketplace. "Material Girl" was crass, vulgar, obvious, charmless, and virtually definitive of the grasping zeitgeist of 1984. It was, naturally, her biggest hit to date, and probably remains so. Around the same time she was fortunate enough to be handed an opportunity well beyond her own contrivance. Susan Seidelman, a little-known but enterprising filmmaker apprenticing, as Madonna had, in the Manhattan bohemia career institute, cast her in *Desperately Seeking Susan* as the mystery woman of the title. The film was halting, turgid, and as instantly irrelevant as any Gidget vehicle. But in its tame exploitation of the downtown-scene mystique it somehow rang the safe-rebellion chime for millions of middle-class youth. Madonna was ideally suited to her role, which called for her to look sultry and jaded and not say a whole lot. The movie earned many times its budget, its title entered the catch-phrase arsenal of headline writers everywhere, and Madonna emerged from the experience having attained a new rung of celebrity, along with a reputation, soon shown to be utterly unfounded, as a major box-office attraction.

The rest, as they say, is history. She married the troubled Sean Penn and succeeded in profiting from his bad press, appeared in a couple of cinematic bombs (*Shanghai Surprise* and *Who's That Girl?*, in case you've forgotten) that did not leave her terribly scathed, issued many song-and-video packages that each involved a new look and a new attempt at a veneer of meaning, made a stab at artistic respectability by appearing in a sub-par David Mamet play, raised middle-American hackles with further Catholic-transgression affectations in the "Like a Prayer" video and with a mock-Sapphic Mutt-and-Jeff talk-show routine with Sandra Bernhard, promptly began being seen with Warren Beatty in as many simultaneous locations as Saint Anthony of Padua, and then embarked on an entirely new round of publicity with The Tour, The Movie, and The Album.

This dawn broke in early spring, as the tour started in Japan and immediately began spinning off magazine spreads. The stage show looked scary in these pictures, a late-modernist casino spectacular involving elements from the Cabaret Voltaire, Salvador Dali's 1939 World's Fair show, *A Clockwork Orange,* Ken Russell movies, and the Alternative Miss World Pageant. Madonna's hairstyle, for which she acknowledged the influence of the mid-1960s "Tressy" doll (you squeezed her stomach and pulled an endless lock through a hole in the top of her head), at the same time suggested styles current on late-night cable-TV commercials for Dial-a-Mistress. The Jean-Paul Gaultier outfits were similarly daunting, redolent of Brunhilde and *Attack of the Amazons* and the homey sinister allure of the 1950s bondage accoutrements immortalized in those little books published by Irving Klaw. Has she gone too far this time? You were supposed to ask.

The show itself was a wink and a nudge, a dance number and a blackout routine. Indeed, in its erotic display it was probably one of the most traditional stage shows to follow the circuit since everybody stopped wondering who killed burlesque. The degree of sexuality present in its set pieces was entirely allusive, twice-removed, and all but obliterated by the massive inverted commas that enclosed every aspect of the production. As a spiritual heir to Barnum, Madonna was in essence executing her version of the sign he famously put up reading "This Way to the Egress," which lured scores of people with active imaginations and small vocabularies right out the door.

For the record: she mock-kicked her female dancers around the stage while insulting them and complaining about the New York attitude (or at least that was the line at the Nassau Coliseum), mimed sodomizing various parties (though you would have missed the allusion had you been thinking Ziegfeld), allowed herself to be mock-ravished by male dancers gotten up as eunuchs during a faux-Oriental version of "Like a Virgin" and by an unseen deity while she struck ecstasy–of–Saint Teresa poses during "Like a Prayer." There was also a song (included on the current album) whose lyrics and production number were devoted to spanking. Oh, yes, and there were those male dancers adorned with breasts that flopped like so many pairs of flaccid phalli while her own set looked like armor-plated projectiles.

There might be said to be a recurring theme here. If truth be told, Madonna herself does not precisely exude sexuality. What she exudes is more like will, iron self-discipline, and, of course, punctuality, that courtesy of monarchs. In her "Ciao, Italia" video, decked out in various gymnastic outfits and body-pumping to the screams of tens of thousands in a soccer stadium in Turin, Madonna looks perfectly able to make the trains run on time. (Do not mistake this for an ethnic slur; her last name could just as easily be O'Flanagan and the setting Oslo or Kalamazoo.) Between the teasing simulation of carnality and the real passion for efficiency lies Madonna's bona fide erotic territory.

All the sexual imagery in the show, behind its rococo and vaudeville trappings, was single-mindedly fixated on power and its representations. The reason that Madonna does not possess much intrinsic sexual appeal, in spite of having raided the symbolic vanity cases of every icon from Harlow to Dietrich to Hayworth to Monroe (and throwing in Elvis for good measure), is that she lacks any trace of vulnerability, a quality that, it should be noted, is essential to the charms of both sexes. Pout and pant and writhe though she might, Madonna is not sexually convincing because her eyes do not register. They are too busy watching the door.

If, at this point, there is any aspect of Madonna's act that seems independent of calculation, it is her preoccupation with the Catholic mysteries. Just such treading of the line between sacred and profane in the "Like a Prayer" video, you will recall, curtailed her lucrative career as a Pepsi-Cola spokesmodel. It seems there was this thing that happened between her and (apparently) Saint Martin de Porres, and then she acquired a case of stigmata, and then. . . . Somehow various people took offense at this rather conventional set of images straight out of the Symbolist fakebook and put pressure on her corporate sponsors to suppress a commercial that by all accounts (it was broadcast exactly once) featured a very different, rather family-oriented story line, even though it was set to the same tune as the video. This incident did not, however, prevent Madonna from including in her stage show a routine suggesting a musical-comedy version of *The Devils of Loudur,* complete with candles, crosses, stained glass, censers, and dancers garbed in mini-cassocks. While it makes for natural theater and automatic naughtiness, and comes equipped with a rich vocabulary of props, costumes, and buzzwords, it is also, how shall we say, parochial, an odd liability for one attempting so earnestly to cover as broad a consumer base as possible.

Perhaps the whiff of scandal accounts for the gusto with which Madonna throws herself into the exploitation of sacerdotal iconography. During her tour in Toronto, plainclothes cops put in an appearance, apparently following up a complaint of lewdness, and although they took no action, Madonna's parent company, Warner Bros., took the incident and ran with it, generating even more publicity from a non-case of censorship manqué. This occurred, with superb commercial timing, within a week of a more serious occasion, the action by the Broward County (Florida) sheriff's office to ban sales and performances of 2 Live Crew's witless but entirely traditional party record. A week or two after that, the National Endowment for the Arts chose to disregard the advice of its own nominating panel and withheld funds from four performance artists whose very earnest and noncommercial work happens to address the concerns of sexual minorities. Meanwhile, in Italy, Madonna succeeded in garnering more publicity from condemnations of her act by religious authorities, and their disapproval either affected ticket sales or provided a cover for sluggish trade. Presumably, Madonna is now free to title her next opus *Like a Martyr.*

And what of the other two legs of Madonna's media-assault troika? The album, *I'm Breathless,* is a departure for her, although not necessarily a very good idea. It functions as a sort of subsidiary sound track tie-in to *Dick Tracy,* and three of the songs included are featured in the movie.The whole is therefore imbued with a 1930s pastiche quality (all except "Vogue," which is fairly generic dance music but possesses considerably more vigor than any of the other tracks). But the current idea of what the 1930s sounded like bears about the same relation to the real thing as the kind of music that is played by men wearing straw boaters and candy-striped shirts and is called "Dixieland" bears to New Orleans jazz.

Whatever interest the songs might themselves contain is disfigured by an excess of cute fillips, the sort of fripperies that at the time were restricted to novelty records. The three songs appearing in the movie are by Stephen Sondheim, which is fine if you happen to share that kind of taste, although it should be pointed out that his penchant for chromatic eccentricities does no favor to Madonna, whose limited vocal equipment is inadequate to the task at hand. As yet another attempt to expand her horizons, this move by Madonna seems ill-advised, as it neither bears her triumphantly into a new area nor capitalizes on her actual strengths—but the thing currently sits at No. 4 on the charts, so who is to say?

The impossibility of second-guessing the vagaries of the American public is emphasized by the appearance of *Dick Tracy,* a film graced by moments of enormous pictorial beauty that otherwise lurches woodenly along—a Red Grooms construction devised by computer or committee—and yet is the hit movie of the summer. Madonna plays one of the four principal roles not calling for grotesque facial prostheses, although Breathless Mahoney is an animated graphic with all the soul of a rubber stamp. Madonna's job is to look, once again, sultry and jaded. Unfortunately she has been given entirely too much to say, and even though her lines consist of strung-together femme-fatale clichés sampled and resequenced from somebody's memory of the works of Mae West, poor Madonna does not manage even a cartoonish conviction. She simply utters, and the lines fall from her mouth and drop on the floor. "I was wondering what a girl had to do to get arrested," she says, with the same inflection she might use to convey her intention of seeing if the mail has arrived.

Madonna, then, is a bad actress, a barely adequate singer, a graceless dancer, a boring interview subject, a workmanlike but uninspired (co)songwriter, and a dynamo of hard work and ferocious ambition. She has thus far been brilliant at imposing herself on the attention of the world, but there is no telling how long she can keep it up. Her pool of ideas, derived from a diligent study of iconology, is limited. There are only so many more myths she can recut to her fit. Her ability to titillate will wane with time; there is a certain age past which pop stars need to affect a serious demeanor or else find another line of work, and perhaps *I'm Breathless,* for all its many teases, represents a rehearsal for this eventuality, a record made for people who stay home at night.

Actually, it is entirely possible that Madonna will be able to coast from wild youth into eminence without an inordinate amount of exertion. To judge by the audience at her recent stage shows, the largest part of her constituency is made up of teenage girls who may not think she's a genius but admire her as a workhorse and a career strategist (and because she scares teenage boys). To these consumers she is already a fixture, who may ultimately be accorded the sort of permanent landmark status currently enjoyed by enigmas like Bob Hope. For the remainder of the public, much of Madonna's success to date has resulted from her function as a ready-made, albeit a very self-willed ready-made. If other decades possessed their blond bombshell superstars, is it not fitting that the present era should have one of its own? From this perspective, Madonna is a star the way Ivory is a soap and Broadway is a street. But while endurance comes naturally to statues, it requires speed and fluidity of humans, and in ever-increasing amounts. Madonna cannot afford to sleep.

JANE MILLER

# MADONNA

1992

*Here's a view of Madonna as performance artist.*—Eds.

She comes out in a white suit of stovepipe pants and short tight jacket and, under the jacket, dark lingerie. She has the habit of throwing her head back and laughing, revealing the split at her two front teeth. Her lips are cherry red and her hair white (for now) and she makes, together with talk-show host Arsenio Hall, a provocative portrait in black and white in America. She is on, at this moment, in forty million homes. Arsenio Hall has just asked her about some spanking going on in the lyrics of her new musical release, *I'm Breathless,* made in conjunction with the film she stars in, *Dick Tracy.* She says a little spanking is all right; and a few weeks later, sex therapist Dr. Ruth joins Arsenio Hall and confirms that, within limits, this is OK.

Not far down the road, Pedro Almodóvar's *¡Atame!* ("Tie Me Up! Tie Me Down!") has opened—a dark comedy about a woman kidnapped by a guy she ends up falling in love with. But not before there's a lot of bruising, tying, and untying, in a fit of macho archetypal behavior, so he can convince her—by the force her resistance has made necessary—that he's a worthy and sensual mate. Indeed, he wishes to "marry her and have two or three children." It's a case of woman-as-object with its tongue very much in cheek. Almodóvar is playing with blood-red set designs, with the convention of the play-within-the-play (here, a director is making his last film), with caricature (the director of the film is a dirty old man in a wheelchair, spinning and salivating), and with conventions of cinematic perspective. In one scene, for example, there is a close-up of a deep-sea diver in clear water; as he propels himself forward by his fins, the camera backs up and we see the diver is a plastic three-inch windup toy, controlled by a woman in a bathtub, and she's got the thing swimming from the far end of the tub toward her open legs.

Almodóvar is playing with women, Madonna is playing with woman; indeed, the whole world likes to play, and in some cases to pay someone to play, with fire. Madonna shocks. Madonna works the line between kitsch and art, between what makes people "feel good" and what makes them emerge transformed. Whether her evolving persona represents what is independent and creative about an artist, or whether her talent is finally, in someone's judgment, inauthentic and banal, or worse, defamatory, she works the Dionysian line. This edge is an archetypal position to be in. It's attractive because creation occurs at just such intersections, and hers, the archetype of the erotic, has the effect of representing them all insofar as eros is the friction of creation.

As pop star, Madonna functions as an archetype directly inside contemporary culture. It goes without saying that her huge success taps an obsession with Christian mythology. She exists in the form of a Black Madonna, not unlike, for example, the polychrome wood statue in Sierra de Montserrat, in Spain, said to date from the twelfth century. According to legend, the figure was found by shepherds in a cave. On this mountain west of Barcelona, the Black Madonna is visited by thousands of pilgrims yearly as the patron saint of Catalonia—a major tourist industry. "Our" pop Madonna—the surety with which she gives herself away!—has revitalized, with élan, with control, with pleasure, powerful iconography (one of the most powerful curses one can snap at another, in Spanish, is still "tu madre"; the same is true in black America). The plastic joy Madonna takes in her illustration of the myth surfaces near the southern French coast, in Vence, in the Chapelle du Rosaire, decorated by Henri Matisse at age seventy-seven as a gift to the Dominican nuns of Monteils who had nursed him through an illness. There, lemon-yellow and sapphire-blue forms float in a large stained-glass window behind a simple altar. A forty-foot crescent-adorned cross rises from the blue-tiled roof. On the side wall, simple black figures painted on white tile. The Madonna holds an infant whose arms are outstretched to simulate a cross. Matisse says,

> What I have done is to create a religious space . . . in an enclosed area of very reduced proportions, and to give it, solely by the play of colors and lines, the dimensions of infinity.[1]

This sounds, to me, like one definition of poetry. Like Madonna, any serious artist is responsible to the archetypes and icons of the species.

One of my favorite titles in modern poetry has always been César Vallejo's "Black Stone Lying on a White Stone." There's something dear and mysterious about it, and no one quite pictures the image the same but the feeling survives wholly. The poem itself is pregnant with detailed foreboding from the start: "I will die in Paris, on a rainy day, / on some day I can already remember. / I will die in Paris—and I don't step aside— / perhaps on a Thursday, as today is Thursday, in autumn."[2] It is reminiscent of Lorca's eerie prophecy:

> . . . I sensed that they had murdered me.
> They swept through cafés, graveyards, churches,
> they opened the wine casks and the closets,
> they ravaged three skeletons to yank the gold teeth out.
> But they never found me.
> They never found me?
> No. They never found me.[3]

Foreboding, prophecy, intimation, insinuation: these borders or barriers are dangerous, brutal. One must not make a mystique of them, but rather survive to celebrate art as their representation. The implications of even an apparently brief border, like a poem title, are large. "Black Stone Lying on a White Stone," as a title, does more for Vallejo's poem, for example, than set an abstraction against a reality, a title astride its poem body. It's true that it adds beauty, grace, and lightness. But there is also something primary and concrete and bold in the title—what size are the stones? Are they like the Japanese pebblelike disks used in their Go game? In fact, "Piedra negra sobre piedra blanca," as translated by John Oliver Simon, is "Black stone over white stone." It refers, Simon reports, "to a pre-Hispanic board game played with stones and found in the ruins of Pachacamac, and black stone over white stone is the move of death."[4] This translation, then, is more evocative and precise; yet, how powerful the original is if for years I have been carrying in my head a translation (Robert Thy's) that is good, that is resonant, but lacking the technical and cultural accuracy. Now any ambiguity has been deleted—the title is more immediate, and the information cast from outside the poem is welcome like the sun. Now I am even more directed to conjure whether the stones are equal in size, more or less; or is the black one enormous but sleek, the white one oval? Fortunately both translators have chosen "stone" over "rock." A rock seems too heavy, less connotative; we are more aware, I think, of a rock's gravity and density than its gesture or form. Before being a philosophical concern, the relationship of rock to stone, or of black to white, is linguistic. One returns, as if one has forgotten a tool for a task, to words.

Poetry, I believe, can be thought of as the black stone on the white stone of culture, and it has enormous power—like a title on a poem—though it seems like a small thing. Where images from American culture and the language to interpret them pervade the electronic, the electric, and the primitive world, the poetic in them adds to those worlds truth, whereas the false or evanescent in them is disruptive in a way that destroys rather than replenishes. Remember the Coke bottle that flew out of the sky in the film *The Gods Must Be Crazy?*[5] Casually discarded from a plane, it lands in the jungle and it takes on larger-than-life proportions in the village. Disruptions can be funny and useful: the bushmen use it to make flute music, to stretch snakeskin, and to pound designs onto fabric, before it becomes the evil thing they fight over, since there is only one—a new and disturbing convention for them. This soft drink, in the form of a Pepsi, is sold on TV by an adolescent man in his thirties, Michael J. Fox (until recently, he played an eighteen-year-old in a sitcom). In the award-winning ad, he lowers himself down a fire escape in a storm to get his female neighbor a soda from a vending machine. He nearly breaks his neck dredging up that great unequalizer, the chivalric code, with the Pepsi. The ad comes across as cute (that lively, American, demoralizing adjective) but contrived and finally false, a small detectable lie, a fiction. Poets struggle to keep the distinction between a truth and a lie. Even though advertising pumps its stuff from the same image pool, the unconscious, it often mystifies, satirizes, distorts. At the core of even a very disturbing poem there has to be a definite calm, the control of the writer at the edge of experience. Eventually, subliminally, the culture, I believe, feels the effects of these poetic goings-on: a logo, or sign, for example, which the audience slips behind or sees through to get to another layer or message. Some particularly resonant ads tap our attraction to and need for the bold assertion of contrariety, an assertion that is poetry's lifeblood. Rap music is the latest version of a consumer product that loves words. Poets also function subliminally and dynamically in the marketplace when they surface as journalists, producers, inventors, and so on, to keep these poetic tools in the system.

Benetton ads pick right up on the tools, whimsically arranging a set of "models"—the word can be used for a person or a thing: the lie begins with irony—of different sizes and shapes and colors, a United Nations of perfect bodies in clothing perfectly unaffordable for most people. Perhaps this is the most unfortunate aspect of "poetic justice," irony used to excuse life rather than reveal it—here is an ad campaign very consciously purporting to be without racial prejudice, without guile, deconstructing the diffident

Hollywood model, yet it, too, is finally cashing in on a concept rather than dislocating our prejudices for altruistic purposes. In the ad, everyone's wearing oversized, stripy, bold new colors, the mauves, chartreuses, and cobalts of a more perfect world. Large black and white polka dots on some legs, and yellow T-shirts and blouses, a layer of flowery prints here, a tight red leather skirt there, and written across it all—the United Colors of Benetton: black and white models all arm-in-arm in a row, black stone, white stone. Again, advertising and television have appropriated the making of swift connections, the poetic metaphor. (Not to mention the appropriation of lighting and cropping from noncommercial still photography, but that is another matter.) But clearly the place where poetic effects have been felt most strongly in the culture is in the music business.

Madonna's success as a songwriter/rock star lies in the timely appropriation of iconography. The transformation of the ancient materials is poetic at the simplest level of function, embodying, through her lyrics and costume, the profane and the sacred. To do this is to politicize, to seize the power of the objects and make it her own. The culture demands, more and more, it would appear, that its sacred symbols be part of the carnal world: the cross hanging down into the bustier. Her song titles come easily out of the Christian terminology: "Like a Virgin," "Like a Prayer," complemented by "Material Girl." Madonna is engaged in blatant, ongoing self-invention, a manipulation of the good/bad girl ("What I do is total commercialism, but it is also art." . . . "Art should be controversial, that's all there is to it").[6] The conceptualized, saucy urban rebel and the chaste stereotype of a blushing bride who affirms the value of true love (see her 1988 video "Like a Virgin") combine to great popular success. The high contrast, as natural and attractive as day and night, is campily and self-consciously conceived. Madonna manipulates her image on her own, playing a version of her downtown self in her debut film *Desperately Seeking Susan,* for example. Recently, too, in David Mamet's play *Speed-the-Plow,* she became unhappy with the light-headed and light-hearted secretary role and eventually quit: "To continue to fail each night and to walk off that stage crying, with my heart wrenched . . . it just got to me after a while. I was becoming as miserable as the character I played."[7]

She is slowly removing the ironic posturing and vamping from her art, the polarized virgin/whore, and becoming the young female presence in pop culture. There is no irony at all in her new video, "Justify My Love" (1991)—it is sexy, it is witty, it flirts with androgyny, it shows a Euro-style powerful woman in heavy makeup and Monroe-esque glamour working the taboos of violence, submission, ménàge a trois, etc., but it is not making fun of itself, not particularly. The video has a confidence and a joy to it. By cutting away the caricature, the satire, there's subsequent fullness. This is the adult and, one might say, the poetic experience, ambivalent but not confused—she knows who she is. She began this artistic growth after her early success with "Material Girl" and *Desperately Seeking Susan.* She chooses consciously, for example, to imitate Marilyn Monroe, reclaiming her. It would have been absurd if it hadn't worked, with her whole identity at stake—this is the risk so familiar and terrifying to the poet—yet Madonna manages the same sensuality and naturalness Monroe inhabited, familiarly entertaining troops at her USO performances. Madonna politicizes the makeover by taking it seriously, not using the image but being it, and, by extension, politicizes Monroe, who finally gets claimed as a woman from-the-inside, and not as an object of veneration/frustration. The poet Judy Grahn did this years ago with a poem that begins, "I have come to claim / Marilyn Monroe's body / for the sake of my own. / Dig it up, hand it over. . . ."[8] Cindy Sherman makes similar claims in her obsessive photographic self-portraits. She photographs herself in different guises and poses without parody. This is a form, perhaps the most blatant form, of reclamation. Madonna momentarily lives out Monroe, literally embodying the poetic gesture, the spirit of an act. From that point on, Madonna has been able to alter the artistic surface, going on to other identities, controlling her vital image, whereas for Monroe what remained was to become a static symbol. That Monroe, despite being manipulated into a persona, was able to be a real presence is a tribute to her greatness, the sheer strength of her personality. Monroe the artist, in *Some Like It Hot,* in *The Misfits,* and other films, controls herself by playing her roles earnestly and lightly, even when they are bimbo roles (with Cary Grant in *Monkey Business*) forced on her by contract.

This control, this pressing the most out of material ("expressing") is essential to the poetic wherever it arises. Obviously, as in Monroe's case, where there is the mix of the poetic and business, there is the possibility of outside exploitation. The poet works essentially alone, without pay, yet it is as possible that he or she loses the frictive moment—where the writer and the fire are one—ending up with unethical or selfish use of material. In returning to nature for signs, it can happen that the poet fails to negotiate with it, merely reassembling the Romantic platform:

> I need to go back into the winter woods
> and climb down through the canyons where the shallow water
> shifts . . .

. . . yes, and any time
when father, husband, good boy, brother, all my voices fail
me
and the fumble for a loving moment falters,
let me go back into the woods in winter
and in summer lie on dry sand[9]

This is precious ("all my voices fail me") and self-conscious ("the fumble for a loving moment falters"—the alliteration here makes the line even more embarrassingly pronounced, adolescent); the adjective "dry" is obvious and, most telling, the winter woods and summer sands are undifferentiated from other woods, other sands, trite, stock images. Why the line break at "water / shifts," other than to assert activity by an enjambment because the verb is weak? Real poetic activity explodes, explores, demystifies. It is not exactly like taking the ore out of a mountain, for the power of the mountain remains in the ore. That is why poetry that is simplistic or overexplains is lost on us. ("I need to go back into the winter woods / and climb down through the canyons"—you do? It may not matter.) The play, the elasticity of control, is a reminder of the essential physicality of the world and is, therefore (like John Oliver Simon's more discriminating translation of Vallejo), a subtle and powerful correction. The poet must charge material or, put another way, respond to charged material—the cause and effect of it hardly matters. I believe many other artists admire the activity of the poet; in the underworld, money is not at stake and the poet is free to work among the signs, revitalizing their many levels of meaning. The following poem of Laura Jensen's is not about a girl, for example, or a veranda, though those appear here, but shows a poet quietly reassessing, rebalancing, black stone on white, the life of spirit and the spirit of life:

does she rush past me
because she is a vital spirit
exploding from flesh
that sees nothing
will necessarily make sense . . .
the children on the veranda
do not know that they are poor
that part of their psychic pain
is because of it
they think of themselves

as themselves
the ones who are intelligent
will struggle all their lives
to calm the pain—
of vital emotional force[10]

The poem tells us, in clipped Dickinsonian brevity, what the condition of emotions is: "pain." The fragment is psychological and political ("psychic pain / is because of it"). Yet these "ideas" are intentionally balanced by, made equal to, the concrete, monosyllabic "does she rush past me"; the hard beats of real running feet. The poet always keeps a measure and control of the times, and that can be heard in the choice of rhythms. Here the poem works the base line of sound and beats, keeping it simple.

"They shot him a final time, with flashbulbs."[11] This is a line from "The Fall of Che," in Eduardo Galeano's *Century of the Wind,* the third volume of his intense history of the world, *Memory of Fire.* Compare the understatement of feeling here that, paradoxically, invites empathy. He is busy at work in just a single line, dismantling one tone for a higher one; the irony that undercuts becomes the irony that thrusts disparate events together, pointing up their tragic, irreconcilable opposition. The reader travels the events that have led to a tragic end. What must the first shooting have been like? The restraint is poetic, and is the line's power. Most importantly, the verb "shot" is itself put to trial, is exposed and compared with its second usage, "shot . . . with flashbulbs." The killing is judged thereby.

The repetition in a line like "It was so beautiful to live when you were living"[12] lends musical compression to an emotional feeling. This is the beginning of poetry. In Galeano's hands, repetition is used with incredible intentionality: "No one is executed without a trial. Each trial lasts as long as it takes to smoke a cigarette."[13] These are, again, lines from Galeano's history of the world, *Century of the Wind,* a poetic history insofar as the actions crystallize without explanation into moral equivalents. The format is the half- or one-page observation/essence of a fact. Galeano spent years as a journalist practicing the art of condensing. He moves like lightning through history and culture, debunking, alerting, revealing, without a line of rhetoric or overstatement. He "doesn't know to what form the work belongs—narrative, essay, epic poem, chronicle, testimony. Perhaps," he goes on to say, "it belongs to all or none."[14] In these capsule histories, the historian-as-poet tests the values of the culture. He moves by intuition, by analogy, detail by detail, reserving a reverent language for space and distances; maintaining a relationship with magic, and between magic and language. There is a sense—in the selection of words, in the swiftness of phrasing, in the momentum—of the experience of freedom in love, and of the practice of drifting in time.

Meanwhile it is three o'clock in a poet's life, in early summer, say. Radio, a memory of a boat crossing, wind, conversation in Spanish about a water pump, glyphs penned on road signs—the culture makes its assault. Events, trends, and ideas break out onto the scene. So, too, it is poetic work to break into consciousness contents that have vanished into the unconscious, or to bring, as Jung says, "new contents, which have never yet been conscious."[15] Some of these remnants and messages, like the very dreams which are often their transmitters, won't have simple explanations, nor will it be valuable to reclaim all of them. This is the freedom of the poet.

A poem title can carry the same connotative power as any subliminal message in our culture, for it hints and presages. Even a straightforward title of description invites conjecture about its possible use beyond a conventional, obvious meaning, since it exists on the periphery, and that border carries with it danger and possibility. The distance between a poem and its title is analogous to the transaction, on a larger scale, made by those great poets who, like Vallejo, find during their own time a transaction between the personal and the mythic. The title of an art piece speaks to this expectation connection. The finished composition itself speaks to the spirit of the time in which it is made, and if it is gregarious, as in the decision to keep her given name Madonna, it speaks to the spirits in general. Similarly, Michelangelo's Pietá in St. Peter's, with its highly polished smooth surface, is very light and very white in the otherwise overwrought cathedral. Carved five hundred years ago, one can see the white marble engendered out of the darkness.

**NOTES**

1. Henri Matisse, quoted in tourist brochure, Matisse Chapel, Vence.
2. Cesar Vallejo, "Black Stone Lying on a White Stone," translated by Robert Thy, *Neruda and Vallejo: Selected Poems* (New York: Beacon Press, 1971).
3. Federico García Lorca, *Poet in New York,* quoted in Edwin Honig's *García Lorca* (New York: New Directions, 1963), p. xiii.
4. John Oliver Simon, "A Glance at Peruvian Poetry," *American Poetry Review,* vol. 18, no. 3 (May/June 1989), p. 10.
5. *The Gods Must Be Crazy,* directed by Jamie Uys, a 20th Century-Fox Release, 1984.

6. "Madonna: The New, Revamped Vamp," Stephen Holden, *The International Herald-Tribune,* Mar. 21, 1989, p. 20.

7. "Madonna," Bill Zehme, *Rolling Stone* magazine, Mar. 23, 1989, p. 180.

8. Judy Grahn, *Edward the Dyke and Other Poems* (New York: Women's Press Collective, 1971).

9. Brooks Haxton, "For the Returning and Remaining Absent," *American Poetry Review,* vol. 18, no. 2 (March/April 1989).

10. Laura Jensen, "What Can We Wish For and Believe We Can Have?" *American Poetry Review,* ibid.

11. Eduardo Galeano, *Century of the Wind* (New York: Pantheon), 1988.

12. Pablo Neruda, speaking to Mathilde Urrutia; quoted in *Century of the Wind.*

13. Galeano, p. 150.

14. Ibid., from the introduction.

15. Carl Jung, *Man and His Symbols* (London: Pan Books, 1978), p. 25.

CATHY SCHWICHTENBERG

# MADONNA'S POSTMODERN FEMINISM: BRINGING THE MARGINS TO THE CENTER

1992

*A well-known and controversial academic critic of Madonna adds her voice to the fray.*—Eds.

*Within the context of ongoing debate between feminism and postmodernism, this essay adopts a postmodern feminist perspective to examine how pop-star Madonna uses postmodern strategies of representation to challenge the foundational "truths" of sex and gender. Specifically, the music videos "Express Yourself" and "Justify My Love" are analyzed to illustrate gender deconstruction and sexual multiplicity. While such a postmodern challenge may not be amenable to feminisms based on an identity politics, it does bring previously marginalized "others," such as gay men and lesbians, to the center as a model from which a multifaceted coalitional politics can be built.*

It is precisely at times such as these, when we live with the possibility of unthinkable destruction, that people are likely to become dangerously crazy about sexuality. . . . Disputes over sexual behavior often become the

Attending the gala premier of *Evita* in Los Angeles. *Courtesy of Vinnie Zuffante, Star File.*

vehicles for displacing social anxieties, and discharging their attendant emotional intensity. Consequently, sexuality should be treated with special respect in times of great social stress. (Rubin, 1984)

On Monday, December 3, 1990, the two most current signifiers of sexuality and destruction were coupled on ABC's *Nightline*. Although Madonna's defense of her sexually explicit "Justify My Love" video ranked a newsworthy first, displacing the war in the Gulf, one followed fast on the other. This pairing was not coincidental. As Gayle Rubin points out, . . . times of great social stress, such as those created by deficit, recession and war, are likely to produce a displacement of anxieties onto sexual values and erotic conduct. The controversy surrounding Madonna's depiction of diverse sexual practices is, perhaps, symptomatic of the contradictions that besiege the core of an American value system that polices "deviant" sexualities but sanctions the violence of war. Madonna, I contend, is involved in a bloodless war. Hers is a "sex war" to be fought on the field of sexual representation.

This episode of *Nightline,* with Forrest Sawyer, established such a confrontation. Following a video montage that featured Madonna "pushing the boundaries of sexuality," Forrest Sawyer issued a paternalistic warning to viewers prior to screening "Justify My Love." Madonna, as interviewee, spoke nervously from within the television frame—a double "frame" established by the normalizing context of the mainstream media. She was forced to justify "Justify" in response to Sawyer's sexual inquisition, which defined the terrain of discussion in terms of moral absolutes. Forrest Sawyer appeared patronizing and self-righteous, constantly referring to boundaries, lines and limits: "Where is that line?" "First, you have to tell me where *you* draw the line." In Sawyer's "newsworthy" discourse on sexuality "the line" established a zone between a sanctified sexual order and the evil, unspeakable acts on the other side. Madonna, with her polymorphous, gender-blending ménage, had clearly crossed into the "danger zone."

While Madonna crosses lines between gender polarities and sexual practices in "Justify My Love," her multiple video incarnations also have been described as a postmodern challenge to aesthetic boundaries. E. Ann Kaplan notes that Madonna's "postmodern feminism is part of a larger postmodern phenomenon which her videos also embody in their blurring of the hitherto sacrosanct boundaries and polarities such as male/female, high art/pop art, film/TV, fiction/reality, private/public" (1987, p. 126). Madonna's shifting persona and stylistically seductive aesthetic are all hallmarks of postmodern commodity culture where modernist notions of authenticity surrender to postmodern fabrication.

Madonna's postmodern reinventions are of particular concern for some feminists who view her multiple personae as a threat to women's socialization which entails the necessary integration of female identity (Goodman, 1990). Yet, such displeasure signals an even larger problematic that pits feminism against postmodernism. Here, perhaps most troubling to feminist criticism is Madonna's role as an envoy of postmodernism which, in its lack of authenticity, unity, and stable categories, challenges the more modernist foundational tenets of feminism itself.

Nancy Fraser and Linda Nicholson (1990) explain that the rift between postmodernism and feminism is the result of two tendencies that have proceeded from opposite directions toward the same objective: to debunk traditional (patriarchal) philosophy in favor of a more politically potent social theory/criticism.

Postmodernists have focused primarily on the philosophy side of the problem. They have begun by elaborating antifoundational and metaphilosophical perspectives and from there have drawn conclusions about the shape and character of social criticism. For feminists, on the other hand, the question of philosophy has always been subordinated to an interest in social criticism (pp. 19–20).

However, while feminists may have willingly subordinated philosophy to social criticism, philosophy as a male preserve has continued to subordinate questions of feminism.

Craig Owens (1983) observes that in the early 1980s women were excluded from the postmodern debate. This debate, which incited grand theorizing from male philosophers and cultural theorists, focused on the postmodern challenge to modernism and enlightenment philosophy without so much as noting women's absence (Habermas, 1983; Jameson, 1984; Lyotard, 1984). In response, feminists impertinently pointed out that while male philosophers and cultural theorists could freely relinquish mastery, foundational truths, and unified conceptions of self, women had to question such relativistic thinking since they had yet to establish an adequate foundation for feminism that could articulate women's multiple identities to a unified social identity. Such an identity could incite collective political action as well as help forge a social theory responsive to the conditions of all women, oppressed under patriarchy specifically by virtue of gender. Postmodernism called on women to relinquish their foundational goals, and seemed to undermine earlier feminist theories that moved in that direction.

According to Fraser and Nicholson (1990), throughout the 1970s feminist thinkers had endeavored to produce expansive social theories that could explain the basis for male/female inequities. In the process, feminist thinkers (the authors cite Chodorow [1978] and Gilligan [1983] as representative) often reified female differences through essentialist (or universal) categories that excluded the determinants of race, class, and sexual preference. Postmodernism, by contrast, focused on the differences between women rather than their sameness, and emphasized the socially constructed (not to mention fluid and ad hoc) nature of all sex/gender categories.

Feminism's newly emergent foundation, forged as an inclusive, woman-centered basis for social thought and political action, confronted a postmodernism without guarantees for feminism, that instead offered a network of potential alliances not necessarily bounded by the category of "woman" and its epistemological entailments. With this as a context, it is easy to see why an alliance between feminism and postmodernism is regarded with skepticism.

Currently, then, postmodernism is thought a political liability for feminism, insofar as postmodernism challenges a unified conception of feminism. Because feminism attempts to posit a unified identity for the category of "woman" as its foundation (as in "women's culture," "feminine writing," or "female discourse"), feminism is compelled to exclude fragmented or multiple identities from its ranks as disruptive signifiers of postmodernism. Thus, both Christine di Stefano (1988) and Kate Soper (1990) argue that postmodernism, with its emphasis on fragmented identities, runs the risk of destroying or subverting feminism which, as gender politics, is based on a unified conception of women as social subjects; while Seyla Benhabib (1984) notes that postmodernism leads to relativism. Susan Bordo, however, cautions against "eschewing generalizations about gender a priori on theoretical grounds" (1990, p. 135), and notes that Madonna's postmodern presentation in a music video like "Open Your Heart" facilitates rather than deconstructs her objectification (1990a).

But postmodernism may not be a political liability for feminism. For instance, "simulation," the key term in Jean Baudrillard's (1983) postmodern theory, is a concept often overlooked in feminist debates. Simulation, which stresses the artificial as "dress-ups," "put-ons," and "makeovers," is not a political liability for a postmodern feminism intent on reclaiming simulation for the "other." In particular, Madonna's political stylistics appeal to lesbians who have long been the "other" as "the skeleton in the closet of feminism" (Case, 1988–89, p. 57). Madonna's gender-bending pinstriped suit and crotch-grabs in "Express Yourself," her scene of Sapphic titillation on *David Letterman,* and her languid French kiss with *l'autre femme* in "Justify," all represent a deconstruction of lines and boundaries that fragment male/female gender polarities and pluralize sexual practices. This is a postmodern, unbounded feminism, that unifies *coalitionally* rather than foundationally.

Thus, I read Madonna's figuration against the backdrop of Baudrillardian theory where simulation is the pivotal term for a postmodern feminism that addresses differences between and among women. Madonna, a postmodern "product," uses simulation strategically in ways that challenge the stable notion of gender as the edifice of sexual difference. Specifically, I analyze Madonna's deconstruction of gender boundaries in the music video "Express Yourself" to illustrate the fragmentation of gender, which is then refashioned through the flux of identities, more conducive to readings of otherness. This, in turn, advances the argument for a radical sexual politics, best exemplified through Madonna's stylistic challenge to an ontological notion of sexuality pluralized in the music video "Justify My Love." Such an excursion into Madonna's protean persona underscores the need (now more crucial than ever) for feminism to "open its heart" to the radical disjunctures informing gender and sexuality as plural invocations for women under the sign of postmodernism.

### Disperse Yourself: Postmodern Gender Simulations

While from the outset, Jean Baudrillard's (1983, 1988, 1988a) bleak postmodern theory may appear to have nothing in it for women, looks are deceiving. Amid his reified surface world, emblematic of a dead culture, is the concept of simulation. Simulation functions as the conceptual linchpin in Baudrillard's theory of the hyperreal, and is operationalized at the moment when the poles of the real and representation contract and collapse into one another. Simulation begins with the liquidation of all referentials, and a new culture of surfaces emerges out of the rubble. This new postmodern culture lacks all reference to a fixed and stable reality. When played out in a postmodern feminist key, this bipolar collapse into fabrication poses a challenge to the male/female polarities of sexual difference, which have by now proved to be an impasse for feminist theory (de Lauretis, 1987; Kaplan, 1985).

Indeed, sexual difference was erected as a binary structure in which woman's differences were posed in opposition to man's. This reliance on gendered binarisms resulted in woman's separate but equal status, or in feminine essentialism, neither of which proved fruitful for theorizing gender beyond the constraints of biological sex. Moreover, the polarities of sexual difference buttressed the edifice of heterosexuality, ostensibly excluding all "others" who did not accede to the male/female couplet (de Lauretis, 1986; 1987). Thus, in the effort to collapse this binary opposition, postmodern feminists can seize the moment of simulation, and read sexual difference against the backdrop of postmodernism, where gender emerges as a process that must be "worked at" and constructed.

Foremost among constructions of gender is "femininity" which, in light of simulation, can be regarded as artifice or masquerade. For instance, psychoanalyst Joan Riviere (1986) notes that "women who wish for masculinity may put on a mask of womanliness to avert anxiety and retribution feared from men." This, she argues, is especially true of women in male-dominated professions where women disguise themselves as "feminine," as disempowered (p. 93). However, while Riviere contends that femininity is *used* as a masquerade in the form of "protective coloration," she is unwilling to assert that all femininity is a "put-on," lacking any essential bipolar foundation in sexual difference. Femininity is marked by the arrangement of signifiers on the body's surface that act in a part-to-whole relationship in the construction of a "look."

The "look" is key, for women simulate appearances. In this regard, Michele Montrelay describes femininity as a masquerade that "takes shape in the piling up of crazy things, feathers, hats, and strange baroque constructions which rise up like so may silent insignias" (1978, p. 93). Indeed, Montrelay, Gayatri Spivak (1976, 1983), Mary Russo (1986), Judith Butler (1990a), and Mary Anne Doane (1982) have all suggested that mutable cultural underpinnings of femininity as an exaggeration in which woman "plays" at herself, playing a part. This suggests a reflexive shift to the surface where femininity is a masquerade that is in excess of itself. In particular, Doane notes that "this type of masquerade, an excess of femininity, is aligned with the *femme fatale*" (1982, p. 82).

The part of the *femme fatale* has been repeatedly performed by Madonna, who organizes her excess of femininity around the drama of vision. Her body functions as a "prop" that simulates the excessive femininity of male projections only to turn that vision against itself. For example, "Open Your Heart," "Borderline," "Material Girl," and "Express Yourself" are all reflexive commentaries on male "looking" countered by a feminine "look." "Open Your Heart" is structured as a cinematic peep show that frames Madonna's play as stripper; "Borderline" is organized around photography and modeling; "Material Girl" refers to the cinematic construction of Marilyn Monroe, deconstructed by Madonna's feminine double-play as a construction of a construction; and "Express Yourself" advances a panopticon-like vision of surveillance, which Madonna underscores in her gyrations against a screen that reduces her figuration to a cartoon-like silhouette.

The exhibitionist knows that the voyeur is watching; thus, Madonna bares the devices of femininity, thereby asserting that femininity is a device. Madonna takes simulation to its limit in a deconstructive maneuver that plays femininity off against itself—a metafemininity that reduces gender to the overplay of style.

If femininity is an excessive performance on one side of the divide, then gender play signals the play of signifiers across the bar. As Wendy Chapkis notes, "Gender and sex increasingly do appear to be areas of fashion and style rather than biology and identity" (1986, p. 138). Gender play is the mix and match of styles that flirt with the signifiers of sexual difference, cut loose from their moorings. Such inconstancy underscores the fragility of gender itself as pure artifice. Thus, gender play takes shape in a postmodern pastiche of multiple styles: masculinity and femininity fractured and refracted in erotic tension.

Gender play is highlighted, in particular, by the play of differences signifying "drag." Indeed, if masquerade is feminine excess, then drag is the ebb and flow of dis-engendered and re-engendered signifiers that are held in suspension. In the case of female impersonators, Esther Newton (1972) notes this as a "double inversion" in which "appearance is an illusion": "Drag says 'my outside appearance is feminine, but my essence inside [the body] is masculine.' At the same time it symbolizes the opposite inversion: 'my appearance outside [my body, my gender] is masculine but my essence inside [myself] is feminine'" (p. 103). Drag foregrounds gender as an imitation that lacks an original through a constant shift of contingent signifiers.

Newton's (1972) formulation is relevant to drag insofar as it stresses the double inversion of polarities; however, drag as a performance of gender goes even further. The stylistics of gesture, posture, movement and pose, as well as the stylization of external adornments, are all signifiers on the loose. These signifiers are in process, transiently coded and highlighted in a bricolage of differences that construct an "imagined body" or "provisional identity." Signifiers touch, create friction, and move about in multiple configurations that fragment gender and eroticize play. Drag consists of an energized surrender and retrieval in which parts in flux never designate the whole, but rather pose gender as an inherently fractured and easily fragmented construction.

For instance, in Madonna's "Express Yourself" video, drag is a deconstructive performance staged against the futuristic, intertextual backdrop of Fritz Lang's *Metropolis*. This revitalized, postmodern backdrop provides a pastiche of sexually loaded signifiers that reference everything from S/M to gay male pornography, thereby setting the stage for a suited Madonna (Curry, 1990). Madonna's performative play has been described approvingly as "a dykey Madonna dancing in a man's suit [and] grabbing her crotch" (Porkorny, 1989, p. 10). Indeed, her drag dance is a de-centering vision that foregrounds the double inversion of drag as a double-play on gender. Drag parodies gender, which is fissured through a doubling back on femininity in a masculinity that is feminized: the body multiply figured as gender's autocritique.

Here, Madonna's body is dynamized in a constant conflict and rearrangement of signifiers. Her excessively *femme* silhouette cuts to a working-class man in silhouette who watches Madonna emerge from the smoke—her monocled and suited transformation, a parodic send-up of "the boss" and the bounds of gendered authority. She throws her body into broad movements—mechanized, abrupt. Madonna's dance freely associates with "masculine" workout moves in a kinetic synchronization that also invokes the dissonantly gendered body of Michael Jackson.

Powerful low-angle shots predominate as Madonna punches the air, grabs her crotch, and spreads her legs. She teasingly opens and closes her jacket, revealing a black lace bra in a dissonant interplay of difference. Here, Madonna's drag dance resonates with postmodern dance, which "directs attention away from any specific image of the body and towards the process of constructing all bodies" (Dempster, 1988, p. 48). Madonna's body, caught in the flux of destabilized identities, deconstructs gender as a "put-on," a sex toy. Madonna concludes the sequence with hand on crotch and finger pointed at the viewer. The viewer is compelled to reread her body as the intersection of converging differences.

This imaginary construction of the body as fragments reflects on the artifice of gender. Madonna's disingenuous figuration signifies, through strategies of simulation, a political core at the heart of play. Her strategies are not alien to the lesbian community. As Joan Nestle (1988, p. 18) notes, "On a good bar night, the variety of self-presentation runs the whole gamut from Lesbian Separatist drag to full femme regalia to leather and chains." So, too, Madonna enacts this multiplicity; her postmodern body, in disguise and in process, is "unstable, fleeting, flickering, transient—a subject of multiple representations" (Dempster, 1988, pp. 48–49). Two of Madonna's representational strategies have been touched upon here as feminine masquerade and drag. Indeed, the surface play of gender suggests plural styles that, under the sign of the postmodern, are made available to multiple discourses.

#### Sexuality: Over the Line and Between the Sheets

If, for postmodern feminism, gender has gone up in smoke in the implosion of sexual difference, then the next step is to deconstruct "sex" as the basis for identity. Sex must be placed on equally fictive footing with gender, for both are mutable and constructed, and thus can be deconstructed and refigured. As Butler insightfully remarks, "If the regulatory fictions of sex and gender are themselves multiply contested sites of meaning, then the very multiplicity of their construction holds out the possibility of a disruption of their univocal posturing" (1990a, p. 32). Indeed, one's biological sex has long been riveted to ontological, essentialist notions of sexuality, with gender as an alibi. Here, Jonathan Ned Katz notes that "feminists have explained to us that anatomy does not determine our gender destinies (our masculinities and feminities)"; however, "we've only begun to consider that biology does not settle our erotic fates" (1990, p. 29). Nature has functioned as the basis for culture and its social practices; thus, exposing the artifice of gender is only half the job: sex still exerts a tenacious hold. It is the last line of defense, harboring "natural," "normal," "immanent" notions of sexuality.

In this society, in particular, compulsory heterosexuality regulates a normalizing frame, for sex (as biology) and gender (as culture) have long been wedded to produce one acceptable form of sexuality as the "natural" derivation of the two. Sexual essentialism, thus rooted in biology, generates sexual determinism as some immanent proclivity towards "proper" erotic aim, object choice, and sexual practice. However, as Katz notes, "The common notion that biology determines the object of sexual desire, or that physiology and society together cause sexual orientation, are determinisms that deny the break existing between our bodies and situation and our desiring" (1990, p. 29).

Thus, I would argue, it is time for a break—a radical break from the impoverished script of a univocal sexuality. Here, the postmodern proliferation of bodies, pleasures, and knowledges advocated by Michel Foucault (1980) deregulates the univocal aim of sexual agency, thereby calling into question the fundamental categories of sex and gender as the basis for a unified identity. As demonstrated earlier, gender can be exposed as artifice through strategies of simulation that collapse binarisms. But sexuality too must be derailed from its track which is locked into a naturalized heterosexual destination.

Once again, the maintenance of gay/straight boundaries categorically reproduces the old dream of symmetry found in the male/female couplet of sexual difference. While gender succumbs to simulation, sexual practices take refuge in sexed bodies from whence those practices originate as homosexual or heterosexual. Not surprisingly, heterosexuality (like the gender-master-term "male") is constituted as a monolithic category against which all other practices are defined as "other," as deviant. Deviance, though, is necessary to the constitution and invention of heterosexuality (Katz, 1990). This tenacious sexual binarism undergirds Forrest Sawyer's compulsion to repeat "lines, limits and boundaries" in his *Nightline* interview with Madonna. In order to protect the heterosexual zone, Sawyer tries to stave off sexual plurality through the erection of discursive boundaries, a symptom of his terror. Thus, when Sawyer stutters "and you have . . . apparently group sex," his referent collapses the video with Madonna, her body the finely honed instrument of multiple practices as simultaneously fucker and fuckee with the video's multiple bodies—all detoured from their assigned routes.

Not surprisingly, "Justify My Love" has been characterized by a moralistic litany of charges against nudity, bisexuality, sadomasochism, and multiple partners (group sex). The video opens up a Pandora's Box of "sexual prohibitions," which are judged as such through the maintenance of a single sexual standard. The kind of sexual morality, whether religious, political, or psychological, that legislates such a standard has, as Rubin (1984) notes, "more in common with ideologies of racism than with true ethics." According to Rubin:

> A democratic morality should judge sexual acts by the way partners treat one another, the level of mutual consideration, the presence or absence of coercion, and the quantity and quality of the pleasures they provide. Whether sex acts are gay or straight, coupled or in groups, naked or in underwear, commercial or free, with or without video, should not be ethical concerns. (p. 283)

Here one's body, and what one chooses to do with it, may be the last bastion of freedom against those discourses that try to restrict it. Even those discourses associated with the progressive agendas of liberalism, socialism, and feminism, which supposedly pride themselves on a politics of cultural diversity, often deny freedom of expression to alternative sexualities.

Perhaps most alarming is the tactical alliance between antiporn feminists and the right wing, of which Rubin notes that, "stripped of their feminist content, much of the language and many of the tactics of persuasion developed by the feminist antiporn movement have been assimilated by the right wing" (Stamps, 1990, p. 9).[1] Thus, feminists concerned with violence against women find themselves strange compatriots with the Moral Majority in a coalition that will not necessarily deter male perpetrated violence, but is likely to place sexual minorities under seige by the state.[2]

Butler (1990) points out that one way to combat this assault on sexual pluralism is proliferation, a Foucauldian strategy that displaces the binary structure of gay/straight as discursively uncontrollable. Rather than succumb to the ontological identities at the core of this sexual binarism, the task is to efface boundaries by refusing the definitional efficacy of the terms themselves—to build up a range of representations and intensify multiple meanings. Such tactics, which push for a democratic morality, have been implemented unwittingly by the mainstream media. In its eagerness to vilify "deviance," the media continues to be complicitous in proliferating sexual representations that invite viewers to question the very basis of a single-standard morality within public discourse.

In this respect, both Madonna's polymorphic video and Robert Mapplethorpe's S/M photographs have served as a vehicle for public controversy. The two share much in common as multidiscursive fragments that have insinuated themselves into our culture's sexual *lingua franca* as so many loaded signifiers. However, they share even more than representational proliferation and an excess of signification, for Richard Meyer (1990, p. 65) notes that Mapplethorpe's visual aesthetic relies on the intrinsic theatricality of S/M, a high stylization that also informs the sexual stylistics of Madonna's "Justify My Love" video.

While "Justify" borrows its *mise-en-scène* from European art cinema, it duplicates Mapplethorpe's preference for black and white to intensify sexual theatrics, which are visually extended by the video's camera work. Vertiginous camera movement tracks Madonna's dizzying walk through mazelike hotel spaces, a subjective sign of the autoerotic extended to glimpses of bodies in spatial dislocation. Fluid cuts on action shift between Madonna's undulating body in the corridor's exaggerated deep space, and the flat staged spaces where leather/lace-clad bodies pose between acts. Here the trope of sadomasochism is complicated through a staged distribution of fetish-signifiers that diffuse the typical binary terms of mastery and subordination. Marked by fluidity and dislocation, this dream scene collapses the boundaries inscribed in spatial and sexual relations. As Eric Michaels notes, "Texts which intend polysemy, which do not police meaning but instead invite it, do not encourage [singular] identification, a psychological response, but displacement, a spatial activity" (1987, p. 91). The polysexual stimulates the polysemic in this dream of dissymmetry where sexual identities are displaced by multiple erotic acts.

Displacement is at the core of the video's transgression where bodies intersect in the infamous bedroom scene. Here, multiple bodies shift positions in a series of displacements, while camera movement simulates the fluidity of erotic activity as it ranges over bodies, undisturbed by substitutions. Core identities surrender to the assumption of erotic roles in a splitting between dark, light, male, female, gay, straight—differences multiplied and compounded. As Butler notes, "Fantasy enacts a splitting or proliferation of identifications that puts the very locatability of identity into question" (1990, p. 110).

Thus, from the outset, in medium shot, Madonna draws her lover, Tony Ward, onto the bed. Space is disrupted as a black, sexually stylized figure enters the frame in a close-up, low-angle shot coded as above Madonna/camera/viewer. A cut reorients space yet again in a medium close-up shot of Madonna prone on the bed, her arms raised in expectation. Splits between spaces break spatiosexual continuity, and Madonna is joined across the divide by a wo/man coded between male/female, light/dark: a coding split between spaces and identities. S/he becomes the third term, interceding between Tony/Madonna, as the "top" to Madonna's "bottom." The triangulated erotic action shifts to Tony Ward, now in the revolving third-term position—voyeur to female performers who, as exhibitionists, break the male gaze in two shot-reverse-shot sequences.

Madonna and the complexly figured wo/man on the bed dislocate and reallocate erotic aims in a polymorphic distribution. As their bodies entwine in a convergence of rhyming black lace, the camera moves horizontally up their bodies toward the locus of categorical rifting, the mouth. Gender and sexuality are placed in question in this crossing of boundaries where a deep, languid kiss is the focal point—a collapse of space and binary terms into the erotic act. As Rosalind Coward notes, "Sexual relations alone regularly transgress the barrier around each individual, and the kiss seals a crossing into this personal zone, a crossing into the empire of the senses" (1985, p. 96). Close-ups of a muscular back, the flesh between edges of black lace, capture the tactility of Madonna's slow caress, mutually enjoyed.

"Justify" maintains these structures of splitting, displacement, and the multiplication of erotic aims rerouted into a sexually plural orbit. This extends to top/bottom relations which, while derived from the terminology of gay S/M, more generally refer to sexual exchanges in which power is eroticized in the enactment of fluid erotic roles. Newton and Walton (1984) note that:

> In any given sexual exchange, the top is the person who conducts and orchestrates the episode. The bottom is the one who acts out or interprets the sexual initiatives and language of the top. How this exchange takes place is not a given. The top might not move much or the bottom might be expressive and physically active, rather than the inert being conjured up by the word "passive." (p. 246)

Throughout the video, top/bottom relations shift, beginning with the wo/man on top of Madonna and Madonna as bottom, initiator of the kiss. Later, Ward is top and Madonna bottom as the camera's horizontal movements simulate intercourse, while still later, these movements are rhymed when Madonna tops Ward, the closeup of her black-laced buttocks matching the earlier shot of the wo/man's black-laced back. Moreover, toward the video's conclusion, the camera moves with Ward down the wo/man's body in a sensual caress rhymed in a later move upward in which Ward embraces Madonna: black lace doubly matched on the vertical as well as horizontal plane. Thus, the video presents a gridlike structure with which to represent multiple points of sexual pleasure as split and dispersed across bodies, between bodies, on top of and beneath bodies: a plural assertion of sexualities.

"Justify My Love" multiplies and proliferates the very terms of sexual identification through top/bottom interchanges and spacial dislocations that refuse to match sex identity with erotic aim and object choice. Indeed, "Justify" issues a challenge to ontological notions implicit in the sex/gender/sexuality triumvirate by producing rifts and breaks between their linkage. As a postmodern vehicle for this insistent rifting, Madonna pries open a space in the mainstream to provide sexual minorities with visibility and confirmation, while provoking feminism to rethink its own lines, limits and boundaries.

"Justify" and Madonna's other videos suggest that the answer is not to delimit the spheres of feminism and postmodernism, but rather to "push the envelope" toward the postmodern possibilites of multifaceted alliances. Her popularity, which crosses the ranks of cross-dressers, drag queens, Dykes for Madonna, and various gay and lesbian sex-radicals, brings the margins to the center of feminist debate through postmodern representational strategies. Feminism, inflected by postmodernism, may be opened up to more radical possibilities. The gay liberation movement is case in point, where, as James Darsey notes, "the rhetoric of gay liberation is unique in being perhaps the most thoroughly postmodern of reform discourses" (1991, p. 44).

Although differentially constituted (and not without internal as well as external conflicts) gay men and lesbians have been at the vanguard of political movements, displacing essentialized notions of identity with "a patchwork of overlapping alliances" (Fraser and Nicholson, 1990, p. 35).[3] Indeed, the material power exerted through postmodern sex/gender representations, as practiced within the gay community and popularized by Madonna, can fracture the notion of "an identity" with a motley pastiche of interests, alignments, and identities that intersect at decisive moments. Such provisional coalitions could present a formidable challenge to patriarchal moralism, which, lacking the presumed immanence of identity categories, would have a more difficult time maintaining social control over "others" aligned in a disparate unity.

### Conclusion: Toward a Postmodern Feminist Politic of Motley Alliances

The politics of sex/gender representations as they relate to identity has not been lost on Madonna. One of her more recent guises, recounted without a trace of irony in *Vanity Fair,* has been that of the lonely chanteuse, nostalgic for domestic "pleasures" such as picking lint from lint screens and mating Sean's socks (Hirschberg, 1991). This domestic construction provides some rifting with her bold persona in *Truth or Dare,* a confrontational performance-documentary that has, among other things, Madonna declaring that the sight of two men kissing gives her a "hard-on." In each case, Madonna confounds prescribed boundaries by, respectively, playing at femininity and simulating male sexuality. Thus, from her disengendering polysexual display in "Justify," to her drag dance in "Express Yourself," to her representation as space-age dominatrix in Blond Ambition, Madonna will continue to simulate and deconstruct the "truths" of sex and gender.

Through strategies of simulation, she transforms the "truth" of gender into drag, a dialectical fragmentation between two terms, and then fissures this destabilized sex identity further by means of splitting and displacement to advance a prodigious sexual plurality. In more general terms, her disingenuous figuration says much about the political promise of postmodern strategies.

The ungrounded ground of postmodern feminist discourse, in particular, can establish alliances based on an eccentric and disparate mobilization aimed at concerted political action. As Butler (1990a, p. 148) insists, "the deconstruction of identity is not the deconstruction of politics; rather, it establishes as political the very terms through which identity is articulated." This reinscription in the plural expands the range for a coalitional politics not determined or fixed by foundationalist frames. Thus, one could "come out," and participate in a range of identities such as a lesbian heterosexual, a heterosexual lesbian, a male lesbian, a female gay man, or even a feminist sex-radical. As Butler notes, "There are structures of psychic homosexuality within heterosexual relations, and structures of psychic heterosexuality within gay and lesbian sexuality and relationships" (1990, p. 121). Once sex and gender are placed on equally fictive footing, the possibilities for multiple identities (and alliances) are enormous.

So, the postmodern era inaugurating simulation and fragmented identities need not be cause for political pessimism—especially in regard to "others" who have lived in the shadows of realist epistemology and sex/gender essentialism. To think otherwise and to entertain multiple styles, surfaces, sexualities, and identities may move us from the margin to the center in coalitional acts of resistance and disruption.

Thus, we return to the center, to the spectacle of Madonna on *Nightline,* rifting the seams that attempt to suture her into a seamless interrogation. At the interview's end, Forrest Sawyer asks her what she will do next, rehearsing the media's desire to know and fix this prolific source of multiplicity. To this, Madonna reflexively replies: "So you want me to promote one of my products, one of my upcoming, button-pushing products?" Madonna thus refuses to divulge the ground or location of her future insurrections. Coalitional politics that lack all truth in appearances can do likewise. So can a strategic postmodern feminism, whose sly deployments multi-Madonna knows only too well.

## NOTES

1. The specifics of what has been called the "sex wars" or the "sex/porn debates" fall outside the scope of this paper. However, the debates between antiporn feminists and sex-radicals continue to be a rich area for further research, particularly around the defeat of the antipornography ordinances in Minneapolis and Indianapolis, which pitted antiporn feminists against the Feminist Anti-Censorship Task Force (FACT). See Leidholt & Raymond (1990) and Caught Looking, Inc. (1988) for opposing points of view.

2. An unlikely and unofficial coalition of fundamentalist religious groups and antiporn feminists have created a discursive climate which encourages state repression of sexual minorities. For example, witness the frightening breach of civil rights in recent police raids on gay/lesbian nightclubs and gatherings as reported in Boston's *Gay Community News* (Nealon, 1990, 1990a; Yukins, 1991).

3. Here, it is important to note that there are gay male and lesbian differences of response to Madonna. While the wealth of material in the gay press suggests that she

is more popular among gay men (Musto, 1991), she has also had a profound impact on the lesbian community (Solomon, 1990), whose views have been underrepresented in print (but not in widespread networks of discussion). I recognize differences, to be sure, and do not wish to essentialize gay discourse or lump together others as the same. However, my project here is a first step toward deconstructing sex/gender presumptions and foundations, for which I find the rich and multiple differences represented by gay men, lesbians, and others, a lived contestation for what often passes in theory as a given.

## REFERENCES


Baudrillard, J. (1983). *Simulations.* (P. Foss, P. Patton, & P. Beitchman, trans.). New York: Semiotext(e).

Baudrillard, J. (1988). *America.* (C. Turner, trans.). London: Verso.

Baudrillard, J. (1988a). *The ecstasy of communication.* (B. & C. Schutze, trans.). New York: Semiotext(e).

Benhabib, S. (1984). Epistemologies of postmodernism: A rejoinder to Jean-Francois Lyotard. *New German Critique 33,* 103–126.

Bordo, S. (1990). Feminism, postmodernism, and gender-skepticism. In L. Nicholson (ed.), *Feminism/Postmodernism* (pp. 133–156). New York: Routledge.

Bordo, S. (1990a). Material girl: The effacements of postmodern culture. *Michigan Quarterly Review 29,* 653–677.

Butler, J. (1990). The force of fantasy: Feminism, Mapplethorpe, and discursive excess. *Differences 2,* 105–125.

Butler, J. (1990a). *Gender trouble: Feminism and the subversion of identity.* New York: Routledge.

Case, S. E. (1988/89). Towards a butch-femme aesthetic. *Discourse 11,* 55–73.

Caught Looking, Inc. (1988). *Caught looking: Feminism, pornography & censorship.* Seattle, WA: Real Comet Press.

Chapkis, W. (1986). *Beauty secrets: Women and the politics of appearance.* Boston: South End Press.

Chodorow, N. (1978). *The reproduction of mothering: Psychoanalysis and the sociology of gender.* Berkeley: University of California Press.

Coward, R. (1985). *Female desires.* New York: Grove Press.

Curry, R. (1990). Madonna from Marilyn to Marlene—pastiche and/or parody? *Journal of Film and Video 42,* 15–30.

Darsey, J. (1991). From "gay is good" to the scourge of AIDS: The evolution of gay liberation rhetoric, 1977–1990. *Communication Studies 42,* 43–66.

De Lauretis, T. (1986). Feminist studies/critical studies: issues, terms, and contexts. In T. de Lauretis (ed.), *Feminist studies/critical studies* (pp. 1–19). Bloomington: Indiana University Press.

De Lauretis, T. (1987). The technology of gender. In T. de Lauretis, *Technologies of gender: Essays on theory, film, and fiction* (pp. 1–30). Bloomington: Indiana University Press.

Dempster, E. (1988). Women writing the body: Let's watch a little how she dances. In S. Sheridan (ed.), *Grafts: Feminist cultural criticism* (pp. 35–54). London: Verso.

Di Stefano, C. (1988). Dilemmas of difference: Feminism, modernity, and postmodernism. *Women and Politics 8,* 1–24.

Doane, M. A. (1982). Film and the masquerade: Theorizing the female spectator. *Screen 23,* 74–87.

Foucault, M. (1980). *The history of sexuality, vol. 1: An introduction.* (R. Hurley, trans.). New York: Vintage Books.

Fraser, N. & Nicholson, L. (1990). Social criticism without philosophy: An encounter between feminism and postmodernism. In L. Nicholson (ed.), *Feminism/Postmodernism* (pp. 19–38). New York: Routledge.

Gilligan, C. (1983). *In a different voice: Psychological theory and women's development.* Cambridge, MA: Harvard University Press.

Goodman, E. (1990, December 18). Multi-Madonna offers wrong answers. *Daily Hampshire Gazette,* p. 8.

Habermas, J. (1983). Modernity—An incomplete project. In H. Foster (ed.), *The anti-aesthetic: Essays on postmodern culture* (pp. 3–15). Port Townsend, WA: Bay Press.

Hirschberg, L. (1991, April). The misfit. *Vanity Fair,* 158–168, 196–198.

Jameson, F. (1984). Postmodernism, or the cultural logic of late capitalism. *New Left Review 146,* 53–92.

Kaplan, E. A. (1985). The hidden agenda: Revision: Essays in feminist film criticism. *Camera Obscura 13/14,* 235–249.

Kaplan, E. A. (1987). *Rocking around the clock: Music television, postmodernism, and consumer culture.* New York: Methuen.

Katz, J. N. (1990). The invention of heterosexuality. *Socialist Review 20,* 7–34.

Leidhoidt, D. & Raymond, J. (eds.) (1990). *The sexual liberals and the attack on feminism.* New York: Pergamon Press.

Lyotard, J.-F. (1984). *The postmodern condition: A report on knowledge.* (G. Bennington & B. Massumi, trans.). Minneapolis: University of Minnesota Press.

Meyer, R. (1990). Imagining sadomasochism: Robert Mapplethorpe and the masquerade of photography. *Qui Parle 4,* 62–78.

Michaels, E. 1987). My essay on postmodernity. *Art and Text 25,* 86–91.

Montrelay, M. (1978). Inquiry into femininity. *M/F 1,* 83–101.

Musto, M. (1991, March 20). Immaculate connection: Madonna and us. *Outweek,* pp. 35–41, 62.

Nealon, C. (1990, September 9–15). Iowa gay fest raided. *Gay Community News,* pp. 1, 7.

Nealon, C. (1990a, September 23–29). Summer of gay raids. *Gay Community News,* pp. 1, 3.

Nestle, J. (1988). Lesbian roundtable. *On Our Backs 5,* 16–19.

Newton, E. (1972). *Mother camp: Female impersonators in America.* Englewood Cliffs, NJ: Prentice-Hall.

Newton, E. & S. Walton (1984). The misunderstanding: Toward a more precise sexual vocabulary. In C. S. Vance (ed.), *Pleasure and danger: Exploring female sexuality* (pp. 242–250). Boston: Routledge & Kegan Paul.

Owens, C. (1983). The discourse of others: Feminists and postmodernism. In H. Foster (ed.), *The anti-aesthetic: Essays on postmodern culture* (pp. 57–82). Port Townsend, WA: Bay Press.

Porkorny, S. (1989, July 30-August 5), Obsess yourself! *Gay Community News,* pp. 8–10.

Riviere, J. (1986). Womanliness as a masquerade. in V. Burgin, J. Donald, & C. Kaplan (eds.), *Formations of fantasy* (pp. 35–44). London: Methuen.

Rubin, G. (1984). Thinking sex: Notes for a radical theory of the politics of sexuality. In C. S. Vance (ed.), *Pleasure and danger: Exploring female sexuality* (pp. 267–319). Boston: Routledge & Kegan Paul.

Russo, M. (1986). Female grotesques: Carnival and theory. In T. de Lauretis (ed.), *Feminist studies/critical studies* (pp. 213–229). Bloomington: Indiana University Press.

Solomon, A. (1990, June 26). Dykotomies: Scents and sensibility in the lesbian community. *Village Voice,* pp. 39–42.

Soper, K. (1990). *Troubled pleasures: Writings on politics, gender, and hedonism.* London: Verso.

Spivak, G. C. (1976). Translator's Preface. In J. Derrida, *Of grammatology* (pp. ix–xc). Baltimore: Johns Hopkins University Press.

Spivak, G. C. (1983). Displacement and the discourse of woman. In M. Krupnick (ed.), *Displacement: Derrida and after* (pp. 169–195). Bloomington: Indiana University Press.

Stamps, W. (1990, September 30–October 6). On the edge, under the gun: A Boston symposium examines the right-wing attack on radical sexuality. *Gay Community News,* p. 9.

Yukins, E. (1991, March 11–17). Vice cops raid lesbian party. *Gay Community News,* pp. 1, 6.

PAMELA ROBERTSON

# GUILTY PLEASURES

1996

*This discussion of "feminist camp" and how Madonna appeals to those who enjoy exaggerated sexual identities is perhaps one of the few academic articles to mention* The Beverly Hillbillies.—Eds.

Beginning with the appearance of her first singles and music videos over a decade ago, Madonna has been a more consistent subject of public debate than virtually any other entertainer in history. She has graced countless magazine covers, ranging from *Vanity Fair* and *Rolling Stone* to *Fortune* and the *National Review,* and has become a fixture in national newspaper editorials and gossip columns. She has appeared on many talk shows, including a memorable 1990 appearance on ABC's *Nightline* with Forrest Sawyer and two notorious appearances on David Letterman's *Late Night* show. She has been the subject of a TV movie-of-the-week and a feature-length documentary, *Truth or Dare* (which was in turn the object of one-hour-long cable TV parody by Julie Brown and another half-hour parody on the TV show *Blossom*). In addition to numerous biographies and picture books of Madonna, and her own book *Sex,* there is a Madonna comic book, a book of women's dreams about Madonna, even *The I Hate Madonna Handbook*. Madonna is as ubiquitous in academic discourse as she is in the popular media. Already the subject of numerous academic essays in the mid-1980s, three collections of essays published in 1993—one devoted exclusively to Madonna's book *Sex*—cemented the institutionalization of a major subdivision of American media studies into Madonna studies.

As Steven Anderson already noted in 1989, the glut of debates revolving around Madonna run the gamut of concerns about the nature of contemporary society itself:

> The tidal wave of Madonna's renown has swept over adulators and detractors. Once a flesh-and-blood superstar, she's now a metaphysic unto herself. Not that she doesn't have feelings, desires, or stomach gas, but she's achieved such ineffable "being-ness" that old controversies—is she Pop incarnate? Glamorized Fuckdoll?—are largely irrelevant. The only aspect left to consider is Madonna's resonance in the minds of the public, for whom—like it or not—she's become a repository for all our ideas about fame, money, sex, feminism, pop culture, even death.

Anderson suggests that "old controversies" about Madonna are dead; but her "resonance" in the public sphere, while serving as a "repository" for ideas about other matters, still manifests itself in replays of these very controversies. For instance, making a joke about the prevalence of opinions about Madonna in all strata of society, jewelry thieves in Quentin Tarantino's *Reservoir Dogs* argue if "Like a Virgin" is about "big dick" or female desire. Hal Hartley's *Simple Men,* similarly, features generally laconic characters engaged in an extended discussion of whether Madonna's self-exploitation is exploitative. And in academia, feminists query whether Madonna represents parody or pastiche, a healthy break from essentialism or a rejection of traditional feminist concerns. A hall-of-mirrors effect occurs in the construction of Madonna's star text: media attention fuels academic discourse, which in turn fuels media discourse, and ultimately all becomes a part of "Madonna." Rather than ask "Can pop culture be critical of society?" or "What is the meaning of feminism today?" cultural critics ask "Is Madonna a glamorized fuckdoll or the queen of parodic critique? Pop incarnate or an artist/provocateur?"

If Madonna serves as the repository for our ideas about "fame, money, sex, feminism, pop culture, even death," those ideas are filtered primarily through academic and media discussions about the political effectiveness of gender parody and the manipulation of negative stereotypes. The "controversies" Madonna generates echo, in short, controversies about the value and appeal of camp. Thus, a February 1993 item in the *New Yorker* announces, "Camp is dead, thanks to Madonna." The article, a brief review of a drag show, proclaims that "gender tripping can't be subversive anymore" because Madonna "has opened all the closets, turning deviance into a theme park." On the one hand, the article signals the prominence and accessibility of the discourse of camp in the eighties and early nineties—related to the mainstreaming of the spectacle of drag culture symbolized by, among other things, the much hyped "secret" of *The Crying Game,* the popularity of video "queen" RuPaul, *Paris Is Burning,* and *The Adventures of Priscilla, Queen of the Desert,* as well as Madonna's use of drag and vogueing in her videos and tours. On the other hand, by hanging such a quick assessment of the condition of camp on the signifier "Madonna," the article also underscores that Madonna's status in the public mind has come to be that of unique author of gender bending, parody, and female masquerade.

Madonna, clearly, did not invent feminist camp nor has she effected any major changes in the production of feminist camp. The open secret of the Madonna phenomenon is that, in large part, it and she are astonishingly uninteresting and unoriginal. As Russell Baker cogently assesses, "Madonna isn't the cultural elite. . . . She's just Mae West for yuppies." She engages in forms of female masquerade and gender parody similar to those of West in the 1930s, who was herself imitating nineteenth-century burlesque and female impersonation. Like West, she foregrounds her identifications with both African American and gay male culture. Her play with drag and gender bending can be traced to lesbian idols Dietrich and Garbo. Her "Boy Toy" and "Material Girl" personae revitalize the knowing masquerade of countless gold diggers from the 1920s, 1930s, and 1950s. Yet no analysis of feminist camp would be complete without an acknowledgment of Madonna's role in bringing camp to the forefront in a transnational consumer society. While aiming to inscribe Madonna in an ongoing tradition of feminist camp, I suggest that Madonna's *difference* from previous instances of feminist camp, including West, has to do with the changing meaning of camp from the 1960s to the present. As Baker suggests, Madonna is not just Mae West but Mae West for *yuppies*. If the stuff of camp has not changed significantly since West, what has changed is the context in which camp is produced, how it is consumed, and who consumes it.

Camp has undergone two important changes since the 1960s to become a more overt, more public sensibility, and a mainstream fashion. The first is the "outing" and "heterosexualization" of camp, its virtual equation with first pop and then postmodernism, coincident with the publication of Sontag's essay. The second is a more recent shift to overtly politicized camp and radical drag, dating back to gay camp's changed status following Stonewall and the 1970s gay liberation movement, and its revitalization in the 1980s with the onset of AIDS and "queer" politics.

The first predominantly heterosexual pop and/or postmodern style of camp applies to Madonna's career as a whole—in her extraordinary self-marketing, her changing images, and her retrocinephilia. The second, more explicitly homosexual and political style of camp inheres primarily in Madonna's explicit references to gay subcultures, especially drag and vogueing, in conjunction with her stated identification with gay men, her flirtation with lesbianism, and her AIDS charity work. In this chapter, I examine these two trajectories of camp through Madonna's star text. My aim is less to provide a history of Madonna's career than to use her as a lens through which to view post-1960s camp. In particular, I explore the debate about Madonna as a debate about camp, so as to determine what this debate tells us about the status of camp today.

**Cashing In on Camp: Camp, Pop, and Postmodernism**

The publication of Susan Sontag's "Notes on 'Camp'" in 1964 disseminated camp to the general populace, attracting attention in such mainstream publications as *Time.* Despite Sontag's identification of camp as a primarily gay male practice, the publicity surrounding "Notes on 'Camp'" gave the camp sensibility currency for heterosexuals, initiating what Paul Rudnick and Kurt Anderson call the "world of heterosexual camp, Camp Lite." According to Rudnick and Anderson, "The most serious woman in America gave her imprimatur to a jolly, perverse sensibility that was, back then and in the main, homosexual and male": "Sontag's essay was like a thrilling, open-ended mother's excuse note to a whole generation of gifted children: *To Whom It May Concern: Johnny has my permission to enjoy TV and Jacqueline Susann books.*" In defining, if only loosely, the camp sensibility, Sontag must certainly be credited with publicizing the term among heterosexuals. In addition, by legitimating camp as a serious object of study, Sontag opened the way for 1970s gay intellectuals—including Richard Dyer, Andrew Britton, and Jack Babuscio—to engage the topic of camp, often in contention with her characterization.

Sontag's influence, however, cannot be separated from the context in which her essay appeared: namely, pop art. As Andrew Ross points out, pop differs markedly from camp, because camp is the "in" taste of a minority elite, while pop "was supposed to declare that everyday cultural currency had value, and that this value could be communicated in a simple language." Nevertheless, pop problematized the question of taste itself, rejecting an elitist past based on cultural acts of judgment and the notion that objects had intrinsic aesthetic value. Pop, in this sense, created a context for the mainstreaming of camp taste—justifying the democratic spirit of camp, its collapsing of high-low boundaries, while opening the sensibility up to a majority audience. In a curious twist, camp taste became the dominant code. Rather than a covert, cult sensibility, camp became a commercialized taste—and a taste for commercialism—a determinedly unguilty pleasure.

Pop, in its broadest sense, was also the context in which notions of the postmodern took shape. Outside its architectural context, the term "postmodern" is by and large a slippery and unstable signifier, defined, as Anne Friedberg notes, largely through its overusage. The term serves, on the one hand, as a kind of historical marker, isolating contemporary society's explosion of technologies, mass-media fragmentation and globalization, and accelerated information access. On the other hand, the sweeping connotations of the term include discourses of style in various media, as well as theories about the period and its cultural objects. While it is tempting to abandon the term "postmodern" altogether, given its semiotic instability, the various values attached to notions of postmodernity need to be acknowledged and accounted for as part of the cultural current that shapes the discourse around contemporary notions of camp, parody, kitsch—and Madonna.

Andreas Huyssen notes the link between Robert Venturi's influential *Learning from Las Vegas* ("one of the most telling documents of the break of postmodernism with the modernist dogma") and the 1960s pop sensibility: "Time and again the authors use pop art's break with the austere canon of high modernist painting and pop's uncritical espousal of the commercial vernacular of consumer culture as an inspiration for their work. What Madison Avenue was for Andy Warhol, what the comics and the Western were for Leslie Fiedler, the landscape of Las Vegas was for Venturi and his group." Venturi's celebration of Las Vegas style furthered the new camp sensibility's emphasis on the ironic, "thus pushing architecture off on its own snickery detour." Ironic, but no longer parodic, camp came to be equated with postmodern pastiche, which Fredric Jameson has famously labeled "blank parody."

If the mainstreaming of camp taste represents a revolution of sorts, that revolution has, in large part, been televised and televisual. Much of the public discourse on drag, vogueing, and transvestites, as well as other "gay" topics, has since the 1970s taken place on the daytime talk shows hosted by Phil Donahue, Oprah Winfrey, and others. At the same time, a form of camp cinephilia, dedicated to film trivia, the showcasing of "Bad Movies We Love" and classical Hollywood cinema, formerly the stuff of revival movie houses and midnight movies, became a frequent feature on locally syndicated stations across the United States and then on cable TV stations like TNT. Television exposed new generations of audiences to Berkeley musicals, historical camp figures like West, and cult figures like Maria Montez, thus providing an additional context for the rise of camp coextensive with Sontag's writing.

More than just serving as a medium for the "outing" of pre- and post-1960s camp, however, television has itself seemingly become the definitive reference point for the Camp Lite sensibility. The "irony epidemic," as Rudnick and Anderson describe it, filters its jokey baby-boomer ambivalence through insider references to television shows and characters from the 1950s forward as much as, if not more than, through its recycling of retro objects and fashions. This ironic sensibility, which eulogizes a fantasy of the baby boomers' American innocence through nostalgia, has its own television station in the cable network Nickelodeon. Nickelodeon's *Nick at Nite* programming, similar in spirit to midnight movies and the camp fetishization of "bad" movies, most closely captures the spirit of Camp Lite. *Nick at Nite* devotes itself exclusively to rebroadcasting syndicated shows from the '50s, '60s, and '70s. Not content to simply broadcast the shows, *Nick at Nite* underscores its ironic attitude toward them, bracketing them with promos using clips from the shows to delineate the use of triple takes and the history of amnesia plots, or subjecting the shows to mock-serious psychoacademic analysis ("What does Rob Petrie's ottoman signify?"), all in the interest of its quasi-ironic mission of "Preserving Our Television Heritage." Despite its ironic jokiness, then, *Nick at Nite* fetishizes and collects TV trivia, promulgating a kind of nightmare vision of E. D. Hirsch's "cultural literacy" with respect to "classic TV." Beyond Nickelodeon, this nostalgia for "classic TV" has now infiltrated Hollywood, which is in the midst of a trend for "based on TV" films—including the *Star Trek* cycle, *The Addams Family, Dragnet, The Fugitive, Boris and Natasha, Wayne's World, The Coneheads, The Flintstones, The Beverly Hillbillies, The Brady Bunch,* and *The Little Rascals.* It can also be seen in the hip citations of "classic TV" in *Dream On, Natural Born Killers,* and *Pulp Fiction.*

Both camp's alliance with pop and its downshifting into the small screen of television could be taken as evidence of its demise. The term Camp Lite, after all, suggests a watering down of camp's critical and political edge. As Christin Mamiya argues, pop art not only drew upon the mechanisms, imagery, and ideology of consumer culture but also helped to legitimize that system: "Pop art not only depicted and reflected this rampant consumption but also appropriated the mechanisms and strategies of corporate society, ensuring the effective marketing of this movement and its absorption into the matrix of consumer institutions." Due to pop's complicity with corporate society, many critics view camp's sublimation into pop as a betrayal of "true" "authentic" camp, an appropriation of a subculture by the culture industry. In a similar vein, for many critics, the mainstreaming of camp in its appropriation by the widely accessible medium of television, and in its related glorification of a television past shared by most Americans, signifies a loss of perspicuity in camp: televisual camp is no longer the province of an elite few, and the range of objects considered camp have similarly lost their specificity as marginal. Camp's relation to dominant culture, however, was always already parasitic. Rather than an avant-garde oppositional stance, camp represents a subculture's negotiated means of access to the dominant culture; it operates as much by taking alternative pleasures in mass-cultural objects as it does by creating its own objects. In this sense, it registers a subculture's recognition of failed access to and not simply a refusal of the culture industry. In legitimating both camp and consumer society, post-1960s pop camp simply makes public the consumerism already implicit in camp.

Madonna, especially in her Boy Toy and Material Girl incarnations, seemed the epitome of the newly defined camp style, embracing crass consumer culture, like pop, and updating it through new media forms. "The ultimate postmodern video star," Madonna appeared on the cultural scene simultaneously with, and depended on, the introduction of MTV, the cable television station that paradigmatically represents the postmodern explosion of technologies, acceleration of images and information, and mass-media access. Her shifting media images, borrowed largely from stereotypes and cinematic images from the past, seemingly embody the postmodern discourse of style. Madonna is most often compared to Monroe, but her sexy images borrow from other film stars, film genres, and photographic styles. For example, the video for "Open Your Heart" (dir. Mondino, 1986) has echoes of Giulietta Masina in Fellini's *Nights of Cabiria* (1957). "Who's That Girl?" (dir. Foley, 1987) updates *Bringing Up Baby* (dir. Hawks, 1938). And the video for "Vogue" (dir. Fincher, 1990) appropriates images from black-and-white 1930s glamour photography of Hollywood stars. A paradigmatic figure from the Reagan-Bush era, Madonna, moreover, typifies 1980s tropes of mobility and consumption. Resolutely commercial, and flaunting it ("we are living in a material world, and I am a material girl"), Madonna represents herself as a self-commodifying commodity for whom pastiche becomes a marketing strategy.

Joyce Millman aptly describes Madonna as "the video generation's Barbie." Like Barbie, Madonna sells because, like Mattel, she continuously updates the model, making her former selves obsolete. It is not enough to own a Barbie doll, one must own the latest Barbie—Bridal Barbie, Aviation Barbie, Barbie for President, etc. Madonna constantly offers new models, all Madonna but each differentiated through her costume and accessories—Boy Toy Madonna, Material Girl Madonna, Thin Madonna, Madonna in Drag, S&M Madonna, and so on. Millman characterizes Barbie as "the Madonna/whore complex molded into shapely plastic," reflecting, in part, "the fallout of sixties social change and the trickle down of seventies permissiveness." Madonna, similarly, portrays herself as a series of teasingly sexual female stereotypes, the Madonna/whore complex made flesh and blood. She does not just embody a pop or postmodern sensibility but takes that sensibility into the terrain of gender and sexual difference, aligning herself with some of the traditional concerns of camp.

As Ross suggests, the "outing" of camp takes hold in the culture not simply due to its affinity with pop and postmodernism but also because Sontag's essay appears in the context of sexual liberation "for which camp played a crucial role in the redefinition of masculinity and femininity." Ross sees the effect of camp on mainstream popular taste in the eroticized spectacle of performance rock. Madonna has sometimes been compared to performance rock stars, especially David Bowie, because of her shifting images and play with gender roles. Gender bending in performance rock was, however, primarily a masculine privilege. The "redefinition" of sex and gender roles in performance and glam rock was the province of a host of male aesthetes—David Bowie, the New York Dolls, Lou Reed, Iggy Pop, and others. In addition, the gender bending in performance rock, linked in many of the performers' star texts to suggestions of bi- and homosexuality, related more closely to drag and female impersonation than to pop or postmodernism.

While exposing camp style to a heterosexual audience, performance rock differed in spirit from the new camp, disdaining the vulgar consumerism and antielitist judgments of pop. Lisa Lewis notes an ideological division between rock and pop music similar to that between high culture and popular culture: "Rock discourse forged a hierarchy within popular music by creating a structure of value against which 'pop' music could be devalued. Rock was made to stand as a higher form . . . as the representative of art and artfulness." While pop music and pop art are not identical, both embrace consumerism and are positioned as the low other to a "high" culture discourse. Performance rock defined itself in opposition to pop-music discourse and stood instead as the representative of artfulness in popular music. Madonna, in contrast, clearly embodies pop-music discourse: "Image and representation . . . are Madonna's playground. She revels in self-promotion, in the creation of an image or images, in being a personality, a celebrity. She accepts artifice as an integral feature of music production and promotion and is comfortable with textual production." Although Andy Warhol influenced Bowie and Reed, his true heir is Madonna. She captures the full force of Warhol's ironic redefinition of fame and celebrity and his creation of the "superstar" (who becomes one once named).

Male performance-rock artists inhabit a quasi-romantic persona (Ziggy Stardust, Aladdin Sane), their changing images reflecting different voices. Madonna, in contrast, creates different images, the meaning of which exists at the level of style. She does not inhabit personae so much as represent them ironically: "I'm just being ironic. . . . That's the joke of it all. It's a luring device, like the whole boy-toy thing. It's playing into people's idea of what's humiliating to women." In embracing pop discourse, rather than rock, and a postmodern malleability, rather than a romantic star persona, Madonna's eroticized images expose image as artifice and play on the negative connotations attached to images of women.

Some of the controversy Madonna generates has to do with her pop reproduction of the lowest forms of aesthetic culture, her commercialism, and the presumably formulaic and trivial pop music she produces. It is, however, largely because she plays on "people's idea of what's humiliating to women" that Madonna has become a controversial figure in academic and popular discourse. Madonna enters the cultural scene following both the 1970s Women's Liberation movement and the 1980s institutionalization of academic feminism and provokes debates about not just postmodernism but "postfeminism" as well.

The status of and need for feminism in the early 1980s especially was extremely foggy. The label "postfeminist" suggested a belief, in the media and especially among younger women, that there was no longer any need for feminist politics, and, subsequently, suggested a feeling among 1970s feminists that activist feminism was losing ground. The debate about postfeminism encompassed many areas—the viability of women's music, for instance, as well as a questioning of certain "feminist orthodoxies around the body and self-presentation: the injunction against feminine adornment and its oppressive signifiers—makeup, high heels, skirts, long hair and so on," which, for postfeminists, seemed "oppressive and trapping in itself." As a female superstar, Madonna challenged a lot of the established positions of academic and activist feminism and functioned on both sides of the "postfeminist" debate as a touchstone for the rearticulation of a host of feminist issues including pornography, fashion, makeup, and sex.

In discussing the negative female stereotypes contained in Madonna's image, feminist critics echo the post-Stonewall debate about the politics of camp for gay men: they ask whether Madonna fuels or dismantles those stereotypes, whether she represents a retrograde and antifeminist image of oppression, or embodies a new vision of powerful and independent femininity. Most of the negative criticism of Madonna relates to her sexuality and gender—her image as a kind of female grotesque and as the antithesis of feminism and feminist identity politics. In a survey of "Madonna-haters," Madonna is called antifeminist and a backward step for women; further, she is likened to a social disease, a narcissist, a succubus, a vampire, and—linking her sexuality and her commercialism—a prostitute. *The I Hate Madonna Handbook* also compares her to a prostitute and features a quiz: "Feminist or Slut?"

Some feminists consider Madonna's postmodernism a liability for feminism insofar as her changing images challenge the unified concept of "woman." However, contrary to Camille Paglia's assertion that she alone recognizes Madonna's permutations as the "future of feminism," many feminists dismiss the charge that postmodern style is apolitical and empty of content and have considered Madonna's use of borrowed styles to be parodic and critical. For example, discussing Madonna's changing images, and particularly her retrocinephilia, Ramona Curry argues that Madonna "functions not as mere imitation or pastiche, but as a *parody* of female star images, indeed of the concept of stardom altogether." Curry notes that the repetition of this parody may seem ultimately to be pastiche, but "what adheres to Madonna's cumulative image from her varied and multiple performances is her status as a kind of meta-masquerade."

The turning point in feminist attitudes toward Madonna and the beginning of her acceptance by an adult female audience, along with her established popularity among teenage "wannabe" fans, seems to have been the video for "Material Girl" (dir. Lambert, 1985). Here, Madonna imitates Marilyn Monroe's "Diamonds Are a Girl's Best Friend" number from *Gentlemen Prefer Blondes* (dir. Hawks, 1953). In a video-within-the-video, Madonna performs "Material Girl" dressed in a pink sleeveless gown that is an exact replica of Monroe's dress. The song simultaneously celebrates and parodies the gold digger's self-commodification as a form of 1980s crass materialism: "The boy with the cold, hard cash is always Mr. Right / Cause we are living in a material world, and I am a material girl."

Because this video invokes a famous text, and especially a famous sex symbol, "Material Girl" could be taken as simple nostalgia or pastiche. The video, however, reproduces elements of the Monroe image (blondness, sexuality, gold digging) and simultaneously recasts that image in a potentially critical manner. First, the flaming narrative suggests that "Madonna" is not really the material girl of the song, differentiating her from the Monroe character. Greg Seigworth cites the video's "self-conscious disjunction of the singer and the song as ironic commentary on the then-predominant image of Madonna as Boy Toy" and asserts that "Madonna was trying to intervene in and influence the shape her own emerging mythology would take." Second, both Madonna's witty performance and the song's pointed lyrics attribute to the Monroe character a knowingness and degree of control absent from most nostalgic treatments of Monroe, which generally remember her as a witless sex object and/or tragic victim. Thus, the video creates a dialectical constellation of Monroe-Madonna, revealing a stronger and more savvy Monroe in the image of Madonna.

Many feminists embrace Madonna not only because her multiple masquerades challenge essentialist notions of identity, but also because, throughout her various incarnations, Madonna asserts her own power and independence, in the economic sphere and in terms of authorship. In claiming Madonna as a parodic text, critics generally cite her presumed control over her own image. Sonya Andermahr claims, "Madonna calls her own shots. . . . [S]he exercises more power and control over the production, marketing and financial value of that image than any female icon before her. She has never been content to be the face that launched a thousand record covers; she has to be the helmswoman too." Similarly, John Fiske observes, "She parodies not just the stereotypes, but the way in which they are made. She represents herself as the one who is in control of her own image and of the process of making it." As one woman who dreamt of Madonna put it, "I had a dream that Madonna's real name was Boswana. . . . It's because she's the boss."

The issue of economic and authorial control relates directly to Madonna's "success in articulating and parading the desire to be desired in an unabashed, aggressive, gutsy manner." In other words, the perception of Madonna's control relates to precisely the same characteristics that lead some to call her a prostitute—her outspokenness in both her songs and press about her own sexual desires and her sexual attractiveness. Many of her videos, including "Open Your Heart," "Borderline," "Express Yourself," and "Material Girl," offer "reflexive commentaries on male 'looking' countered by a feminine 'look.'" Revolving around a drama of vision, Madonna's videos subvert and complicate the primacy of classical Hollywood's structured male gaze. Gazed at by a bevy of men, Madonna returns the gaze, asserting her own desires and desirability, her status as sexual subject and not merely a sex object. Extratextually, contesting her frequent comparison to Marilyn Monroe, Madonna says, "I take the preconceived notion of what a sex goddess is and throw it back in your face and say I can be a sex symbol, but I don't have to be a victim."

Madonna's initial popularity among teenage girls has been attributed to fans' identification with her power and independence. According to both Fiske and Lewis, for instance, "Madonna as a site of meaning" offered teenage girls a means of resisting the powerlessness and subordination in their own lives. Teenage "wannabes" imitated Madonna's style in the mid-1980s in order to appear sexy and because they admired and identified with her independence, self-reliance, and presumed resistance to patriarchy.

In the same year that "Material Girl" was released, Susan Seidelman's *Desperately Seeking Susan* further broadened Madonna's appeal among adults, especially women. Addressed to young adult women, the film suggests that Madonna's adult female fans, like her teenage fans, identify with her as a figure of power and desire (a suggestion supported by the dreams collected in *I Dream of Madonna*). In the film, Rosanna Arquette's bored suburban housewife functions as an obsessive "wannabe" in relation to Madonna's thinly veiled self-portrait, Susan. Arquette's Roberta voyeuristically tracks Susan's romantic life via newspaper classifieds, spies on and follows her through the city, wears her clothes, and carries a photo of her—even into the bathtub. Roberta's identification with Susan is literalized in the portion of the film when her amnesia causes her to "become" Susan. Ultimately, through her identification with Susan, Roberta gets the courage to become her own person, leaving behind her unsatisfactory marriage, bland suburban life, and unhip clothing. The only narrative film that has succeeded because of, and not despite, Madonna, *Desperately Seeking Susan* not only targeted a more mature audience for Madonna but determined, in large part, the way in which that audience would respond to her.

Critics argue that many gay men and lesbians, similarly, identify with Madonna's power and independence. Michael Musto observes, "Her pride, flamboyance, and glamour reach out to gay guys as much as her refusal to be victimized strikes a chord in lesbians." If gay male identification with female stars had been, as Ross claims, "first and foremost, an identification with women as *emotional* subjects in a world in which men 'acted' and women 'felt,'" Madonna, for Musto, offers a more equitable model. He continues: "It's not the divisive old Judy story, with guys weeping along with the diva as she longs to go over the rainbow and track down the man that got away, while women cringe." A diva of a different sort, gay men, lesbians, and straight women can take equal pleasure in Madonna and identify with her as a figure of desire and power. In this sense, she offers camp pleasure without the guilt of affirming negative stereotypes.

The perception of Madonna's power and independence relates not only to her outspoken sexuality but also to her use of politically controversial imagery in her textual productions. Lisa Henderson ties Madonna's popularity among gays and lesbians to her status as a political figure: "The heart of Madonna's appeal to lesbian and gay audiences . . . include[s] her willingness to act as a political figure as well as a popular one and to recognize that such fraught domains as sex, religion, and family are indeed, political constructions, especially for lesbian and gay people." Madonna both parodies sexual stereotypes and blasts the patriarchal institutions that construct those stereotypes. In videos, songs, commercials, and public-service announcements she has taken on such embattled territories as the Catholic church, the family, abortion, condoms, big business (Pepsi), and the American flag. She has, moreover, made public statements about the censorship battles in the United States and abroad and become a symbol of that struggle due to her banned Pepsi commercial, banned video for "Justify My Love," and threatened boycotts and closings of her live concert tour in Rome and Toronto.

### Queer as You Wanna-Be: Camp and Identity Politics

Madonna's self-presentation and reception among gays and lesbians as a political figure links her to the second tendency of post-1960s camp I mentioned earlier—its shift to overtly politicized camp and "queer" politics. This trajectory springs directly from and closely resembles pre-1960s gay camp. It differs, however, from earlier "traditional" gay camp in crucial ways because the historical meaning of camp changes for gays after Stonewall. As I noted in the introduction, for many gay intellectuals after Stonewall, camp was initially viewed largely as an embarrassment affirming the dominant culture's negative perception of the gay community. Even theorists like Richard Dyer who valorized camp did so largely from a historical perspective, arguing that camp had functioned as a kind of dress rehearsal for liberation politics and "coming out," but not claiming that it should substitute for politics after Stonewall.

At the same time, though, flamboyant drag and cross-dressing began to be used in the 1970s in Gay Pride parades to signify being "out" in a visible public ritual. By taking on the dominant culture's negative perception of gay men as "queens," the use of camp style in public—much like the use of the slogan "We're Here, We're Queer, Get Used to It"—could assert gay pride, identity, community, and history. If pop camp exposes one side of camp—recognizing the camp subculture's consumerism and desire for access to the dominant culture—queer camp emphasizes the other side—camp's ability to signal difference and alienation from the dominant. Here, rather than make public camp's parasitic relation to the dominant culture, queer camp recodes the subculture's own history to reconceive itself as adversarial.

In the 1980s, camp became a key strategy in gay activist politics aimed at asserting gay rights, and not simply gay pride. Gay activists, in the wake of the AIDS crisis, work to improve AIDS awareness among homosexual and heterosexual communities; to demand more government funding for research and treatment centers, faster FDA approval for drugs, better access to experimental drugs, and nonprejudicial insurance coverage policies; and to combat the increasing problem of gay-bashing and hate crimes spawned by AIDS paranoia. With particular attention to the latter, the gay activist group Queer Nation has adopted what Lauren Berlant and Elizabeth Freeman describe as a "camp counterpolitics" in which Queer Nation engages in a "kind of guerrilla warfare." Queer Nation embodies a mobile sense of queerness. According to Berlant and Freeman, it shifts "between a utopian politics of identity, difference, dispersion, and specificity and a pluralist agenda, in the liberal sense, that imagines a 'gorgeous mosaic' of difference without a model of conflict." Staging public events, like Queer Nights Out in bars and parades in shopping malls, Queer Nation claims safe spaces and adopts camp strategies to create visible public spectacles: "Its tactics are to cross borders, to occupy spaces, and to mime the privileges of nationality—in short, to simulate 'the national' with a camp inflection." Queer Nation's use of camp strategies, as well as the prominence of drag in Gay Pride parades, and other overt manifestations linked to gay identity politics, have redefined and revitalized camp within the gay community. The new queer camp style takes on the signs and practices of camp without the pathos, adopting camp not as a mark of oppression but as an index of pride, signaling a refusal to accept oppression anymore.

Andrew Ross rightly claims that for most academics and sex radicals Madonna functions "like what environmentalists call a charismatic mega-fauna: a highly visible, and lovable, species, like the whale or the spotted owl, in whose sympathetic name entire ecosystems can be protected and safeguarded through public patronage." In large part, Madonna's status as a political figure depends upon her willing identification as a "queer" supporter. She has consistently aligned herself in public with gay culture and politics. Madonna had a gay following early on partly because she made African American–style dance music after the demise of disco. In numerous interviews, she states her identification with gay men, self-identifying as a "fag hag" and describing gay men as "just a f__k of a lot more sensitive than most of the straight men I know. They're more fun to be around. They're freer. I also feel that they're persecuted and I can relate to that." Interviews and biographies refer constantly to Madonna's relationship with her gay dance teacher, Christopher Flynn, who was both mentor and close friend and who introduced Madonna to the world of gay discos in Michigan. Madonna is also one of the earliest well-known celebrities who performed in AIDS benefits, and she included safer-sex instructions and a condom in the packaging for her album *Like a Prayer.*

Moreover, in Madonna's gender bending, she identifies herself with a wide range of sex and gender roles, expanding the range of erotic representation and identification. In masculine suit, grabbing her crotch for "Express Yourself" (dir. Fincher, 1989), she imitates Michael Jackson's already androgynous (and parodic?) interpretation of phallic masculinity. In "Justify My Love" (dir. Mondino, 1990), she occupies multiple sexual subject positions, leaving open whether we are to read them as lesbian, straight, and/or bisexual. Beyond videos, Madonna invites us to be confused about her "real-life" sexual identity, in joking about and refusing to clarify the nature of her "friendship" with Sandra Bernhard on *Late Night with David Letterman,* or in offering us *Sex,* her book of fantasies, presumably her own, which features pictures of Madonna with lesbian skinheads, posing in gay and lesbian clubs.

Madonna takes advantage of the pop or postmodern mainstreaming of camp to introduce elements of queer politics into popular culture. John Leland argues that "in exchange for her genuine affection, [Madonna has] raided gay subculture's closet for the best of her ideas." Although each of Madonna's videos contain some element of gender parody, and her career as a whole can be read as meta-masquerade, the video for "Vogue" (dir. Fincher, 1990), in particular, articulates a relationship between gay subcultures, Hollywood stars, and feminist camp. The video mainstreams the subcultural gay practice of vogueing in which African American and Latino gays combine quasi-breakdance movements with impersonations of specific female stars, as well as generic male and female types (e.g., the executive, the schoolgirl). The song and video obscure vogueing's racial and homosexual specificity while opening the practice out to a larger audience. The video shows the men in suits, not drag, and the lyrics exclaim, "It doesn't matter if you're black or white, if you're a boy or a girl." While mainstreaming this practice, however, the video makes sex and gender roles ambiguous enough that its affiliation, and Madonna's, with a gay subculture cannot be ignored or erased.

"Vogue" uses gay subcultural references in conjunction with postmodern pastiche and retrocinephilia to create a queer camp effect. Although the men do not cross-dress, Madonna does. Each time she appears with the male dancers, she wears a dark masculine suit. Her use of drag mixes gender signs—she wears an enormous cone-bra with a man's suit, for instance—and underscores her status as a female female impersonator when she appears singly in various glamorous female guises in other sections of the video. She reappropriates female images from the male dancers, who vogue but do not dress in drag, and yet maintains vogueing's sense of parody and fun. Because no single image-identity seems to be her own, and because she exaggerates and heightens the pose—wearing a ridiculous Veronica Lake wig and reflecting that image in a mirror, for example—she flaunts the masquerade as masquerade.

Madonna's poses in "Vogue" could be taken as simply nostalgic, since the black-and-white glamour photography refers directly and indirectly to well-known Hollywood stars and famous photographs of them. But the song ironizes these star images, even while paying homage to them. After repetitions of the phrase "beauty's where you find it," Madonna raps a catalogue of select Hollywood stars ("ladies with an attitude, fellows that were in the mood") who have overlapping gay camp, straight camp, and nostalgic associations: "Greta Garbo and Monroe. / Dietrich and DiMaggio. / Marlon Brando. Jimmy Dean. / On the cover of a magazine. / Grace Kelly. Harlow, Jean. / Picture of a beauty queen. / Gene Kelly. Fred Astaire. / Ginger Rogers. Dance on air. / They had style, they had grace. / Rita Hayworth gave good face. / Lauren, Katharine, Lana, too. / Bette Davis, we love you." The monotone rap flattens out the differences between these stars and their different camp and nostalgic attributes and empties them of content (in a manner similar to Warhol's portraits of celebrities). Rather than emphasize Monroe's tragic connotations, Hepburn's androgyny, or Astaire's talent, Madonna confines them all and the pleasure we take in them ("we love you") to the reduced categories of beauty, style, grace, and "attitude." Instead of the mournful aura of nostalgia, or the complexities of a star matrix, they, like Warhol's "superstars," are invested with the status of brand names for a way of being, giving good face, which is easily accessible to all of us: "Strike a pose, there's nothing to it." The lyrics let us imagine that we too can strike the pose, while they emphasize that these star images represent nothing but a pose. "Vogue" suggests that women and gay men alike can gain access to their desires by recognizing and manipulating the illusion, seeing through the mask and giving good face.

Of course, for many critics, Madonna's politics are empty of content. *The I Hate Madonna Handbook* claims that Madonna's politics are "as phony as her hair color." Similarly, in parodying *Truth or Dare,* both Julie Brown and *Blossom* suggest that Madonna's sexual politics are just fuel for more publicity. Making fun of Madonna's politics, Julie Brown's *Medusa: Dare to Be Truthful* parodies "Vogue" in a song called "Vague." After deliberately exposing her "muffin" to delighted cops who have threatened to arrest her, Medusa sings, "I'm not thinking nothing. / C'mon get vague, / Let your body move without thinking. / C'mon get vague, / Let your IQ drop while you bop." Instead of Madonna's catalogue of cult stars, Medusa raps a list of has-beens and mediocre talents ("Brooke Shields. / Dawber, Pam. / Personality of Spam."). Brown sums up their appeal, and, by implication, Madonna's: "Ladies with no point-of-view. / Fellas who don't have a clue. / If they're stars, then you can do it. / Just be vague, there's nothing to it." For Brown, and others, Madonna is not so much a political spokesperson as a narcissist who mouths a "vague" politics to mask a mediocre talent—a claim Madonna obliquely supports in *Truth or Dare* when she tells her backup singers that she knows she is not the most talented singer or dancer, but rather is interested in "pushing people's buttons."

Many critics recognize that Madonna does indeed "push people's buttons" but still find her politics "vague." In particular, many see Madonna's appropriation of gay, racial, and ethnic subcultural practices as an appropriation of style rather than a substantive politics. Marcos Becquer and José Gatti argue, for example, that Madonna's "escape to the polymorphous perversity of an idealized universally available dance floor" in "Vogue" subsumes the gay/Other under the myth of equality. Like those feminists who criticize Madonna's postmodernism for challenging feminism's unified concept of "woman," for Becquer and Gatti, Madonna's pluralist queerness, as opposed to gay or feminist identity politics, translates multiculturalism's "gorgeous mosaic" into an unattainable fantasy. In ignoring real difference ("it doesn't matter"), Madonna's "Vogue" denies real antagonisms and real struggles.

More than just a cranky assessment of one video, the opinion put forth by Becquer and Gatti provides a useful point of entry into a whole series of questions about the politics of, not just Madonna, but of contemporary queer camp. These questions, perhaps unanswerable, have to do with the relationship between camp, popular culture, postmodernism, commodification, and politics. How, for example, does camp today negotiate difference? If camp is rooted in a culture of oppression and struggle, is it possible to articulate anything but a power hierarchy through camp? And, once mainstreamed, does camp, even explicitly gay camp, simply become a means for heterosexual performers and spectators to go slumming? To begin to address these questions, or at least to understand what is at stake in them, requires a reconsideration of Madonna's star text, especially of the issue of power as it relates to camp.

As I have suggested, the issue of power is key to Madonna's star text and fan identification with her. Madonna's cultural clout and the controversies she generates are deeply rooted in perceptions of her as powerful. As Lynne Layton notes, "Madonna's art and its reception by critics and fans reflect and shape some of our culture's anxieties about identity and power inequalities. Madonna disturbs the status quo not only because she is an outspoken, sexy woman, but because she has a lot of social and economic power." Layton suggests that the critics' focus on gender relations in Madonna's textual productions functions to obscure a focus on power relations. For Layton, "Madonna presents the perplexing case of someone who accepts the concept of a natural hierarchy of power but attacks the version of the concept that excludes women, gays, and minorities." By this account, Madonna's gender bending simply reverses the structure of patriarchal power relations. The female takes the gaze from the male, the weepy diva becomes dominatrix. Gender relations are still predicated on a master-slave model, but now the slaves subjugate the master. Madonna's power may well enable her to function as an important symbol of interventionist politics, but if we understand that power is privilege and that Madonna speaks from a privileged position—related to her economic power, whiteness, and influence—we need to consider what, if any, access we and others have to the kind of mobile and flexible subjectivity inherent to Madonna's project.

Madonna masks the actual powerlessness of subcultural groups through her performance of agency and power. To adapt Kaja Silverman's reading of what Foucault calls "discursive fellowships," Madonna compensates for a lack of agency by pretending to occupy the positions of both speaking and spoken subject: "Discourse always requires a speaking position (a position from which power-knowledge is exercised) and a spoken subject (a position brought into existence through the exercise of power-knowledge)." According to Silverman, the male subject is capable of occupying both positions. The female subject, by contrast, is "automatically excluded from all current discursive fellowships except those like feminism, which have grown up in opposition to the dominant symbolic order." When Madonna argues, in her interview with Forrest Sawyer, that the video for "Express Yourself" (dir. Fincher, 1989) does not exploit women because she chained herself to the bed, she asserts her ability to control current stereotypical, pornographic, and hierarchical discourses, thus obscuring the fact that she is spoken by those discourses and incapable of speaking them. Silverman allows for the possibility of the "unusual" woman who gains admittance to a discursive fellowship. However, even if we take Madonna to be an "unusual" woman, the exception to the rule, her "unique" deviation from the female norm merely confirms the larger rule of exclusion.

David Tetzlaff astutely captures the ideological effect of Madonna's privileged position as an "unusual" woman: "The discourses engaged by Chameleon Madonna have no claim on her. How could she be free for her ultimate self-actualization if she were bound to the historically rooted struggles of the subaltern groups who populate her videos? . . . She has won for herself an unlimited ticket for subcultural tourism—she can visit any locale she likes, but she doesn't have to live there." Here, Tetzlaff suggests that Madonna does not reverse power relations so much as ignore and, therefore, mask them. Madonna's masquerade lacks the pathos of oppression—taking camp pleasure in dismantling stereotypes without camp's guilty self-recognition in stereotypes. It is not, however, the case that these stereotypes have been rendered defunct. Rather, Madonna's individual economic and social power removes her from the conditions and struggles of subaltern groups so that her appropriation of these subcultures and stereotypes, no matter how well intentioned, can never be more than a form of subcultural tourism at the level of style. As Douglas Crimp and Michael Warner assert, "She can be as queer as she wants to, but only because we know she's not."

At worst, Madonna's own focus on power and independence leads her to adopt a patronizing attitude toward all those less powerful than herself, causing Bell Hooks to compare her to a modern-day plantation mistress. Hooks notes how, after choosing a cast of characters from marginalized groups (white gays, straight and gay nonwhites) for her "Blond Ambition" tour, Madonna, in *Truth or Dare,* publicly describes them as "emotional cripples." John Champagne, similarly, observes that *Sex* reinstantiates middle-class privilege because it expresses the same revulsion toward sexuality that it claims to contest—presenting portraits of sexual freaks instead of highlighting the sensuality of the images. Champagne notes how the photographs emphasize Madonna's separation from the sexual activity taking place around her. The book features, for instance, images that create a sharp contrast between Madonna's blond glamour and the dark-haired, pierced, and tattooed lesbian skinheads or between her whiteness and African Americans Naomi Campbell and Big Daddy

Kane. Further, Madonna is pictured as the lone female and lone sexual subject at the Gaiety Theater; Madonna is at the center of virtually every image, foregrounded, and mugging for the camera.

This condescension becomes, at times, positively sinister when Madonna simply fails to recognize her privileged position with respect to different groups and different individuals. It becomes increasingly difficult to attribute to Madonna a genuinely progressive or coalition politics, for instance, when she ignores the hairdresser who has been drugged and raped in *Truth or Dare,* seeing in the young woman's ordeal only a reflection of her own greatness (assuming by some strange logic that the woman was attacked because she was with the tour), or when she claims in *Sex* that abused women "must be digging it" and that women are not degraded in pornography because the models choose to pose (as if her decision to make *Sex* mirrors the average porn model's options). These moments, in Kate Tentler's words, "are the glitches that make a feminist cringe, the ruptures in my faith. Can her life, her songs, her videos really stand in as the visuals for my feminist politics?"

The point here is not to rake Madonna over the coals for failing to live up to my political ideals or to ask of her that she be a role model. Instead, I take Madonna to be as representative of the limitations of camp as she is of its potential. While we can see a difference between pre-1960s and post-1960s camp, between Mae West and Madonna, it would be a mistake to view the history of camp as a lapsarian narrative. Rather than assume a linear history of camp's fall from authenticity, we need to examine pre- and post-1960s camp in a constellation, to read Mae West through Madonna and vice versa. In this way, we can see the dormant affinity between West and Madonna, and, in their similarity, locate the utopian promise in Madonna and the dystopian aspects of West. Madonna and West are both "unusual" women struggling to situate themselves in a discursive fellowship to which they have no access, while at the same time, they offer a view of how a female subject might be imagined as speaking and not merely as spoken.

If Madonna represents the death of camp, it is not because camp itself has changed but because camp's context and mode of consumption have changed. Camp's always-already parasitic relation to the dominant culture surfaces in post-1960s camp. At issue is a conflict in camp between a subculture's desire for access to the mainstream and that subculture's desire for a unique identity. In Madonna, these two sides of camp engage in a kind of internal warfare. The desire on the part of Madonna's advocates for her to articulate an identity politics through camp, to assert difference, conflicts with the desire for the mainstream, for equality and admittance to the dominant culture.

The difficulty posed by Madonna's status as an "unusual" woman overlaps with the difficulty posed by the mainstreaming of camp: namely, the issue of appropriation. Discussing the fact that *Sex* does not seem queer enough because Madonna's queerness feels like appropriation, Crimp and Warner address the "inevitable ambivalence" of the term: "Appropriation is a weird term, though, because in a way you always win these battles by being appropriated. If you're going to conquer cultural turf and gain a certain amount of legitimacy, how else is it going to happen except through the appropriation of certain rhetorics by people who haven't hitherto been part of the minority culture?" The issue of appropriation lurks in virtually every analysis of, not just Madonna, but camp in general, usually obscuring the fact that camp itself operates largely through appropriating objects from dominant culture. Camp's advocates and opponents alike, myself included, are continuously beleaguered by the question, "Who does camp belong to?" Is camp strictly a gay male sensibility? Can lesbians camp? Is "straight" camp still camp? The question remains, however, whether the appropriation of camp connotes the erasure of identity or the acceptance of difference. To gain acceptance without loss of identity, we cling to the notion of a subculture while still yearning to be part of mainstream culture.

What is finally at stake here is the value of difference in identity politics. As Alexander Doty observes, "[W]e queers have become locked into ways of seeing ourselves in relation to mass culture that perpetuate our status as subcultural, parasitic, self-oppressive hangers-on: alienated, yet grabbing for crumbs or crusts and wishfully making this into a whole meal." Camp and queer alike can only be defined in opposition to the noncamp and nonqueer. Queers cannot be overly interested in multiplying themselves or their camp sensibility because they require the other for their self-definition and for their self-conception as resistant or alternative. In searching for a "whole meal," self-defined queers face a quandary: How to demand simultaneously the right to maintain a unique identity and gain equal rights, justice, and access to power?

Doty's tentative solution to this problem would be to emphasize the porousness of culture, to redefine the dominant, and recognize the queerness in and of mass culture so that the notion that what is mass or popular is "straight" would become "a highly questionable given" in culture. This solution suggests that dominant culture cannot appropriate or subsume our difference because that difference already permeates the dominant—both through the dominant culture's appropriation of what is queer and through the queer and camp appropriation of objects from the dominant culture for queer or camp readings. Perhaps Doty is right, and the ultimate blandness of the Madonna phenomenon testifies to just this. However, to assert that queerness is everywhere still assumes necessarily that such a thing as nonqueer exists: it merely reverses the power relation to assert that what is nonqueer is less rather than more prevalent than what is queer.

We can just as easily reverse the direction of Doty's argument to emphasize the porousness of identity. We could argue, in other words, that the ultimate blandness of the Madonna phenomenon inheres in the ultimate blandness of queer difference instead of the ultimate complexity or queerness of dominant culture. If queerness has been posited as unique and other because dominant culture wants it that way, then perhaps the ultimate move of de-essentializing would be to say not that queers are just like "straights" or that "straight" culture is really queer, but that sex and gender identities are porous and that queer difference is largely a matter of self-conception. This solution, however, begs the question of the value of difference in queer self-conceptions: If difference has been reified by queer and nonqueer culture alike, that is because we still cling to some belief that there are real differences and that some of these matter deeply.

In this perhaps unresolvable problematic, we are caught once again in the either/or "dominant versus resistant" model of cultural politics, replayed now on the field of identity politics. Just as before we faced a theoretical duality between ascribing an unqualified power to either texts or readers, with the subsequent reification of pleasure as wholly good or wholly bad, here we face a similar duality between mainstream culture and its subcultures, with the potential reification of difference. What is needed then is a means of reconceiving sex and gender identities in such a way as to maintain the difference we value in both our self-definition and our social roles without sliding into either vulgar essentialism or vulgar constructionism.

What makes the Madonna phenomenon interesting is, perhaps, its restaging of this controversy in cultural criticism as a controversy in the area of identity politics. Madonna and her reception provide a caution about too easily conflating camp with progressive politics. Madonna's reception, both positive and negative, suggests that camp can still be a political and critical force—perhaps even more so since becoming a more public sensibility—yet suggests that the pool of persons with access to those forces is still severely restricted. The mainstreaming of camp taste in contemporary culture may help articulate a queer subjectivity and coalitional politics, but it may also serve to obscure real difference and to reduce gay politics to a discourse of style. Perhaps, in the future, camp will be dead—if the conditions of oppression are gone and there is no longer any need for camp as a survival strategy. But, in the meantime, we need to scrutinize our camp icons, and our own camp readings and practices, to ensure that we do not naively substitute camp for politics.

MARK WATTS

# ELECTRIFYING FRAGMENTS: MADONNA AND POSTMODERN PERFORMANCE

1996

*Here Madonna's self-imagery is seen from a "postmodern" perspective.*—Eds.

*The rise and (perceived) decline of Madonna has gone, so to say, hand-in-hand with that of postmodern theory—slightly* démodé *just at present, but nonetheless pervasively influential for that. The singer's two most recent albums were critical successes, and the controversy in Argentina over the choice of the star to play Eva Perón testifies to her continuing capacity to attract notoriety. But in what does that notoriety consist? How is the persona that is all we know of Madonna constructed, and how does it work? How is she able to make such distinctive use of the emergent potential of multimedia? What constitutes the* coherence *of Madonna's image? Mark Watts, a graduate in Film and Literature of the University of Warwick, here analyzes the appeal of the singer-actress in terms of the concept of* punctum, *defined by Barthes (in opposition to the rational, linear understanding of* studium*) as the "electrifying fragment" that seizes and ravishes the imagination.*

It is often said that pop stars make lousy actors, though this might be seen as a paradox in an age when to succeed as a pop star you need to make great videos. No one represents this paradox as well as Madonna: she is often perceived as living her whole life as a performance, and her live performances are critical successes while her big-screen performances are panned.

This should not come as a great surprise. Madonna's postmodern performance style perfectly suits her approach to videos and concerts, but is uneasily contained by conventional narrative structures. Her most exceptional films, *In Bed with Madonna* [a.k.a. Truth or Dare] and *Desperately Seeking Susan,* both rely heavily on video aesthetics.

I want to take as my point of departure comments Andy Medhurst has made about Madonna's greatest-hits video, *The Immaculate Collection:*

> When the history of pop video (the first cultural form to be *nothing but* punctum) is written, this will be its *Iliad,* its Old Testament. Madonna condenses decades of stardom into a wardrobe of outfits, fuses cold ambition with dance-floor transcendence, and disguises her heartlessness with sheer semiotic acumen.[1]

Medhurst introduces the idea of punctum by saying:

> Barthes once outlined two ways of reading a text—*studium,* a rational, linear understanding, and *punctum,* the electrifying fragment that seizes and ravishes the imagination.[2]

This concept has captured my imagination, and I find myself wanting to explore it. I will concern myself with postmodernism (which Medhurst evokes without mentioning) as an essential grounding, before looking more closely at punctum. The reference to semiotics gives me an excuse to concentrate more on how the meaning of "Madonna" is created than on what "Madonna" means.

Madonna Louise Ciccone is obviously a person whom I don't know, have no real insight into, and have no qualifications for commenting on. The Madonna I talk of, then, is the "persona," which is constantly growing and transforming—added to by the songs, videos, films, posters, interviews, concerts, everything we see or read about her. Although it would be impossible to experience all these facets, the general impression is almost always the same, and constitutes the star's *coherence.*

Medhurst might be considered guilty of confusing the persona with the person, his talk of "cold ambition" echoing the title of Madonna's Blonde Ambition tour in the same way as many magazines dub her "The Material Girl" she declares herself in the song of the same name. But how can we be sure that Madonna is in reality "heartless"—some of her songs might suggest otherwise? And talking of her "semiotic acumen" reminds me of a line from the *Times:* "If the Madonna created in the heads of academics existed she would have to carry Foucault in her handbag and have Derrida at her bedside."[3]

**Madonna, Persona, Aura**

The persona can be said to be the signified of the word "Madonna." It embodies the indescribable combination of ideas that enters our mind when we think "Madonna"—singer, star, exhibitionist, whatever.

What go to make up this signified, then, are the signifiers—the songs, or photos. Of these signifiers, I would like to concentrate on what I will call primary signifiers—those which come from the presence of Madonna (image, voice, etc.)—rather than the secondary signifiers (what we read about her in the tabloids, or in academic discourse). In theorizing how the signified is created, it is necessary to split these signifiers into two aspects, those of performance and technology. For I would argue that it is only by multiplying the two that the signified might be recast as the "aura."

To demonstrate this I will describe my own experience at Wembley Stadium in 1990 at a performance during the Blonde Ambition tour. I was at the front and had a very clear view of Madonna—Madonna the performer, the persona personified. However, despite my excellent view of the stage, I found myself constantly looking at the image of Madonna (the projection of her performance) on the giant video screen—the performance as mediated by the technology. It was not the Madonna on the stage but the Madonna on the video screen who was the more authentic.

This would appear to be in direct contrast to the view of authenticity (and thus aura) offered by Walter Benjamin, who in his essay of 1935, "The Work of Art in the Age of Mechanical Reproduction," claims that "the whole sphere of authenticity is outside technical—and of course not only technical—reproducibility," thus equating a work of art's aura with its uniqueness. He goes on to say: "The cult of the movie star . . . preserves not the unique aura of the person but the 'spell of the personality,' the phony spell of a commodity."[4]

I would argue that the break between modernism and postmodernism comes at the point where "aura" is not lost because of technology but depends upon it—where the aura surrounds the image and not the reality. Hence iconic power is at a higher level than ever, and punctum becomes more dominant than studium. This would bear out theories that in the late (or third) stage of capitalism the most fetishized commodity has become the image (seen as symptomatic of postmodernism.)

My quotation from Medhurst did not mention the term postmodernism at all, despite its construction of Madonna as a postmodern being. This is clear from the reference to videos as pure punctum (which I will discuss below), a cultural form symptomatic of short attention spans and image/commodity fetishism, and their content—Madonna's ability to collapse history, "condensing decades of stardom into a wardrobe of outfits," and so on.

This perhaps demonstrates that it is almost impossible to exclude postmodernism (as a concept if not a word) from discourse on Madonna. For this reason we will use the term as a convenient label to pull together various ideas that will help illustrate how Madonna is both symptomatic of the culture we live in and shapes and reinforces that culture.

Postmodernism is, then, a concept that has no stable definition. It derives its name from the facts that the period of "art" (and other cultural production) known as "modernism" is past, and that we live now in an era that not only comes after it, but is dependent upon its existence. Yet the phrase is a misleading one, because we cannot in fact be past modernity: in truth, we may only be able to judge postmodernism, and indeed Madonna, from sufficient historical distance.

Some theorists have argued that we are at the end of history—where nothing can happen but endless repeats, where instead of new genres we have pastiche. Architecture no longer looks to the future but to the past. Systems of values have broken down—so that it is no longer fashionable to argue that Beethoven is a "greater artist" than Madonna. We live in an age of plurality where it is possible to have multiple interpretations.

Music videos are often made to invite more than one reading, and often stand in contrast to the lyrics or apparent intention of the song. However, even a video with what we might call a classical narrative style, such as "Papa Don't Preach," is open to a number of approaches. For example, E. Ann Kaplan says of this video:

> Madonna has touched upon issues confronting many teenagers today, particularly the lower classes, which her video (set as it is in a section of New Jersey facing New York City's skyline) obviously addresses.[5]

Yet Sean Cubitt stands in opposition to this, arguing that the address "is to the wealthy child, toying with the adventurousness of being streetwise."[6] In fact, the video incorporates both middle- and working-class addresses: it has a plural address.

**The Plural Address**

Madonna thus manages to speak to different people on different levels. She has so welded such plurality into her persona that a certain incoherence has become a coherent part of her image. Thus we feel we can never trust what Madonna says in her interviews, and in a so-called documentary like *In Bed with Madonna* we are never sure what is true and what is fiction (reminding me of Schechner's view that postmodern performance "lies always on the threshold of life and the theatre itself"). In one sense it might be argued that Madonna is foregrounding the manipulation of the media (as in the fast editing of that film), but she does so in a way that seems to celebrate this manipulation.

Madonna's pop videos can be considered postmodern in two senses. Firstly, the form of video is in itself postmodern, belonging to a culture of mass communication, transmitting a three-minute sound/image recording all over the world to be repeatedly recycled in the flow of media space (the single "Like a Prayer" debuted as a Pepsi-Cola advert in forty different countries). Secondly, they are postmodern in content, not least in terms of their intertextuality (e.g., "Material Girl" as pastiche of *Gentlemen Prefer Blondes*) and self-referentiality (e.g., showing the cutting room in that video with an "editor" saying: "This girl is going to be a big star").

The video for "Express Yourself" exemplifies how Madonna uses star iconography, costume, and performance which we can relate to her persona and her music. The video is set against the backdrop of Fritz Lang's film of 1926, *Metropolis*—a pastiche rather than social comment, a future only out of the past.

Madonna appears in no less than seven costumes, with different hairstyle and makeup as well as dress, once as a photo looking in on the action. No image adds particularly to our understanding of the linear narrative meaning of the video, nor to the song itself. In each incarnation (and it is by no means sure whether each costume change is intended to be the same character within the diegesis) she is clearly referring to something, though it is not always clear to whom or what she is referring.

The point is not that you get the connection (or are in on the joke) but that you realize she is making a reference. It is the act of referring to something that is important, not what is being referred to. The referentiality of the text thus becomes almost meaningless—referring for the sake of referring.

The video thus gives an (empty) symbolic meaning to the images—images of the cat, the men fighting, etc.—that make one ask: what was that about? Madonna once said, "My idea is to take these iconographic symbols . . . and say, here's another way of looking at it."[7] In this video, then, instead of demythologizing "high" iconography (like the cross), she is mythologizing "low" iconography (such as bondage gear).

This is not, however, to say that it is impossible to make meanings from the juxtapositions of sounds and images. Madonna evoking Dietrich in "Express Yourself" is of course Madonna evoking a strong woman (an icon of mixed sexuality, gender-crossing, etc.) not afraid to express herself. But it is also an example of Madonna at play with one of her favorite icons. Is one of these meanings more important than the other?

"Express Yourself" is made up of image after image. It does not afford a rational, linear understanding of the text, and the only way to make sense of images which appear out of sequence (e.g., the pouring of milk over the male character before he arrives) is to concede that they don't really make sense. They are made up of punctum: full of electrifying fragments.

### The Point about "Punctum"

The point about punctum is that it is these fragments that give the songs/videos/images their specificity. As Patrice Pavis says of image notation in the theatre: "The images we retain are not necessarily the most important ones in the performance, but they make up the framework of our perception and of what we remember, and therefore exert enormous influence on how we structure the plot and the production of meaning."[8]

The electrifying fragment might be a single image in a video (the way Madonna kicks a lamppost in the video of "Borderline"—a unique bit of performance mediated through the camera in terms of lighting, composition, etc.), a photo in a book full of photos (e.g., *Sex,* with Madonna as Marilyn biting a man's bare arse), or in the songs themselves (lyrics such as "Romeo and Juliet, they never felt this way I bet").

Tellingly, these are (I think) personal to me—that is, I do not claim these instances to be some magic that everyone will find, accounting for Madonna's success. She works in an area of contemporary cultural production that does indeed throw up an extraordinary amount of potential punctum. And there is enough for everyone. Of all the images that are thrown at us in a video like "Express Yourself," at least one is likely to capture the imagination.

However, Medhurst's description of pop videos as "the first cultural form to be nothing but punctum" needs to be qualified. Barthes used punctum in relation to photography, and so we might expect the still photo to be the natural home of punctum. The reproducibility of the mass media means that punctum can be removed from its source (movie, video, stage performance) and reproduced as the electrifying fragment without the whole: pure punctum. In this way it becomes a commodity (poster, postcard, etc.), and we that find its reproducibility increases its power (or "aura") rather than diminishing it.

Pop videos owe a debt to this, and we find the slowing down and in fact freezing of the "moving" image to be a common feature in Madonna videos. This can be seen from early examples, not only with the dancing in "Lucky Star" but the opening and closing shots of Madonna putting on/taking off her shades, through "Papa Don't Preach" (to emphasize the notion of love at first sight), to its most prominent in "Cherish" (directed by Herb Ritts, usually associated with photography), which consists mainly of shots of Madonna's body, most in close-up, many shot in slow motion, some almost frozen—closing on a frozen image of her face. The credo of "Vogue" is to "strike a pose."

These illuminate aspects of postmodern performance for us not only because of their self-referentiality in terms of Madonna's body (the common feature in all her videos so far) but because of their use of extensive close-up. Artaud saw the gestural as the fundamental code of the theatre, and in a close-up the slightest gesture can look huge, completely changing our interpretation (and the tone) of the text. These videos not only foreground gestures, but are able to freeze them in order to be reproduced (and fetishized).

Interestingly, Madonna does not just reproduce images, but reproduces already reproduced images. Thus, Tom Kalin sees her referring not to Monroe herself, but to the Monroe of Warhol.[9] We might see a comparison with American artist Cindy Sherman, who puts herself into a number of roles in "untitled movies" foregrounding how we construct identity from the imagery and stereotypes of the mass media. The video for "Bad Girl" looks more like a video from a movie than "just" from a record.

### How to Achieve Longevity

Away from visual imagery, pop songs themselves have always relied on a high degree of punctum, especially in the chorus lines of pop songs and the guitar riff in rock. Madonna songs can also be intertextual: in "Rescue Me" she sings "R.E.S.C.U.E.ME" in the same way as Aretha Franklin sings "R.E.S.P.E.C.T.," and at the end of "Deeper and Deeper" she sings, "You've got to just, let your body move to the music, you've got to just, let your body go with the flow" straight out of her previous hit, "Vogue." She identifies punctum and appropriates it, whether using somebody else's, creating her own, or using her own. She turns the electrifying into the already said, and the already said into the electrifying.

While pop songs have always involved a high degree of punctum, pop videos multiply the possibilities, combining them with potential for imagery punctum and packaged for the three-minute attention span. Pop video punctum towers over the still photograph because it puts punctum back into a context, but instead of putting it back into its proper place, it juxtaposes it with other punctum.

Madonna's music might be good (great even) but it is usually to her image that her success is attributed, her emergence coinciding with the emergence of MTV. It has been argued that video was very important in establishing her as a star, the *Like a Virgin* album thus going triple platinum without even a hint of a tour.[10] And the film *Desperately Seeking Susan* made her a visual star just as her music career was gaining its own momentum. Her costume made her appealing to men and, more importantly, to the young girls who were to form her core audience at the time—the fact that these "wanna-bes" often dressed like her and that she was able to set up her own clothes label, "Boy Toy," emphasizing how important the image was in establishing her as a star.

But, as Will Straw has noted, a permanent condition of celebrity, post 1982, is "oversaturation and burnout." This he attributes to changes in the record industry, so that the turnover of singles became higher than ever before, with star biographies no longer felt to be of use in interpreting the songs themselves.[11] Ten years on, for Madonna to have remained a "star," not only selling a relatively high number of songs, videos, and posters worldwide, but still generating media interest (even if it is, say, a full page in the *Daily Mail* to cover the fact that they will *not* cover her new tour!) is a rare achievement.

It has been said that Madonna achieves longevity by changing her image, but actually this is not quite the case. Madonna has done it by peddling punctum. An advert for the album *Like a Prayer,* which appeared in the movie magazine *Empire* in January 1990, seemed designed to promote Madonna (the signified—the face of the eighties) rather than the album (a signifier.)

The poster shows images of Madonna, covering different media, including album covers (e.g., *True Blue, You Can Dance*), movie stills (*Who's That Girl?, Desperately Seeking Susan*), video stills ("Express Yourself") and singles covers ("Dear Jessie"). This advert explains to me why Madonna can achieve longevity where others, who merely "change" their image, have failed. "Changing" her image *is* Madonna's image.

The power of the image of Madonna as Mickey Mouse is thus in its play with American iconography combined with performance (the gestures of Madonna's hand and face) as mediated through the camera, and presented (here at least) out of its original context. The image is recycled so many times it is hard to know what its original context was: it was also the advert for a single, a poster, a front cover of the American music magazine *Rolling Stone,* and has been included in a retrospective of the best of *Rolling Stone* photography (thus, it finally ends up as "art").

Once these images are recycled in the culture, they also get out of Madonna's control and can be appropriated by the "public" for their own ends (which can also help us understand how the culture makes sense of the images).

## Images, Fantasies, Pluralities

As examples, take two posters that were in wide circulation at the University of Warwick in the summer term of 1993. The first advertised for students wanting summer work in the U.S.A. and Canada, and used a full-page image of Madonna as an electrifying fragment (on boards filled with more boring notices) to capture the imagination and bring you forward to sell you the idea. The picture, Madonna naked, comes from many circulated to advertise the book *Sex.*

It might therefore be seen as proof that Madonna is an icon of sex. Yet the *GQ* generation no longer considers Madonna as a favorite sex symbol, citing instead Sharon Stone or Cindy Crawford. However, the poster catches the eye not only because of the position Madonna is standing in, but in that it offers a chance to be submissive under a dominant woman—the idea of being a sex slave to Madonna more than just the idea of having sex with her. The words and imagery of this poster tap into male fantasy.

The second poster was advertising a LesBiGay disco. Madonna has become a gay icon (though interestingly only in certain images—the first poster has no hint of lesbian or gay iconography). The images of Madonna in this outfit, echoing both Marlon Brando in *The Wild One* and also male gay iconography, were shot to accompany the single "Justify My Love," also as video covers, posters, postcards, and advertising. The video did include sequences of same-sex kissing, as has been associated with Madonna's playing at lesbianism—dancing with Sandra Bernhard on American television, using gay dancers in her live shows, and as foregrounded in some scenes of *In Bed with Madonna.* She has done a lot to bring gay culture into the mass media (voguing originates from the black gay subculture). Though she denies being a lesbian in "real" life, Madonna plays with different sexual identities (often in self-confessed fantasies, as in *Sex*) and it is this use of fantasy that underlies her iconography.

It should not be ignored that the image on this poster is not only an icon of queerness but an icon of disco—of the dance-floor transcendence that Medhurst evokes. "Into the Groove" was *the* disco anthem of 1985—its lyrics instantly recognizable to a generation who sing along with nostalgia at night clubs today. "Only when I'm dancing can I feel this free" does indeed sum up the freedom that a dance floor can bring—the dancers happy to "just let the music set them free." In "Vogue," a dance floor is a place for getting away, where

> It makes no difference if you're black or white,
> If you're a boy or a girl,
> If the music's pumping it can bring you new life,
> You're a superstar, yes, that's what you are.

A dance floor is a place of freedom for the gay community when they really can be who they want to be, uninhibited from normal restrictions. At the Rubber Ball in 1993, Madonna was the only mainstream artist the DJ played. The partiers here lived out their fantasies on the dance floor, dressed—in rubber, leather, or very little at all—in ways that expressed themselves as they could not do in normal society. This explains Madonna being taken up as a gay icon, her image of playing gay, of performance, of fantasy.

### Ravishing the Imagination

It is the phrase "ravishes the imagination" that is the key to understanding punctum. It is hard to rationalize why (in "Rescue Me") Madonna singing "And right while I am kneeling there I suddenly begin to care" should make the hair on the back of my neck stand up. The rhyme gives me pleasure and it also startles me: is Madonna singing about oral sex? If she is, the line seems out of context. But the thought, the connection by implication seems to make this line stand out, in the same way as I read a sequence of music in "Dear Jessie" as metaphor for premature ejeculation. Madonna seems to put the pun into punctum.

Punctum always engages our imagination. Drying her armpits by the hand drier in the public toilets in *Desperately Seeking Susan* taps into our utopian dreams—wouldn't it be great to be that free, to know no divisions between private and public spaces? While such images have been claimed by women and gay men especially, they represent, I feel, universal hopes. So Madonna's plurality means that she seems to address us individually; the fact that we take the images and make them our own reinforces their electrifying possibilities.

Sometimes we are shocked by what we make of the images/lyrics—but this too can create punctum. Fantasy, by pushing reality into the background, can be a large source of pleasure for both sexes, and Madonna in her images and songs can be said to indulge our fantasies. ("Devour your fantasy here with me," she sings in "Into the Groove.") But, in good postmodern fashion, she seems to blur the boundaries and bring fantasy closer to reality. Hence some theorists have argued that Madonna is a postfeminist icon, and women find in Madonna feelings of emancipation and even of empowerment.[12]

In a culture of plurality, we can all read into Madonna what we like ("All you need is your own imagination, so use it, that's what it's for"—"Vogue") to make our own meanings. As Tom Kalin suggests, "'Open Your Heart' . . . either destabilizes the voyeuristic male gaze or cynically regurgitates arty pornography, depending upon who bends your ear."[13] She is a truly democratic icon.

One of the most interesting aspects of the Medhurst quote is that not only does he exclude the term postmodernism from his analysis of *The Immaculate Collection,* but he places the video collection at the *start* of something, using the *Iliad* and the Old Testament as analogues. This ties in with Charles Jencks's idea that the term "postmodernism" is an intermediate step between modernism and what is still to come, generating optimism about the possibilities of video culture. Whilst my analysis might echo Baudrillard's notion of *simulacrum,* where image has no relation to a basic reality, or Debord's notion of a "society of spectacle," it is not intended to be so pessimistic.

Madonna on stage uses the aspects of postmodern performance seen in her videos. Each song is a set piece like an individual video, though usually her stage performance of a song will exist in stark contrast to the video performance. We can watch her on large video screens, which emphasize her gestures (and manipulation of her image) and fragment the performance as a whole. However, it is not just the video screens that are on display at a Madonna concert, but the cameras that transmit the pictures. Thus the whole process of video making is acknowledged and integrated into the performance.

Madonna does believe in the redemptive power of music. This clearly carries over to images, and she performs a series of images as if they were notes in a song. Her performance style incorporates the contents of her frozen images—irony, playfulness, and good old-fashioned decoration. By addressing a wide and diverse audience (though, as I have argued, in a seemingly personal way), she gets us to confront what such images might mean for us, and thus we are forced to find our own path through the intertextual maze.

Stephen Connors sees as a negative tendency of postmodernist culture that "80,000 or more regularly attend concerts to watch videos, albeit 'live' videos."[14] But this is to ignore the utopian possibilities presented to the audience at a pop concert. I would argue that one of the principle pleasures of the stadium rock concert is the atmosphere, the feeling of solidarity with other human beings—which video culture supposedly turns its back on. And, ironically, it is within this mass that individuals can actually feel free, dancing their own way (the bigger the mass, the harder it is to be self-conscious), the music and images emancipating them from modern life. Madonna in concert understands this well, and dance-floor transcendence is the principle behind all her songs, videos, and images.

## NOTES AND REFERENCES

1. Andy Medhurst, in "Film on Video: the Essential 100," supplement to *Sight and Sound,* 1993.
2. Ibid.
3. Kate Muir, the *Times,* 4 August 1992.
4. Walter Benjamin, "The Work of Art in the Age of Mechanical Reproduction," in Mast, ed., *Film Theory and Criticism* (Oxford University Press, 1992), pp. 667, 674.
5. Quoted in Sean Cubitt, *Timeshift* (Routledge, 1991), p. 54.
6. Ibid., p. 55.
7. *Time,* 20 May 1991, p. 66.
8. Patrice Pavis, "Theatre Analysis: Some Questions and a Questionnaire," *New Theatre Quarterly* I, no. 1 (May 1985), p. 211.
9. Tom Kalin, "Media Kids (on Pussy Power)," *Artforum* XXX (September 1991), pp. 19–21.
10. This point is raised by Lisa A. Lewis, in "Being Discovered" in Frith, Goodwin, Grossberg, eds., *Sound and Vision* (Routledge, 1993), p. 131.
11. Will Straw, "Popular Music and Postmodernism in the Eighties," in Frith, Goodwin, Grossberg, op. cit.
12. Nancy Friday in *Women on Top* feels that "only women can liberate other women," while Madonna "stands hand on crotch, preaching to her sisters—masturbate." E. Anne Kaplin has frequently argued that Madonna represents the "postfeminist heroine."
13. Kalin, op. cit., p. 20.
14. Connors, op. cit., p. 152.

New 'Doo, 1998. *Courtesy of Vinnie Zuffante, Star File.*

# Selected Discography

Titles in parentheses are background music, which do not feature vocals by Madonna.

**Albums**

**July 1983** *Madonna* **Sire**

Lucky Star; Borderline; Burning Up; I Know It/Holiday; Think of Me; Physical Attraction; Everybody

**November 1984** *Like a Virgin* **Sire**

Material Girl; Angel; Like a Virgin; Over and Over; Love Don't Live Here Anymore/Into the Groove; Dress You Up; Shoo-Bee-Doo; Pretender; Stay

**June 1986** *True Blue* **Sire**

Papa Don't Preach; Open Your Heart; White Heat; Live to Tell/Where's the Party; True Blue; La Isla Bonita; Jimmy, Jimmy; Love Makes the World Go Round

**August 1987** *Who's That Girl?* **Sire**

Who's That Girl?; Causing a Commotion; The Look of Love; (24 Hours/Duncan Faure); (Step by Step/Club Nouveau)/(Turn It Up/Michael Davidson); (Best Thing Ever/Scritti Politti); Can't Stop; (El Coco Loco [So So Bad]/Coati Mundi)

**November 1987** *You Can Dance* **Sire**

Spotlight; Holiday; Everybody; Physical Attraction/Over and Over; Into the Groove; Where's the Party

**March 1989** *Like a Prayer* **Sire**

Like a Prayer; Express Yourself; Love Song (w/ Prince); Till Death Do Us Part; Promise to Try/Cherish; Dear Jessie; Oh Father; Keep It Together; Spanish Eyes; Act of Contrition

**May 1990** ***I'm Breathless*** **Sire**

He's a Man; Sooner or Later; Hanky Panky; I'm Going Bananas; Cry Baby; Something to Remember; Back in Business; More; What Can You Lose (w/ Mandy Patinkin); Now I'm Following You, Part I (w/ Warren Beatty); Now I'm Following You, Part II (w/ Warren Beatty); Vogue [*N.B.:* Vogue was not on the original *I'm Breathless* release. It was added to the CD after the song became a hit single.]

**November 1990** ***The Immaculate Collection*** **Sire**

Holiday; Lucky Star; Borderline; Like a Virgin; Material Girl; Crazy for You; Into the Groove; Live to Tell/Papa Don't Preach; Open Your Heart; La Isla Bonita; Like a Prayer; Express Yourself; Cherish; Vogue; Justify My Love; Rescue Me

**October 1992** ***Erotica*** **Sire**

Erotica; Fever; Bye Bye Baby; Deeper and Deeper; Where Life Begins; Bad Girl; Waiting; Thief of Hearts; Words; Rain; Why's It So Hard; In this Life; Did You Do It? (w/ Mark Goodman and Dave Murphy); Secret Garden

**October 1994** ***Bedtime Stories*** **Sire**

Survival; Secret; I'd Rather Be Your Lover; Don't Stop; Inside of Me; Human Nature; Forbidden Love; Love Tried to Welcome Me; Sanctuary; Bedtime Story; Take a Bow

**November 1995** ***Something to Remember*** **Sire**

I Want You (w/ Massive Attack); I'll Remember (theme from the film *With Honors*); Take a Bow; You'll See; Crazy for You; This Used to Be My Playground; Live to Tell; Love Don't Live Here Anymore (remix); Something to Remember; Forbidden Love; One More Chance; Rain; Oh Father; I Want You (orchestral, w/ Massive Attack)

**November 1996** ***Evita: The Complete Motion Picture Music Soundtrack*** **Sire**

**March 1998** ***Ray of Light*** **Maverick/Warner Bros.**

Little Star; Skin; Sky Fits Heaven; Swim; Nothing Really Matters; Shanti/Ashlangi; Frozen; Power of Good-Bye; To Have and Not to Hold; Mer Girl; Candy Perfume Girl; Drowned World

### Singles

Madonna has released 39 singles commercially in the United States, all of which have made the *Billboard* Hot 100 Singles Chart (long held as the authority of music charts). Her lowest-peaking single is "Love Don't Live Here Anymore," which stalled at #78, while her biggest #1 single is "Take a Bow," which spent seven weeks at the top of the chart.

"Frozen" was Madonna's 39th commercially available single. It was her 31st single to hit the Top 10. She is currently in third place (behind Elvis Presley and the Beatles), on the all-time list of artists with the most Top-10 singles.

Madonna has placed a single in the Top 10 of the *Billboard* Hot 100 every year since 1984 (except 1988, when she did not release anything).

Madonna and Janet Jackson are tied with the most consecutive Top-10 singles (17 apiece).

Madonna has 16 gold singles—the second-highest number for any female artist. She trails Janet Jackson, who has 18 to her credit, "Together Again" being her most recent certification. One of Jackson's gold singles is "Scream," a duet with her brother Michael. All of Madonna's singles are solo efforts.

What follows is a listing of every commercially released Madonna single, including debut dates, chart peaks, weeks on the chart, Gold/Platinum certification information, title, B-side information, Hot-100 airplay and sales peaks, catalog numbers, and label information.

| Debut Date | Peak Position | Weeks on Chart | Gold/Platinum Certification | Title | Hot 100 Airplay Peak | Hot 100 Sales Peak | B-Side | Label/Catalog Number |
|---|---|---|---|---|---|---|---|---|
| 10/29/83 | 16 | 21 | — | Holiday | — | — | I Know It | Sire 29478 |
| 3/10/84 | 10 | 30 | — | Borderline | — | — | Think of Me | Sire 29354 |
| 8/24/84 | 4 | 16 | — | Lucky Star | 3 | 6 | I Know It | Sire 29177 |
| 11/17/84 | 1 (6 wks) | 19 | Gold | Like a Virgin | 1 (5 wks) | 1 (4 wks) | Stay | Sire 29210 |
| 2/9/85 | 2 (2 wks) | 17 | — | Material Girl | 2 | 3 | Pretender | Sire 29083 |
| 3/2/85 | 1 (1 wk) | 21 | Gold | Crazy for You[1] | 1 (1 wk) | 2 | No More Words (Berlin) | Geffen 29051 |
| 4/27/85 | 5 | 17 | Gold[2] | Angel | 4 | 9 | (dance mix edit) | Sire 29008 |
| 8/17/85 | 5 | 16 | — | Dress You Up | 3 | 12 | Shoo-Bee-Doo | Sire 28919 |
| 4/12/86 | 1(1 wk) | 18 | — | Live to Tell[3] | 1 | 2 | (instrumental) | Sire 28717 |
| 6/28/86 | 1 (2 wks) | 18 | — | Papa Don't Preach | 1 (3 wks) | 1 (2 wks) | Pretender | Sire 28660 |
| 10/4/86 | 3 | 16 | — | True Blue | 3 | 4 | Ain't No Big Deal[4] | Sire 28591 |
| 12/6/86 | 1 (1 wk) | 18 | — | Open Your Heart | 1 (2 wks) | 1 (1 wk) | White Heat | Sire |
| 3/21/87 | 4 | 17 | — | La Isla Bonita | 3 | 3 | (instrumental mix) | Sire 28425 |
| 7/11/87 | 1 (1 wk) | 16 | — | Who's That Girl?[5] | 1 (2 wks) | 1 (1 wk) | White Heat | Sire 28341 |
| 9/12/87 | 2 (3 wks) | 18 | — | Causing a Commotion[6] | 2 | 2 | Jimmy Jimmy | Sire 28224 |
| 3/18/89 | 1 (3 wks) | 16 | Platinum | Like a Prayer | 1 (3 wks) | 1 (3 wks) | Act of Contrition | Sire 27539 |
| 6/3/89 | 2 (2 wks) | 16 | Gold | Express Yourself | 3 | 2 | The Look of Love | Sire 22948 |
| 8/19/89 | 2 (2 wks) | 15 | — | Cherish | 2 | 2 | Supernatural[7] | Sire 22883 |
| 11/11/89 | 20 | 13 | — | Oh Father | 22 | 16 | (Pray for) Spanish Eyes | Sire 22723 |
| 2/3/90 | 8 | 13 | Gold | Keep It Together | 7 | 7 | (instrumental) | Sire 19986 |
| 4/14/90 | 1 (3 wks) | 24 | Double Platinum | Vogue[8] | 1 (3 wks) | 1 (2 wks) | (Bette Davis dub) | Sire 19863 |
| 6/30/90 | 10 | 11 | Gold | Hanky Panky[9] | 11 | 13 | More | Sire 19789 |
| 11/17/90 | 1 (2 wks) | 16 | Platinum | Justify My Love | 2 | 1 (5 wks) | Express Yourself (remix) | Sire 19485 |
| 3/2/91 | 9 | 8 | Gold | Rescue Me | 5 | 11 | (alternate single mix) | Sire 19490 |
| 7/4/92 | 1 (1 wk) | 20 | Gold | This Used to Be My Playground[10] | 2 | 3 | (long version) | Sire 18822 |
| 10/17/92 | 3 | 18 | Gold | Erotica | 2 | 4 | (instrumental) | Maverick/Sire 18782 |

| Debut Date | Peak Position | Weeks on Chart | Gold/Platinum Certification | Title | Hot 100 Airplay Peak | Hot 100 Sales Peak | B-Side | Label/Catalog Number |
|---|---|---|---|---|---|---|---|---|
| 12/5/92 | 7 | 17 | — | Deeper and Deeper | 8 | 15 | (instrumental) | Maverick/Sire 18639 |
| 2/20/93 | 36 | 11 | — | Bad Girl | 44 | 36 | Fever | Maverick/Sire 18650 |
| 7/24/93 | 14 | 20 | — | Rain | 11 | 31 | Waiting | Maverick/Sire 18505 |
| 4/2/94 | 2 (4 wks) | 26 | Gold | I'll Remember[11] | 22 | — | Secret Garden | Maverick/Sire18247 |
| 10/8/94 | 3 | 22 | Gold | Secret | 1 | 13 | (instrumental) | Maverick/Sire 18035 |
| 12/17/94 | 1 (7 wks) | 30 | Gold | Take a Bow | 1 (9 wks) | 4 | (InDaSoul mix) | Maverick/Sire18000 |
| 4/22/95 | 4 | 27 | — | Bedtime Story | 68 | 27 | Survival | Maverick/Sire17924 |
| 6/24/95 | 46 | 15 | — | Human Nature | 58 | 35 | Sanctuary | Maverick/Sire 17882 |
| 12/9/95 | 6 | 20 | Gold | You'll See | 10 | 6 | (instrumental)/ Live to Tell (live) | Maverick/Warner Bros. 17719 |
| 4/20/96 | 78 | 8 | — | Love Don't Live Here Anymore | — | — | (album remix) | Maverick/Warner Bros. 17714 |
| 11/16/96 | 18 | 20 | — | You Must Love Me[12] | 25 | 14 | Rainbow High | Warner Bros. 17495 |
| 2/22/97 | 8 | 16 | — | Don't Cry for Me Argentina[13] | 5 | 11 | (maxi-single, with various remixes) | Warner Bros. |
| 3/21/98 | — | — | — | Frozen | — | — | Shanti/Ashtangi | Maverick/Warner Bros. |

1 "Crazy for You" is from the film *Vision Quest* and was not on any Madonna album until *The Immaculate Collection* in 1990. It was only found on the *Vision Quest* soundtrack along with another Madonna track, "Gambler."

2 The gold certification for "Angel" is for its 12-inch single (Sire 20335). The B-side of that single is "Into the Groove."

3 "Live to Tell" is from the film *At Close Range,* starring Madonna's then-husband Sean Penn.

4 "Ain't No Big Deal" is a previously unreleased track. It was originally slated for her first album.

5,6 "Who's That Girl?" and "Causing a Commotion" are both from the film *Who's That Girl?,* starring Madonna. Those songs (as well as two other new Madonna tracks) can be found on the *Who's That Girl?* soundtrack.

7 "Supernatural" was an unreleased track until this point. It also made an appearance on the AIDS benefit album *Red, Hot and Dance.*

8,9 "Vogue" and "Hanky Panky" are both from the album *I'm Breathless—Music from and Inspired by the Film* Dick Tracy. "Vogue" is neither from nor inspired by the film. It was originally intended as the B-side to "Keep It Together," but Warner Bros. executives thought the track was too strong to be relegated to simply a B-side, so it was released on its own. It was tacked on to the *I'm Breathless* album after the fact, mostly to spur on sales.

10 "This Used to Be My Playground" is from the film *A League of Their Own,* starring Tom Hanks, Geena Davis, and Madonna. The song plays over the closing credits of the film. It is not on the film's soundtrack album. At the time, this track was only available on the summer olympics benefit album *Barcelona Gold.* It later appeared on Madonna's album *Something to Remember.*

11 "I'll Remember" is the theme from the film *With Honors,* starring Joe Pesci and Brendan Fraser. Alek Keshishian *(Truth or Dare)* directed the film, and Patrick Leonard (who has cowritten and coproduced with Madonna before) did the music.

12 Both "You Must Love Me" and "Don't Cry for Me Argentina" are from the film *Evita,* starring Madonna, Antonio Banderas, and Jonathan Pryce. "You Must Love Me" won both the Golden Globe and Academy Award for Best Original Song. The song was written specifically for the film version and marked the first time songwriters Tim Rice and Andrew Lloyd Webber had collaborated in over 15 years.

13 "Don't Cry for Me Argentina" was only released as a maxi-single. The catalog number reflects this.

# Videos

| Video | Director | Album on Which Song First Appeared | Year Released |
|---|---|---|---|
| Everybody | Ed Steinberg | *Madonna* | 1982 |
| Burning Up | Steve Barron | *Madonna* | 1983 |
| Holiday[1] | (unknown) | *Madonna* | 1983 |
| Borderline | Mary Lambert | *Madonna* | 1984 |
| Lucky Star | Arthur Pierson | *Madonna* | 1984 |
| Like a Virgin | Mary Lambert | *Like a Virgin* | 1984 |
| Material Girl | Mary Lambert | *Like a Virgin* | 1985 |
| Crazy for You[2] | Harold Becker | *Vision Quest—Original Motion Picture Sound track* | 1985 |
| Into the Groove[3] | Susan Seidelman | *You Can Dance* | 1985 |
| Dress You Up (live)[4] | Danny Kleinman | *Like a Virgin* | 1985 |
| Gambler[5] | Harold Becker | *Vision Quest—Original Motion Picture Sound track* | 1985 |
| Like a Virgin (live)[6] | Danny Kleinman | *Like a Virgin* | 1985 |
| Live to Tell | James Foley | *True Blue* | 1986 |
| Papa Don't Preach | James Foley | *True Blue* | 1986 |
| True Blue (non-U.S. version)[7] | James Foley | *True Blue* | 1986 |
| Open Your Heart | Jean-Baptiste Mondino | *True Blue* | 1986 |
| La Isla Bonita | Mary Lambert | *True Blue* | 1987 |
| Who's That Girl? | Peter Rosenthal | *Who's That Girl?—Original Motion Picture Sound track* | 1987 |
| Like a Prayer | Mary Lambert | *Like a Prayer* | 1989 |
| Express Yourself[8] | David Fincher | *Like a Prayer* | 1989 |
| Cherish | Herb Ritts | *Like a Prayer* | 1989 |
| Oh Father | David Fincher | *Like a Prayer* | 1989 |
| Dear Jessie (non-U.S. version)[9] | (unknown) | *Like a Prayer* | 1989 |
| Vogue | David Fincher | *I'm Breathless—Music from and Inspired by the Film* Dick Tracy | 1990 |
| Justify My Love[10] | Jean-Baptiste Mondino | *The Immaculate Collection* | 1990 |
| Like a Virgin (live)[11] | Alek Keshishian | *Like a Virgin* | 1991 |
| Holiday (live)[12] | Alek Keshishian | *Madonna* | 1991 |
| This Used to Be My Playground | Alek Keshishian | *Barcelona Gold* | 1992 |
| Erotica | Fabien Baron | *Erotica* | 1992 |
| Deeper and Deeper | Bobby Woods | *Erotica* | 1992 |

| Video | Director | Album on Which Song First Appeared | Year Released |
|---|---|---|---|
| Bad Girl | David Fincher | *Erotica* | 1993 |
| Fever | Stephane Sednaoui | *Erotica* | 1993 |
| Rain | Mark Romanek | *Erotica* | 1993 |
| I'll Remember | Alek Keshishian | *With Honors—Original Motion Picture Sound track* | 1994 |
| Secret | Melodie McDaniel | *Bedtime Stories* | 1994 |
| Take a Bow | Michael Haussman | *Bedtime Stories* | 1994 |
| Bedtime Story[13] | Mark Romanek | *Bedtime Stories* | 1995 |
| Human Nature | Jean-Baptiste Mondino | *Bedtime Stories* | 1995 |
| I Want You | Earle Sebastian | *Inner City Blues—The Music of Marvin Gaye* | 1995 |
| You'll See | Michael Haussman | *Something to Remember* | 1995 |
| Love Don't Live Here Anymore | Jean-Baptiste Mondino | *Something to Remember* | 1996 |
| You Must Love Me[14] | Alan Parker | *Evita—The Complete Motion Picture Sound track* | 1996 |
| Don't Cry for Me Argentina[15] | Alan Parker | *Evita—The Complete Motion Picture Sound track* | 1996 |
| Frozen | Chris Cunningham | *Ray of Light* | 1998 |

1 Though a low-budget video was made, "Holiday" was never officially released.

2, 5 Both "Crazy for You" and "Gambler" were fashioned from film footage from *Vision Quest.*

3 "Into the Groove" was made up entirely of clips from *Desperately Seeking Susan.*

4, 6 In 1985 "Like a Virgin" got its second release, though this time it was a live version, taken from *Madonna Live: The Virgin Tour.* The "Dress You Up" clip was also culled from the tour.

7 There are two different videos for "True Blue." MTV held a Make My Video contest, asking viewers to make their own video for "True Blue." The winners were Angel Garcia and Cliff Guest, and their video was the U.S. release. Madonna's version, directed by James Foley, was the international release.

8 When "Express Yourself" was completed, it was the most expensive video ever made (estimated cost, $1 million). In addition, it was the first time Madonna worked with director David Fincher, who would later go on to direct *Alien 3, Seven,* and *The Game.*

9 The video for "Dear Jessie" was only released overseas. The video was animated and featured pink elephants. Madonna does not appear in the video.

10 "Justify My Love" was banned from MTV and subsequently released as the first-ever commercially available video single.

11, 12 "Like a Virgin" and "Holiday" were released in 1991 as part of a promotional push for *Truth or Dare.* The videos were the performances taken directly from the film.

13 At the time of its making, "Bedtime Story" was the most expensive video ever made (estimated cost, around $2 million).

14 When "You Must Love Me" was shot, Madonna was eight months pregnant with her daughter, Lourdes Veronica. In the video, Madonna's stomach is hidden behind a piano.

15 "Don't Cry for Me Argentina" is made up entirely of scenes from *Evita.* In fact, the video sequence matches the film exactly.

# *Filmography*

NOTE: Sometimes Madonna is credited as Madonna Ciccone.

**As Actress**

*Chicago* (1999) . . . Velma Kelly

*Ambrose Chapel* (1998)

*Recycle Hazel* (1998)

*Happy Birthday Elizabeth: A Celebration of Life* (1997) (TV) . . . Herself

*Evita* (1996) . . . Eva Perón

*Girl 6* (1996) . . . Boss #3

*Blue in the Face* (1995) . . . Singing Telegram

*Four Rooms* ("The Missing Ingredient" segment) (1995) . . . Elspeth

*The History of Rock 'n' Roll, Vol. 10* (1995) . . . Herself
. . . aka *Up from the Underground* (1995)

*Dangerous Game* (1993) . . . Sarah Jennings
. . . aka *Snake Eyes* (1992) (working title)

*Body of Evidence* (1993) . . . Rebecca Carlson
. . . aka *Deadly Evidence* (1993)

*A League of Their Own* (1992) . . . Mae Mordabito

*Shadows and Fog* (1992) . . . Marie

*Madonna: Truth or Dare* (1991) . . . Herself
. . . aka *Truth or Dare* (1991)
. . . aka *In Bed with Madonna* (1991)

*Dick Tracy* (1990) . . . Breathless Mahoney

*Madonna: Blond Ambition World Tour '90* (1990)
. . . aka *Blond Ambition* (1990)

*Bloodhounds of Broadway* (1989) . . . Hortense Hathaway

*Who's That Girl?* (1987) . . . Nikki Finn

*Shanghai Surprise* (1986) . . . Gloria Tatlock

*Desperately Seeking Susan* (1985) . . . Susan

*A Certain Sacrifice* (1985) (as Madonna Ciccone) . . . Bruna

*Vision Quest* (1985) . . . Special Appearance
. . . aka *Crazy for You* (1985)

**As Composer/Performer**

*With Honors* (1994) (song "I'll Remember")

*A League of Their Own* (1992) (theme song "This Used to Be My Playground") (uncredited)

*Who's That Girl?* (1987) (theme song "Who's That Girl?")

*At Close Range* (1986) (theme song "Live to Tell")

*Desperately Seeking Susan* (1985) (song "Into the Groove")

*Vision Quest* (1985) (theme song "Crazy for You")
. . . aka *Crazy for You* (1985)

Producer Filmography

*Going Down* (1999)

*Recycle Hazel* (1998)

*Madonna: Truth or Dare* (1991) (executive)
. . . aka *Truth or Dare* (1991)
. . . aka *In Bed with Madonna* (1991)

**Notable Television Guest Appearances**

*Saturday Night Live* (1975), playing Musical Guest (episode 18.11) 1/16/1993

*Saturday Night Live* (1975), playing Host (episode 11.1) 11/9/1985

*Saturday Night Live* (1975), playing herself in episode "1991"

*Saturday Night Live* (1975), playing Liz Rosenberg in episode "1992"

*Saturday Night Live* (1975), playing Marilyn Monroe in episode "1993"

# Selected Bibliography

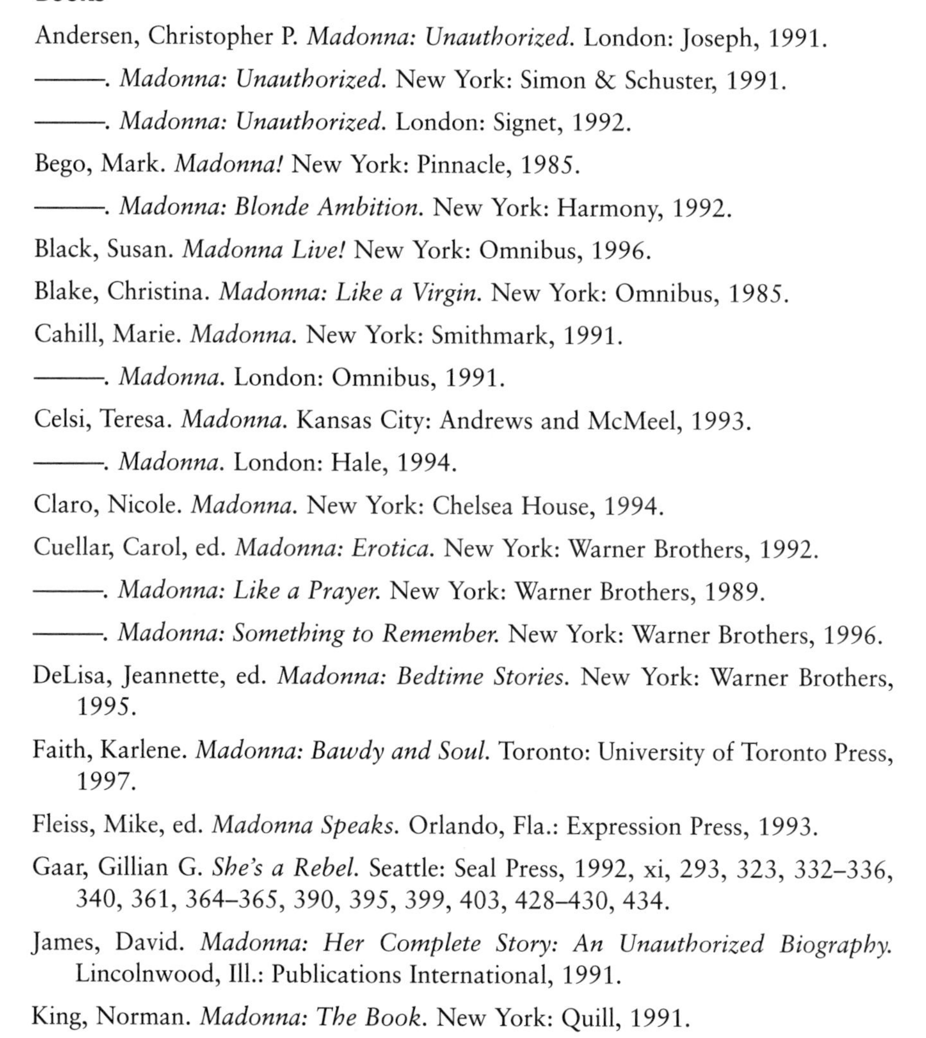

### Books


Andersen, Christopher P. *Madonna: Unauthorized.* London: Joseph, 1991.

———. *Madonna: Unauthorized.* New York: Simon & Schuster, 1991.

———. *Madonna: Unauthorized.* London: Signet, 1992.

Bego, Mark. *Madonna!* New York: Pinnacle, 1985.

———. *Madonna: Blonde Ambition.* New York: Harmony, 1992.

Black, Susan. *Madonna Live!* New York: Omnibus, 1996.

Blake, Christina. *Madonna: Like a Virgin.* New York: Omnibus, 1985.

Cahill, Marie. *Madonna.* New York: Smithmark, 1991.

———. *Madonna.* London: Omnibus, 1991.

Celsi, Teresa. *Madonna.* Kansas City: Andrews and McMeel, 1993.

———. *Madonna.* London: Hale, 1994.

Claro, Nicole. *Madonna.* New York: Chelsea House, 1994.

Cuellar, Carol, ed. *Madonna: Erotica.* New York: Warner Brothers, 1992.

———. *Madonna: Like a Prayer.* New York: Warner Brothers, 1989.

———. *Madonna: Something to Remember.* New York: Warner Brothers, 1996.

DeLisa, Jeannette, ed. *Madonna: Bedtime Stories.* New York: Warner Brothers, 1995.

Faith, Karlene. *Madonna: Bawdy and Soul.* Toronto: University of Toronto Press, 1997.

Fleiss, Mike, ed. *Madonna Speaks.* Orlando, Fla.: Expression Press, 1993.

Gaar, Gillian G. *She's a Rebel.* Seattle: Seal Press, 1992, xi, 293, 323, 332–336, 340, 361, 364–365, 390, 395, 399, 403, 428–430, 434.

James, David. *Madonna: Her Complete Story: An Unauthorized Biography.* Lincolnwood, Ill.: Publications International, 1991.

King, Norman. *Madonna: The Book.* New York: Quill, 1991.

———. *Madonna: The Book.* New York: William Morrow, 1992.

Lagerfeld, Karl. *Madonna, Superstar: Photographs.* New York: Norton, 1988.

———. *Madonna, Superstar: Photographs.* New York: Norton, 1991.

Lloyd, Fran, ed. *Deconstructing Madonna.* London: Batsford, 1993.

*Madonna.* Collector's ed. New York: New American Library, 1985.

*Madonna: Blond Ambition World Tour.* Boy Toy/Music Tours, Inc., 1992.

*Madonna. Sex.* New York: Warner Brothers, 1992.

*Madonna.* New York: Smithmark, 1996.

*Madonna Live!* London/New York: Omnibus Press. Exclusive distributors, Music Sales Corp., 1987.

*Madonna: Portrait of a Material Girl.* Philadelphia: Courage, 1993.

*Madonna, The Girlie Show: World Tour.* New York: Callaway, 1994.

*Madonna, The Rolling Stone Files: The Ultimate Compendium of Interviews, Articles, Facts, and Opinions from the Files of Rolling Stone.* New York: Hyperion, 1997.

Matthew, Gordon. *Madonna.* New York: Simon & Schuster, 1985.

Matthew-Walker, Robert. *Madonna: The Biography.* London: Sidgwick & Jackson, 1989.

———. *Madonna: The Biography.* Rev. ed. London: Pan, in association with Sidgwick & Jackson, 1991.

———. *Madonna: The Biography.* 2d ed. Philadelphia: Trans-Atlantic Publications, 1991.

McKenzie, Michael. *Madonna: Her Story* (formerly *Lucky Star*). Rev. ed. London: Bobcat, 1987.

———. *Madonna: Her Story.* New York: Omnibus, 1996.

———. *Madonna, Lucky Star.* Chicago: Contemporary Books, 1985.

———. *Madonna: Lucky Star.* London: Columbus, 1985.

———. *Madonna, The Early Years: 65 Classic Photographs of Madonna and Friends.* New York: Worldwide Televideo Enterprises, 1993.

O'Brien, Glenn. *Madonna: The Girlie Show World Tour.* London: Prion, 1994.

O'Brien, Lucy. *She Bop: The Definitive History of Women in Rock, Pop and Soul.* New York: Penguin, 1996, esp. 214–22.

Randall, Lee. *The Madonna Scrapbook.* Secaucus, N.J.: Carol Publishing Group, 1992.

Rettenmund, Matthew. *Madonnica: The Woman and the Icon from A to Z.* New York: St. Martin's, 1995.

Riley, Tim. *Madonna Illustrated.* 1st ed. New York: Hyperion, 1992.

Rosenzweig, Ilene. *The I Hate Madonna Handbook.* New York: St. Martin's, 1994.

St. Michael, Mick. *Madonna in Her Own Words.* London; New York: Omnibus, 1990.

———. *Madonna Speaks Out: Madonna in Her Own Words.* London: Omnibus, 1993.

Sexton, Adam, ed. *Desperately Seeking Madonna: In Search of the Meaning of the World's Most Famous Woman.* New York: Delta, 1993.

Smith, Paul, ed. *Madonnarama: Essays on Sex and Popular Culture.* Pittsburgh, Penn.: Cleis Press, 1993.

Syn, Cardinal. *Madonna's Sexiest Jokes.* New York: Sure Seller, 1994.

———. *The Sexiest Jokes about Madonna.* New York: S.P.I. Books, 1994.

Thompson, Douglas. *Like a Virgin: Madonna Revealed.* London: Smith Gryphon, 1991.

———. *Madonna Revealed.* Secaucus, N.J.: Carol Publishing Group, 1991.

———. *Madonna Revealed: The Unauthorized Biography.* Dorchester, 1992.

———. *Madonna Revealed: [The Unauthorized Biography].* New York: Leisure Books, 1992.

Turner, Kay. *I Dream of Madonna: Women's Dreams of the Goddess of Pop.* San Francisco: Collins, 1993.

Voller, Debbi. *Madonna: The Illustrated Biography.* London/New York: Omnibus, 1988.

———. *Madonna: The New Illustrated Biography.* New York: Omnibus, 1990.

———. *Madonna: The Style Book.* London: Omnibus, 1992.

West, Joey. *The I Hate Madonna Joke Book.* New York: Windsor, 1993.

### Chapters in Books

Lewis, Lisa A. "Consumer Girl Culture: How Music Video Appeals to Girls." In *Television and Women's Culture: The Politics of the Popular.* Ed. Mary Ellen Brown. London: SAGE, 1993, 89–101.

Paglia, Camille. "Madonna as Gauguin: Mark Bego's *Madonna: Blonde Ambition*" (book review). In *Vamps and Tramps: New Essays.* New York: Vintage, 1994, 370–74. Reprinted from *Notes: Quarterly Journal of the Music Library Association* 50, 1 (September 1993): 88–90.

———. "Madonna in the Shadows: Madonna's *Sex*" (book review). In *Vamps and Tramps: New Essays.* New York: Vintage, 1994, 367–369. Originally appeared in *Us* magazine as a review of Madonna's book *Sex.*

Udovitch, Mim. "Madonna." In *The Rolling Stone Book of Women in Rock: Trouble Girls.* Ed. Barbara O'Dair. New York: Random House, 1997, 340–47.

## Periodicals

Ansen, David. "Madonna: Magnificent Maverick." *Cosmopolitan* 208, 5 (May 1990): 308–11.

Aspden, Peter. "Desperately Seeking Meaning" (profile of Madonna as a music performer and her cultural role). *Times* Higher Education Supplement, Nov. 5, 1993, 13.

Brown, Jane D., and Laurie Schulze. "The Effects of Race, Gender, and Fandom on Audience Interpretations of Madonna's Music Videos" (interpretation of videos "Papa Don't Preach" and "Open Your Heart"). *Journal of Communication* 40, 2 (Spring 1990): 88–102.

Brown, Mary Ellen, and John Fiske. "Romancing the Rock: Romance and Representation in Popular Music Videos" (analysis of two videos, A-Ha's "Take on Me" and Madonna's "Material Girl"). *OneTwoThreeFour: A Rock 'n' Roll Quarterly* 5 (1987): 61–73.

"Evita or Madonna: Whom Will History Remember?" (interview with Argentine writer Tomas Eloy Martinez). *New Perspectives Quarterly* 14, 1 (Winter 1997): 32–33.

Ferguson, Andrew. "Bad Girls Don't Cry." *National Review* 46, 10 (May 30, 1994): 72.

Flick, Larry. (Cover story). "WB Expects Madonna to 'Light' Up Int'l Markets." *Billboard* 110, 8 (February 21, 1998): 1, 83.

Greeley, Andrew M. "Like a Catholic: Madonna's Challenge to Her Church." *America* 160, 18 (May 13, 1989): 447–449.

Harris, Daniel. "Make My Rainy Day." *Nation* (June 8, 1992): 790–93.

Hayes, Jarrod. "Madonna in Living Color: Race, Color, and Sexuality in Music Videos" (Madonna and the issues of race and gender in the Alek Keshishian film *Truth or Dare*). *Found Object* 1 (Fall 1992): 26–35.

Herman, James Patrick. "Seeing the Light." *Elle* 13, 8 (April 1998): 106.

Hirschberg, Lynn, and Steven Meisel. "The Misfit." *Vanity Fair* 54, 4 (April 1991): 158–169+.

Hirshey, Gerri. "Madonna." *Rolling Stone* 773 (November 13, 1997): 98–100.

Hofler, Robert. "An Affair to Remember: Madonna Makes Love to the Camera." *Life* 9 (December 1986): 50–62.

Holden, Steven. "Madonna: I Want to Bring Back Glamour." *Seventeen* 45 (October 1986): 160+.

Kelly, Michael. "Playgirl of the Western World." *Playboy* 38, 3 (March 1991): 82–84+.

Kowalski, Rosemary. "Madonna: Woman Is the Message." *OneTwoThreeFour: A Rock 'n' Roll Quarterly* 3 (Fall 1986): 59–73.

Krupp, Charla. "Meet Madonna, Multimedia Star." *Glamour* 83 (February 1985): 144+.

Leung, Linda. "The Making of Matriarchy: A Comparison of Madonna and Margaret Thatcher." *Journal of Gender Studies* 6, 1 (March 1997): 33–42.

Lubow, Arthur. (The '80s: Madonna). "Heaven Can Wait." *Savvy Woman* 10, 10 (October 1989): 66–67+.

"Madonna's Private Diaries" (written during production of *Evita*). *Vanity Fair* 435 (November 1996): 174–188, 223–232.

McClarty, Susan. "Living to Tell: Madonna's Resurrection of the Fleshy" (Madonna considered within the context of gender issues in the music industry; also analysis of videos "Open Your Heart" and "Like a Prayer"). *Genders* 7 (March 1990): 1–21.

Orth, Maureen. (Cover story). "Madonna in Wonderland." *Vanity Fair* 55, 10 (October 1992): 204+.

Pareles, Jon. "[Cyndi] Lauper vs. Madonna: Who's Better?" *Mademoiselle* 92 (December 1986): 102, 232.

Price, Richard. (The Fifty Most Powerful Women in America). "Madonna Flexes Her Muscles." *Ladies Home Journal* 107, 11 (November 1990): 198, 282.

Rochlin, Margy. "Madonna." *Harper's Bazaar* 123, 3342 (June 1990): 100–105.

Rohrer, Trish Deitch. "Madonna Down and Dirty" *(Truth or Dare)*. *GQ—Gentlemen's Quarterly* 61, 5 (May 1991): 65–69.

Schifrin, Matthew, and Peter Newcomb. "A Brain for Sin and a Bod for Business." *Forbes* 146, 7 (October 1, 1990): 162–166.

Schwartz, Joel D. "Virgin Territory: How Madonna Straddles Innocence and Decadence." *New Republic* (August 26 1985): 30–32.

Shewey, Don. "The Gospel According to St. Madonna." *Advocate* 577 (May 21, 1991): 40–45.

———. (Cover story). "Madonna: The Saint, the Slut, the Sensation . . ." *Advocate* 576 (May 7, 1991): 42–51.

Simels, Steve. "My Madonna Problem (and Yours)." *Stereo Review* 56, 4 (April 1991): 95.

Sischy, Ingrid. (Cover story). "Madonna and Child." *Vanity Fair* 451 (March 1998): 204–213, 266, 268–270.

Sobran, Joseph. "Single Sex and the Girl: Meet Madonna, Scourge of the Pharisees, Defender of Artistic Integrity, Exposer of Christian Charity." *National Review* 43, 14 (August 12, 1991): 32–35.

Thornton, Lawrence. "The Two Faces of Eva" (comparison between Madonna and Eva Perón). *George* (December 1996): 76–77.

Walters, Barry and Victoria DeSilverio. "Madonna Chooses Dare." *Spin* 14, 4 (April 1998): 70.

Woods, Vicki. "Madonna Holds Court." *Vogue* 179, 5 (May 1989): 342–51.

# Chronology

**1958** Madonna Louise Veronica Ciccone is born in Rochester, Michigan, on August 16, 1958.

**1963** Madonna's mother, Madonna Ciccone, dies in Michigan in December.

**1977** Goes to New York City, studies dance with choreographer Alvin Ailey, and does modeling work.

**1979** Moves to France to join disco singer Patrick Hernandez in a show.

**1980** Establishes a group called Emmy with Detroit-native drummer Steve Bray. Begins film career with small role in a B-movie, *A Certain Sacrifice*.

**1982** Records club hit single "Everybody," produced by New York disc jockey Mark Kamins.

**1984** Breaks out from the dance scene and expands into mainstream pop with hit single "Holiday," written and produced by John "Jellybean" Benitez. The song makes the Top 20 in the United States and the Top 10 in Europe. Also releases singles "Borderline," "Lucky Star," and "Like a Virgin."

**1985** Singles "Material Girl," "Crazy for You," "Angel," "Dress You Up," and "Into the Groove." Marries actor Sean Penn. The Virgin Tour. Starring role in film *Desperately Seeking Susan*. Performs in Live Aid concert.

**1986** Singles "Live to Tell," "Papa Don't Preach," "True Blue," and "Open Your Heart." Appears with husband Sean Penn in movie *Shanghai Surprise*.

**1987** Singles "La Isla Bonita" and "Causing a Commotion." "Who's That Girl?" single ties in to movie comedy of the same name, starring Sir John Mills. The Who's That Girl? Tour.

**1988** Separates from husband Sean Penn. Appears in Broadway play *Speed-the-Plow,* by David Mamet.

**1989** Singles "Like a Prayer," "Express Yourself," and "Cherish." Controversial video "Like a Prayer" is condemned by the Vatican and prompts Pepsi-Cola to cancel an advertising contract. Album *Like a Prayer,* produced with Patrick Leonard, is an international best-seller. Divorces Sean Penn.

**1990** Singles "Oh Father," "Keep It Together," "Vogue," and "Hanky Panky." Costars with Warren Beatty in the movie *Dick Tracy.* The Blond Ambition Tour.

**1991** Singles "Justify My Love" and "Rescue Me." Release of the film *Truth or Dare: On the Band Behind the Scenes, and in Bed with Madonna,* which documented the Blond Ambition tour.

**1992** Singles "This Used to Be My Playground" and "Erotica." Signs a deal with Time Warner, which assures release of albums, movies, and books produced by her production company, Maverick. Appears in baseball film *A League of Their Own.* Publication of best-selling book *Sex.*

**1993** Singles "Deeper and Deeper," "Bad Girl," and "Rain." The Girlie Show Tour.

**1994** Singles "I'll Remember" and "Secret." Controversial appearance on television talk show *Late Night with David Letterman.*

**1995** Singles "Take a Bow," "You'll See," "Bedtime Story," and "Human Nature."

**1996** Singles "You Must Love Me" and "Love Don't Live Here Anymore." Stars in leading role as Eva Perón in the film *Evita.* Gives birth to a daughter, Lourdes Maria, on October 14.

**1997** Single "Don't Cry for Me Argentina." Madonna and *Evita* win several awards at the 1996 Golden Globe show. Madonna turns 39 on August 16. Madonna reacts to the death of Princess Diana and condemns the paparazzi, particularly at the 1997 *MTV Video Music Awards* held at Radio City Music Hall in New York City.

**1998** Single "Frozen." Releases *Ray of Light* and announces a new spirituality in a series of interviews.

# Permissions

"Madonna" by J. D. Considine. From *The Rolling Stone History of Rock and Roll: The Definitive History of the Most Important Artists and Their Music*, ed. Anthony DeCurtis and James Henke.

"Like a Virgin" album review. From *People* magazine, January 1, 1985. © 1985 by Time–Life, Inc. Reprinted by permission.

"Concert Review: Universal Ampitheater, Los Angeles (1985)" from *Variety* 319 (May 8, 1985). Reprinted by permission.

"Madonna Is Nobody's Toy" by Robert Hillburn. From the *Los Angeles Times*, July 6, 1986. Copyright 1986 *Los Angeles Times*. Reprinted by permission.

"Like a Veteran: Madonna's Tour Reveals Her Savvy, Show–biz Side" by Brett Milano. From *The Chicago Tribune*, July 26, 1987. Reprinted by permission of *The Chicago Tribune*.

"Ex–'Boy Toy' Madonna Transforms Herself into Adult on Like a Prayer" by Jonathan Takiff. From the *Atlanta Journal Constitution*, March 24, 1989. © 1989 *The Atlanta Journal Constitution*. Reprinted by permission.

"Concert Review: Hollywood Los Angeles Sports Arena" from *Variety* 339 (May 30, 1990). Reprinted by permission.

"Without the Videos, Her Albums Just Aren't the Same" by Greg Kot. From *The Chicago Tribune*, May 13, 1990. Reprinted by permission of *The Chicago Tribune*.

"The Madonna Pornucopia: *Sex* for the Coffee Table and *Erotica* for the Ears" by Richard Harrington. From *The Washington Post*, October 21, 1992. © 1992, *The Washington Post*. Reprinted with permission.

"Madonna Goes to Camp" by Richard Corliss. From *Time* magazine, October 25, 1993. © 1993 by Time–Life, Inc. Reprinted by permission.

"Pillow Talk" by Steve Dollar. From the *Atlanta Journal Constitution*, October 25, 1994. © 1994 *The Atlanta Journal Constitution*. Reprinted by permission

"Madonna Captures the Moment and See the Spiritual Light" by Joan Anderman. Reprinted by permission of the author.

"Madonna: She's One Lucky Star" from *Teen* magazine 29 (January 1985). Reprinted by permission.

"Madonna" by Denise Worrell. From *Time* magazine, May 27, 1985. © 1985 by Time–Life, Inc. Reprinted by permission.

"Madonna Cleans Up Act but Her Music Remains True Blue to Controversy" by Stephen Holden. From *The New York Times*, July 10, 1986. Copyright © 1986 by The New York Times Co. Reprinted by permission.

"Confession of a Catholic Girl" by Becky Johnston. From *Interview* 19, 5 (May 1989). Reprinted with permission.

"Face–to–Face with Madonna" by Edna Gundersen. Copyright 1996, USA TODAY. Reprinted with permission.

"New Tune for the Material Girl: I'm Neither" by Ann Powers. From *The New York Times*, March 1, 1998. Copyright © 1998 by The New York Times Co. Reprinted by permission

"Madonna Rising: The Wild and Funky Early Years in New York" by Christopher Anderson. Copyright, 1991, *New York* magazine. Distributed by Los Angeles Times Syndicate. Reprinted with permission.

"Madonna Rocks the Land" by John Skow. From *Time* magazine, May 27, 1985. © 1985 by Time–Life, Inc. Reprinted by permission.

"A Mad, Mad World of 'Madonnas'" by Mary Rourke. From the *Los Angeles Times*, May 31, 1985. Copyright 1985 *Los Angeles Times*. Reprinted by permission.

"Virgin Territory: How Madonna Straddles Innocence and Decadence" by Joel D. Schwartz. From *The New Republic* 193 (August 26, 1985). Reprinted by permission of *The New Republic*, © 1985, The New Republic, Inc.

"Single Sex and the Girl" by Joseph Sobran. From *The National Review* 43, 14 (August 12, 1991). Reprinted by permission.

"Madonna Sells Her Soul for a Song" by Ed Siegel. Copyright 1989 by *The Boston Globe*. Reprinted with permission.

"Why Madonna Can't Keep Her Clothes On" by William Cross. From *McCall's* magazine 120, 4 (January 1993). Reprinted by permission.

"Playing the Shock Market" by Matthew Gilbert. From *The Boston Globe*, October 11, 1992. Copyright 1992 by *The Boston Globe*. Reprinted with permission.

"Madonna and Other Arthurs" by Molly Ivins. Reprinted by permission from *The Progressive*, 409 E. Main Street, Madison, WI 53703.

"Madonna" by Steve Allen. Reprinted from *Journal of Popular Culture* 27, 1 (Summer 1993) by permission.

"Venus of the Radio Waves." From *Sex, Art, and American Culture* by Camille Paglia. Copyright © 1992 by Camille Paglia. Reprinted by permission of Vintage Books, a Division of Random House, Inc.

"Immaterial Girl?" by Tamara Ikenberg. From the *Los Angeles Times*, April 9, 1998. Copyright 1998 *Los Angeles Times*. Reprinted by permission.

"Like a Critiqued: A Postmodern Essay on Madonna's Postmodern Video 'Like a Prayer'" by Stephen E. Young. Reprinted from *Popular Music and Society* 15, 1 (Spring 1991) by permission.

"Face–Off: Madonna's 'Like a Prayer'" by Liz Rosenberg and Donald Wildmon. Copyright 1989, USA TODAY. Reprinted with permission.

"Our Lady of MTV: Madonna's 'Like a Prayer'" by Carla Freccero. From *boundary 2*, 19:2 (Summer 1992). Copyright 1992, Duke University Press. All rights reserved. Reprinted with permission.

"Justify My Ideology: Madonna and Traditional Values" by Janelle L. Wilson and Gerald E. Markle. Reprinted from *Popular Music and Society* 16, 2 (Summer 1992) by permission.

"Animality and Artifice." From *Sex, Art, and American Culture* by Camille Paglia. Copyright © 1992 by Camille Paglia. Reprinted by permission of Vintage Books, a Division of Random House, Inc.

"Make My Rainy Day" by Daniel Harris. Reprinted by permission from the June 8, 1992, issue of *The Nation* magazine.

"Gender Politics and MTV: Voicing the Difference" by Lisa A. Lewis. © 1993 by Temple University. Reprinted by permission of Temple University Press.

"Unlike a Virgin" by Luc Sante. Reprinted by permission of *The New Republic*, 1990, The New Republic, Inc.

"Madonna" by Jane Miller. From *Ploughshares* 17, 4 (Winter 1991–1992). © 1991 Jane Miller. Reprinted by permission.

"Madonna's Postmodern Feminism: Bringing the Margins to the Center" by Cathy Schwichtenberg. Reprinted by permission of the publisher of *The Southern Communication Journal* l, Southern States Communication Association, SCJ, vol. 57, no. 2 (Winter, 1992): 120–31.

"Guilty Pleasures" by Pamela Robertson. In *Guilty Pleasures: Feminist Camp from Mae West to Madonna*, pp. 115–38. Copyright 1996, Duke University Press. All rights reserved. Reprinted with permission.

"Electrifying Fragments: Madonna and Postmodern Performance" by Mark Watts. First published in *New Theater Quarterly* 12, 46 (May 1996) by Oxford University Press. Special Thanks to Clive Barker. Reprinted by permission of the author.

# Index

Page numbers in *italics* refer to illustrations.


ABBA, 7
academic analyses, 140, 219–30
  co-option of Madonna, 219–25
  as cultural imperialism, 222
  of feminist camp, 268–90
  of "Justify My Love" video, 206–13
  of "Like a Prayer" video, 171–81, 184–203
  of Madonna as capitalist, 232–40
  of Madonna as performance artist, 240–49
  of meaning of Madonna, 291–301
  political/feminist, 226–32
  unsympathetic overview of, 219–25
Act of Contrition, 12, 188
*Addams Family, The* (television series and film), 273
*Adventures of Priscilla, Queen of the Desert, The* (film), 269
advertising images, 243–44
African Americans
  Italian Americans and, 190–91
  and "Like a Prayer" video, 189–90, 192–93, 194, 197–98
  Madonna's ties with, 126, 196, 270
  and *Sex,* 186–87
  and vogueing, 282
  white musicians' guilt toward, 195
*Agnes of God* (film), 193
AIDS, 11, 20, 126, 270, 281, 282
Aiello, Danny, 48–49
Ailey, Alvin, xiv, 88
"Airotica," 20
Aladdin Sane, 275
albums
  debut, xiii, 31, 34, 104, 119. See also *Madonna*
  *Evita* sound track, 75
  Madonna's creative control of, 231–32
  recording of first, 104
  retrospective *You Can Dance,* 16
  reviews of, 3, 6–7, 12–14, 15–16, 18–20, 23–24, 24–27
  sales decline of, 21
  sales of first, 111, 119
  sales of second, 119–20
  *True Blue* as career turning point, 6–7
  *See also specific album titles*
Allen, Steve, 144–57
Allen, Woody, 130
*All That Jazz* (film), 20
Almodóvar, Pedro, 240
Alter, Adam, 95, 96, 97, 98
Althusser, Louis, 189
Alvin Ailey American Dance Center, 88–89
Alvin Ailey American Dance Theater, 33, 40
Alvin Ailey Dance Company, xiv, 187, 205
American Family Association, 53, 181, 197
American Foundation for AIDS Research, 11
Andermahr, Sonya, 278
Anderman, Joan, 24–27
Anderson, Christopher, 87–108
Anderson, Kurt, 271, 272
Anderson, Steven, 268–69
Anti-Defamation League (ADL), 154–55
anti-Semitism, 126, 154–55
appropriation, 288–89

Arbuckle, Fatty, 145
Archer, Anne, 156
*Around the World in a Day,* 5
Arquette, Rosanna, xv, 107, 108, 111, 279
Association, 13
*!Atame!* (film), 240–41
*At Close Range* (film), 49
Austin, Dallas, 23, 24
Ayers, Anne, 10

Babuscio, Jack, 271
Babyface, 23
"Bad Girl" (single), 19
"Bad Girl" (video), 296
*Bad as I Wanna Be* (Rodman), 78
Baker, Russell, 270
Baker, Susan, xv
Ball, Tyla, 117
*Baltimore Sun,* 9
Banderas, Antonio, 75, 78–79
Barbie doll, 274
Barbone, Camille, 95–100, 101, 103
Barkin, Ellen, 108
Barr, Roseanne, 202n.25
Barthes, Roland, 290, 295
Basquiet, Jean-Michel, 103–4
Baudrillard, Jean, 171, 176, 177, 178, 220, 253–54, 300
Bay City, Michigan, 38, 53, 187, 205
Beastie Boys, 115, 121
Beatles, 12, 13, 80
Beatty, Warren, xv, 12, 55, 57, 108, 124, 236
  on Madonna's public personality, 127, 136
"Be a Clown," 22
Becquer, Marcos, 284
*Bedtime Stories,* 23–24
Bell, Daniel, 178
Bell, Erica, 100–102, 104, 105, 107
"Be My Baby," 7
Benatar, Pat, 226, 229
Benetton advertising, 243–44
Benhabib, Seyla, 253
Benitez, John ("Jellybean"), xiv, *4*, 104–6, 107, 108
Benjamin, Walter, 392
Berlant, Lauren, 281
Bernhard, Sandra, 124, *137*, 138, 236, 282, 298
Betts, André, 19
*Beverly Hillbillies, The* (television series and film), 273
Beverly Hills, California, 118
Bieber, David, 134
Bil and Gil, 90
*Billboard* charts, 75, 111, 119–20
"Billie Jean," 49
*Biograph,* 133
bisexuality, xvi, 165, 259, 275
Black Harlem, 190, 196
Black Madonna, 241
Black Sheep, 19
"Black Stone Lying on a White Stone" (Vallejo), 241–42
"blank parody," 272
Blond Ambition Tour, 236–37, 263
  authenticity of performance, 292–93
  marginalized cast members, 286
  *Truth or Dare* documentary on, 124, 136
  Vatican disapproval of, 126, 140, 204
  See also *Truth or Dare*
*Bloodhounds of Broadway* (film), 73
*Blossom* (television program), 268, 284
*Blue Angel* (film), 189
Blue Angel (Lauper rock act), xiii
*Body of Evidence* (film), 17, 21, 134, 138, 156
bondage, xvi, 17, 18, 19, 240
Boone, Debbie, 122
"Borderline" (single), xiii, 9, 15, 34, 104
"Borderline" (video), xiv, 34, 295
  fashion ingredients, 169
  and Madonna's star quality, 163
  and male "looking" vs. feminine "look," 255, 278
Bordo, Susan, 224–25, 253
*Boris and Natasha* (film), 273
"Born to Be Alive," xiv, 91
*Born Yesterday* (play and film), 113
*Boston Globe,* 139
  on "Like a Prayer" controversy, 131–34
  review of *Ray of Light,* 24–27
  on *Sex* and *Erotica,* 137–41
Bowie, David, 7, 81, 139, 234, 275
"Boy Toy" belt buckle, xv, 5, 6, 45–46, *84*, 110, 116, 234, 270, 276, 277, 297

Boy Toy collection, 116
Bradby, Barbara, 220
*Brady Bunch, The* (television series and film), 273
Brando, Marlon, 298
bra straps, 170
Bray, Stephen, xiv, 7, 49, 70, 97, 102, 228, 229
  as African American, 191, 228
  arrival in New York, 94, 95
  on Madonna's autonomy, 152, 231
  on Madonna's East Village walk-up, 88
breakdance, 282
Breakfast Club (band), xiv, 33, 93–94, 228
breast envy, 220
*Bringing Up Baby* (film), 274
Britton, Andrew, 271
Broward County, Florida, 238
Brown, Julie, 268, 284
Brown, Tina, 139
Bryson, Peabo, 10
Bubman, Alice, 118
burlesque, 22, 270
burning crosses, 59, 193–94, 196–97
"Burning Up" (single), xiv, 5, 15, 34, 95, 112
"Burning Up" (video), 34, 162
Burroughs, Norris, 90
bustier, 164, 168
Butler, Judith, 255, 258, 260, 261, 263–64
"Bye Bye Baby," 19
Byrne, David, 102

Cabala, 80
*Cabaret* (film), 189
Cabaret Voltaire, 236
Cagney, James, 7, 11, 50
Camel cigarettes, 134
Camillucci, Gregory, 92–93
camp, 268–90
  and appropriation, 288–89
  cult figures, 272
  death of, 269, 273, 287–88, 290
  elements of, 272
  feminist, 269–70
  heterosexualization of, 270, 271, 275
  and identity politics, 280–90
  ironic sensibility of, 272–73
  mainstreaming of, 188, 270–73, 275, 289–90
  politicization of, 270, 280–90
Campbell, Joseph, 186
Campbell, Naomi, 18, 138, 286
"Camp Lite" sensibility, 271, 272–73
"Candy Perfume Girl," 26
Cannes Film Festival, 124–25
Caras, Adriana, 117
Carter, Elliott, 172
Catholicism
  as continuing influence on Madonna, 65, 77–78, 83, 165, 187, 205, 237–38
  *Like a Prayer* use of, 188
  and *Like a Prayer* controversy, 12, 125, 170, 183–84, 191
  "Like a Virgin" use of, 235
  Madonna on personal beliefs, 44–45
  and Madonna's perceived blasphemous images, xv, xvi, 125, 149, 152, 153
  Madonna's rebellion against, 64–65, 66, 126–27, 140, 205
  Madonna's upbringing in, 38, 40, 53, 69, 126, 226
  Madonna's use of imagery of, 59–60, 87, 126, 126–27, 128, 187
  "popular religiosity" symbols, 191, 193
  song titles and terminology of, 244
  Vatican denunciation of Madonna's act, 126, 140, 204, 238
"Causing a Commotion" (single), 8, 14, 162
Cavani, Liliana, 216
CBGB (club), 103
censorship
  as creating media attention, 206
  and defense of "Like a Prayer" video, 182
  Madonna's statements against, 280
  Madonna's view as defining art, 130, 140
  by MTV of "Justify My Love," xvi, 105, 125, 153, 165, 170, 204, 206, 213, 215
  Paglia's defense of MTV ban, 125, 215

*Century of the Wind* (Galeano), 247–48
*Certain Sacrifice, A* (film), 3
Champagne, John, 286
"Chapel of Love," 49
Chapkis, Wendy, 256
charity (as virtue), 127
Chavez, Ingrid, 20
"Cherish" (single), 12, 13, 221
"Cherish" (video), 296
Chicago, Illinois, 8, 9
*Chicago Tribune,* 15–16
Chodorow, N., 253
Christian mythology, 241, 244. *See also* Catholicism
"Ciao, Italia" (video), 237
Ciao Italia tour, 188
Ciccone, Madonna (mother), 31, 37–38, 44, 65–66, 82, 187
Ciccone, Madonna Louise Veronica. *See* Madonna
Ciccone, Silvio/Tony (father), 31, 35–37, 106, 124, 127
  background of, 35–37, 187, 226
  and Madonna's concert tours, 124, 127, 189–90
  and Madonna's East Village living conditions, 90
  remarriage of, 38, 66
  upward mobility of, 37, 187, 190
Clapton, Eric, 133, 134
Clay, Andrew Dice, 139, 144
*Clockwork Orange, A* (film), 236
Club 57, 103
club scene
  Goth look, 168
  and Madonna's demo tape, 102, 114, 228
  Madonna's rise in, 100–107, 233–34
Coca-Cola, 131, 183, 185
Collins, Phil, 111
Commes des Garcons, 46
concert tours
  Blond Ambition, 124, 136, 236–37, 292
  Chicago Soldiers Field, 8–11
  Ciao Italia, 188
  costumes, 116–17, *117*
  Girlie Show, 21–22, *154*, *158*
  Los Angeles reviews, 4–5, 14
  Madonna's postmodern performance style, 291, 300–301
  male backups, 115
  paraphernalia sales, 111–12
  sell-outs, 111
  show description, 114–16
  threatened closings, 280
  Virgin, 9, 119, *119*, 187, 189–90
  warm-up band, 115, 121
condoms, 282
*Coneheads, The* (film), 273
Connors, Stephen, 301
Considine, J. D., 9, 10
Conte, Louis, 10
Continental Club, 100
Cooke, Sam, 13
Cooper, Abraham, 154
"Cop Killer," 139
Corliss, Richard, 21–22
"corp-rock" generation, 185
Cosby, Bill, 131
*Cosby Show, The* (television program), 231
Costello, Elvis, 111
Coward, Rosalind, 261
Crawford, Joan, 164
"Crazy for You," 111
Crimp, Douglas, 286
Cross, William, 134–36
cross-dressing, 152, 262, 280, 283. *See also* drag culture
cross-shaped earrings, 110, 111, 117
crucifixes and rosaries, 5, 106, 117, 119
  as blasphemy vs. fashion accessories, xv
  as dominant symbol in "Justify My Love" video, 211
  Madonna on her motives for using, 45, 205
  Madonna quoted on "sexiness" of, 149, 183
*Crying Game, The* (film), 269
Cubitt, Sean, 293
"cultural literacy," 273
"Cupid," 13
Curry, Ramona, 277

*Daily Mail,* 297
Dali, Salvador, 236

*Damned, The* (film), 216
dance-pop, xiv, 25
Danceteria, 33–34, 101, 102, 103, 107, 114, 205, 228, 233
*Dark Side of Love, The* (Goldberg), 135
DARP Studios, 23
Darsey, James, 262–63
Dean, James, 49–50
"Dear Jessie," 13, 299
Debord, Guy, 300
deconstruction, 223, 224, 254, 256, 258, 263–64
"Deeper and Deeper," 20, 296
DeLory, Donna, 14
DeMann, Freddy, 104, 113
De Mornay, Rebecca, 108
De Niro, Robert, 147
*Desperately Seeking Susan* (film), 34, 41, 120
  as best Madonna film, 163
  "Into the Groove" from, 8
  Madonna persona revealed in, 52, 98, 113, 163, 244, 299
  Madonna's audition for, 107–8
  success of, xv, 6, 9, 111, 112, 213n.1, 235, 279, 297
  video aesthetics of, 291
  women's identification with, 279
Detroit, Michigan, xiv, 12, 31, 87, 88, 106–7, 187
*Detroit News,* 156
deviant behavior (as concept), 147–48
"Diamond's Are a Girl's Best Friend," 58, 277
*Dick Tracy* (film), xv, 12, 55, 57–58, 73, 213n.1
  *I'm Breathless* album and, 238, 240
  Madonna's performance in, 239
  Sondheim songs in, 14, 15, 58, 238
"Did You Do It?," 19
Dietrich, Marlene, 22, 164, 170, 189, 283, 295
DiMaggio, Joe, 148, 170, 283
disco, xiv, 104, 121, 141, 281, 282, 299
  Madonna as typifying, 162
  disco-trance, 27
  displacement, 261–62
  di Stefano, Christine, 253
  Doane, Mary Anne, 255
  Dolce & Gabanna, 168–69
  Dollar, Steve, 23–24
  dominatrix, 17–18, 21, 165
  Donahue, Phil, 272
  "Don't Go for Second Sex, Baby" (Morton), 223
  *Do the Right Thing* (film), 196
  Doty, Alexander, 288–89
  drag culture
    Madonna signifiers, 256, 270, 275, 283
    mainstreaming of, 269, 272, 280, 281
    *See also* cross-dressing
*Dragnet* (television series and film), 273
drag queens, 163, 165, 166, 216, 262
*Dream On* (film), 273
"Dress You Up" (single), 11, 15
"Dress You Up" (video), 166
"Drowned World," 82
Duran, Duran, 169
Durham, North Carolina, 88
Duvall, Robert, 147
Dyer, Richard, 271, 280
Dykes for Madonna, 262
Dylan, Bob, 9, 80, 133
Dynell, Johnny, 105

E! (Entertainment Television), 168
Ebersole, C. R., 142
Ebert, Roger, 156
*ecce homo* tradition, 191
Edelman, Hope, 135
electronica, 81–82
Elliot, Brian, 7, 48
*Empire* (magazine), 297
"end of history" theory, 293
Entertainers Merchandise Management Corp., 116
*Entertainment Tonight* (television program), 138
*Erotica* (album), 16, 25, 78
  Harrington review of, 18–20
  sadomasochistic lyrics of, 137–38
  sales of, 21
  as self-exploitative, 87
  sound of, 19
"Erotica" (single), 19

"Erotica" (video)
description of, 17–18, 139
and Madonna's style, 141, 170
MTV late-night-only showing of, 16, 138, 170
"Everybody" (single), xiv, 34, 103, 114, 233–34
*Evita* (film), 25, 74, 78–79, *250*, 290
Madonna's desire for role, 72, 75–76
"Express Yourself" (concert production), 22
"Express Yourself" (single), 13, 14
deconstructionist analysis, 223
"Express Yourself" (video), 165, 206
drag dance in, 257, 263
fashion look of, 170, 294
gender-boundary blurring in, 253–54, 282
iconography of, 294–95
Madonna's defense of, 285–86
and male "looking" vs. feminine "look," 256, 278
as pastiche, 294–95

*Face, The* (British magazine), 107
"Fall of Che, The" (Galeano), 247
Falwell, Jerry, 177
*Fashion Emergency* (television program), 168, 169
*Fashion Reviews* (television program), 168
Fellini, Federico, 274
female impersonators, 256, 270, 275
Madonna as, 283
femininity
camp redefinitions of, 275
as gender construction, 255, 256
"look" of, 255
Madonna and, 163, 188, 230
Madonna on, 42, 67, 68
feminism
analysis of "Like a Prayer" video, 184–203
analysis of Madonna's life and career, 226–32
antipornography campaign, 259–60
collective nature of, 203n.33, 253, 254
debates on significance of Madonna, 269
detractors of Madonna, 163, 164, 165, 166, 214, 215, 276–77
distrust of postmodernism, 252, 253
Madonna's challenges to, 276
Madonna's postmodern strategies and, 249–64, 277, 300
Madonna's sexual fantasies and, 18
Madonna's style as expression of, xv, 42, 115
Paglia critique of American ideologues, 215–16
Paglia on Madonna's true expression of, 125, 213n.5, 215–16, 277
postfeminist label, 276
reclamation of Madonna, 184–203, 278
turning point in view of Madonna, 277
view of Madonna's materialist self-parody, 110, 225
feminist camp, 269–70, 282
*femme fatale,* 255
"Fever," 20
Fiedler, Leslie, 272
Fifth Dimension, 175
film
camp cinephilia, 272–73
*Desperately Seeking Susan* as career boost, xv, 111, 112
European sadomasochistic images, 216, 240, 260
Madonna's failures, xv, 75, 291
Madonna's parody of female star images, 277, 283
Madonna's re-creation of studio-era star glamour, 164, 166, 170, 274
male gaze concept, 189
possible Madonna projects, 106, 113
video references to vintage photography, 177, 270, 274
vogueing impersonations of stars, 282
*See also* video; *specific film titles*
First Amendment rights, 140, 145, 182, 183. *See also* censorship
Fiske, John, 185, 186, 212, 224, 278–79
*Flintstones, The* (television series and film), 273
Flynn, Christopher, 39–40, 99, 103, 282

Fonda, Bridget, 165
Fonda, Jane, 148
*Forbes* (magazine), 12
"Forbidden Love," 23
Fosse, Bob, 20
Foucault, Michel, 220, 258, 260, 285
Fox, Michael J., 243
fragmentation, 253, 254, 257, 261, 264, 271, 295–96
Francis, Connie, 121
Frank, Dave, 97
Franklin, Aretha, 13, 296
Fraser, Nancy, 252–53
Freccero, Carla, 184–203
freedom of speech. *See* First Amendment rights
Fresh 14 (club), 105
Freud, Sigmund, xv, 216, 220
Friedberg, Anne, 271
"Frozen" (single), 26, 27
"Frozen" (video), 82
  Ikenberg review, 167–68, 170
*Fugitive, The* (television series and film), 273
Fundador, Roman ("Fundy"), 99
fundamentalists, 182, 191, 197
Fun House (club), 104
funk, xiv

Gabriel, Peter, 175
Galeano, Eduardo, 247–48
Galliano, 168, 170
Garber, Marjorie, 220
Garbo, Greta, 170, 283
Gates, Henry, 143, 144
Gatti, José, 284
Gaultier, Jean-Paul, 46, 168, 236
gay culture
  camp and, 270, 271, 280–90
  Madonna's identification with, 126, 141, 216, 270, 279, 281–82, 298–99
  Madonna's popularity with, 204, 262–63, 279–80
  queer politics, 270, 280–90
  *See also* drag culture; gender boundaries; lesbians
gay liberation movement, 216, 262–63, 270, 280
Gay Pride parades, 280, 281
gay rights, 281
gender boundaries, 251, 253–54
  camp and, 275
  constructions of, 254–56, 259, 263–64
  fragmentation and, 254, 261, 263
  Madonna's bending of, 254, 259, 269, 270, 275, 278, 282, 285, 299
  parody of, 270, 282
  performance rock and, 275
gendered binarisms, 254–56
gender play, 256
gender politics, 253, 285–86
General Dynamics, 37
*Gentlemen Prefer Blondes* (film), 235, 277, 294
Gere, Richard, 80, 103
Gilbert, Matthew, 137–41
Gilligan, Carol, 253
Gilroy, Dan, 90–91, 92, 93, 94, 228
Gilroy, Ed, 90, 92, 93, 94, 228
"girl culture," 184
Girlie Show Tour, 21–22, *154*, *158*
"Girls Just Want to Have Fun," xiii
Glass, Philip, 172
Glendale Galleria, 118
*Gods Must Be Crazy, The* (film), 243
"Going Bananas" (concert performance), 22
Goldberg, Jane, 135
gold diggers, 270
Golden Section (GS), 180n.5
Goldstein, Richard, 153
good/bad girl. *See* madonna-whore complex
Goodman, Ellen, xiii
Gordon, John, 97
Gore, Tipper, xiii
Gotham Productions, 95, 96, 97, 98
Goth look, 168, 169, 170
Gracida, Bishop, 197
Graham, Martha, 33, 88
Grahn, Judy, 245
Granat, Arny, 9
Grant, Cary, 245
Grateful Dead, 9
Greeley, Andrew M., 83
Green, Grant, 23
Greer, Germaine, xiii

Griffith, Melanie, 108
Guerra, GiGi, 169
Gulf War, 251
Gumbel, Bryant, 156
Gundersen, Edna, 74–79
*Guys and Dolls* (musical), 15

Hajdik, Teresa, 115
Hall, Arsenio, 240
Hall, Delores, 102
Hall, Leon, 168, 169
Hamill, Peter, 126
Hancock, Herbie, 23
Haring, Keith, xiv, 105, 153
Harlow, Jean, 141
Harrington, Richard, 16–20
Harris, Daniel, 219–25
Harris, Niki, 14
Harry, Debbie, 141
Hartley, Hal, 269
Hatch, Cary, 10
Henderson, Lisa, 279–80
Hernandez, Patrick, xiv, 91
Herra, James, 10
heterosexual camp, 270–71, 275
heterosexuality, 255, 258, 259
Hilburn, Robert, 6–7
hip-hop, xiv, 19, 23
hippie-punk scavenger aesthetic, 234
Hirsch, E. D., 273
Hitchcock, Alfred, 211
Holden, Stephen, 48–52
"Holiday" (single), xiv, 8, 9, 34, 104, 115
  lyrics and flavor of, 234
Holliday, Judy, 40–41, 113, 164
Hollywood. *See* film
Hollywood Hills, California, 55
Hollywood Los Angeles Sports Arena, concert review, 14
Holman, Libby, 113
homosexuality. *See* gay culture; gender boundaries; lesbians
hooks, bell, 286
*House of Games* (film), 73
Hulsether, Mark D., 203n.29
"Human Nature" (single), 24
"Human Nature" (video), 169
Hurrah's (club), 103
Hurrell (photographer), 166
Huyssen, Andreas, 272
hyperreal (Baudrillard concept), 254

Ice-T, 139
identity politics, 249, 278, 280–90
*I Dream of Madonna* (anthology), 279
*I Hate Madonna Handbook, The,* 177, 268, 283–84
Ikenberg, Tamara, 167–70
*Iliad* (Homer), 300
"Images of Race and Religion in `Like a Prayer'" (Scott), 224
*I'm Breathless,* 14, 24, 137, 238, 239, 240
  review of, 15
*Immaculate Collection, The* (album), 206
*Immaculate Collection, The* (video), 291, 300
*In Bed with Madonna.* See *Truth or Dare*
*I Never Saw Another Butterfly* (dance), 89
"Inside Me," 23
"In the Still of the Night," 7
intertextuality, 296
*Interview* (magazine), 52–74
"In This Life," 20
"Into the Groove," 8, 299, 300
ironic sensibility
  camp and, 272–73, 275–76
  Madonna and, 54, 120, 121–23, 206, 212–13, 275–76, 277–78, 283
*Island Magazine,* 105
Italian-American culture, 186–91, 194–96
  as Madonna's background, 35, 126, 189–90, 226
  relationship with African Americans, 190–91, 195, 196
Italian Harlem, 190, 194, 195, 196
Italy, 126, 188, 189, 235, 238
"It's a Family Affair," 13
Ivins, Molly, 142–44
"I Want Your Sex," 183

Jackson, Michael, 49, 111, 202n.25, 257, 282
  *Victory* tour, 9, 10

Jagger, Mick, 110, 112, 141
Jameson, Fredric, 171–72, 179, 272
Jam Productions, 9
*Jane* (magazine), 169
Jellybean. *See* Benitez, John
Jenck, Charles, 300
Jensen, Laura, 246–47
Jews, 126, 154–55
"Jimmy Jimmy" (single), 7, 49
"Jinglin' Baby," 19
Joel, Billy, 13
Johnson, Betsey, 119
Johnston, Becky, 52–74
Joplin, Janis, 141, 175
Jung, Carl, 248
"Justify My Love" (concert performance), 22
"Justify My Love" (single), 18, 298
  lyrics, 207, 208–9
  seen as anti-Semitic, 154
"Justify My Love" (video), 18, 138, 139
  academic reading of, 204–5, 206–13
  as adult, poetic experience, 244–45
  androgyny in, 216, 282
  as avant-garde, 215
  controversy surrounding, xvi, 251, 259, 260
  decadence of, 125, 165, 215, 216
  displacement and identification splitting in, 261–62, 282
  eroticism of, 210, 213
  fragmentation of gender in, 254, 259
  ideological criticism of, 211–13
  lesbian eroticism in, 165, 170, 254
  Madonna's defense of, 125, 215, 251, 264, 268
  MTV ban on, 125, 153, 165, 170, 204, 205, 213, 215, 280
  multiple interpretations of, 206, 212
  *Nightline* interview on, 125, 206, 215, 251, 259, 264, 268, 285
  Paglia on, 125, 215–16
  sales of, 206
  sexual explicitness of, 206, 213
  sexual morality and, 259–60
  traditional themes in, 210–11
  video analysis flow sheet, 208–9
  visual look of, 211, 216, 260
"Just for the Night," 10

Kalin, Tom, 296, 300
Kamins, Mark, xiv, 102–3, 104, 114, 228, 229, 233
Kane, Big Daddy, 18, 138, 286
Kansas City (club), 96
Kaplan, E. Ann, 176, 177, 212, 219, 222, 224, 251, 293
Katz, Jonathan, 258
Kaye, John, 97
Keaton, Diane, 107
Keeler, Christine, 165
"Keep It Together," 13, 14, 188
King, Ben E., 13
King, Evelyn, 10
kitsch, 241, 272
Klaw, Irving, 236
Klein, Calvin, 18, 139
*Klute* (film), 148
Konowitch, Abbey, 206
Kot, Greg, 15–16
Krauthammer, Charles, 183
Kravitz, Lenny, 20
Ku Klux Klan, 59, 196–97

Lacan, Jacques, 220
LaFace Records, 23
"La Isla Bonita" (concert performance), 22
"La Isla Bonita" (single), xvi, 8, 49, 165
Lambert, Mary, xvi, 59, 60, 191, 202n.21
Lang, Fritz, 14, 170, 294
Lang, Pearl, 33, 88, 89, 103
*Last Temptation of Christ, The* (film), 175, 177, 183
Las Vegas style, 272
*Late Night with David Letterman* (television program), 254, 268, 282
Latinos, 282
Lauper, Cyndi, xiii, xiv, 3, 22, 111, 216, 219, 226, 234
Layton, Lynne, 285
*Learning from Las Vegas* (Venturi), 272
LeBon, Simon, 169
Lee, Peggy, 20
Lee, Spike, 196
Leigh, Jennifer Jason, 108
Leland, John, 282
Leon, Carlos, 76, 77, 82

Leon, Lourdes Maria Ciccone (daughter), 74–75, 77, 78, 80, 82, 168
Leonard, Elmore, 143, 144
Leonard, Patrick, 7, 8, 10, 11, 15, 25, 49, 70
on Madonna's musical sensibilities, 231–32
lesbians
academic discourse on, 220
eroticism in "Justify My Love," 165, 170, 213, 254
innuendos about Madonna and, 124, 139, 270, 282, 298–99
Madonna's popularity with, 253–54, 257–58, 262, 279–80
Letterman, David, 254, 268, 282
Lewicki, Stephen, 93
Lewis, Jerry Lee, 175
Lewis, Lisa A., 184, 226–32, 275, 278–79
*Like a Prayer* (album), 24, 53, 57, 138
advertising for, 297
as autobiographical, 187–88
condom packaged with, 282
cover, 177, 188, 201n.13
development of, 70–71
as emotionally jarring, 55
Italian-American family as theme, 187–88
live studio musicians used for, 70–71
and Pepsi commercial controversy, 131, 133
Prince and, 177
religious imagery in, 60, 188
review of, 16
*Village Voice* put-down of, 186
"Like a Prayer" (Pepsi commercial), 53, 58–59, 131–34, 166, 191, 294
"Like a Prayer" (single), 131, 133, 221, 244
academic musical analysis of, 222–23
lyrics of, 179
as representation of rebelliousness, 206
"Like a Prayer" (video)
academic analyses of, 171–80, 184–203, 224
controversy surrounding, xvi, 53, 59–60, 125, 131–34, 161, 170, 187, 191, 236, 237
as disdaining religious beliefs, 183–84
fashion look of, 170
as female empowerment fantasy, 195
images described, 173–74, 194–95
images of Italian-American culture in, 187, 194–95
as indictment of white male patriarchal Christianity, 191
oppositional dyads in, 178
Paglia analysis of, 163–64, 166
political and spiritual interpretation of, 194–99
postmodern essay on, 171–80
religious symbolism in, 59–60, 87, 166, 174, 175, 183, 237
scheduled MTV debut of, 133
social messages found in, 224
story line (Madonna version), 191–94
story line (postmodern version), 182
sub-texts, 174–77
symbolism of African Americans in, 190–91
sympathetic interpretation of, 182
"Like a Rolling Stone," 133
"Like a Thesis' (Wells), 225
*Like a Virgin* (album), xvi, 8, 15, 34, 83, 108, 138
cover of, 116
and Madonna's production input, 231
reviews of, 3, 12–14, 15
sales of, 9, 21, 49, 111, 119–20, 297
"Like a Virgin" (live performance)
on Chicago Soldier Field bill, 11
fashion ingredients, 169–70
irony of, 121–22, 206
and Madonna's autoeroticism, 124, 130
Madonna's father and, 127
Madonna's introductory outfit, xiv–xv, 115, *117*, 168
"Like a Virgin" (single), 49, 69, 110, 133, 244, 269
irony of, 121–22
sales of, 111
teenage fans, 169
"Like a Virgin" (video), 235, 244
"Like a Virgin-Mother?: Materialism and Maternalism in the Songs of Madonna" (Bradby), 220

lingerie, 164, 168, 170
*Little Rascals, The* (television series and film), 273
Little Richard, 121
Live Aid, 9, 11, *51*
"Live to Tell" (single), 14, 15, 27, 49, 69
"Living to Tell: Madonna's Resurrection of the Fleshly" (McClary), 222–23
L. L. Cool J, 19
Lloyd Webber, Andrew, 25, 27
Lofton, John, 153
Lombard, Carole, 40–41
Loren, Sophia, 148
Los Angeles, California, 4–5, 14
*Los Angeles Times,* 6–7, 167–70
Los Feliz, California, 75
Love, Courtney, 25
"Love Makes the World Go Round" (single), 7, 11, 50
"Love Song," 12
Lucas, Reggie, 114, 229
Luce, Clare Boothe, 147
"Lucky Star" (single), xiii, 15, 31, 104
"Lucky Star" (video), xiv, 162–63, 296
Lucky Strike (club), 100
Lymon, Frankie, 50

MacLaine, Shirley, 80
Madison Square Garden, 11, 144
Madonna, *4*, *6*, *51*, *56*, *63*, *129*, *132*, *137*, *150*, *151*, *173*
  academics' co-option of, 219–25
  academic "texts" on, 140, 171–81, 184–203, 206–301
  acceptance of artifice by, 275
  as actress, 71–73, 90, 98, 239
  aggressiveness of, 88, 96
  on ambitions, 41, 94
  art and, 128, 130
  artistic growth of, 245
  attention-seeking by, 101–2, 124–25, 130, 226–27
  audience for, 123–24, 262–63, 277–78, 285. *See also* Madonna wannabes
  audience segments alienated by, 153–55, 164
  audition for *Desperately Seeking Susan,* 107–8
  aura of, 102, 114, 292–93
  as avant-garde, 141, 163, 177, 215
  backlash against, 6, 144–49, 156, 164, 169, 230–31
  belly button exposure, xiv, 45, 115, 163, 177, 188
  birthdate and place, 205
  body of, 88, 89, 90, 92, 115, 118, 166
  body used as prop by, 255, 257–58
  "Boy Toy" persona, xv, 5, 6, 45–46, 110, 270, 274, 276, 277, 297
  Breakfast Club band of, 93–94
  as calculatingly magnetic, 125–26
  camp and, 269–70, 274–90
  as capitalist, 232–40
  and Catholicism. *See* Catholicism
  childhood rebellion by, 64
  childhood role models, 67
  comedic talent of, 112, 113, 164
  and commercialism, 274
  contradictory images projected by, 212–13, 263
  control of own career and image by, 141, 152, 213n.1, 216, 230, 231, 278
  controversial image of, ix-x, xiii, 25, 48, 53, 87, 204, 213n.2, 268–69, 276
  courting of controversy by, 48, 87
  couture designers favored by, 46, 168–69
  on criticism and bad press, 57, 156
  cross-dressing by, 269, 283
  crucifixes and rosaries used by, xv, 5, 45, 106, 117, 119, 205
  cult appeal of, 122–23
  as cult trend-spotter, 25
  as cultural icon, 204
  cultural resistance to, 164
  dance as mode of expression, 161
  dance-pop sensibilities, 25
  dance training, xiv, 33, 38, 39–40, 50, 62, 88, 90, 113, 187, 205, 227
  as decadent, 165
  defenders of, 125, 136, 161–70, 213n.5, 215–16
  defense of "Justify My Love" video by, 215, 251, 264, 268

Madonna (*continued*)
DeMann as agent, 104
demo tape played at Danceteria, 102, 114, 228
as depraved, 144, 147–49, 152, 153
detractors of, ix, xv, xv–xvi, 10, 110, 119, 144–57, 164, 221, 276–77, 283–84, 286–87
disco style, xiv, 121, 141, 162
divorce from Penn, 54
drug rejection by, 44
as drummer, 92, 94, 113
early career, xiv, 33–34, 87–108, 113–14, 227–28, 233–35
early comparison with Lauper, xiii, xiv, 3, 216, 219, 234
early idols, 40–41
and Eastern thought and music, 26
and *Evita* role, 72, 75–76, *250*
exercise regime of, 62
exhibitionism of, 134–36, 138–39, 140, 142
on fame, 42, 44
fame of, 53, *54–55*, 140, 275, 297
family background, xiv, 12, 31, 33, 35–38, 53, 65–67, 187, 188–89, 190, 205, 226
on fans, 42
fans' views of, ix, 50, 52, 111, 188, 239, 278–79, 285
"fanzine" interview, 31–35
father's influence on, 13, 31, 35–37, 38, 66, 67, 90, 127, 140, 187–88, 190, 226, 227
fear of assassination onstage, 99
and female empowerment, 184
and feminine wiles, 36, 38–39, 226–27
on femininity, 42, 67, 68
and femininity fabrications, 163, 188, 230, 255, 256
as feminist, xv, 18, 115, 125, 140, 184, 203n.33, 213n.5, 215–16, 278
feminist analysis of, 226–32
feminist critics of, 163, 164, 165, 225, 276–77
*femme fatale* performances, 255
film career, xv, 6, 52, 75, 93, 106, 113, 291
first album, 104
first film, 93
first recording contract, 98, 99, 102–3, 228
first two singles, xiv
first video, 162
flamboyance of, 125
forceful personality of, 110
and gay culture, 141, 216, 262–63, 270, 281–82, 298–99
genre jumping by, xvi
hair styles and colors of, 35, 46, 48, 92, 117–18, 119, 141, 166, 167, 170, 195, 236, 240, *302*
houses, 55, 75
iconography of, 244–45
on image, 41
image shifting by, xvi, 8, 9, 10, 12, 23, 25, 48, 52–54, 69, 81–82, 168–70, 186, 225, 229, 230, 244, 270, 274, 275–76, 278, 294–95, 297
images of, 297–99
income of, 12
individuality of, 102
instinctive intelligence of, 161
interviews given by, 31–83
irony of, 54, 120, 121–23, 206, 212–13, 275–76, 277–78, 283
Italian-American cultural influences on, 35, 126, 186–90, 226
kissing skill, 101
lesbian innuendos about, 124, 139, 165, 270, 282, 298, 299
and line between kitsch and art, 241
longevity of celebrity of, 297
on love, 46, 74, 130
mainstream reviewers vs. academic critics on, 221
on marriage, 46
marriage to Penn, xv, 13, *52*, 54, *54*, 130, 235
and masturbation, xiii, 124, 125–26, 130, 136, 152
as megastar, xiii, 96
and motherhood, 25–26, 74–75, 76, 77, 78, 80, 168
and mother's early death, xiv, 37–38, 65–66, 77, 82, 98, 99, 126, 135, 187, 188, 205, 226

and mother's grave, 127, 136
and mother's religious influence, 188
motifs of, 188–89
and multimedia contract, xvii
and multiple lovers, 104, 106, 108, 114, 228
musical career inception, 90–91, 92, 113, 228
musical influences on, 13, 50
musical styles of, 121
name source, xiv, 31, 44, 117, 152, 206, 248
and "New Madonna" concept, 10, 14, 25, 52–53, 54
nude modeling by, 89–90, 231, 233
nude *Playboy* and *Penthouse* photos of, xv, 6, 11, 120, 152, 231
odd jobs held by, 92–93, 97, 187
as outrageous, 136
in Paris, xiv, 91–92
parodies of, 268, 284
as parodying culture, 212, 269, 277
as patronizing those less powerful, 286–87
as perfectionist, 24
performance style of, 290–301
personality projection by, 15
on personal moral code, 45
persona meaning of, 291–94
persona plurality of, 294–95
physical evolution of, 166–67
political both/and position, 186, 286–87
as political figure, 281–84
politically controversial imagery of, 279–80
as pop culture symbol, 50, 120
pop style of, xiv, 25, 229–30
on pornography, 17, 287
and postfeminist debate, 276, 300
postmodern feminism of, 249–64
and postmodern performance, 290–301
postmodern sensibility of, xiv, xvi, 140, 212, 225, 252, 274, 277
power and agency of, 188, 278–80, 285–86
power as focus of, 237
press manipulation by, 55, 107, 119–24, 140
producing credits of, 231–32
professionalism of, 108
as prostitute, 149, 157, 277, 278
psychic powers believed by, 99
psychoanalytic views of, 135–36
relationship with Barbone, 96–100
relationship with Basquiet, 103–4
relationship with Beatty, xv, 108
relationship with Bell, 100–102
relationship with Benitez, 104–6, 107, 108
relationship with Bray, 94, 95, 228
relationship with Gilroys, 90–91, 92, 94, 228
relationship with Kamins, 102–3, 114, 228
relationship with Leon, 76, 77, 82
relationship with Newman, 105–6
resourcefulness of, 101
retrocinephilia of, 277
reviews of, 3–27
rock community's early views of, xiii
on Rodman affair, 78
as safe shocker, 139
self-assessment by, 60, 113
self-creation of, 55
self-discipline of, 52, 61–62, 108
on self-examination, 82
self-parody by, 3, 110, 113
self-promotion image and skill of, xvi, 55, 102, 134–35, 229, 234, 239, 270, 274, 275, 278
on self-revelation, 81
semiotic analysis of, 191–93
sensuality of, 93, 167
sex-as-power message of, xv, 68, 216, 278
and sex roles, 163, 189, 282
and sexual fantasies, xvi, 17, 18, 138, 299
and sexual glamour, 164–65, 274
sexuality of, 67–68, 69, 102, 105, 108, 141
as sexually artificial, 149, 237
and sexual self-exploitation, 87, 134, 165, 276–77
and sexual stereotypes, 274
sexy image of, xvi, 4–5, 16–20, 25, 39, 41, 117
shock power of, 152

Madonna (*continued*)
and siblings, 31, 38–39, 65, 66–67, 77, 187, 205, 226
singing voice of, 10, 15, 16, 26, 50, 82, 110, 112, 166, 234
social conscience of, 11
songwriting by, 92, 93, 97
sound antecedents of, 49
in *Speed-the-Plow,* 12, 72–73, *109,* 244
stardom goal of, 52, 92, 102
star quality of, 96, 163
star status of, xv, xiii
on stepmother, 38, 65, 66
style changes of, 48, 52, 54, 55, 57, 167–69, 274
style and costumes of, xiv–xv, *xviii,* 5, 8, 22, 31, *32,* 35, *43,* 46, *47,* *84,* 87, 92–93, 96, 100, 106, 110, 113, 115, 116–20, *117,* 141, 142, 162–63, 234–35, 297
style inception of, 38
style ingredients of, 116–17, 141, 162–63, 164
and style as statement, 40, 42
symbolic self-determination of, 230
transformational states of, ix, 26
unauthorized biography of, 87–108
as uninhibited, 105
"unusual" woman status of, 286, 288–89
use of people by, 40, 88, 94, 99–100, 106, 228
vegetarianism of, 89
video's importance to, x, xiv, 7, 161–216, 235, 297
on virginity, 39
visualization of music by, 7
and vogueing, 269
as vulgar, 149
work ethic of, 187
on writing song lyrics, 70
on yoga and spirituality, 79, 80–83
*Madonna,* xiii, 31, 34
Madonna's one-woman promotion of, 104
Madonna's production input, 231
review of, 15
sales of, 111, 119
*Madonna Connection, The* (Schwichtenberg), 140, 222
*Madonna of 115th Street, The: Faith and Community in Italian Harlem, 1880–1950* (Orsi), 186–87
Madonna phenomenon, 87–158
as academic label, 219–20, 221
blandness of, 189–90
camp and, 273–90
early New York years of, 87–108
exhibitionism and manipulation theories on, 119–42
identity politics and, 289–90
as repository for other cultural ideas, 269
as uninteresting and unoriginal, 270
and young fans, 109–19
"Madonna's Postmodern Feminism" (Schwichtenberg), 221
Madonna wannabes, xv, 14, 52, 87, 109–12, 114, 116–19, 143, 204
accessories, 8, 109–10, 111–12, 116, 116–19, 117–18, 119
decline of, 21, 169
identification with daughterly position by, 188
identification with Madonna's power and independence by, 278–79
look of, 21, 120, 162, 234, 297
Madonna's appeal to, xv, 115, 277
Madonna's assessment of, 42, 61
role-playing by, 123–24
madonna-whore complex, xv, 10, 69, 165, 212–13, 244, 274
male gaze, 189, 190, 220, 223, 255, 278, 285, 300
Mamet, David, 12, 73, 236, 244
Mamiya, Christin, 273
Mantegna, Joe, 73, *109*
Mapplethorpe, Robert, 18, 216, 260
Marcus, Greil, 139
marginalization, 249
(Marilyn) Monroe Doctrine, xiv
Markle, Gerald E., 204–14
Martin de Porres, Saint, 193, 237
Martinez, Bobby, 108
Marxist Madonna, 220
Mary, the Blessed Virgin, 165, 187, 195

Mary Magdalene, 126, 165
masculinity, 275
Masina, Giulietta, 274
Massive Attack, 26
master-slave model, 285–86, 298
masturbation, xiii, 124, 125–26, 130, 136, 152, 170, 206
"Material Girl" (concert performance), 5, 11, 115–16
"Material Girl" (single), 3, 15, 58, 112, 121, 235, 244
  academic close reading of lyrics, 220
  debates on meaning of, 122, 123
  as Madonna persona, 270, 274
  Madonna's work ethic and, 187
  as self-parody, 110
"Material Girl" (video), xiv, 235
  ambiguity and contradictions in, 212
  fashion ingredients of, 170
  irony of, 206, 277–78
  and Madonna's comedic flair, 164, 277
  and male "looking" vs. feminine "look," 278
  Marilyn Monroe image and, 135, 164, 170, 255–56, 277–78
  negative assessment of, 235
  as pastiche, 294
  as turning point in attracting female fans, 277
"'Material Girl': The Effacements of Postmodern Culture" (Bordo), 224–25
Matisse, Henri, 241
Maverick Records, 81
*McCall's* (magazine), 134–36
McClary, Susan, 184, 189, 196, 222–23
McGillis, Kelly, 108
McRobbie, Angela, 184, 227
Meadow, Phyllis W., 136
Medhurst, Andy, 291, 293, 295, 299, 300
media
  censorship seen fueling attention from, 206
  "fanzine" type interview, 31–35
  interaction with academic discourse, 269
  Madonna interviews, 31–83
  Madonna's manipulation of, 55, 107, 119–24, 140
  postmodernism and, 271–72, 274
*Medusa: Dare to Be Truthful* (Brown parody), 284
*Meeting of Minds* (television program), 147
mehndi tattoos, 167, 168, 170
Meisel, Steven, 17, 18, 138
Melvoin, Susannah, 26
*Memory of Fire* (Galeano), 247
"Mer Girl," 82–83
metaphor, poetic, 244
*Metropolis* (film), 14, 22, 170, 294
Mezan, Peter, 135
Miami, Florida, 9
Michael, George, 183, 185
Michaels, Eric, 260–61
Michelangelo, 248
Michelob beer, 133
Midler, Bette, 22, 106, 141
Milano, Brett, 8–11
Miller, Arthur, 148
Miller, Henry, 146
Miller, Jane, 240–49
Miller, Lee, 72
Millman, Joyce, 274
Minnelli, Liza, 189
Miranda, Carmen, 22
*Misfits, The* (film), 245
*Mississippi Burning* (film), 59, 194
M.K. (club), 103
modernism
  pop art's break from, 272
  postmodernism vs., 171, 172, 252, 292, 293
Moffitt, Jonathan, 10
*Monkey Business* (film), 245
Monroe, Marilyn, 7, 40–41, 48, 110, 283, 296
  dress style of, 46, 128, 141, 170
  Madonna compared with, 274
  Madonna contrasted with, 148, 149, 164, 278
  Madonna's politicization of, 245
  "Material Girl" deconstruction of, 255–56, 277–78
  "Material Girl" as homage to, 135, 164, 170
  reclamation of, 245
Montez, Maria, 272

Montrelay, Michele, 255
moral anarchism, 146
Moral Majority, 260
Morrison, Jim, 141
Morton, Melanie, 220, 223
Motown, 49
MP. *See* Madonna phenomenon
*Ms.* (magazine), 215–16
MTV
attempted academic analyses of, 225
ban on "Justify My Love" video, 105, 125, 153, 165, 170, 204, 206, 213, 215, 280
and "Erotica" video, 16, 138, 170
global cultural imperialism of, 185
importance to Madonna, xiv, 4, 141
and "Like a Prayer" video, 53, 172
Madonna as creation of, 110, 161, 205–6, 235, 274, 297
and Madonna's avant-garde sensibility, 163
postmodern style of, 185, 198, 222, 274
*MTV Video Music Awards* (1985 telecast), xiv-xv, 168
Mudd Club, 103
Mulvey, Laura, 189
Music Building (New York City), 95
music videos. *See* video
Musto, Michael, 279

*Nashville* (film), 99
National Endowment for the Arts, 238
*Natural Born Killers* (film), 273
Nestle, Joan, 257
New Critics, 224
Newman, Steve, 105
*New Musical Express,* 17
New School (New York City), 89–90
Newton, Esther, 256, 262
Newton, Helmut, 18, 216
New York City, Madonna's years in, 33, 40, 87–88, 113–14, 187, 227–28, 233–34
*New York Daily News,* 125
New York Dolls, 275
*New Yorker* (magazine), 269
*New York Post,* 167
*New York Times,* 205
Nicholson, Linda, 252–53
*Nick at Nite* (television feature), 273
Nickelodeon (cable channel), 273
*Nightline* (television program), 125, 206, 215, 251, 259, 264, 268, 285
*Night Porter, The* (film), 216
*Nights of Cabiria* (film), 274
"Notes on Camp" (Sontag), 270, 271, 275

O'Connor, Sinead, 139, 141
"Oh Father," 188
Old Testament, 300
"Open Your Heart" (video)
Italian-American cultural images in, 187, 188–89, 190
Italian cinematic influence on, 274
as Madonna's greatest video, 164–65, 166, 167
and male gaze concept, 189, 300
and male "looking" vs. feminine "look," 255, 278
as postmodern, 253
reflecting lethal lingerie period, 170
story and images, 189–90
Orion Pictures, 107, 108, 112
Orsi, Robert, 186–87, 191, 192, 193, 195
other (concept), 253, 255
"other woman," 197
Owens, Craig, 252

Pacino, Al, 147
Paglia, Camille, xiii, 198, 203n.33
on Madonna as true feminist, 213n.5, 215–16, 277
praise for Madonna's videos, 125, 161–70
"Papa Don't Preach" (single), xvi, 7, 14, 16, 82
academic theorists on, 221
controversial topic of, 48, 49, 165
Italian-American family motif of, 188
political both/and position of, 186
"Papa Don't Preach" (video), 296
fashion look of, 170
irony of, 206
multiple interpretations of, 293
power of, 48–49

Paradise Garage (club), 107
Parents' Music Resource Center, xv
Paris, France, xiv, 91–92, 187
*Paris Is Burning* (film), 269
Parker, Alan, 74, 75–76
parody
  as camp element, 272
  of Madonna, 268, 284
  by Madonna, 212, 269, 277, 283
  vogueing as, 283
Parton, Dolly, 148, 149
pastiche, 293, 294
Paterson, Vincent, 14
Patinkin, Mandy, 15
patriarchal codes of feminity, 188
patriarchal family structure, 187
patriarchal philosophy, 252, 280
Pattison, Robert, 175
Patton, Cindy, 220
Pavilion (Chicago), 9
Pavis, Patrice, 295
Pearl Lang's Dance Company, 89
Pellerin, Jean Claude, 91, 92
Pellerin, Madame, 92
Penn, Sean, xv, 13, 49, 52, 54, *54*, 70, 114, 130, 235, 263
*Penthouse* (magazine), 183
  nude layout, xv, 6, 120, 152, 231
*People* (magazine)
  on bad reviews for *Body of Evidence,* 156
  review of *Like a Virgin,* 3
Pepsi-Cola
  boycott threats against, 191
  deal with Madonna, 12, 133, 183
  "Like a Prayer" commercial, 53, 58–59, 131–34, 185, 191, 197–98, 294
  Madonna's unveiling of commercial, 53
  Michael J. Fox commercial, 243
  withdrawal of Madonna commercial, xvi, 166, 170, 180, 191, 237
performance rock stars, 275
Perón, Eva, 74, 290
Peters, John, 106
Pettibone, Shep, 19
"phallic woman" gesture, 202n.25
photography
  Madonna as nude model, 89–90
  punctum concept, 295–97
  *Sex* book, 17, 18
"Physical Attraction," 34
Pietá (Michelangelo), 248
Pittsburgh, Pennsylvania, 187
Platters, 175
*Playboy* (magazine), nude layout, xv, 6, 11, 120, 138, 152, 231
poetic justice, 243–44
poetry, 241–48
political camp, 270, 280–90
Pontiac, Michigan, 187
Pop, Iggy, 275
pop art, 271, 272, 273, 275
pop music styles
  early 1980s, xiii-xiv, 234
  interpretation of Madonna's association with, 229–30
  Madonna as embodiment of, 275, 276
  Madonna's fusion of, 162
  punctum and, 296–97
  rock's ideological division from, 229, 275
popular culture
  academic approaches to, 219–25
  academic sentimentalization of, 220–21, 222
  baby-boomers' immersion in, 162
  behavioral models, 178
  camp appropriated by, 270, 282
  inappropriate transfer of high-culture study tools to, 223–24
  Madonna and ideology of, 227
  Madonna as archetype of, 241
  Madonna as symbol of, 50, 244
  Madonna controversies and, 269
  pop art and, 271
  positive functions of, 198–99
  postmodernism and, 172
  protopolitical in, 184, 198
  queer politics introduced into, 282
popular spirituality, 187
pornography
  feminist and right-wing campaigns against, 165, 259–60
  Madonna's view of, 17, 287
  Paglia's defense of, 215

Porter, Cole, 22
postfeminism, 276, 300
postmodernism
as both reactionary and leftist, 185–86
broad connotations of term, 271–72, 393
camp style, 270, 271
conceptual limits of, 220, 223
critical views of, 171–72, 220, 252
critique of "Like a Prayer" video, 172–80
definition of, 171
feminist rift with, 252, 253
fragmented identities emphasis of, 253
insufficiency as cultural analysis vehicle, 222, 223–25
Madonna as phenomenon of, xiv, xvi, 140, 212, 225, 252, 274, 277
Madonna's feminism as, 249–64, 277
Madonna's performance as, 290–301
MTV style and, 185, 198, 222
in pop art context, 271
technological dependence of, 292
*Postmodern Videos* (television program), 185
poststructuralism, 171
Pottasch, Alan, 131
"Power of Goodbye, The," 26, 27, 82
Powers, Ann, 79–83
Presley, Elvis, 99, 120
press. *See* media
Pribram, E. Deirdre, 225
Prince, 5, 12, 110, 112, 138, 177
Private Eye (club), 114
Profumo affair, 165
"Promise to Try," 13, 188
Promising Female Artist sweepstakes, xiii
prostitution, 148–49, 157, 165, 277, 278
Protestantism, 153, 165
Pryce, Jonathan, 75
*Pulp Fiction* (film), 273
punctum (Barthes concept), 290–93, 295–97, 299–300
punk rock, 172
Q-Tip, 19
Queer Nation, 204, 281
queer politics, 270, 280–90
Quinn, Aidan, xv

R&B, 191, 228
Radio City Music Hall, 111
Rage, Christopher, 18
"Rain," 19–20, 22
rap, 19, 243, 283
*Ray of Light,* 79–83
Anderman review, 24–27
"Frozen" video from, 167
loss themes, 82
Madonna on, 79, 81
Reed, Lou, 275
Reich, Steve, 172
"Rescue Me," 296, 299
*Reservoir Dogs* (film), 269
"Respect," 13, 296
Revelation, book of, 126, 154
"Revolution No. 9," 12
rhythm-and-blues, 191, 228
Rice-Davies, Mandy, 165
right wing (political), 259–60
Riley, Bob, 97
Ritts, Herb, 166, 296
Riviere, Joan, 255
Robertson, Pamela, 268–90
Robinson, Leon, 194, 197
Robinson, Smokey, 22
rock music
commercialism and, 133, 134
ideology of authenticity, 123, 229
as informing baby-boom generation, 162
Madonna seen violating discourse of, 123, 229
performance-rock male artists, 275–76
postmodernism and, 172
Rodgers, Nile, 3, 4–5, 231
Rodman, Dennis, 78
Rogers, Will, 149
*Rolling Stone* (magazine), 69, 78, 89
Madonna cover photos, 230, 298
on Madonna's exploitation of people, 228
on Madonna's exploitation of sex, xv-xvi

on Madonna's fame, 53
on Madonna's violation of rock discourse, 229
Rolling Stones, 188
Ronstadt, Linda, 112
rosaries. *See* crucifixes and rosaries
Rosenberg, Liz, 9, 11, 53, 180–81
Rosenblatt, Michael, 102–3
Ross, Andrew, 184, 198, 271, 275, 281
Ross, Diana, 50
Ross, Herbert, 113
Rossellini, Isabella, 138
Rostova, Mira, 98
Rourke, Mary, 116–19
Rubber Ball (club), 299
Rubin, Gayle, 251, 259–60
Rudnick, Paul, 271, 272
Ru Paul, 269
Rushdie, Salman, 182
Russell, Ken, 236
Russian Tea Room, 92–93
Russo, Mary, 255
Ruth, Dr., 240
*Ruthless People* (film), 106

Sade, Marquis de, 147
sadomasochism
"Erotica" and, 17–18, 19, 137–38, 170
European film images of, 216, 240, 260
"Justify My Love" video and, xvi, 165
Madonna criticized for images of, 149, 152
Madonna on "mutuality" of, 17
*Sex* and, 21, 134
visual aesthetic of, 169, 260
Salzman, Eric, 172
"Sanctuary," 23
Sanskrit, 80
Sante, Luc, 232–40
*Saturday Night Live* (television program), 139
Sawyer, Forrest, 215, 251, 259, 264, 268, 285
*Scandal* (film), 165
Scharf, Kenny, xiv
Schoenberg, Arnold, 172
Schreiber, Martin, 89–90
Schwartz, Joel D., 119–24
Schwichtenberg, Cathy, 220, 221, 222
"Madonna's Postmodern Feminism," 249–67
Scott, Ronald, 224
Scott-Heron, Gil, 199
"Secret Garden," 20
Seidelman, Susan, 52, 107, 108, 112, 163, 235, 279
Seigworth, Greg, 277
semiotics, 171, 185, 186, 291
sex
gender vs., 254–58, 259, 263–64
as identity basis, 258–63
*Sex* (Madonna book), 25, 298
academic essays on, 268
appropriation and, 288
description of, 18, 138
lesbian images in, 18, 282
Madonna on, 78
price of, 16, 138, 142
review of, 16–18
sales of, 21
seen expressing middle-class privilege, 286–87
as self-exploitative, 87, 134
sexual fantasies, xvi, 17, 18, 138, 282, 299, 300
sexual glamour, 164–65
sexuality
biology and, 258–63
camp redefinitions of, 275
social anxieties and, 249, 251, 260
*See also* gender boundaries
*Sexual Personae* (Paglia), 136
Shalom, Robert, 114
*Shanghai Surprise* (film), xv, 23, 52, 76, 236
"Shanti/Ashtangi," 26
"She Bop," xiii
Sherman, Cindy, 171, 245, 296
*She's So Unusual,* xiii
Shirelles, 115
"Shoo-Bee-Doo," 3
Siegel, Ed, 131–34
*Siesta* (film), 202n.21
Silberkleit, Allison, 118
Silver, Ron, 73, *109*

Silverman, Kaja, 285, 286
Simon, John Oliver, 242, 245
Simon, Paul, 103
Simon Wiesenthal Center (Los Angeles), 126, 154
*Simple Men* (film), 269
simulacrum (Baudrillard concept), 300
simulation (Baudrillard concept), 253–54, 256, 259, 263, 264
Sinatra, Nancy, 41
singles
  academic overinterpretation of, 223–24
  first two, xiv
  sales of, 4, 111
  successes, xvi
  *See also specific song titles*
Sire label, 14, 102, 103, 133, 228, 233–34
'60s girl-group sound, 49, 50
"Skin," 27
Skow, John, 109–16
SkyDome (Toronto), 21–22
Slick, Grace, 141
Smit, Angie, 93, 94
Sobran, Joseph, 124–30
Soldier Field (Chicago ), 8, 9
*Some Like It Hot* (film), 245
Sondheim, Stephen, 14, 15, 58, 238
Sontag, Susan, 270, 271, 272, 275
"(Sooner or Later) I Always Get My Man," 14
Soper, Kate, 253
soul, xiv
"Spanish Eyes," 13
"Spanish Harlem," 13
*Speed-the-Plow* (Mamet), 12, 72–73, *109*, 244
*Spin* (magazine), 63
Spivak, Gayatri, 197, 255
Sports Arena (Los Angeles), 14
Springsteen, Bruce, 9
Stark, Ray, 113
Stark, Susan, 156
Starr, Blaze, 113
*Star Trek* (television series and film), 273
Stein, Seymour, 103, 233–34
Steinberg, Ed, 103
Stewart, Marlene, 116, 117
*Sticky Fingers,* 188
stigmata, 166, 170, 191, 193, 237
Stone, Sly, 13
Stonewall rebellion (1969), 270, 280
*Strange Cargo,* 26
Straw, Will, 297
Streep, Meryl, 147
Streisand, Barbra, 106, 147, 167
*Subversive Intent: Gender, Politics and the Avant-Garde* (Suleiman), 136
Suleiman, Susan Rubin, 136
Supremes, 50
"Survival," 23
Swaggart, Jimmy, 197

"Take a Bow" (video), 170
Takiff, Jonathan, 12–14
Talking Heads, 172
Tarantino, Quentin, 269
"Tears of a Clown," 22
*Teen* (magazine), 31–35
television
  camp sensibility and, 272–73
  Madonna and, 268
  *See also* MTV; *specific program titles*
Tentler, Kate, 287
"There Ain't Nothing Out There," 10
"These Boots Are Made for Walkin'," 41
"Thief of Hearts," 20
Thomas, Norman, 203n.26
thrift-shop chic, 46, 87, 109, 110, 116
Thurber, James, 155
Thy, Robert, 242
*Tie Me Up, Tie Me Down!* (film), 240–41
"Till Death Do Us Part," 13, 16, 188
*Time* (magazine), xv, 53
  Madonna mid-1980s cover story, 35–46, 228–29
  on Madonna's *Evita* performance, 75
  review of *Girlie Show* tour, 21–22
Times Square, 33, 40, 87
"Times They Are A-Changin', The," 133
Time Warner, xvii, 153
*Today* (television program), 156
"To Have and Not to Hold," 26
Toronto, Canada
  *Girlie Show* tour, 21–22, 238

threatened closing of tour, 280
*Truth or Dare* sequence on police interaction, 125–26, 136
tours. *See* concert tours
Tracks (club), 102
trance music, 81–82
transsexuality, 216
transvestism, 165, 189, 272
Travolta, John, 80
Tricky and Goldie, 81–82
trip-trance music, 26
*True Blue* (album), xvi, 8, 10
as career turning point, 6–7
Madonna's production control of, 231
reviews of, 6–7, 16
songs, 48–50
"True Blue" (video), 170
Truman, James, 107
Trump, Ivan, 143, 144
*Truth or Dare* (documentary), xvii, 21, 140, *150*, *151*, 167, 298
assessment of, 124–30
bold persona of, 263
as expression of female independence, 206
Madonna's shifting image in, 225, 294
parodies of, 268, 284
video aesthetics of, 291
view of Madonna revealed by, 136, 163, 286, 287
Turner, Tina, 112, 117, 122, 141
2 Live Crew, 238

U2, 81
Ulmer, Gregory, 172
Universal Amphitheater, Los Angeles, 4–5
University of Michigan, xiv, 33, 88, 89, 113, 187, 205, 227
*US* (magazine), 127
USA (United Support of Artists) for Africa, 111
*USA Today,* 10, 74–79, 180–81, 182

"Vague," 284
Vallejo, César, 241–42, 246
Vanilla Ice, 18
*Vanity Fair* (magazine), 126, 127, 128, 140, 141, 263
Van Lieu, Jean, 91, 92
*Variety,* 4–5, 14
Vatican, 126, 140, 204, 238
Venice, Italy, 235
Venturi, Robert, 272
"Veronica Electronica," 167–68
Versace, 168
*Victory* tour (Jackson), 9, 10
video, 161–216
cinematographic images of, 274
controversial themes of, 206
deconstructed texts of, 224
as fashion pulpit, 169–70
freezing of image, 296
gay subculture as influence on, 282
gender parody in, 282
Ikenberg overview of each, 169–70
intertextuality of, 294
interview on "Papa Don't Preach," 48–52
"Lucky Star" as breakthrough, 162–63
Madonna's comic send-ups, 112
Madonna's first, 162
Madonna's greatest-hits, 291
Madonna's image constructions, 230
Madonna's mastery of, x, xiv, 7, 205–6, 235, 297
Madonna's postmodern performance style, 297, 300–301
male "looking" and feminine "look" juxtaposition, 255, 278, 285
multiple readings of, 293
oppositional readings of, 186–99
overinterpretation of, 224
Paglia's assessment of, 161–70
as pornographic and decadent, 125
as posed and not shocking, 139
postmodernism and, 291, 292, 293, 294–95
punctum and, 297
self-referentiality of, 294
of Virgin Tour, 235
*See also specific video titles*
*Video Music Awards* (MTV), xiv-xv, 168
*Village Voice,* 185, 186
Virgin Tour, 9, 119, 187, 189–90
video, 235
VIRGIN T-shirts, 110

virgin/whore. *See* madonna-whore complex
Visconti, Luchino, 216
*Vision Quest* (film), 34, 106
Vodnoy, Mimi, 117–18
*Vogue* (British magazine), 52–53
"Vogue" (single), 14, 15, 18, 141, 238, 283, 296, 300
"Vogue" (video), 166, 274, 296, 299
  fashion look of, 170
  gay subcultural references, 282–83
vogueing, 269, 270, 272, 282–83, 298–99

"Waiting for You," 19
Walton, S., 262
"War," 139
Ward, Tony, xvi, 261, 262
Warhol, Andy, 52, 272, 275, 283, 296
Warner, Michael, 286
Warner Books, 16
Warner Bros. Records, 49, 99, 133, 154–55
  defense of "Like a Prayer" video, 181–82
  Madonna's signing with, 99, 102–3, 104
  and Toronto police incident, 238
  *See also* Sire label
Warner Reprise Video, 206
*Washington Post,* 16–20
"Watermelon Man," 23
Watts, Mark, 290–301
*Wayne's World* (film), 273
WBLS (radio station), 234
"We Are the World," 111
Webber, Bruce, 18
Weintraub, Camille, 118
Wells, Charles, 220, 221, 225
Wembley Stadium, 292
West, Mae, 18, 270, 272, 287
Westwood, Vivienne, 46
Whalley-Kilmer, Joanne, 165
"What Can You Lose," 15
"Where Life Begins," 19
"Where's the Party," xvi, 50
*White Heat* (film), 7, 50
"White Heat" (song), 7, 8, 50
"White Heat" (video), 11
*Who's That Girl?* (film), xv, 8, 24, 75, 162, 170, 236
  as updating of *Bringing Up Baby,* 274
"Why's It So Hard," 20
Wild, David, 168, 169
Wildmon, Donald, 53, 181, 182, 197
*Wild One, The* (film), 298
Williams, David, 10
Wilson, Janelle L., 204–14
Winding, Jai, 10
Winfrey, Oprah, 272
Winwood, Steve, 133
Women's liberation movement, 226, 227, 276
Wonder, Stevie, 50
"Words," 19
"Work of Art in the Age of Mechanical Reproduction, The" (Benjamin), 392
Worrell, Denise, 35–46

*Yellow Submarine,* 13
*You Can Dance,* 16
Young, Nell, 185
Young, Stephen E., 171–81

Ziggy Stardust, 275